# Buying or R

# a Home in

# Switzerland

## ● A Survival Handbook ●

David Hampshire & Anne-Marie Travers

**Survival Books ● London ● England**

First published 2010

Copyright © Survival Books 2010
Cover photograph © Ben Zastovnik (🖥 www.dreamstime.com)
Illustrations and maps © Jim Watson

Survival Books Limited
9 Bentinck Street, London, W1U 2EL, United Kingdom
☎ +44 (0)20-7788 7644, 🖶 +44 (0)870-762 3212
✉ info@survivalbooks.net
🖥 www.survivalbooks.net

British Library Cataloguing in Publication Data
A CIP record for this book is available
from the British Library.
ISBN: 978-1-905303-51-9

Printed and bound in India by Ajanta Offset

# Acknowledgements

The authors would like to thank the many people who contributed to the successful publication of *Buying or Renting a Home in Switzerland*. These include Dianne Hauptli (research & editing), Tania Gulekjian Mobayed (finance and mortgages), Lilac Johnston (proof-reading and research), Di Tolland (DTP and research) and Grania Rogers (research), and the many people – unfortunately too numerous to mention – who provided advice and information. Finally, a special thank you to Jim Watson for the cover design, illustrations and maps, and to the many photographers (listed on page 318) whose beautiful images add colour and bring Switzerland to life.

Chillon Castle, Vaud

# What readers & reviewers have said about Survival Books:

'If you need to find out how France works then this book is indispensable. Native French people probably have a less thorough understanding of how their country functions.'

**Living France**

'It's everything you always wanted to ask but didn't for fear of the contemptuous put down. The best English-language guide. Its pages are stuffed with practical information on everyday subjects and are designed to compliment the traditional guidebook.'

**Swiss News**

'Rarely has a 'survival guide' contained such useful advice – This book dispels doubts for first-time travellers, yet is also useful for seasoned globetrotters – In a word, if you're planning to move to the US or go there for a long-term stay, then buy this book both for general reading and as a ready-reference.'

**American Citizens Abroad**

'Let's say it at once. David Hampshire's Living and Working in France is the best handbook ever produced for visitors and foreign residents in this country; indeed, my discussion with locals showed that it has much to teach even those born and bred in l'Hexagone – It is Hampshire's meticulous detail which lifts his work way beyond the range of other books with similar titles. Often you think of a supplementary question and search for the answer in vain. With Hampshire this is rarely the case. – He writes with great clarity (and gives French equivalents of all key terms), a touch of humour and a ready eye for the odd (and often illuminating) fact. – This book is absolutely indispensable.'

**The Riviera Reporter**

'A must for all future expats. I invested in several books but this is the only one you need. Every issue and concern is covered, every daft question you have but are frightened to ask is answered honestly without pulling any punches. Highly recommended.'

**Reader**

'In answer to the desert island question about the one how-to book on France, this book would be it.'

**The Recorder**

'The ultimate reference book. Every subject imaginable is exhaustively explained in simple terms. An excellent introduction to fully enjoy all that this fine country has to offer and save time and money in the process.'

**American Club of Zurich**

'The amount of information covered is not short of incredible. I thought I knew enough about my birth country. This book has proved me wrong. Don't go to France without it. Big mistake if you do. Absolutely priceless!'

**Reader**

'When you buy a model plane for your child, a video recorder, or some new computer gizmo, you get with it a leaflet or booklet pleading 'Read Me First', or bearing large friendly letters or bold type saying 'IMPORTANT - follow the instructions carefully'. This book should be similarly supplied to all those entering France with anything more durable than a 5-day return ticket. – It is worth reading even if you are just visiting briefly, or if you have lived here for years and feel totally knowledgeable and secure. But if you need to find out how France works then it is indispensable. Native French people probably have a less thorough understanding of how their country functions. – Where it is most essential, the book is most up to the minute.

**Living France**

A comprehensive guide to all things French, written in a highly readable and amusing style, for anyone planning to live, work or retire in France.

**The Times**

Covers every conceivable question that might be asked concerning everyday life – I know of no other book that could take the place of this one.

**France in Print**

A concise, thorough account of the Do's and DONT's for a foreigner in Switzerland – Crammed with useful information and lightened with humorous quips which make the facts more readable.

**American Citizens Abroad**

'I found this a wonderful book crammed with facts and figures, with a straightforward approach to the problems and pitfalls you are likely to encounter. The whole laced with humour and a thorough understanding of what's involved. Gets my vote!'

**Reader**

'A vital tool in the war against real estate sharks; don't even think of buying without reading this book first!'

**Everything Spain**

'We would like to congratulate you on this work: it is really super! We hand it out to our expatriates and they read it with great interest and pleasure.'

**ICI (Switzerland) AG**

# Important Note

S witzerland is a diverse country with many faces. It has four national languages, both federal and cantonal laws, a variety of religions and customs, and continuously changing rules and regulations – particularly with regard to foreigners.

Always check with an official and reliable source (not always the same) before making any major decisions or taking an irreversible course of action. Don't, however, believe everything you're told or read, even, dare I say it, herein!

To help you obtain further information and verify data with official sources, useful addresses and references to other sources of information have been included in all chapters, and in **Appendices A** and **B**. Important points have been emphasised throughout the book, some of which it would be expensive or foolish to disregard. **Ignore them at your peril or cost.**

Unless specifically stated, a reference to a company, organisation or product doesn't constitute an endorsement or recommendation, unless specifically stated.

# Contents

# Authors' Notes

♦ Frequent references are made in this book to the European Union (EU), which comprises Austria, Belgium, Bulgaria, Cyprus, the Czech Republic, Denmark, Estonia, Finland, France, Germany, Greece, Hungary, Ireland, Italy, Latvia, Lithuania, Luxembourg, Malta, the Netherlands, Poland, Portugal, Romania, Slovakia, Slovenia, Spain, Sweden and the UK. The European Economic Area (EEA) includes the EU countries plus the European Free Trade Association (EFTA) countries of Iceland, Liechtenstein and Norway. Although Switzerland isn't a member of the EEA, it's a member of the EFTA and enjoys the same privileges and rights as EEA members.

♦ All times are shown using the 12-hour clock; times before noon are indicated by the suffix 'am' and times after noon by 'pm'.

♦ Unless otherwise stated, all prices quoted are in Swiss francs (CHF) and include VAT. They should be taken as estimates only, although they were mostly correct at the time of publication and fortunately don't change overnight in Switzerland.

♦ His/he/him also means her/she/her (please forgive me ladies). This is done to make life easier for both the reader and the author, and isn't intended to be sexist.

♦ British English and spelling is used throughout the book. Names of Swiss towns and foreign words are generally shown in their English spelling, e.g. Basle (Basel), Berne (Bern), Geneva (Genève), Lucerne (Luzern) and Zurich (Zürich).

♦ Warnings and important points are printed in **bold** type.

♦ The following symbols are used in this book: ☎ (telephone), ▤ (fax), 💻 (Internet) and ✉ (email).

♦ Lists of **Useful Addresses** and **Useful Websites** are contained in **Appendices A** and **B** respectively.

♦ For those unfamiliar with the metric system of **Weights & Measures**, conversion tables are included in **Appendix C**.

♦ The airlines serving Switzerland from the UK and USA are listed in **Appendix D**.

♦ A map showing the Swiss cantons is inside the back cover. Other physical, road and rail maps are shown in **Appendix E**.

♦ Glossaries of property terms in French-English and German-English are included in **Appendix F**.

# Introduction

If you're planning to buy or rent property in Switzerland or even just thinking about it, this is **THE BOOK** for you! Whether you're seeking a modern apartment, a period house or a chalet, a holiday or a permanent home, ***Buying or Renting a Home in Switzerland*** will help make your dreams come true. The aim of this book is to provide you with the information necessary to help you choose the most favourable location, and most appropriate home to satisfy your personal requirements – and at the right price. Most importantly, it will help you avoid the pitfalls and risks – not that there are many – associated with buying a home in Switzerland

You may already own or rent a home in another country; however, buying or renting a home in Switzerland (or in any 'foreign' country) is a different matter altogether. One of the most common mistakes many people make when buying or renting a home abroad is to assume that the laws and procedures are the same as in their home country. **This is rarely, if ever, the case!** Buying property in Switzerland is generally very safe, particularly when compared with some other countries. However, if you don't follow the rules provided for your protection, a purchase can result in a serious financial loss, as some people have discovered.

For most foreigners, buying or renting a home in Switzerland has previously been a case of pot luck. However, with a copy of ***Buying or Renting a Home in Switzerland*** to hand you'll have a wealth of priceless information at your fingertips – information derived from a variety of sources, both official and unofficial, not least the hard won personal experiences of the authors, their friends, colleagues and acquaintances.

This book doesn't contain all the answers – but what it will do is reduce the risk of making an expensive mistake that you may regret later, and help you make informed decisions and calculated judgements, instead of costly mistakes and uneducated guesses (forewarned is forearmed!). **Most important of all, it will help you save money and will repay your investment many times over.**

Buying or renting a home in Switzerland is a wonderful way to make new friends, broaden your horizons and revitalise your life, and – if you're a non-resident – it will provide a welcome bolt-hole to recuperate from the stresses and strains of modern life. I trust that this book will help you avoid the pitfalls and smooth your way to many happy years in your new home in Switzerland, secure in the knowledge that you've made the right decision.

**Viel Glück/Bon courage!**

*David Hampshire &*
*Anne-Marie Travers*

January 2010

Madonna del Sasso, Orselina, Ticino

# 1.
# MAJOR CONSIDERATIONS

**B** uying or renting a home in Switzerland isn't only a major financial commitment, but is also an undertaking that can have a huge influence on many other aspects of your life, including your health, security and safety; your family relationships and friendships; and your lifestyle, opinions and outlook. You also need to bear in mind any restrictions that may affect your choice of location and type of property, such as whether you'll need (or be able) to learn another language or dialect; whether you'll be able (or be permitted) to find employment or start a business; whether you can adapt to and enjoy the climate; whether you'll be able to take your pets with you; and, not least, whether you'll be able to afford the kind of home (and lifestyle) that you want. In order to ensure that you're making the right move, it's as well to confront these and other major considerations before making any irrevocable decisions.

## WHY SWITZERLAND?

Switzerland is one of the most beautiful countries in Europe, and one of the most captivating, with an abundance of ravishing landscapes and charming towns and villages. It's a country of huge variety, offering something for everyone: magnificent unspoiled countryside for nature-lovers; a wealth of historical towns and ancient cities for history buffs; an abundance of mountains, lakes and rivers for sports enthusiasts; lively nightlife for the jet set in the major cities and resorts; excellent wines and cuisine for gourmets; a profusion of painting, sculpture and music for art lovers; and relaxation and tranquillity for the stressed. Few other countries in the world offer such an exhilarating mixture of beauty, culture, history, sophistication and style.

Furthermore, it has exceptional political, social and economic stability; excellent communications and transport infrastructure; quality homes and efficient public services; outstanding education and health systems; low taxation; a beautiful, clean and safe environment; a tolerant multicultural, cosmopolitan society where English is the *lingua franca*; and the highest quality of life and standard of living in the world. Put simply, it's one of the most attractive countries in the world in which to to invest, do business, live or work.

When buying or renting property in Switzerland, you aren't simply buying a home, but a lifestyle. As a location for a holiday, retirement or permanent home, it has few rivals, and offers a wide choice of high quality property and a fine climate for most of the year, particularly if you're a winter and/or summer sports enthusiast.

However, despite the many excellent reasons for buying or renting a home in Switzerland, it's important not to be under any illusions about what you can expect from a home there. The first and most important question you need to ask yourself is **exactly** why do you want to buy a home there? Obviously if you'll be working in Switzerland then you'll need somewhere to live and most employees initially rent a home there.

If you're seeking a holiday or retirement home, then you'll be able to choose from a much wider area, but will face many other decisions. For example, if you're seeking a second home, will it be used mainly for long weekends or for longer stays? Do you plan to let it to offset some of the mortgage and running costs? Are you primarily looking for a long-term investment or do you plan to work or start a business in Switzerland in future?

Often buyers have a variety of reasons for buying a home in Switzerland; for example, some people buy a holiday home with a view to living there permanently or semi-permanently when they retire. If this is the case, there are many more factors to take into account than if you're 'simply' buying a holiday home that you'll occupy for just a few weeks a year, when it may be wiser not to buy at all! If, on the other hand, you plan to work or start a business in Switzerland, you'll be faced with a whole different set of criteria.

Can you afford to buy a home in Switzerland, where property is relatively expensive? What of the future? Is your income secure and protected against inflation and currency fluctuations? In recent years, many people purchased holiday homes abroad by taking out second mortgages on their family homes and stretching their financial resources to the limit. Not surprisingly, when the recession struck in 2008, many people had their homes repossessed or were forced to sell at a huge loss when they were unable to maintain the mortgage payments. Another danger is taking out a mortgage in Swiss francs when your income is in another currency, such as £sterling, US$ or Euros, which could be devalued against the Swiss franc, leading to a huge hike in mortgage payments.

The Swiss aren't very mobile and they move house much less frequently than the Americans and British, which (along with historically low inflation) is reflected in the stable property market. Nevertheless, prices in some regions have increased considerably in the last decade, driven up by foreign buyers and speculators; in the major cities, fashionable resorts and most popular regions, prices rise faster than average, which is usually reflected in much higher purchase prices (see **Cost of Property** on page 196).

You shouldn't expect to make a quick profit when buying property in Switzerland, but look upon a property purchase as an investment in your family's future happiness, rather than merely in financial terms.

Unless you know exactly what you're looking for and where, it's sensible to rent a property for a period (see **Chapter 6**) until you're more familiar with the country or a particular region. As when making any major financial decision, it isn't wise to be in too much of a hurry. Many people make expensive (even catastrophic) errors when buying property abroad, usually because they don't do sufficient research and are too hasty, often setting themselves ridiculous deadlines (such as buying a home during a long weekend break or a week's holiday). Not surprisingly, most people wouldn't dream of acting so rashly when buying property in their home country! It isn't uncommon for buyers to regret their decision after some time and wish they'd purchased a different kind of property in a different region – or even in a different country!

---

☑ **SURVIVAL TIP**

Before deciding to buy a home in Switzerland, you should do extensive research (see page 103), study the possible pitfalls and be prepared to rent for a period (see Chapter 6).

---

## Advantages & Disadvantages

There are both advantages and disadvantages to buying or renting a home in Switzerland, although for most people the benefits far outweigh the drawbacks.

### *Advantages*

◆ guaranteed summer sunshine (most of the time) and winter snow in high-altitude resorts – Switzerland is one of the world's foremost winter and summer playgrounds;

◆ relatively good value for money (provided you avoid the most fashionable areas);

◆ unparalleled build quality and fixtures and fittings;

◆ a very secure and stable property market;

◆ a good long-term investment with sustainable growth prospects;

◆ historically and consistently low interest rates, with one the world's strongest and most stable currencies;

- safe purchase procedures (scams are almost unknown) and the honesty and integrity of (most) licensed real estate agents and notaries;

- an excellent country in which to establish or run a business with low corporate and personal taxes, state-of-the-art telecommunications and infrastructure;

- situated at the heart of Europe with excellent transport links, both domestically and internationally;

- a multicultural, multilingual and international society, where English is widely spoken;

- a gentle, slower pace of life in rural areas;

- a very high standard of living and quality of life, with excellent education and health facilities;

- comparatively low taxation, especially if you qualify for lump-sum taxation;

- one of the world's most stable countries – both economically and politically;

- a beautiful, clean and safe environment.

### *Disadvantages*

- restrictions regarding buying, renting and selling a holiday home for non-residents;

- long waiting lists for permits for holiday homes in some cantons for non-residents;

- high cost of property (and rents) compared with many other countries;

- relatively high home running costs compared with some other countries;

- high cost of living (although this is usually offset by high salaries and relatively low taxes);

- unexpected renovation and restoration costs if you buy an old home and don't do your homework;

- possible currency risks if your income isn't in Swiss francs;

- overbearing bureaucracy and paperwork (which was invented to prevent the Swiss having paradise on earth!);

- overcrowding in the major cities and popular tourist areas;

- the risk of overpaying for a home and being unable to sell it and recoup your investment;

- the expense of getting to and from Switzerland if you don't live in a nearby country or a country with inexpensive air or rail connections.

## CLIMATE

It's almost impossible to provide a general description of the Swiss climate, as it varies considerably from region to region (like the Swiss themselves); probably no other country in Europe has such diverse weather conditions in such a small area.

The Alps, extending from east to west, form a major weather division between the north and south of Switzerland, and separate weather forecasts are usually given for each area. The climate north of the Alps is continental with hot summers and cold winters, although prolonged periods when the temperature is below freezing are rare during daytime (unless you live on top of a mountain).

In winter, the average daytime temperature at higher elevations is often below zero and can be freezing, although the sun can be very hot and you can get sunburnt easily. In winter it usually snows everywhere at some time, even in the lowlands, although Basle gets an average of just 11 days snow per year and it rarely snows in Geneva (around nine days a year) and it usually melts within a day or two. At higher altitudes, it generally thaws by spring,

except above 2,000m (6,561ft). Many areas experience heavy fog and mist, caused by temperature inversions, particularly in autumn. In winter, avalanches are common but they rarely occur in towns or villages or on ski pistes where there's extensive avalanche protection (slopes where there's a danger of avalanches are cleared by blasting). Mudslides, rockfalls and floods are a danger in some areas in spring (with the winter thaw) and in summer.

In Ticino, south of the Alps, a mild Mediterranean climate prevails and even in winter it's significantly warmer here than elsewhere in Switzerland. Spring and autumn are usually mild and fine in most areas. Generally, Switzerland has more rainfall than most other regions of Europe (although Valais is particularly dry) and the country is noted for its low humidity and lack of wind. Most areas suffer occasionally from the *foehn*, a warm oppressive south wind often blamed for headaches, fatigue, vertigo, bad tempers and other minor irritating complaints (you can even buy a gadget to ease its unpleasant effects).

The daily weather forecast in winter includes the snowfall limit (*Schneefallgrenze, limite des chute de neige*), which is the lowest level (in metres) where snow will fall and where freezing point will occur (*Nullgradgrenze, limite du degré zéro*). Generally, Swiss weather forecasts are highly accurate. Average afternoon temperatures in Centigrade and Fahrenheit (in brackets) are shown in the table below:

The Swiss weather forecast is available by telephone (☎ 162 – CHF 0.50 plus 0.50 per minute) in the local language, on the Swiss television teletext service, via the internet (e.g. 💻 www.meteocentrale.ch/en and www.wetter.ch) and in daily newspapers. The pollen count (*Pollenbericht, indice de pollen*) is reported from March to July on the Swiss television teletext service, in daily newspapers and at 💻 www.meteoschweiz.ch (under Health). Avalanche bulletins are given on telephone service number ☎ 187 (CHF 0.50 plus 0.50 per minute) and in English on the website of the Swiss Federal Institute of Snow and Avalanche Research (💻 www.slf.ch/english/en).

## ECONOMY & TRADE

Despite its limited size and lack of raw materials, Switzerland is one of the most productive, competitive and prosperous countries in the world. Swiss products are renowned for their quality, reliability and after sales service, with a strong emphasis on the refinement and finishing of products, and high quality specialisation. Switzerland's success is due to a combination of technical know-how, enterprising spirit, hard work, virtually no strikes, high investment in plant and equipment, and an overriding pro-business mentality. Like Japan, it's largely dependent on imports, particularly raw materials, semi-finished and finished products, energy sources and food. Many Swiss companies are leaders

| Temperature/Rainfall Averages | | |
|---|---|---|
| Average Temperature °C (°F) | Rainfall in mm (inches) | |
| City | January | July |
| Basle     0.9 (33.6) | 18.5 (65.3) | 778 (30.6) |
| Berne     1.0 (33.8) | 17.5 (63.5) | 1,028 (40.5) |
| Geneva     1.0 (33.8) | 19.3 (66.7) | 822 (32.4) |
| Lucerne     0.2 (32.4) | 17.9 (64.2) | 1,545 (60.8) |
| Lugano     2.6 (36.7) | 21.1 (70.0) | 1,171 (46.1) |
| Sion     0.8 (33.4) | 19.1 (66.4) | 598 (23.5) |
| Zurich     0.5 (32.9) | 17.6 (63.7) | 1,086 (42.8) |

Source: 💻 www.meteoschweiz.ch.

in their fields and a 'Made in Switzerland' label has a certain cachet to many buyers, who gladly pay a premium for Swiss quality, durability and reliability.

One of Switzerland's most important industries is precision mechanical and electrical engineering, which produces highly specialised equipment and tools, particularly machine tools, and textile and printing machinery. Many Swiss companies are also world leaders in the fields of life sciences (biotech, MedTech, pharmaceuticals), information and communication technologies (ICT), and micro- and nanotechnology. Other major industries include watch-making, chemicals and pharmaceuticals, tourism, and the textile and clothing industries. The Swiss food industry is also prosperous and Swiss chocolate and cheese, among other foods, are exported throughout the world (Nestlé is the world's largest food company). Despite the fact that only a quarter of Switzerland's surface area is productive, Swiss farmers produce around 70 per cent of the country's food.

It's the service sector, however, which contributes most towards balancing the budget, in particular Swiss banks and insurance companies. The tourist industry is also important and is one of the country's largest employers, providing work directly or indirectly for some 250,000 people. Tourism is Switzerland's third-largest export earner (after the machine and chemical industries) with foreign tourists spending some CHF 15bn annually (around 3 per cent of GDP). The Swiss workforce consists of around 4.4mn people or around 55 per cent of the population (55 per cent men and 45 per cent women), some 25 per cent of whom are foreigners, mostly from the EU. Around 70 per cent are employed in the services sector, 25 per cent in industry, trades and construction, and 5 per cent in agriculture and forestry.

It was feared that Switzerland's rejection of European Union membership would prove an obstacle to future growth and prosperity, as few western countries are so dependent on the outside world for their economic survival. However, Switzerland has negotiated a series of bilateral trade treaties with the EU, and most EU citizens have the right to live and work freely in Switzerland (Swiss citizens have the same rights in EU countries). As a trading partner, Switzerland is the third-largest goods supplier and second-largest customer of the EU, and some 45 per cent of Swiss direct investment is in EU countries. The Swiss can therefore enjoy the benefits of EU membership without the bureaucracy and expense (nobody said the Swiss weren't smart!).

Switzerland cannot afford any kind of isolation, either with regard to energy or raw materials, or in relation to its capital and labour markets. For this reason, Switzerland's foreign exchange system has always been based on a free market, opposition to all forms of protectionism, and a policy of low customs duties with almost no restrictions on imports. It's ranked fourth in the world for economic freedom – behind Hong Kong, Singapore and New Zealand – and first in Europe.

Agricultural products are virtually the only exception. Most food imports are subject to high duties in order to protect the livelihood of Swiss farmers and ensure sufficient food production in times of need (due to their high production costs, Swiss farmers cannot compete with imports). Swiss farmers receive a large part of their income from federal subsidies, although there are regular battles over milk prices and production quotas. Despite the duties on imported food, Switzerland imports more agricultural products per capita than any other European country. Other important benefits of the Swiss farming policy are safeguarding the traditional Swiss way of life, particularly in mountainous regions, and the protection of the environment.

Agriculture is considered a vital prerequisite for the tourist industry. Nevertheless, each resident pays some CHF 500 a year to subsidise Swiss farmers.

The Swiss economy remains strong and competitive, despite the strength of the Swiss franc, high labour costs and ever-increasing competition. However, Swiss companies have felt the pinch in recent years and are increasingly being forced to move production and other facilities abroad, reduce prices and shave their profit margins. The Swiss economy is among the world's most open (number three) and most competitive (number eight), and its GDP per head (US$42,000) is the third-highest in the world, thanks primarily to high-value-added services, specialized industries, and a highly qualified workforce.

Switzerland spends more per capita on research and development, science and education than any other country, had the third-highest number of computers per head in 2008, and is a world leader in advanced technology exports. The Swiss economy is among the world's most open and most competitive – in 2009 it knocked the US off the top spot – and its exports as a percentage of GDP are the world's highest. The Swiss have also produced (per capita) more Nobel Prize winners and registered more patents than any other country.

### Recession

Switzerland's economic growth was relatively strong from 2004 to 2007, with average annual GDP growth of 2.9 per cent, although it slowed to 1.6 per cent in 2008 with the onset of the global financial crisis. Switzerland entered recession in early 2009, but wasn't as badly affected as many other countries, such as Germany, Japan, the UK and the US; and although exports fell by around 17 per cent in the first eight months of the year, the domestic economy remained relatively robust. The country's GDP contracted by around 2 per cent in 2009, although it's forecast to grow by 0.5-1 per cent in 2010.

The Swiss unemployment rate reached 4.2 per cent in November 2009 (around 150,000) – a five-year high – and is expected to reach around 5 per cent in 2010, an unprecedented level for a country that for many years officially had zero unemployment! The country's average inflation was just 0.89 per cent from 1994 to 2007, but rose to 2.4 per cent in 2008 due to high global food and fuel costs. Switzerland experienced deflation of around -0.4 per cent in 2009 and the forecast for 2010 is inflation of around 1 per cent.

## GOVERNMENT

Switzerland is the most politically stable country in the world. The Swiss constitution (reviewed and updated in 2001) provides both the Confederation and cantons with the system of a democratic republic, in the form of direct or representative democracy. Switzerland's foreign policy is neutral. A number of important recent referendums (e.g. EEA membership and Swiss UN troops, both of which were rejected) have shown only too clearly that the Swiss government is increasingly out of step (at least in terms of foreign policy) with its people. However, Switzerland's foreign policy isn't entirely isolationist and in 1992 it became a member of the IMF and the World Bank (it's also a member of the Council of Europe, GATT and the OECD). In 2002, the Swiss voted to become a member of the United Nations (after 57 years!).

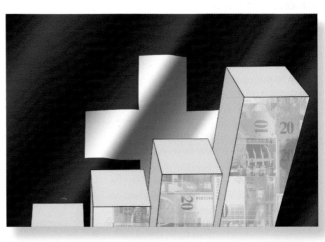

In Switzerland, power flows upwards from some 3,000 communities (Gemeinde, commune), each of which has a local council or municipal authority.

A Swiss citizen is first and foremost a citizen of a community (written in his passport), which remains ultimately responsible for his welfare throughout his life. In a community, the executive is the administrative council headed by the mayor, with legislative matters handled by the municipal council. The community levies local taxes and has self-rule in all matters that aren't the responsibility of either the federal government or the canton. These include the administration of public property such as forests; water, gas and electricity supplies; bridges, roads and administrative buildings; schools (primary education); and the civil defence, fire, health and local police departments. Several communities make up a borough or county (Bezirk, district).

Next in line are the 26 cantons (Kanton/ Stände, canton) – see **Chapter 2** – six of which rank as 'half-cantons' (half a canton is better than none). Each canton has its own written constitution and is in effect a sovereign state subject to federal law. The cantonal governments consist of an executive state council of five to nine members (each head of a department) and a legislative grand council of varying size, depending on the canton. Each canton is responsible for its own civil service; citizenship; church matters; education; finances and income tax; labour department; land usage; law and order; libraries; public health; public transport; roads; stock exchange supervision; and water and electricity supply.

The federal government is directly responsible for the armed forces; civil, criminal and industrial law; currency; customs and federal taxes; fishing, forestry and hunting (shared with the cantons); foreign policy; hydroelectric and nuclear power; monetary controls; pensions; post and communications services; and railways. Legislative power is exercised by the federal assembly (Bundesversammlung, Assemblée Fédérale), consisting of two chambers of equal status:

◆ **The Council of States** (Ständerat, Conseil des Etats) comprises 46 representatives of the cantons. The 20 'full' cantons have two representatives each and the six half-cantons one each.

◆ **The National Council** (Nationalrat, Conseil National), is elected for a four-year term and consists of 200 direct representatives of the people. The number of members allocated to each canton depends on their size and population, e.g. Zurich has 34 seats, while cantons Appenzell-Ausserrhoden, Appenzell-Innerrhoden, Glarus, Nidwalden, Obwalden and Uri have just one seat each.

Both chambers hold four regular sessions a year, each of three weeks duration, and bills must be debated and passed by both chambers. Members aren't professional politicians and hold other jobs, although most are self-employed or high-ranking corporate executives with the time and money to be part-time politicians. Politicians are paid around CHF 70,000 a year.

Traditionally, relatively few federal politicians have been women (possibly because they've only had the right to vote since 1971), although this is changing; in 2009, almost 30 per cent of Nationalrat members, 22 per cent of Ständerat members and three of the seven federal councillors were women. (In 2010, the President of Switzerland will be a woman, and both chambers – Nationalrat and Ständerat – will be presided over by women.) The misogynist men of half canton Appenzell-Innerrhoden steadfastly refused to give women the right to vote in community and cantonal elections, until being overruled by the federal government in 1990.

The federal assembly elects the seven federal councillors (comprising the federal executive, who serve for four years and head the departments of foreign affairs; the interior; justice and police; defence and sport; finance; economics and environment; and transport and energy (including communications). Re-election of federal councillors is permitted. Each year the assembly elects a councillor as president of the Confederation (who remains anonymous to everyone but his/her spouse). The highest judicial authority is the Federal Supreme Court, which sits in Lausanne and consists of 30 members elected by the federal assembly.

The Swiss system of democracy, although not perfect, is among the best ever devised. Almost everyone is represented through proportional representation (with the notable exception of the 1.7mn foreigners who comprise around 22 per cent of the population). Local communities and cantons have real powers that cannot be usurped or vetoed by the federal government, and all important decisions must be decided by the people through referendums. The system functions well because politicians of all parties work together for the greater benefit of the majority, rather than indulging in petty squabbling and party politics.

However, Swiss politics are also terminally boring for most foreigners, although the EEA/EU issue injected a modicum of interest in recent decades and the Swiss are beginning to debate issues with some passion (and invariably vote the opposite way in referendums from what their elected representatives would like – such as the vote in November 2009 to ban the building of minarets).

If you're an insomniac, you can find out more about Swiss politics at 🖳 www.socio.ch/poli.

## PERMITS & VISAS

Before making any plans to live or work in Switzerland, you must ensure that you have a valid passport (with a visa if necessary) and the appropriate documentation to obtain a residence permit. The laws regarding work and residence permits for European Union nationals (plus nationals of the European Economic Area/EEA – which includes the EU countries plus Iceland, Liechtenstein and Norway) changed in 2002, when the bilateral treaty between Switzerland and the EU/EEA was introduced. **Henceforth the acronym EU is used to refer to both the EU and the EEA, unless otherwise noted.** There are now two distinct categories of foreigners living and working in Switzerland: EU citizens, who in many ways have similar rights to Swiss citizens, and non-EU citizens, for whom it has become more difficult to obtain work and/or residence permits.

Foreigners entitled to live or work (or both) in Switzerland are issued with a residence permit (*Aufenthaltsbewilligung, autorisation de séjour*) in a plastic cover entitled 'foreigners' permit' (*Ausländerausweis, livret pour étrangers*). Although it isn't mandatory, it's advisable to carry your Swiss residence permit, passport or other official form of identification with you at all times within Switzerland.

Older children without residence permits should carry passports or identity cards to verify their age, for example to purchase reduced price public transport tickets and cinema tickets for age-restricted performances. Secondary school children are often issued with a school identity or student card (*Schülerausweis/Studentenausweis, carte d'identité scolaire/carte d'étudiant*). Foreigners working for international organisations in Switzerland are issued with an identity card (*Identitätskarte, carte de légitimation*) but not a residence permit, and aren't subject to quotas or the same regulations as people working for Swiss employers.

>  **Caution**
>
> Infringements concerning residence permits or registration of foreigners are taken very seriously by the Swiss authorities. There are penalties for breaches of regulations, including permit revocation and deportation for flagrant abuses.

### Visas

Some foreigners require a visa to enter Switzerland, whether as a visitor or for any other purpose. This includes most, so-called, third-world nationals – a term used by the Swiss authorities to refer to anyone who isn't a citizen of an EU or Schengen (see below) member country. **It doesn't mean nationals of third-world countries.** If in doubt, check with a Swiss embassy or consulate.

#### Visitors

If you aren't a national of a Schengen member country (see below) or a country on the Schengen visa-free list (see 🖳 http://

switzerland.visahq.com/requirements), you'll need a Schengen visa (⬛ www.schengenvisa. cc), costing CHF 60, to visit Switzerland. This also allows you to travel freely within all Schengen countries for up to 90 days in a six-month period or 180 days a year. If you have a multiple-entry visa, you can enter and leave the Schengen area any number of times within the 180-day period. There are also Schengen transit and short stay visas.

**Schengen visa holders aren't permitted to live permanently or work in Switzerland** (or any Schengen member country); business trips aren't considered to be employment. Foreigners who intend to take up employment or self-employed activity in Switzerland (or any Schengen country) may require an employment visa (see below), even if their nationality is listed on the Schengen visa-free list.

To extend a stay beyond three months without leaving Switzerland, you must apply to the local canton's 'aliens police' and be registered by your landlord with the local community if your stay exceeds three months. If you wish to establish temporary residence for longer than six months a year, you must apply at a Swiss embassy or consulate before arriving in Switzerland.

Non-EU nationals aren't permitted to visit Switzerland as tourists and seek employment, because applications for work permits are only considered when a non-EU national is outside Switzerland. However, you can visit Switzerland to meet prospective employers or attend interviews.

### Schengen Agreement

Switzerland is a signatory to the Schengen agreement, an open-border policy between 25 European countries. Switzerland officially became a member on 12th December 2008, and all land border controls between Switzerland and the other 24 member countries were removed (air border controls were removed in March 2009).

Other Schengen members are Austria, Belgium, the Czech Republic, Denmark, Estonia,

Finland, France, Germany, Greece, Hungary, Iceland, Italy, Latvia, Lithuania, Luxembourg, Malta, the Netherlands, Norway, Poland, Portugal, the Slovak Republic, Slovenia, Spain and Sweden. Bulgaria, Liechtenstein and Romania are planning to implement the agreement later. The United Kingdom and Ireland aren't members, but are signatories to the Schengen police and judicial cooperation treaty.

Under the Schengen agreement, immigration checks and passport controls take place when you first arrive in a member country from outside the Schengen area, after which you can travel freely between member countries.

### Work Permits

The latest work permit regulations are outlined below. For more information, see our sister publication, *Living and Working in Switzerland*.

#### EU Citizens

On 1st June 2002, a new permit system was introduced for most EU citizens under a bilateral agreement between Switzerland and the EU. This agreement applies to EU/EEA nationals from Austria, Belgium, Cyprus, Denmark, Finland, France, Germany, Greece, Iceland (EEA), Ireland, Italy, Liechtenstein (EEA), Luxembourg, Malta, the Netherlands, Norway (EEA), Portugal, Spain, Sweden and the UK.

Other EU countries (the Czech Republic, Estonia, Hungary, Latvia, Lithuania, Poland, Slovakia and Slovenia – termed the EU-8 countries – plus Bulgaria and Romania) are

United Nations, Geneva

excluded from the bilateral agreement for the time being, and considered to be non-EU citizens with regard to work permits in Switzerland. The transitional period for the EU-8 excluded countries will end on 30th April 2011, after which they will be allowed unrestricted access to work permits in Switzerland. For citizens of Bulgaria and Romania (termed the EU-2 countries), the transitional period will apply for a maximum of seven years, i.e. until 2014.

The agreement will eventually (expected in 2014) culminate in all EU citizens having complete freedom of movement within Switzerland, and Swiss citizens having the same rights within EU countries – unless the Swiss decide otherwise in a referendum. Under the agreement, Swiss employers are no longer required to prove that they cannot find a Swiss person to do a job before employing an EU citizen, and employers aren't required to disclose salaries to the authorities.

Companies registered in an EU country can send their employees to work in Switzerland for a maximum of 90 days each calendar year without obtaining a work permit. They must, however, register employees with the Federal Office for Migration (🖥 www.bfm.admin.ch), and provide the same conditions with regard to working time, salary and holidays as are mandatory in Switzerland.

For stays of up to 12 months and extendable for an additional six months, an L-EC/EFTA permit is issued, which can be transferred between employers and can be renewed if employment continues or a new job is found after that time. L-EC permit holders can also bring their families to Switzerland.

EU citizens with an employment contract for an unlimited term receive a B-EC/EFTA permit that's valid for five years, which allows employees to change jobs or cantons without any restrictions. If a B-EC/EFTA permit holder loses his job, he can stay in Switzerland for the duration of his permit, provided he has sufficient funds to live on and doesn't become dependent on social security. He can also claim unemployment benefits under the same conditions as a Swiss citizen, look for a new job or become self-employed. After five years the B-EC/EFTA permit is automatically converted to a permanent residence 'C' permit (*Niederlassungsbewilligung, permis d'établissement*).

### Non-EU Citizens

Non-EU citizens – so-called third world nationals – (and EU citizens who don't qualify under the new rules – see above) must obtain an 'assurance of a residence permit' (*Zusicherung der Aufenthaltsbewilligung, assurance d'autorisation de séjour*) before entering Switzerland to take up employment. This is an official document issued by the Swiss federal government stating that you've been offered a position with a Swiss employer or have been given permission to live in Switzerland, and that you'll be granted a residence permit after your arrival. The assurance must be obtained before arrival in Switzerland to take up residence.

Since the introduction of the Swiss-EU agreement, it has become more difficult for non-EU nationals to obtain work permits. Before applying for an annual permit for a non-EU national, a Swiss employer must have previously advertised the job vacancy in Switzerland. There are strict annual permit quotas in each canton, plus a federal government quota that can be used in exceptional circumstances. Each canton's quota is based on economic factors and manpower requirements in the canton. In deciding whether to grant a permit, the authorities consider the provision of essential services and supplies, economic necessity due to lack of personnel, and the promotion of commercial development. The authorities can usually exercise their discretion within the bounds of the law.

There are quotas in all cantons for non-EU nationals, including American citizens, and your success in applying for a work permit varies according to the canton, and often depends on the number of unemployed people in a particular canton. Other factors include the level of demand in certain fields.

Although a prospective employer may tell you in good faith that he can obtain a permit, he cannot guarantee that approval will be granted. It's impossible to state absolute rules as the criteria for the granting of permits are many and varied, and include qualifications, experience, profession, quotas, cantonal and federal government approval, the nationality of the applicant and his spouse, and the particular canton.

If the aliens' registration office rejects an application for a permit, the reason will be given in writing to the prospective employer, who will inform you of any right of appeal, the relevant appeal authority and any time restrictions that apply.

It can take up to three months for a non-EU national to obtain a residence permit to live or work in Switzerland – from the initial job application, interview and written job offer, until receipt of your permit approval. You must enter Switzerland within three months of the date of issue of your residence permit approval; if you're unable to take up employment within this period, you should inform your prospective employer so that he can apply for an extension.

Third-world nationals who are resident in Switzerland (or in any other Schengen country – see above) can travel freely to all Schengen member countries without a visa, simply by showing their Swiss residence permit or Schengen ID card (issued to new third-world nationals resident in Switzerland) and a valid travel document, e.g. a passport.

## Residence for Investors

If you're from a non-EU country, you can qualify for residence as an investor (EU citizens can qualify as retirees – see below). In order to qualify, you must invest at least CHF 500,000 in a small to medium-sized company situated in the canton where you intend to live. The investment can be a loan or an equity investment or a combination, and must last as long as you remain in Switzerland. The company cannot be listed on a stock exchange and you cannot invest in a bank account, real estate or a bogus company, but in a real company with real employees. The investment must bring economic added value for the area by fostering job creation. Other conditions (that also apply to the standard residence permit for retirees) are that you must be retired with no day-to-day responsibilities and have an annual income of over CHF 100,000.

You're expected to live in Switzerland for most of the year (over 180 days a year) and you won't qualify if you live abroad most of the time and only spend, for example, the summer or winter in Switzerland. Finally, unless you're a famous artist (actor, singer, sportsperson, etc.) you need to show some ties to Switzerland such as previous trips or periods spent in the country, close Swiss friends, relatives living in Switzerland or other ties.

Investors receive a B permit which is renewed annually and gives you the right to live in Switzerland with your family (wife and children), buy real estate for your own use, and pay taxes under the lump sum taxation system.

## Fiscal Deal

The fiscal deal permit (*Pauschalbesteuerung, forfait fiscal*) is a variant of the class B permit and is primarily for wealthy individuals who wish to live in Switzerland off income earned outside the country; e.g. international sports' players such as tennis players and Formula 1 racing drivers, who have no need or desire to work in the country. To obtain a fiscal deal permit you need certified net wealth of at least CHF 2mn and must spend at least 180 days a year in the country.

The fiscal deal permit allows you to pay considerably less tax (see page 180) than a

Swiss national with the same income would usually pay, as the assessment for tax isn't based on your actual worldwide income, but on a much lower notional amount. The amount of tax payable is a matter of personal negotiation with the canton where you reside; not all cantons issue fiscal deal permits and some, such as Zurich, have voted to abolish them. If you qualify, it usually takes about three months to obtain a fiscal deal permit.

### Retirees

Nationals from an EU-15 country (Austria, Belgium, Denmark, Finland, France, Germany, Greece, Ireland, Italy, Luxembourg, the Netherlands, Portugal, Spain, Sweden and the United Kingdom) can obtain Swiss residency as a retiree, i.e. someone 'without employment or gainful activity', whether in Switzerland or any other country. There's no longer an age limit for EU-15 nationals (which used to be 55), although you must have a minimum annual income equal to CHF 60,000. **However, non-EU-15 nationals must be aged at least 55 in order to retire in Switzerland.** You aren't permitted to work in Switzerland, although you can be semi-active, with limited activities abroad. The spouse of the principal applicant can be any age, and you can also bring children with you who are below the age of 18, i.e. of school age.

You must live in Switzerland for most of the year (over 180 days a year) and it isn't possible to qualify if you live abroad most of the time and only spend, for example, the summer or winter in Switzerland. Finally, unless you're a famous artist (actor, singer, sportsperson, etc.) you need to show some ties to Switzerland, such as previous trips or periods spent in the country, close Swiss friends, relatives in Switzerland or other ties. Bear in mind that the cantonal authorities may apply stricter rules; for example, an applicant who meets the federal requirements can still be refused a residence permit for other reasons, such as to maintain the balance of Swiss and foreign residents.

If you're a retiree you receive a B permit which is renewed annually and gives you the right to live in Switzerland with your family (wife and children), buy real estate for your own use, and pay taxes under the lump sum taxation system (see page 190).

## PETS

If you plan to bring a pet (*Haustier, animal domestique*) with you to Switzerland, check the latest regulations beforehand and ensure that you have the correct documents, not only for Switzerland but for all the countries that you must pass through to reach Switzerland, e.g. if travelling by road. If you need to return prematurely, even after a few hours or days, to a country with strict quarantine regulations, your pet could be put into quarantine.

### Swiss Regulations

There's generally no quarantine priod for animals in Switzerland. For entry into Switzerland, all dogs and cats over five months old must have an international health certificate stating that they've been vaccinated against rabies (*Tollwut, rage*). You must have an official letter stating that your pet was in good health before the vaccination, which must have been given at least 30 days and not more than one year before entering the country. Certificates are accepted in English, French, German and Italian. A dog or cat must also be microchipped or have a tattoo.

Dogs and cats under five months of age may be imported from many countries, i.e. most European countries (except Turkey and

Bernese mountain dog

the former USSR states), Australia, Canada, New Zealand and the USA, without a rabies vaccination, but a veterinary attestation of their age and good health is required. Dogs and cats from countries that don't require rabies vaccinations (e.g. Australia and New Zealand) can be imported without a vaccination certificate. Swiss residents aren't allowed to import dogs with cut ears or cropped tails, although those coming to live in Switzerland can import such dogs when they enter the country.

Dogs and cats arriving by air at Swiss airports are examined on arrival (fee CHF 88). If they don't have the required documentation or fail the examination, they're kept at the airport until the owner arranges a return flight, which must be done within ten days otherwise the animal will be put to sleep. Dogs and cats from Malaysia and cats from Australia are subject to additional regulations.

Birds (except canaries) need a special import licence, obtainable from the Federal Veterinary Office (see box), and are quarantined until it's established that they don't have parrot fever (psittacosis). Rabbits also need special permission and must undergo a quarantine period of around 15 days, but guinea-pigs, golden hamsters, rats, mice, aquarium fish and canaries may be imported without a health certificate. An import licence and a veterinary examination is required for some domestic animals, e.g. horses. Dangerous animals (e.g. poisonous snakes, man-eating tigers, etc.) require a special import licence.

> For the latest regulations concerning the importation or keeping of pets in Switzerland, contact the Federal Veterinary Office (Bundesamt für Vetrinärwesen, Office Vétérinaire Fédéral, Schwarzenburgerstr. 155, CH-3003 Berne, ☎ 031-323 30 33, 🖳 www. bvet.admin.ch).

## British Regulations

The Pet Travel Scheme (PETS – now under the auspices of the EU pet passport scheme), replaces quarantine for qualifying cats and dogs. Under the scheme, pets must be micro-chipped (i.e. have a microchip inserted in their neck), vaccinated against rabies, undergo a blood test and be issued with a health certificate (passport). In the UK, EU pet passports are issued only by Local Veterinary Inspectors (LVI), while in other EU countries passports can be issued by all registered vets. Allow plenty of time, as they can take months to be issued.

The scheme is restricted to animals imported from rabies-free countries and countries where rabies is under control, which includes most European countries plus many non-European countries including Australia, Canada, New Zealand and the USA (see the DEFRA website below for a complete list).

Pets exported from Britain must travel by sea via any major British ferry port, by rail via the Channel Tunnel or via any current and future UK and EU airports utilised by Easyjet. Only certain routes and carriers (listed on the website of the Department for the Environment, Food and Rural Affairs/DEFRA – 🖳 www. defra.gov.uk/wildlife-pets/pets/travel/pets) are licensed to carry animals. Contact DEFRA for further information (☎ 0870-241 1710, ✉ quarantine@animalhealth.gsi.gov.uk).

British pet owners must complete an Application for a Ministry Export Certificate for dogs, cats and rabies susceptible animals (form EXA1), available from DEFRA at the above address. DEFRA will contact the vet that you've named on the form, who will perform a health inspection. You'll then receive an export health certificate, which must have been issued no more than 30 days before your entry into Switzerland with your pet.

## General Information

Switzerland is now officially rabies-free, and dogs no longer require a rabies (*Tollwut, rage*) vaccination unless they travel to countries outside Switzerland, when they must have had a rabies vaccination at least six weeks before travelling and thereafter every two years. A vaccination for distemper (*Staupe, morve/ maladie carré*) is recommended every two years, but isn't mandatory.

A dog needs a licence when it's six months old, available from your local community office or the dog control office in major cities, on production of its international health certificate.

Owners now require private liability insurance (see page 234) in all cantons before a dog licence is issued. A card is issued by the insurance company, which must be produced when applying for a licence.

Licences must be renewed annually (the date varies depending on the community, which will make an announcement in local newspapers) and cost between CHF 60 and 180 a year depending on your community. If you have two or more dogs, the cost of licences can be astronomical in some areas. Owners of unlicensed dogs are fined. If you move home within Switzerland, you must re-register your dog in your new community, but you aren't required to pay the dog tax again if you've already paid in your previous community.

All dogs must be microchipped, and dogs arriving from abroad must have this done within ten days and be registered with the Animal Identity Service (ANIS, Morgenstrasse 123, CH-3018 Bern, ☎ 031-371 35 30, 💻 www.anis.ch). If the ownership changes, the owner moves home or the dog dies, it must be reported to ANIS. If a dog's found lost or roaming the streets, it's taken to an animal shelter (*Tierheim, refuge pour animaux*) and the owner is notified (through the microchip data).

If you plan to leave a pet at a kennel or cattery (*Tierpension, pension pour animaux*), book well in advance, particularly for school holiday periods. Dogs left at kennels must be inoculated against kennel cough (*Zwingerhusten, toux canine*), and all vaccinations must be registered with your veterinary surgeon (*Tierarzt, vétérinaire*) and listed on your pet's international health certificate.

Dogs must be kept on a lead (*an der Leine, être tenu en laisse*) in all public places. There are special areas and parks where dogs are allowed to roam free. Owners of dogs that foul public footpaths may be fined, so take a small shovel and plastic bag with you when walking your dog (no joke!). In some 75 per cent of communities there are special green containers (Robidog), around the size of a garbage can, which are for the disposal of dog waste (they also dispense plastic bags which can be used as gloves).

Brackets or hooks are provided outside many shops and in shopping centres, where you can secure your dog by its lead while shopping (most shops and public buildings such as post offices don't allow dogs entry). When dogs are prohibited, it may also be shown by a round sign with a red border and a white background with a black image of a dog in the centre. Dogs require half-price tickets on public transport and are (surprisingly) admitted to many restaurants.

---

### ☑ SURVIVAL TIP

Since September 2008, new dog owners have been required to attend dog-owner classes and dogs must also attend dog obedience school.

---

## Miscellaneous Information

Note also the following:

◆ Some apartments have regulations forbidding the keeping of dogs, cats and/or other animals.

◆ Most major cities and towns have veterinary hospitals (*Tierspital, hôpital pour animaux*) and a veterinary surgeon is usually on 24-hour call for emergencies. Ask the telephone operator (☎ 1811) for the number.

◆ A brochure regarding the keeping of dogs is published by some cantons.

◆ In some cantons you require special permission to keep a dog of a potentially dangerous breed, e.g. American Staffordshire Terrier, Bull Terrier, Dobermann, Dogo Argentino, Fila Brasileiro, Japanese Tosa, Pitbull Terrier, Staffordshire Bull Terrier and Rottweiler, and crosses of these breeds.

◆ A new federal law requires all dog bites to be reported to the police, and it's now mandatory to have liability insurance for your dog in all cantons.

◆ The death of a dog or horse must be reported to your community and your vet – they may have a special department. Your community or vet will arrange to collect and cremate the body for a fee, as you aren't permitted to bury a large dead pet in Switzerland; burying cats and other small pets is generally acceptable. You can also have a pet cremated privately and keep the ashes.

♦ Dogs and cats may travel on public transportation. Cats and small dogs (no larger than 30cm/12in at the shoulder) can be transported in a cage or basket when they travel free, otherwise they require a half fare ticket and must remain at your feet.

♦ If you take your dog to some countries, e.g. Italy, it must wear a muzzle.

If you want to take your pets from Switzerland to a country that doesn't have rabies, e.g. Australia, Ireland, New Zealand or the UK, it may need to go into quarantine for a period. Check with the authorities of the country concerned.

## LANGUAGE

An important consideration for anyone considering buying or renting a home in Switzerland may be the local language, which varies with the region. However, it isn't so important for tourists or retirees, provided you speak English. Switzerland has four official languages: German, spoken by around 70 per cent of the population (but note that the spoken and written languages differ – see **German** below), French (20 per cent), Italian (7 per cent) and Romansch (Rhaeto-Roman), which is spoken by around 35,000 people (0.5 per cent of the population) in the canton of Graubünden. The remainder are foreigners who don't speak one of the official Swiss national languages.

Although all official languages are equal in principle, this is often not the case in practice, and the German language and German speakers dominate most areas of public life, to the displeasure of the French-speaking Swiss. The cultural and linguistic division between the German- and French-speaking Swiss cantons is referred to as the *Röstigraben/rideau de rösti* (the 'fried potato cake' divide). Italian is usually relegated to a distant third place (except in Ticino).

Although English could be called the *lingua franca* of Switzerland, most official publications, forms, warning signs, etc., are printed in French, German and Italian, and seldom in English. However, English is a mandatory subject in most state schools from the age of 13 or later and is widely spoken by the middle-aged and youths, although less so by the elderly and in rural areas. Nevertheless, it's an important business and commercial language, even within Switzerland. Some 15 per cent of Switzerland's workforce uses English at work, with the German-speaking Swiss more likely to use it than French or Italian speakers. Wherever you work, you'll be inundated with forms, documents, memos and other communications written in the local language. Don't ignore them, as some will be important. The same applies to private mail – don't throw it away unless you're sure it's junk!

Berne, Fribourg and Valais are officially bi-lingual and have both French and German-speaking areas. Graubünden is tri-lingual, where people speak German, Italian and Romansch. Some Swiss towns are totally bi-lingual and languages are even alternated during conversation (the Swiss are very

democratic). In the national parliament, members are free to speak their mother tongue, which may explain why governmental decisions take so long (it's said that the Swiss get on so well because they don't understand each other). The problem of which language to use on stamps and currency is solved by using the Latin name for Switzerland, *Helvetia*.

Probably nothing will affect your lifestyle (and possibly your career prospects) in Switzerland more than your ability to speak the local language(s). What's more, in an emergency, being able to make yourself understood in a foreign language could make the difference between life and death!

## German

The language spoken in German-speaking areas of Switzerland is Swiss German (*Schwyzertüütsch*, *suisse allemand*). It bears little resemblance to the High German (*Schriftdeutsch/Hochdeutsch*, *bon allemand*) of Germany, which is a foreign language to the Swiss – although not half as foreign as Swiss German is to Germans, let alone the French- and Italian-speaking Swiss! There are over 100,000 recorded Swiss German words, and although many have their origin in High German, the Swiss have successfully managed to make them unrecognisable to anyone but themselves. To the casual listener, Swiss German sounds like someone trying to

speak while gargling and is often described as 'not so much a language as a throat disease.' There are many dialects of Swiss German, and sometimes inhabitants of neighbouring villages, let alone cantons, have trouble understanding each other.

Most native High German speakers are initially just as confused as other foreigners. Most Swiss German speakers do, however, speak High German (after a fashion) and, when talking to foreigners, many attempt to speak it, or at least will do so when asked. Note, however, that the Swiss don't particularly like speaking High German and many prefer to speak English.

Even if you don't understand what the locals are saying, the written language in Switzerland is High German, therefore if you understand High German you'll at least be able to read the newspapers. Strictly speaking, Swiss German isn't a written language and it's never used in official communications (the most common usage is in advertising). Most people write Swiss German using completely arbitrary phonetic spelling, and the Swiss cannot even decide how to spell *Schwyzertüütsch* (Swiss German). Nevertheless, there are a few children's books in Swiss German dialects and some poets and authors use it. (It's all a fiendish plot to prevent foreigners from understanding what's going on.) All cantons, except those listed under **French** and **Italian,** below, are Swiss German-speaking (some are bi-lingual with French or Italian).

### Swiss German

It's rarely necessary for foreigners to master Swiss German (*Schwyzertüütsch*, *suisse allemand*), although you may find yourself excluded from everyday life in German-speaking Switzerland if you don't understand it. You'll find that speaking Swiss German opens doors, both in business and socially, and it's particularly important if you plan to settle permanently in a German-speaking area of Switzerland or are thinking of applying for Swiss citizenship.

Opinion is divided over whether it's an advantage to speak High German before attempting to learn Swiss German. If your High German is poor, learning Swiss German won't help you speak, read or write High German, and may even be a hindrance. There are a significant number of foreigners in Switzerland who can speak Swiss German reasonably fluently but are unable to speak, read or write High German properly.

There are many language schools offering Swiss German classes, such as Migros Club School (*Klubschule Migros, École-club Migros,* 🖥 www.klubschule.ch) and the People's High School (*Volkshochschule, université populaire*), both of which run Swiss German classes in many areas (see above). For 'Züritüütsch' (Zurich Swiss-German) classes as well as audio courses (which you can order online), see 🖥 www.schweizer-deutsch.ch.

Various books are available for students of Swiss German, including *Schweizerdeutsch für alle* by Urs Dörig and *Wörterbuch Schweizerdeutsch-Deutsch* (Swiss-German – German dictionary) by Gerd Haffmans as well as *Hoi - your Swiss German Survival Guide* by Sergio J. Lievano & Nicole Egger (Bergli Books).

## French

French is spoken in the cantons of Geneva, Jura, Neuchâtel and Vaud, in addition to the bi-lingual cantons of Berne, Fribourg and Valais. In French-speaking Switzerland (*Westschweiz, suisse romande*) the language is almost the same as in France, with few Swiss idiosyncrasies. The accent is clear and good French is spoken, the purest in Neuchâtel, although the same claim is often made for the French of Geneva and Lausanne.

If you work in a French-speaking region, it's usually necessary to speak French at work. Social life in French-speaking areas of Switzerland can also be difficult without at least basic French, although in cities such as Geneva and Lausanne, English is widely spoken.

## Italian

Standard Italian is spoken in the canton of Ticino and parts of Graubünden (as well as 'High Italian' and some local dialects). It would be almost impossible to work in Ticino without speaking Italian. Socially, the language isn't

such a problem, as Ticino is a popular tourist area where people are used to dealing with foreigners. German is widely spoken in Ticino, mainly due to the influx of German and Swiss German tourists and retirees.

## HEALTH

One of the most important aspects of living in Switzerland (or anywhere else for that matter) is maintaining good health. The Swiss are generally very healthy and have one of the highest life expectancies in the world (84 for women and 79 for men) and also one the lowest infant mortality rates (around four deaths in the first year for every thousand live births). There are no special health risks in Switzerland and no immunisations are required unless you arrive from an area infected with yellow fever. You can safely drink the water (unless there's a sign to the contrary), although many people prefer bottled water.

However, the famous Swiss air isn't always as fresh as the guidebooks would have you believe. Despite strenuous efforts to reduce pollution, impure air and high ozone levels in summer in the major Swiss cities cause health problems (mainly respiratory ailments and allergies), particularly among children. Nevertheless, compared with what passes for fresh air in most countries, Swiss city air is pure oxygen. Pollution is also caused by smokers, as Switzerland rates highly in the world smoking league (per head of population) and has a relatively high proportion of young women smokers. The main causes of death in Switzerland are cardiovascular disease and cancer.

The Swiss are prominent in the lucrative 'immortality' business, which includes plastic surgery, rejuvenation and regeneration clinics, spa treatment centres and therapies by the dozen. Cellular rejuvenation (a bargain at around US$10,000) is especially popular, where patients are injected with live sheep cells – Switzerland abounds with geriatrics prancing around like spring lambs. Complementary medicine is also popular in Switzerland (particularly homeopathy) and is usually covered by Swiss health insurance.

Switzerland has courted controversy in recent years with its assisted suicide law and is one of the few countries in the world where it's legal (see 🖥 www.dignitas.ch).

Switzerland spends around 11 per cent of its GDP (a total of over CHF 50,000bn a year) on health, which is one of the highest percentages in the OECD. Although Swiss health insurance is expensive (only North Americans spend more on health care) and becoming more so every year, the country's health services are excellent and among the best in the world. Switzerland has a wealth of modern hospitals, highly-trained doctors (the highest ratio of doctors to patients in the world) and experienced nurses, and employs the latest equipment and medical techniques. There are generally no waiting lists for operations or hospital beds and the standard of treatment is second to none. If you must get sick, you could hardly choose a better place – provided of course you're insured or can afford to pay the bill!

Hospital facilities are excellent throughout Switzerland, although they're limited in rural areas, where the nearest hospital may be some distance away. There are usually no waiting lists for specialist appointments and non-urgent operations, as there are in many other countries. Switzerland's provision for disabled travellers is good and above average, particularly wheelchair access to buildings and public transport.

## Pre-Departure Health Check

If you're planning to take up residence in Switzerland, even for just part of the year, it's wise to have a health check before your arrival, particularly if you have a record of poor health or are elderly. If you're already taking regular medication, you should ask your doctor for the generic name, as the brand names of medicines vary from country to country. If you wish to match medication prescribed abroad, you'll need a current prescription with the medication's trade name, the manufacturer's name, the chemical name and the dosage. Most medicines have an equivalent in other countries, although particular brands may be difficult or impossible to obtain in Switzerland.

It's possible to have medication sent from abroad, when no duty or value added tax is usually payable. If you're visiting a holiday home in Switzerland for a short period, you

should take sufficient medication to cover your stay. In an emergency, a local doctor will write a prescription that can be filled at a local pharmacy, or a hospital may refill a prescription from its own pharmacy. It's also wise to take some of your favourite non-prescription medicines (e.g. aspirins, cold and flu remedies, lotions, etc.) with you, as they may be difficult or impossible to obtain in Switzerland or be much more expensive. If applicable, you should also take spare spectacles, contact lenses, dentures and a hearing aid, which will be much more expensive to replace in Switzerland.

## Health Insurance

It's particularly important to ensure that your family has comprehensive health insurance in Switzerland, whether you're visiting or living or working there permanently. If your current health insurance won't cover you in Switzerland, you should take out a travel or holiday insurance policy.

Basic health insurance (*Krankenversicherung, assurance maladie*) is compulsory for everyone living in Switzerland for three months or more (and their dependants), with the exception of international civil servants, foreign diplomats and employees of international organisations (and their families). They can, however, apply to join the Swiss health insurance system within six months of taking up residence in the country. Foreigners must obtain health insurance within three months of their arrival in Switzerland and babies must be insured within three months of their birth. Employees are usually insured from their first day of work in Switzerland.

Some large companies have their own health insurance schemes which offer advantageous conditions and reduced premiums for employees and their families. If you're a member of a health insurance scheme sponsored by your employer or a professional association, premiums may be deducted at source from your salary. Private health insurance premiums may be paid annually, quarterly or monthly by standing order from a bank account. Your employer may pay part or all of the cost of your health insurance, although this isn't usual.

Health insurance in Switzerland can be taken out with a health fund (*Krankenkasse, caisse maladie*) or a private health insurance company (*Krankenversicherung, assurance maladie*), similar to BUPA in the UK and BlueCross/BlueShield in the US. Health funds try to exert some control over doctors' and hospital fees, and are the cheapest form of health insurance in Switzerland. It's important to shop around as costs vary considerably between the cheapest and most expensive insurance companies in different cantons, which you can do online at 🖥 www.comparis.ch. The premiums of those with low incomes are subsidised by cantons, although you must make an application.

All insurance companies must offer identical basic cover as prescribed by law, which includes treatment by doctors, chiropractors, midwives and certain other practitioners (e.g. nurses and physiotherapists) when treatment is approved by a doctor; medication and laboratory tests; dental treatment necessary as the result of an accident or illness; hospitalisation in a general ward; and emergency treatment abroad. Existing conditions cannot be excluded from the basic cover, including pregnancy, although supplementary insurance can be refused.

Hospital treatment in a general ward is usually restricted by health funds to hospitals in your canton of residence, although you can choose to pay extra to be treated in a public hospital outside your canton of residence and for a half-private (two-bed) or private room. A health fund pays for treatment in a private clinic only when similar treatment isn't available locally in a general hospital.

A private health insurance scheme usually includes half-private or private hospital cover as standard, and may include medical services and medicines that aren't covered by a health fund. You can sign up for basic health insurance with one insurance company and have additional coverage (e.g. half-private or private) with another.

Standard cover (e.g. a general hospital ward) from a health fund usually costs between CHF 230 and 500 per month for an adult, depending on the insurer, where you live, your age, which deductible you choose, and whether or not you (or your spouse or partner) are covered for accidents by an employer (employees who work more than eight hours a week are insured by their employer against occupational and non-occupational accidents).

Premiums have been increasing in leaps and bounds in recent years, particularly private and half-private hospital cover (which can double your premium), and vary depending on your canton and whether you live in a city (where premiums are higher). Premiums for private and half-private cover can be reduced by payment of an excess or deductible (*selbstbehalt, franchise*). The minimum compulsory excess is CHF 300 per year for adults (zero for children), although you can choose to pay up to CHF 2,500 (the maximum). Patients must pay 10 per cent of all non-hospital costs (treatment, medicines, etc.) above the excess.

Health insurance companies offer various plans, designed to save you (and the insurance company) money. One plan (which saves you 10 to 15 per cent) limits your free choice of doctors (you choose from a list) and requires you to consult your GP before, for example, consulting a specialist. Another, called 'Telmed' or 'Premed24', requires you to call a hotline before making an appointment with a doctor. This is useful, as hotline staff can advise on medical issues and may even save you a trip to the doctor – if necessary they will authorise a doctor's visit and also save you around 8 per cent. Hotlines are staffed by registered nurses, and doctors are available for consultation when necessary. However, plans will only save you money if you follow the rules. If, for example, you visit a doctor without obtaining authorisation on the 'Telmed' plan, you'll be charged more – unless it's an emergency.

Standard health cover is valid worldwide and pays a maximum of twice what the same treatment would cost in Switzerland, which could be a problem in the US, where it's advisable to take out supplementary cover or travel health insurance. However, under bilateral treaties between Switzerland and the EU, Swiss and EU citizens travelling to an EU country receive only the cover that's compulsory in that country, which may be different from Switzerland. It's therefore advisable to have additional travel insurance, which can be obtained from many Swiss insurers for an annual premium of around CHF 150-200 for a family.

If you live and/or work in Switzerland, you may also wish to consider becoming a member of the Swiss air rescue service (known as REGA, 🖳 www.rega.ch), whose services may not be fully covered by your health or accident insurance.

## European Health Insurance Card

The European Health Insurance Card (EHIC) allows EEA residents to access state-funded healthcare in Switzerland and all EEA countries at a reduced cost or sometimes even free of charge. Applications for an EHIC are free, and it's valid for up to five years. If you're resident in an EEA country, you can apply for an EHIC and should carry it with you when travelling in Europe – but don't forget to check that it remains valid.

The EHIC only entitles you to treatment that's urgent or medically necessary during a temporary visit to Switzerland – **under the Swiss health insurance scheme (excluding private practitioners)** – and it doesn't allow you to visit Switzerland specifically to obtain medical care. The EHIC allows you access

to the same state-provided healthcare in Switzerland (including medicines on the official list) as a resident. Maternity care, renal dialysis and managing the symptoms of pre-existing or chronic conditions that arise while abroad are also covered by the EHIC. However, dental treatment isn't covered unless it results from a serious illness or an accident.

If you require treatment, you must show your EHIC card and usually pay for the full cost of treatment and services, but can claim a refund afterwards from the Gemeinsame Einrichtung KVG (**Gibelinstrasse 25, Postfach, CH-4503 Solothurn, ☎ 032-625 30 30, 🖳 www.kvg. org**). However, if you're admitted to a public hospital, the invoice will go directly to the Gemeinsame Einrichtung KVG. You must pay a fixed charge (CHF 92 for adults and CHF 33 for children) for each 30-day period of treatment. This is known as the excess charge, deductible or patient's contribution, and isn't refundable in Switzerland, but you may be able to seek reimbursement from your home country's public health service.

Note that the EHIC isn't an alternative to travel insurance. It won't cover private medical healthcare or the cost of things such as mountain rescue in ski resorts or repatriation. For these reasons and others, it's important to have both an EHIC and private travel insurance. Some insurers now insist that you have an EHIC and may waive their excess if you have one.

If you live in Switzerland you can obtain an EHIC from your Swiss insurance company and use it when travelling to EEA countries, when medical costs are charged directly to the Swiss insurance system. Without an EHIC (or private international insurance) you must pay doctors' or hospital fees yourself, and apply for a refund from your insurance company or national health service – usually a time-consuming process!

## International Health Policies

If you're living or working in Switzerland for less than three months (e.g. on a contract basis) and aren't covered by Swiss compulsory health insurance, you'll need an international health insurance policy. These usually offer members a choice of premiums: to cover average health costs or to provide cover in countries with high medical costs, which usually includes Switzerland. Besides the usual doctors' and hospital fees, claims can generally be made for body scans, convalescence, home nursing, outpatient treatment, health checks and surgical appliances. With an international health insurance policy, you may be able to renew your cover annually, irrespective of your age, which could be important. If you already have private health insurance, you may be able to extend it to cover your family in Switzerland.

Fortress Aarburg, Aargau

Lake Zurich

# 2.
# THE BEST PLACE TO LIVE

**H**aving decided to buy or rent a home in Switzerland, you need to choose the region, canton and town – and what sort of home you want. If you're looking to buy a home but are unsure about where and what to buy, the best decision is usually to rent for a period (see Chapter 5). You may be fortunate and buy the first property you see without doing any research and live happily ever after. However, a successful purchase is much more likely if you thoroughly investigate the towns and communities in your chosen area, and compare the types and prices of properties and their relative values. It's a lucky person who gets his choice absolutely right first time; however, there's a much better chance if you do your homework (i.e. due diligence) thoroughly.

The 'best' place to live in Switzerland obviously depends on your preferences and whether or not you'll be working. There are beautiful – and affordable – places to live, even in the most expensive cantons (such as Geneva, Vaud and Zurich), although you'll need to avoid the most fashionable areas and – if you're working – you may have to travel a bit further to the 'office' than you would wish to. In the last few decades there has been a dramatic increase in the number of people moving to a lower cost canton or area and commuting to work. On the other hand, if you planning to buy a holiday home, you should consider the accessibility of a region or area from your home country, as well as local public transport.

This chapter contains an overview of Switzerland's regions and a survey of each canton, plus comprehensive information (see **Choosing the Location** on page 71) about the local, practical issues a family needs to consider when choosing where to live in Switzerland.

## GEOGRAPHY

Switzerland is a landlocked country (it has been described as the only island in the world surrounded entirely by land!) situated in the central Alpine region of central Europe, with borders with five countries: Italy (734km/456mi) to the south, Austria (164km/102mi) and the Principality of Liechtenstein (41km/25mi) to the east, Germany (334km/207mi) to the north and France (573km/356mi) to the west. Some two-thirds of its frontiers follow the natural contours of mountain ridges, lakes and rivers, with around 25 per cent of its area consisting of scenic high Alps, lakes and barren rock. Switzerland is a small country of 41,290km$^2$ (around 15,940mi$^2$), with a maximum distance from east to west of 348km/216mi and just 220km/137mi from north to south. The Alps, mainly in the central part of the country, reach altitudes of over 4,000m (13,123ft).

Geographically, Switzerland can be divided into three main regions:

♦ The alpine massif, which includes the whole of southern Switzerland, covers some 60 per cent of the country and is home to around 20 per cent of the population. Approximately 20 per cent of the total alpine range lies within Switzerland.

♦ The central plateau (Mittelland), north of the alpine massif, consists of some 30 per cent of the land area and is where some two-thirds of the population lives.

♦ The Jura mountains in the north-west make up the remaining 10 per cent of Switzerland and around 15 per cent of the population.

The highest point in Switzerland is the Dufour Peak of the Monte Rosa (4,634m/15,203ft) and the lowest Lake Maggiore, on the border with Italy (195m/639ft above sea level). The Swiss Alps contain the crossroads formed by the St. Gotthard, Grimsel, Furka and Oberalp passes, and are the source of both the Rhine and Rhône rivers. Due to its central position, Switzerland has long been an important link in communications and transport between northern and southern Europe, a fact that has been decisive in determining the course of Swiss history.

Communications and telecommunications are excellent and among the best in the world, with extensive motorway and rail networks with multiple connections with all its neighbours, and three major airports (Zurich, Geneva and Basle) and several minor regional airports, providing direct connections with most major international destinations.

Maps of Switzerland showing the cantons (also below), major cities, geographical features and communications, are included in **Appendix E**.

Switzerland is divided into 26 states, called cantons, which are described below.

## CANTONS

The old Swiss Confederacy was the precursor of modern-day Switzerland. The *Swiss Eidgenossenschaft*, as the Confederacy was called, was a loose federation of largely independent small states, called cantons. In the 16th century, the old Swiss Confederacy was composed of thirteen sovereign cantons, six land (or forest) cantons and seven city (or urban) cantons. Although they were technically part of the Holy Roman Empire, they had become *de facto* independent states when the Swiss defeated Emperor Maximillian in 1499. The six forest cantons were democratic republics, while the seven urban cantons were oligarchic republics controlled by noble families.

The old Swiss Confederacy existed from the late 13th century (the establishment of Switzerland is traditionally dated to 1st August 1291, on which Swiss National Day is celebrated) until 1798, when it was invaded by the French Republic, who transformed it into the short-lived Helvetic Republic.

Today there are 26 Swiss cantons comprising the federal state of Switzerland, many of which were originally fully independent states from the Treaty of Westphalia in 1648

Arosa, Graubünden

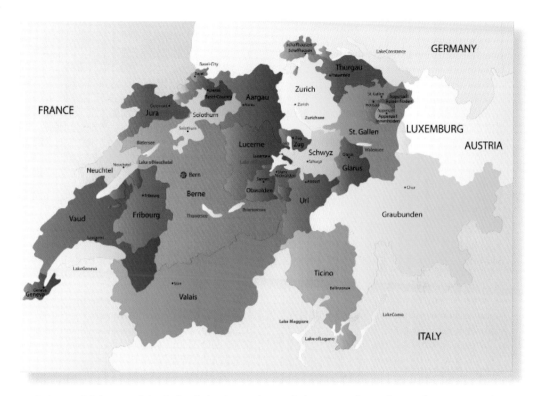

until the establishment of the Swiss federal state in 1848. (The country's formal name is *Schweizerische Eidgenossenschaft* in German, *Confédération suisse* in French, *Confederazione Svizzera* in Italian and *Confederaziun svizra* in Romansh.) The cantons are often referred to by their language groupings: the French-speaking cantons are *Suisse romande* or *Romandie* (Geneva, Jura, Neuchâtel and Vaud, plus the bi-lingual cantons of Berne, Fribourg and Valais); the Italian-speaking canton of Ticino is *Svizzera Italiana*; and the German-speaking cantons (the remainder) are *Deutschschweiz*.

Switzerland is a country that's held together by common ideals and objectives, rather than a common culture, language or religion. Its 26 cantons are sovereign 'states', i.e. autonomous, politically independent entities within the framework of a federal constitution, and each community or municipality (*Gemeinde*, *commune*) within a canton also enjoys broad autonomy. Although many things are harmonised and treated uniformly throughout the country, there remain a number of important areas (e.g. taxes) where regulations vary, depending on the canton and even the community.

Each canton has its own constitution, courts, legislature and government, most of which are unicameral parliaments with one house or chamber, varying between 58 and 200 seats. Cantonal governments consist of an executive state council of five to nine members (each head of a department) and a legislative grand council of varying size, depending on the canton. Under the Swiss Federal Constitution, the cantons are sovereign to the extent that their sovereignty isn't limited by federal law, although some powers are delegated to the Confederation by the constitution. The cantons are responsible for healthcare, welfare, law enforcement and education, and also retain the power of taxation. The cantonal constitutions determine the degree of autonomy accorded to the municipalities, which varies but usually includes the power to levy taxes and pass municipal laws.

As at the federal level, all cantons provide for direct democracy, whereby citizens may demand a popular vote (referendum) to amend the cantonal constitution or laws, or to veto laws or spending bills passed by the cantonal parliament. General popular assemblies (*Landesgemeinde*) – where citizens meet in an open-air gathering to decide on laws, council expenditure and to elect the council, and vote by a show of hands – are still held in the cantons of Appenzell-Innerrhoden and Glarus, while in all other cantons, democratic rights are exercised by secret ballot.

The cantons are listed below (in alphabetical order) with their two-letter abbreviation – widely used, e.g. on car license plates – capital towns and official languages.

An overview of each canton is shown below.

### Cantons

| Canton | Abbrev. | Capital | Official Language(s) |
|---|---|---|---|
| Aargau (Argovia) | AG | Aarau | German |
| Appenzell-Ausserrhoden | AR | Herisau | German |
| Appenzell-Innerrhoden | AI | Appenzell | German |
| Basle-City (Basel-Stadt) | BS | Basle | German |
| Basle-Country (Basel-Land) | BL | Liestal | German |
| Berne (Bern) | BE | Berne | French, German |
| Fribourg (G: Freiburg) | FR | Fribourg | French, German |
| Geneva (Genève) | GE | Geneva | French |
| Glarus | GL | Glarus | German |
| Graubünden (F: Grisons) | GR | Chur | German, Italian, Romansch |
| Jura | JU | Delémont | French |
| Lucerne (Luzern) | LU | Lucerne | German |
| Neuchâtel | NE | Neuchâtel | French |
| Nidwalden | NW | Stans | German |
| Obwalden | OW | Sarnen | German |
| St. Gallen (St. Gall) | SG | St. Gallen | German |
| Schaffhausen | SH | Schaffhausen | German |
| Schwyz | SZ | Schwyz | German |
| Solothurn | SO | Solothurn | German |
| Thurgau (Thurgovia) | TG | Frauenfeld/ Weinfelden | German |
| Ticino | TI | Bellinzona | Italian |
| Uri | UR | Altdorf | German |
| Valais (G: Wallis) | VS | Sion | French, German |
| Vaud | VD | Lausanne | French |
| Zug | ZG | Zug | German |
| Zurich (Zürich) | ZH | Zurich | German |

**Note: F = French and G = German.**

# Aargau

Aargau (capital Aarau, pop. 15,000) became a member of the Swiss Confederation in 1803 and was the former seat of the Habsburg dynasty; in 1798, five years before Berne became the federal capital, Aarau was the capital of Switzerland for six months. Situated in the north of Switzerland bordering Germany, Aargau comprises the lower course of the river Aare, from which it gets its name (meaning Aare district), covering an area of 1,404km² (542.1mi²). Water is depicted in the canton's coat of arms and three major rivers, the Rhine, the Aare and the Reuss, trace the natural borders of the canton. The population of Aargau is 591,632 (January 2009), of which 123,983 (21 per cent) are foreigners, who are fairly evenly split between Catholics (40 per cent) and Protestants (37 per cent). German is the most common language, spoken by 87 per cent of the population.

The canton is one of the least mountainous, forming part of a great table land to the north of the Alps and the east of the Jura mountains, above which rise low hills. The landscape is beautifully diversified, undulating tracts and wooded hills alternating with fertile valleys (watered by the Aare and its tributaries) and meadows.

For centuries, two villages in the canton of Aargau, Endingen and Lengnau, were the only places in Switzerland where Jews were permitted to live, although they weren't permitted to own houses or live under the same roof as Christians.

The farmland of the canton of Aargau is some of the most fertile in Switzerland – dairy farming, cereal and fruit farming are among the major economic activities. Aargau is heavily developed, with around 15 per cent of its land used for housing or transportation, and is Switzerland's most industrialised canton, notably in the fields of electrical engineering (the Swiss headquarters of ABB are situated in Baden), precision instruments, iron, steel and cement. Three of Switzerland's five nuclear power plants are also located in Aargau (Beznau 1 & 2 and Leibstadt) and the canton's many rivers (including the Rhine, Aare, Limmat and Reuss) provide power for a number of hydroelectric power plants within the canton.

Many residents commute to Zurich, which is just across the cantonal border, and to nearby Basle. Tourism is significant, particularly the hot springs at Baden, Schinznach Bad and Zurzach, ancient castles (Hallwyl castle is one of the most beautiful moated castles in Switzerland) and the canton's many museums. Aargau is noted for its art and culture and is home to some 70 museums offering exhibitions on a wide variety of themes, including the Dinosaur Museum in Frick, the Children's Museum in Baden, and the Art Gallery of Canton Aargau (Aarau), designed by the Swiss architects Herzog & de Meuron and home to one of the most comprehensive collections of modern Swiss art.

Aargau has excellent motorway connections via the A1, A2 and A3, and has direct rail links with Basle (49kkm/30mi) and Zurich (47km/29mi) and beyond; fast trains run every half hour from Zurich to the capital, Aarau, and regional trains serve other main towns. Travelling times from Aarau are: Basle (35mins), Berne (60mins) and Zurich (26mins). Zurich-Kloten International Airport (49km/30mi) can be reached by car from Aarau in 35 minutes and by train in one hour (trains run every half an hour), while Basle Airport (55km/34mi) is 55mins by road and 65mins by train (half an hour service).

---

### Aargau

**Official website:** 🖥 www.ag.ch (German only).

**Tourist office:** Aargau Tourismus, Schlossplatz 1, 5000 Aarau (☎ 062 823 00 73, 🖥 www.aargautourismus.ch/en).

## Appenzell-Ausserrhoden

Appenzell-Ausserrhoden (capital Herisau, pop. 15,500) has been a member of the Swiss Confederation since 1513 (the 13th member), when it was part of the canton of Appenzell (until 1597). In 1597, the Protestant canton of Appenzell was divided into two, for religious reasons: Appenzell-Ausserrhoden (sometimes called Appenzell Outer Rhodes in English) and Appenzell-Innerrhoden (see below), which are today officially designated half-cantons, with only one representative on the Council of States. The canton is situated in the northeast of Switzerland, bordering the cantons of St Gallen and Appenzell-Innerrhoden, with a population of 53,054 (January 2009) of which 7,279 (14 per cent) are foreigners. Due to the split of Appenzell, the majority of the population is Protestant (51 per cent) with Catholics comprising 31 per cent.

The Appenzell region is dominated by Säntis peak (2,502m/8,209ft) and the Alpstein, which consists of three mountain chains and is the most popular mountain-walking area in Eastern Switzerland, with a huge number and variety of hiking trails. Appenzell is a popular tourist destination, attracting both summer and winter sports enthusiasts, and is also noted for its folk traditions such as folk dancing, yodelling and mountain sports. *Silvesterchlausen*, a male custom dating back to the 16th century performed on Old Sylvester's Day (New Year's Day on the Julian calendar) in Urnäsch is world famous. The Appenzell region is famed as 'Heidiland', where Johanna Spyri was inspired to write 'Heidi'.

There's little industry in the canton. From the 16th century onwards, linen production was widespread, and developed into a larger textile industry that later diversified into weaving and embroidery, which collapsed in the '20s and '30s. In 2008, to attract new companies, Appenzell-Ausserrhoden lowered its corporate tax rate to 6 per cent, which is the lowest in Switzerland (matched by Obwalden).

Appenzell-Ausserrhoden is well connected to other areas of Switzerland, via the A1 motorway (Gossau and St Gallen-Wilkeln exits). Herisau is served by frequent trains from St Gallen (less than 10mins). The nearest international airport is Zurich (77km/48mi).

### Appenzell-Ausserrhoden

**Official website:** 🖵 www.ar.ch (German only).

**Other websites:** 🖵 www. appenzellerland.ch (German only).

**Tourist office:** Appenzellerland Tourismus AR, Bahnhofstrasse 2, 9410 Heiden (☎ 071-898 33 00, 🖵 www.appenzell. ch/en, ✉ info.ar@appenzell.ch).

## Appenzell-Innerrhoden

Appenzell-Innerrhoden (capital Appenzell, pop. 5,500) joined the Swiss Confederation in 1513 (the 13th member) and was part of the canton of Appenzell until 1597, when it was split into two (half) cantons – Appenzell-Ausserrhoden and Appenzell-Innerrhoden – for religious reasons. Due to the split, the population consists mostly of Catholics (over 80 per cent), with just 10 per cent Protestants. As a half canton, Appenzell-Innerrhoden (sometimes called

Appenzell Inner Rhodes in English) has only one representative in the Council of States. The population is 15,549 (January 2009) – the lowest of any canton – of which 1,565 (10 per cent) are foreigners.

Citizens assemble on the last Sunday in April for the *Landesgemeinde* (general assembly), where they meet in an open-air assembly to decide on laws, council expenditure and to elect the Governing Council by a show of hands (the only other canton where this traditional form of democracy is still practiced is Glarus). For men the 'polling card' still consists of a sidearm, usually a form of bayonet passed down through the family. The *Landesgemeinde* is an integral part of their political culture, through which the people of Innerrhoden identify with their state and its authorities. Appenzell-Innerrhoden is one of Switzerland's most traditional cantons, where women didn't have the right to vote at the cantonal level until 1990, and only then after it was imposed on them by the Federal Supreme Court of Switzerland.

Appenzell-Innerrhoden is situated in the northeast of the country, south of Lake Constance, and has borders with St. Gallen and Appenzell-Ausserrhoden. Nowhere else in Switzerland is the transformation from the hilly landscapes of the Swiss Mittelland to the rock-dominated alpine world so stark as in the Alpstein region. Appenzell's most famous peak is Mt Säntis (2,502m/8,209ft), which although well below the highest alpine peaks is nonetheless the highest point for miles around. The canton covers an area of 173km² (67mi²) and is the second-smallest canton by area (only Basle-City is smaller).

Most of the canton is pastoral, despite being mountainous, and cattle breeding and dairy farming are the main agricultural activities; it's most famous product, Appenzeller cheese, is widely available throughout Switzerland and abroad. The region is also famous for its weaving and embroidery. Tourism is a major earner and the canton is particularly popular among hikers and climbers, with the Säntis peak in the Appenzell Alps one of the main attractions. In the last decade, the idyllic countryside became popular with nudist hikers, which led to residents prohibiting naked hiking at the 2009 *Landesgemeinde*!

The region is noted for its independent culture, fashioned by long-held rural folk customs and religious traditions, such as mountain (folk) dancing, masked new year processions, yodelling and mountain sports; Gonten is the scene of the cantonal *Schwingen* (traditional wrestling) championships, held in late June. The traditional costume of the women of Appenzell-Innerrhoden is considered the finest in the country.

In a report published by Credit Suisse in 2008, Appenzell-Innerrhoden enjoyed the highest levels of disposable income after tax and fixed costs such as housing (it was also in first place in 2006). The report said that the canton was 'the most appealing place to live for the broad middle classes, thanks to relatively low real estate prices, moderate tax rates and the country's lowest health insurance premiums.'

It's common for cars rented in Switzerland to be registered in Appenzell-Innerrhoden, thus having license plates starting with 'AI', due to the canton having the lowest automobile tax rate in Switzerland.

For centuries the region was relatively isolated from the rest of Switzerland, but nowadays modern roads and cable cars ferry sightseers across the otherwise inaccessible terrain. Appenzell-Innerrhoden is well connected to other areas of Switzerland via the A1 motorway from the north and the A13 from the east. There's a frequent local train service to Appenzell from Gossau (40mins) and St. Gallen (around 50mins). The nearest international airport is Zurich (96km/60mi).

---

### Appenzell-Innerrhoden

**Official website:** 🖥 www.ai.ch/en.

**Other websites:** 🖥 www. appenzellerland.ch (in German only).

**Tourist office:** Appenzellerland Tourismus AI, Hauptgasse 4, 9050 Appenzell (☎ 071-788 96 41, 🖥 www.appenzell.ch/en, ✉ info.ai@appenzell.ch).

## Basle-City

Basle-City (capital Basle, pop. 165,000), which includes the municipalities of Bettingen and Riehen, joined the Swiss Confederation in 1501, when it was part of the canton of Basle. The cantons of Basle-City and Basle-Land were created when the canton of Basle was split into two in 1833, creating two half cantons. The division itself was instigated by the canton of Basle-Land (see below) and the constitution of Basle-City doesn't officially recognise the other half canton to this day! As a half canton, Basle-City has only one representative on the Council of States (although it's lobbying to become a full canton). In a survey conducted by Credit Suisse in 2008, Basle-City was ranked as having the second-highest cost of living in Switzerland after Geneva (Basle-Land was only marginally cheaper).

The canton of Basle-City is situated in the north of Switzerland, bordering France and Germany to the north, and Basle-Land to the south, at the so called 'knee' of the River Rhine where the little Birsig River joins the Rhine. The canton covers just 37km² (14mi²), making it by far the smallest, with a population of 186,672 (January 2009) of which 57,382 (some 31 per cent) are foreigners; Basle-City has the highest population density in Switzerland, at over 5,000 inhabitants per km² (1,930 per mi²). The population is fairly evenly split between Catholics (25 per cent) and Protestants (27 per cent), while some 10 per cent are classed as 'other religion', leaving almost 40 per cent who don't belong to any organised religion (perhaps to avoid church tax!).

Basle is a European cultural centre and the self-appointed 'cultural capital of Switzerland', with some 40 museums, including the world-renowned Beyeler Foundation and the Kunstmuseum (the first public museum in the world in 1661), numerous galleries, over 40 cinemas, 25 theatres, a wealth of music venues, and opera and ballet companies. The city hosts Art Basle in June, one of the world's leading contemporary art fairs, while the Basle carnival (*Basler-Fasnacht*, 🖥 http://fasnacht.ch), held over three days in February/March, is a major cultural event and the largest in Switzerland. Basle is also Switzerland's oldest university city (founded 1460).

Basle is the most economically dynamic region in Switzerland (and one of the most productive worldwide) and one of the country's richest cities. Its major industries are chemicals and pharmaceuticals, which include a number of multinationals, such as Novartis, Roche and Syngenta, attracting workers from both cantons

Basle City Panorama

of Basle and from across the border in France and Germany. Banking and finance are also important, as is the service sector in general, and it's also a major convention centre (the Basle Messe convention centre is host to a number of international events, including Baselworld, the world's most important watch and jewellery show).

The most popular places to live in Basle are along the banks of the river Rhine, St. Alban in Grossbasel, Wettstein in Kleinbasel, Gellert with many old and grand estates, and Bachletten (near the Zoo) and elevated Bruderholz on the southern edge of the city. The two suburbs of Riehen and Bettingen are also popular, both of which have their own distinct characters; Riehen is a wealthy small town with an excellent infrastructure, while Bettingen is a pretty village high above the city, but just 15mins away. You could also live in the canton of Basle-Land (see below) – which has lower taxes – some parts of which are closer to the centre of Basle than some areas of Basle-City. For example, Allschwil and Binningen (both on tram routes and within easy cycling distance of Basle-City), are situated in Basle-Land and take less time to get to the city than, for example, from Riehen.

Its location at the crossroads of three countries (*Dreiländereck*), where Switzerland, Germany and France meet, has made Basle a major transport hub, with excellent road and rail connections with its neighbours and the rest of Switzerland. Basle is a major rail intersection and is connected to Paris, Brussels and Berlin, with direct fast trains to all major Swiss cities. The city is served by the international EuroAirport of Basle-Mulhouse-Freiburg (6km/3.7mi), which is situated 4km inside French territory but has customs-free access from Basle. There's also a shipping port at Basle on the river Rhine, which is of major significance to landlocked Switzerland, providing the country's only direct connection to the sea. Local public transport is excellent, with extensive tram, regional railway (S-Bahn) and bus networks.

---

### Basel-City

**Official website:** 🖥 www.bs.ch (German only).

**Other websites:** 🖥 www.basel.ch/en, www.baselarea.ch/en, http://baselexpats.com.

**Tourist office:** Basel Tourismus, Aeschenvorstadt 36, 4010 Basle (☎ 061-268 68 68, 🖥 www.basel.com/en, ✉ info@basel.com).

## Basle-Land

Basle-Land (capital Liestal, pop. 13,000) joined the Swiss Confederation in 1501, when it was part of the canton of Basle. The cantons of Basle-City and Basle-Land were created when the canton of Basle was split into two in 1833, creating two half cantons. As a half canton, Basle-Land (also know as Baselbiet) has only one representative on the Council of States, although it (and Basle-City) are trying to change the Swiss constitution so that they can become full cantons.

In 1830, the people of the Basle countryside became increasingly distrustful of the city of Basle, which although it had a smaller population, dominated the cantonal parliament. When their demands for greater representation were refused, it led to a number of armed conflicts between the city and country dwellers, culminating in the Battle of Hülftenschanz (near Frenkendorf), where the city's troops were defeated. The split was now irreconcilable and the Swiss Confederation was successfully petitioned to create a new canton in August 1833. There have been frequent attempts to re-unify the two cantons, which were 'finally' defeated in a referendum in 1969 when the people of Basle-Land voted to retain their independence. When the canton of Jura was created in 1979, the district of Laufental became an enclave of the canton of Berne, but in 1980 the people voted to join the canton of Basle-Land, which finally came about in 1994.

The canton of Basle-Land is situated in the extreme north of Switzerland, bordering cantons Aargau, Basle-City, Jura and Solothurn, along with France (Alsace) and Germany (Baden-Württemburg). It covers an area of 518km² (200mi²), making it one of the smallest Swiss cantons (18th). Most of its landmass consists of undulating hills,

rather than mountains, although the canton is traversed by the Jura mountains; the highest point is Hinteri Egg (1,169m/3,835ft) and the lowest the River Birs (246m/807ft). It's home to 271,214 peo, 'e (January 2009), of which 50,247 (or 18.5 per cent) are foreigners, and is predominantly German-speaking. The main religion is Protestantism (43 per cent), while around a third are Catholics.

The capital, Liestal, is a picturesque medieval town with a car-free centre. On the Sunday night after Mardi Gras, *Chienbâse* is celebrated with a spectacular parade of people carrying burning bundles of pinewood chips, and carts carrying bonfires, from which the celebration takes its name. The tradition dates back to at least the 16th century, although its origins are unknown.

In its heyday, Augusta Raurica, a Roman Rhine-side provincial capital around 20km/12mi east of Basle near the modern village of Kaiseraugst, was home to some 20,000 people, and today comprises the largest Roman ruins in Switzerland.

The main agricultural produce of the canton is fruit, dairy farming and cattle, while other important industries include textiles, metals and chemicals. The canton is part of the economic centre around the city of Basle, which includes parts of France and Germany, as well as both cantons of Basle. Although tourism isn't a major industry, Basle-Land is famous for its Roman and Jurassic remains (sharks' teeth have been found dating back 160mn years), and charming, perfectly-preserved villages, and it's also one of the best hiking and cycling regions in Switzerland.

Basle-Land has excellent communications with other areas of Switzerland, via motorways A2 and A3, and frequent rail links with Basle (Liestal 10-15mins, direct service) and Zurich (Liestal around 1hr, with a change in Aarau or Olten). The nearest international airports are Basle-Mulhouse-Freiburg (23km/14mi to Liestal) and Zurich (83km/52mi to Liestal). The port of Basel-Land on the Rhine handles some 4,000 ships annually, and the canton also controls the largest railway marshalling yard in Switzerland, while the oldest Swiss tunnel goes under the Hauenstein Pass.

## Basel-Land

**Official website:** 🖳 www.baselland.ch (German only).

**Other websites:** 🖳 www.baselarea.ch/en, www.liestal.ch (German only).

**Tourist office:** Baselland Tourismus, Altmarktstrasse 96, 4410 Liestal (☏ 061-927 64 84, 🖳 www.baselland-tourismus. ch, ✉ info@ baselland-tourismus.ch).

## Berne

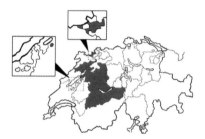

The canton of Berne joined the Swiss Confederation in 1353, and the city of Berne (pop. 123,000) is the capital of the canton and of Switzerland. Like most regions of Switzerland, Berne has a chequered history, and the boundaries of the canton have changed considerably over the centuries. Some towns/regions that were part of the canton include Aargau (1415), Aigle and Grandson (1475), Vaud (1536), and the *Pays d'En-Haut* including Château-d'Oex (1555). From 1798 to 1802, the Oberland was a separate canton of the Swiss Confederation called the 'canton of Thun', with Thun as its capital. Some French-speaking parts of the canton broke away as recently as 1979, when the Canton of Jura (see page 53) was formed.

The canton of Berne is officially bilingual – some 84 per cent are German-speaking and around 8 per cent French-speaking – with a population of 969,299 (January 2009), of which 123,649 (almost 13 per cent) are foreigners. The German-speaking majority speaks its own dialect of Swiss German (Bernese German), while most French-speakers live in the northern part of the canton in the Bernese Jura, where Biel/Bienne is a bilingual city. In the government and administration, both French and German are official languages with equal standing. The capital is home to barely 130,000 people – fewer than Zurich, Geneva, Basle and Lausanne.

Berne is located in west-central Switzerland and is the second-largest Swiss canton (after Graubünden), covering an area of 5,959 km$^2$ (2,301mi$^2$). It's commonly divided into three areas: the Bernese Oberland, the mountainous region lying to the south; the Berner Mittelland, the most densely populated region situated on a hilly plateau north of the Alps (home to the capital city); and the Bernese Jura, the northernmost and lowest-lying part of the canton situated south of the canton of Jura. Here lies the Three Lakes Region (*Seeland*), concentrated around Lake Biel (the other two lakes are Neuchâtel and Murten), rising from the plain up to the Jura mountains.

Berne is generally mountainous, with steep cliffs, glaciers and waterfalls, and is renowned for its scenic beauty and the charm of its historic towns and numerous villages. The highest mountain in the Bernese Oberland is the Finsteraarhorn (4,274m/14,020 ft), although the summits of the Eiger (3,969m/13,020 ft) and Jungfrau (4,158m/13,640 ft) are the most famous. The canton is home to many of Switzerland's most famous ski resorts, including Adelboden, Grindelwald, Gstaad (a rival to Davos, St Moritz and Zermatt for attracting the jet-set), Kandersteg, Lenk, Mürren (car-free), Saanen, Wengen (car-free) and Zweizimmen. The canton is also home to some of Switzerland's foremost hiking areas, which are centred around Interlaken and Thun.

Most Bernese are Protestants (some two-thirds) belonging to the Swiss Reformed Church, while Catholics comprise around 16 per cent of the population. There are also many other religions represented in Berne, which is one of the most religiously diverse of all Swiss cantons.

Not many cities have managed to retain their historic features as successfully as the medieval (12th century) city of Berne, which is a UNESCO Cultural World Heritage site. The medieval air of this city is unique, with its many 16th century fountains, sandstone facades, narrow streets, historic towers and its 6km/4mi of arcades (*Lauben*) – comprising one of the longest weather-sheltered shopping promenades in Europe. However, the city doesn't live in the past, and since the '70s has been considered the home of Swiss rock music and is one of the country's major international sports centres.

Tourism (it's the third most-important canton in Switzerland) is the main source of income in the Bernese Oberland, while other important sectors are agriculture, especially cattle breeding and dairy farming (cheese making), and hydroelectric power generation. The Bernese Emmental cheese (with holes), which gets its name from the Emme valley, is world famous and recognised as the quintessential Swiss cheese (although as the name is unprotected, it's imitated in many other countries). In the Bernese Mittelland, agriculture is of great importance, although this region is also the most industrialised. The three French-speaking districts of the Bernese Jura and the bilingual district of Biel/Bienne are famous as a major centre of the Swiss watch-making industry and high precision machinery.

Berne is well connected to other regions of Switzerland via motorways A1, A6 and A12, and has excellent rail connections. It's directly connected to the international train system and is serviced by high-speed international trains (the French TGV and the German ICE) and has direct services to all major Swiss cities. There's also a direct rail link to the international airports of Geneva (1hr 10mins) and Zurich (1hr 30mins). The regional airport, Bern-Belp (9km/6mi), has good domestic services, although international flights are limited; Zurich international airport is 126km/78mi away and Geneva airport is 161km/100mi.

The region boasts the highest train station in Europe (Jungfraujoch, 3,471m/11,388ft) and has an extensive network of cable cars and funiculars, including the longest funicular in Europe (Niesen) and the longest gondola cableway in the world (Männlichen). The city of Berne also has extensive tram and bus networks.

## Berne

**Official website:** 🖵 www.be.ch (French/German only).
**Other websites:** 🖵 www. berneroberland.ch.
**Tourist office:** Bern Tourismus, Bahnhofplatz 10A, Postfach, 3011 Berne (☎ 031-328 12 12, 🖵 www.berninfo.com, ✉ info@berninfo.com).

## Fribourg

The canton of Fribourg (Freiburg in German) joined the Swiss Confederation in 1481 and its current borders were established in 1803, when Murten (Morat in French) was acquired. The canton of Fribourg (capital Fribourg, pop. 32,000) joined the separatist league of Catholic cantons (*Sonderbund*) in 1846, but the following year its troops surrendered to the federal army. The population is 268,537 (January 2009), of which 46,066 (or 17 per cent) are foreigners, and predominantly Catholic (70 per cent) with a Protestant minority (15 per cent).

The canton is officially bilingual and is situated on the Swiss linguistic frontier (*Röstigraben, rideau de rösti*), with two-thirds of the population speaking French (in the west) and one-third speaking German (the Alemannic dialect) in the east (on the east bank of the River Saane, which forms the language 'border'). Fribourg is the only place in Europe where you can be educated from kindergarten to university in both French and German. The town's radio station has two separate channels, many streets have two names and almost everyone is instinctively bilingual.

The canton of Fribourg lies in the west of Switzerland, bounded in the west by the Lake of Neuchâtel and to the east by the canton of Berne, while to the west and south lies the canton of Vaud. The canton has a number of enclaves within other cantons; two in Vaud and one within the canton of Berne, as well as a larger exclave on the lake. Fribourg covers an area of 1,669km² (644.4mi²), including its enclaves, and lies on the elevated Swiss Plateau, with flat lands in the west rising to a hilly region towards the southeast. It's commonly referred to as pre-Alps but is actually part of the Bernese Alps, the highest point being Vanil Noir at 2,389m (7,838ft).

The capital Fribourg is picturesque and characterful, set on a forested peninsula in a meander of the River Sarine (Saane), with an attractive, almost perfectly preserved, medieval old town, steep, cobbled streets, wrought-iron lamp standards, ornate inn signs and a number of ancient bridges. The fortifications of Fribourg form the most important medieval military architecture in Switzerland, consisting of 2km (1.5mi) of ramparts, 14 towers and one large bulwark.

Fribourg University was the first in a Catholic canton in Switzerland (founded 1889) and is the only bilingual university in Switzerland.

Agriculture is an important industry (there are some 3,500 farms employing 10 per cent of the population), particularly cattle breeding and dairy farming in the north – La Gruyère is home of the famous cheese of the same name (and fondue) – tobacco, fruit cereals and forestry. There's some light industry concentrated around the capital Fribourg and many small and medium-sized businesses in the service sector, while the district of La Sarine is home to a number of electricity power plants. Tourism is also an important sector, particularly in the lake regions.

Fribourg is well connected to the north and south of the country via the A1 (east to west) and A12 (which links Berne to Vevey) motorways, and it's also on the country's main railway axis, which links Geneva to Zurich and Basle. The regional airport of Bern-Belp (34km/21mi) is around 30mins away, while the country's three main airports (Basle, Geneva and Zurich), are all around 150km/93m (1hr 30mins) distant. Fribourg originally had a tram network but it was replaced by trolley buses in 1949.

---

### Fribourg

**Official website:** 🖥 www.fr.ch (French/German only).

**Other websites:** 🖥 www.fribourgregion.ch/en.

**Tourist office:** Fribourg Tourisme, Avenue de la Gare 1, Case postale 1120, 1701 Fribourg (☎ 026-350 11 11, 🖥 www.fribourgtourisme.ch/en, ✉ info@fribourgtourisme.ch).

---

## Geneva

Geneva (capital Geneva, pop. 177,500) is the westernmost canton – or republic, as it likes to style itself – of Switzerland, situated in the southwestern corner of the country. It joined the Confederation in 1815, when its current borders were established. Geneva was an independent republic until 1798, but had been an ally of the Swiss Confederation since 1584. It was annexed and occupied by France during the Napoleonic wars, but after its liberation in

1813 joined the Confederation as the 22nd canton.

Geneva covers an area of 282km² (108.9mi²) and has the distinction of sharing just 4.5km/3mi of its land border with Switzerland (Vaud) and 103km/64mi with France. The population is 446,106 (January 2009), of which 170,094 (38 per cent) are foreigners, making it the most cosmopolitan and multicultural Swiss canton, home to some 200 nationalities. It's the sixth-smallest canton and has the highest population density at almost 1,500 people per km² (579 per mi²).

As a centre of the Calvinist Reformation, the city and canton of Geneva has traditionally been a Protestant stronghold, although today it's one of the most secular areas of the country. Over the latter part of the 20th century, the proportion of Catholics (40 per cent in 2000) rose considerably, primarily due to immigration from Southern Europe, and they now outnumber Protestants (17 per cent), although the canton is still officially considered Protestant. The University of Geneva, the second-largest in Switzerland (after Zurich), was founded by Jean Calvin.

The canton boasts magnificent countryside, lying between the Jura mountain range and the Salève, and the Alps and Lake Geneva (the northern shores are dubbed the 'Swiss Riviera'). The city of Geneva has the most beautiful of locations, centred around the point where the River Rhône flows out of Lake Geneva (*Lac Léman* in French, *Genfersee* in German), flanked on one side by the Jura ridges and on the other by the first peaks of the Savoy Alps. The city is also renowned for its fine old town, magnificently wooded parks along the lakeside, Rose Garden and Botanical Gardens. The symbol of the city is the illuminated Jet d'eau (1891), a fountain at the periphery of Lake Geneva with a 140-metre-high water jet. Geneva is one of Switzerland's leading cultural centres with some 40 museums, many theatres, an orchestra, opera and ballet companies; it's also a convention and congress centre, and a leading venue for international trade fairs and exhibitions.

The Gallic influence is what defines the city, tempered by a streak of Calvinism, so ingrained that the conservative Genevois, surrounded on all sides by decadent and delectable temptations, cannot quite bring themselves to indulge, leaving the high living largely to the international jet-set who live on the lakeside hills. Geneva has become the businessperson's city *par excellence*, unflappable, efficient, and packed with high-class hotels and excellent restaurants. However, it also has the most expensive real estate in Switzerland and a very tight housing market, with a vacancy rate below 0.5 per cent. Apartments and houses typically cost twice as much to buy or rent here than in most other

Geneva

cantons – and are twice as difficult to find! The cost of living is also among the highest in Switzerland. Not surprisingly, in a survey conducted by Credit Suisse in 2008, Geneva was ranked as having the highest cost of living in Switzerland.

The city is noted for its humanitarian traditions and cosmopolitan flair, and is the canton's centre of commerce, trade and finance, and also an international financial centre. A large number of Swiss banks are located here, particularly in the area of private banking; the banking sector includes some 140 banks, 2,600 finance companies and 1,000 trust companies. Geneva is also one of the main trading centres for raw materials, particularly crude oil, sugar, cotton and cereals, and offers cutting edge expertise in many high-tech fields such as watch-making, pharmaceuticals, chemistry, biotechnology, micromechanics and precision instruments (including medical instrumentation). Agriculture is also an important sector – farmland comprises some 50 per cent of the canton – particularly wheat, vegetables and wine.

The service industry is significant in Geneva, which houses the headquarters of some 250 non-governmental organisations and over 30 international organisations, including the United Nations (UN), the International Committee of the Red Cross (ICRC) – inspired by Henry Dunant, a Geneva businessman and the first person to be awarded the Nobel Peace Prize – the International Labour Organization (ILO), the World Health Organization (WHO), the World Trade Organization (WTO) and the European Organization for Nuclear Research (CERN). Some 30,000 French *frontaliers* commute daily to their workplaces in Geneva from dormitory towns just over the border, thus benefiting from both high Swiss salaries and relatively low French living expenses – and equally large numbers of Genevois save money by doing their shopping in France!

Geneva has excellent road, rail and air connections, both internationally and domestically. The canton is served by French TGV high speed trains to Geneva and Lausanne, and is linked by road to the rest of Switzerland via the A1 motorway. Geneva-Cointrin airport offers flights to over 100 destinations, of which around 80 are in Europe

(the airport has a 'French sector' allowing passengers to enter and exit France, without having to transit through Switzerland). The airport is 7km/4mi from the city centre, taking 6mins by train and 10mins by road. The city of Geneva has extensive tram and bus networks.

---

### Geneva

**Official website:** 🖵 www.ge.ch (French only).

**Other websites:** 🖵 www.geneve-communes.ch, www.geinfo.ch, www.geneve.ch, www.geneva.com, www.ville-ge.ch, www.whygeneva.ch.

**Tourist office:** Genève Tourisme & Bureau des Congrès, rue du Mont-Blanc 18, Case postale 1602, 1211 Geneva1 (☎ 022-909 70 00, 🖵 www.geneve-tourisme.ch, ✉ info@geneve-tourisme.ch).

---

## Glarus

The canton of Glarus (capital Glarus, pop. 6,000 – the smallest cantonal capital) is situated in eastern central Switzerland and joined the Confederation in 1352. Between 1798 and 1803 it was part of the Canton of Linth, which was established and occupied by Napoleon, but in 1836 the constitution was adapted to unite the region and establish one *Landesgemeinde* (popular assembly), which continues to this day on the first Sunday in May.

The population is 38,370 (January 2009), of which 7,430 (19 per cent) are foreigners, and is mostly German-speaking and fairly evenly split between Protestants (44 per cent) and Catholics (37 per cent), who now live peacefully together after having fought bitterly for supremacy over the centuries. Glarus is surprisingly progressive, and in 1864 introduced the first European labour law prohibiting workers from working more than 12 hours a day, while in 2007 it was the first Swiss canton to lower the voting age to 16.

The area of Glarus covers 685km² (264.5mi²), of which around half is productive, the rest being mountainous; the highest peak in the Glarus Alps is the Tödi at 3,614m (11,857ft), followed by Hausstock (3,158m/10,361ft) and Glärnisch (2,910m/9,547ft). The large (24.19km²/9.34mi²) lake of Walensee (or Walenstadt) is situated in the northeast, two-thirds of which is in St Gallen and one-third in Glarus. On its way from Lake Zurich through the Linth Plain, the deeply carved Glarus valley branches southwards shortly before the Walensee. Not far from the capital is the hiking region of the Klöntal and the Klöntalersee, a beautiful valley surrounded by mountains.

Some two-thirds of Glarus town was destroyed in a disastrous fire in 1861, after which it was rebuilt on a grid plan.

In the 18th century, textiles (e.g. printed fabrics), paper mills, and metal and machinery factories were important industries. Today the factories are largely just a tourist attraction, along with winter sports, hiking, mountain climbing and cycling. Other important industries include hydroelectric plants, plastics, printing, forestry, cattle breeding and dairy farming; *Glarner Schabziger*, a local cheese, is one of the oldest branded products in the world. Surprisingly, Glarus is one of the most industrialised Swiss cantons, with some 80 per cent of its products exported.

Glarus is served by direct trains from Zurich (55mins) and to Chur (one change) in 1hr 5mins. Access to Glarus by road is via the A3 (exit: Niederurnen-Näfels-Glarus) or A2 motorway (exit: Altdorf); Zurich (70km/44mi) is just 40mins away by road and it also has the nearest airport (81km/50mi).

### Glarus

**Official website:** 🖥 www.gl.ch (German only).

**Other websites:** 🖥 www.stadt-glarus.ch (German only).

**Tourist office:** Glarnerland Tourismus, Raststätte, 8867 Niederurnen (☎ 055-610 21 25, 🖥 www.glarusnet.ch, ✉ tourismus@glarusnet.ch).

## Graübunden

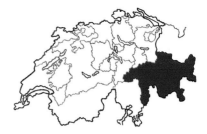

Graubünden (capital Chur, pop. 32,000), or Grisons in French, joined the Swiss Federation in 1803. It's the largest and easternmost canton of Switzerland, covering an area of 7,105.2km²/2,743.3mi² bordering Austria, Italy and Liechtenstein. The population is 190,459 (January 2009) – the most sparsely populated – of which 29,619 (or 16 per cent) are foreigners; the inhabitants are split fairly evenly between Catholics (47 per cent) and Protestants (41 per cent). The capital, Chur, is Switzerland's oldest settlement, with archaeological remains dating to the Pfyn culture (Neolithic period, 3900-3500 BC).

The name Graubünden translates as 'Grey Leagues/Unions' and refers to the canton's origin in three local alliances, the League of God's House, the Grey League (from the homespun grey clothes worn by the people at the time) and the League of Ten Jurisdictions.

Graubünden is Switzerland's only tri-lingual canton with three official languages: German or *Bündnerdeutsch* (68 per cent), mostly in the northwest; Romansh (15 per cent) in the Engadin and around Disentis/Muster; and Italian (10 per cent) in the southern valleys (the remaining 7 per cent speak French and other languages). The canton has many bilingual communities and the Romansh language and culture is an important part of its character; author and politician Heinrich Zschokke once remarked that Graubünden was 'Switzerland within Switzerland'.

Graubünden is almost entirely mountainous, comprising the highlands of the Rhine and Inn river valleys – many consider it the most beautiful part of the country. The highest peak in the Grison Alps is Piz Bernina (4,049m/13,284ft) and there are 11 glaciers in the canton. Some 90 per cent of the canton is above 1,200m (3,937ft), while the average peak is 2,100m (6,890ft); the mountain ranges in the central area also contain some of the deepest valleys (some 150) in Europe.

Tourism is the main pillar of the economy and the most important in Switzerland, employing over a third of the canton's workforce. Graubünden is a popular year-round tourist destination and is home to some of Switzerland's most famous resorts, including Davos, Klosters and St Moritz (where the Via Suvretta is one of the world's most expensive streets), plus Arosa, Flims, Laax, Pontresina, Scuol and Sils. Many of the canton's most scenic areas are part of the Swiss National Park (home to chamois, ibex and marmots) or the Ela Nature Park, while the Benedictine Convent of Saint John at Müstair, the Swiss Tectonic Arena Sardona and the Albula/Bernina railway are all UNESCO World Heritage sites.

Only a third of the canton is productive land, with forests covering over 25 per cent of the area and less than 2 per cent arable land. Agriculture (mostly mountain farming) includes forestry and mountain pasturage in summer, particularly sheep and goats, wine production (around Chur), maize and chestnuts. Chur is also an industrial centre.

Graubünden is well connected to other areas of Switzerland, via the A13 motorway from St. Gallen/Bodensee in the north and Lugano/Milan in the south, and also via the A3 to Basle and Zurich (1h 15mins). Chur has a direct rail connection from Zurich (1hr 17mins). The nearest international airport is Zurich (130km/81mi), with a direct rail connection (1hr 40mins). There's also a private airport (Engadin) Samedin) at St Moritz-Samedan, which is the highest in Europe, handling some 20,000 charter and private flights annually.

Local public transport in the difficult mountain terrain is provided by an integrated timetable of postbuses and trains. The Swiss Federal Railways only extend a few kilometres into the canton, to the capital, Chur, where passengers transfer to the Rhaetian (a Latin name for the area) Railway (RhB), with its famous Glacier and Bernina Express trains. The RhB has UNESCO World Heritage status and operates the largest narrow-gauge railway network in Switzerland (the cantonal government is the largest shareholder). Switzerland's most scenic railway, the Glacier Express – the slowest express in the world – connects St Moritz and Davos with the Valais resort of Zermatt.

---

### Graubünden

**Official website:** 🖥 www.gr.ch/en.

**Other websites:** 🖥 www.graubunden.com/en.

**Tourist office:** Graubünden Ferien, Alexanderstrasse 24, CH-7001 Chur (☎ 081-254 24 24, 🖥 www.graubunden.ch, ✉ contact@graubunden.ch).

---

## Jura

Jura (capital Delémont, pop. 11,500) is the most recently created canton, which separated from the canton of Berne in 1979 and became the 26th canton of the Swiss Confederation. The Jura region is French-speaking and

Catholic, whereas the canton of Berne was (and is) mostly German-speaking and Protestant. The people of the Jura region called for independence and in 1978 the Swiss people gave their consent in a referendum. However, the southern part of the Jura region, which is also predominantly French-speaking but with a Protestant majority, chose not to join the newly-formed canton and remained part of Berne. This area is now known as Bernese Jura.

The word Jura is used to refer to both Canton Jura and to the combined territory of Canton Jura and Bernese Jura, and is the name of the mountain range running from Geneva to Basle and also partly in France.

Situated in the northwest of Switzerland, Jura covers an area of 838km² (324mi²) and borders the cantons of Basle-Land, Berne and Solothurn, and France (Doubs), and consists of parts of the Jura Mountains in the south and the Jura plateau in the north. The population of 69,822 (January 2009), of which 8,440 (12 per cent) are foreigners, is almost entirely French-speaking, with just one German-speaking municipality (Ederswiler). The vast majority (75 per cent) of the population is Catholic, with a small Protestant minority (13 per cent).

The capital, Delémont (German: Delsberg), lies between the towns of Basle and Biel in the northwest of Switzerland, near the French border. This historic town is embedded in the densely forested, hilly Jurassic landscape, where mediaeval buildings, neat facades and interesting museums are features of the attractive old town. The Wenger knife factory was founded in Delémont in 1893 and is one of only two companies that manufacture official Swiss army knives, the other being its rival Victorinox (which acquired Wenger in 2005). However, Jura's prize is the charming mediaeval town of Saint-Ursanne on the banks of the River Doubs, whose treasures include collegiate churches, a cloister, castle ruins and a hermitage.

Agriculture is an important industry in Jura, including dairy farming (cheese), tobacco, and cattle and horse breeding, while the main industries (employing 40 per cent of the workforce) include watch-making (the Jura styles itself 'Watch Valley'), micro-technology, automation and textiles. However, economically, Jura is one of Switzerland's poorest cantons.

Delémont is around 45mins from Basle (42km/26mi) and an hour's drive from Berne (59km/37mi), Lucerne (104km/65mi) and Zurich (118km/73mi), and will be connected directly to the Swiss motorway network when the A16 motorway is extended to Biel/Bienne (scheduled for completion in 2016). Basle is 35-40mins by direct train from Delémont. Canton Jura will eventually be connected to the TGV Rhine-Rhone line, by linking the Biel-Delémont-Belfort route to the future French station in Meroux, situated just a few kilometres from the Swiss border. Jura also has its only local railway company, *Chemins de fer du Jura* (CJ), with 85km/53mi of lines; CJ also operates local bus services. The canton is around 40mins from the EuroAirport of Basle-Mulhouse-Freiburg.

---

### Jura

**Official website:** 🖳 www.jura.ch (French only).

**Tourist office:** Jura Tourisme, Place du 23-juin, 2350 Saignelégier (☎ 032-420 47 70, 🖳 www.juratourisme.ch/e, ✉ info@ juratourisme.ch).

---

## Lucerne

Lucerne (capital Lucerne, pop. 57,500) became the fourth member of the Swiss Confederation in 1332 and was the first city

Lucerne

to join. Situated in the centre of Switzerland on the northern foothills of the Swiss Alps (Urner Alps), the canton's highest point is the Brienzer Rothorn (2,350m/7,710ft). The canton covers an area of 1,493km²/576mi², with a mainly German-speaking population of 368,742 (January 2009), of which 59,735 (16 per cent) are foreigners. During the Reformation, Lucerne remained Catholic and is Rome's greatest ally in Switzerland; the *papal nuncio* resided here from 1601 to 1873. Today over 70 per cent of the population are Catholics, with just 12 per cent Protestant. Unlike Geneva and Zurich, Lucerne didn't support the Reformation and has always remained a stronghold of Catholicism, along with the rest of central Switzerland.

Situated between the Alps central plateau and mountains, lakes and rivers, Lucerne encompasses the traditional and the modern, the city and the countryside. The canton has various climatic zones and while the weather in the Napf and Pilatus region is rather humid, tropical fruit and palm trees thrive at the foot of the Rigi. By virtue of its unique topographic location and its eight lakes and six rivers, the canton has significant water reserves. Lucerne is the ideal starting point for excursions to the highlights of central Switzerland or a trip up one of Lucerne's regional mountains, Pilatus (2,132m/6,995ft) or Rigi (1,752m/5,748ft) – the queen of mountains – which straddles cantons Lucerne and Schwyz.

Queen Victoria came for a long holiday in August 1868, checking in under a pseudonym.

The beautiful city of Lucerne – many believe it's Switzerland's most attractive city – is an important cultural centre, with some

40 museums, a world-famous Culture and Convention Centre (KKL) that stages a number of renowned music festivals, and a celebrated Fasnacht carnival in February. Lucerne is also one of Switzerland's most charming and picturesque cities, with its unique 14th century Chapel Bridge (*Kapellbrücke*) and mediaeval old town, and Europe's largest fleet of steamships on Lake Lucerne. Tourism is an important sector and apart from being a popular destination in its own right, Lucerne is a gateway to holiday resorts in the nearby Alps and also a thoroughfare for much of the transit traffic between Germany and Italy.

The main sources of income are agriculture, industry and tourism. Some 55 per cent of the land is used for agriculture, primarily crops, fruit, tobacco and cattle breeding, while a further 30 per cent is forested; the remainder is either developed or unproductive (lakes, rivers or mountains). Industry includes textiles, machinery, paper, wood and metallurgical goods.

Located at the heart of Switzerland, Lucerne has excellent connections with other regions of Switzerland, via the A2 motorway, and has direct rail links with Basle (1hr 10mins), Geneva (2hrs 50mins) and Zurich (50mins). The international airports of Zurich (67km/42mi), Basle (103km/64mi) and Geneva (264km/164mi) are only a few hours by road from Lucerne, and can also be reached by direct express trains (Zurich 1hr 45mins). Local public transport consists of buses and trolleybuses.

---

### Lucerne

**Official website:** 🖥 www.lu.ch (German only).

Other websites: 🖥 www.lucerne.ch, www.luzern.org/en.

**Tourist office:** Luzern Tourismus AG, Zentralstrasse 5, 6002 Lucerne (☎ 041-227 17 17, 🖥 www.luzern.com/en, ✉ luzern@luzern.com).

## Neuchâtel

The canton of Neuchâtel (capital Neuchâtel, pop. 31,500) – Neuenburg in German – joined the Swiss Confederation in 1815, and has a population of 170,924 (January 2009), of which 40,593 (24 per cent) are foreigners – one of the highest percentages in Switzerland. The people are almost entirely French-speaking (they claim to speak Switzerland's 'purest' French) and historically have been strongly Protestant, although there has been an influx of Catholics in recent decades who now comprise 31 per cent of residents, compared with 38 per cent Protestants.

Neuchâtel was one of the first cantons to grant women the vote (in 1959) and also to give the vote to foreigners holding a residence permit and domiciled in the canton for at least five years (2002), as well as lowering the voting age to 18.

Neuchâtel is located in the west of the country (bordering Berne, Vaud and France in the northwest) and covers an area of 803km² (310mi²). Lake Neuchâtel lies southeast of the canton in the central area of the Jura Mountains, although the highest region is the Neuchâtelois Mountains (900-1,065m/2,953-3,494ft). From the lake to the ridges of the Jura mountain range, the canton offers a surprising variety of landscapes. Built of yellow sandstone, the charming university town of Neuchâtel is located on the northern shore of Lake Neuchâtel, nestling against the Jura hills. Other important towns include La-Chaux-de-Fonds (the third-largest French-speaking town in Switzerland) and Le Locle, both watch-making centres, which have received UNESCO World Heritage status in recognition of their exceptional universal value.

The canton is well-known for its wines, grown along Lake Neuchâtel, and also for dairy farming and cattle and horse breeding in the valleys; it also produces the world's best Absinthe (the 'green fairy'), made in Val-de-Travers, and which can be consumed legally nowadays. Watch-making is a long-established industry, which has evolved into a wealth of technical expertise in other high-tech fields such as micro- and nanotechnology, microchip production, machine tools, biotechnology and medical technology. Tourism (particularly eco-tourism) is also important and Neuchâtel has a wealth of hiking trails, cycle routes and nature reserves. It offers a wide range of cultural activities, including music and film festivals, excellent museums, street fairs and other festivals – a total of over 1,500 events are organised annually throughout the canton!

Neuchâtel

Neuchâtel is well connected to other areas of Switzerland via the A5 motorway and has direct rail connections with Basle (1hr 35mins), Berne (48mins), Geneva (1hr 20mins) and Zurich (1hr 50mins), and by TGV to Paris (3hrs 50mins). The nearest international airports are Geneva (122km/76mi) and Zurich (153km/95mi).

---

### Neuchâtel

**Official website:** 🖥 www.ne.ch (French only).

**Other websites:** 🖥 http:// en.neuchatelville.ch.

**Tourist office:** Tourisme Neuchâtelois, Hôtel des Postes, Case postale 3176, 2001 Neuchâtel (☎ 032-889 68 90, 🖥 www.neuchateltourisme.ch/e, ✉ info@ne.ch).

---

## Nidwalden

Nidwalden (capital Stans, pop. 7,500) jined an alliance with Obwalden, Schwyz and Uri in 1291 – the original four forest cantons (*Vier Waldstätten*) – which was considered the foundation of the Swiss Confederation. At this time Nidwalden, along with Obwalden, formed Unterwalden, which lasted until around 1330. Today, Nidwalden and Obwalden are officially designated 'half-cantons', with just one representative on the Council of States (rather than the two of a 'full' canton). Unlike Appenzell-Innerrhoden and Glarus, Nidwalden abolished its annual general assembly (*Landesgemeinde*) in 1997.

The population of Nidwalden is 40,737 (January 2009), of which 4,303 (11 per cent) are foreigners; over 75 per cent are Catholic and 12 per cent Protestant (Swiss Reformed Church). The vast majority of the population (over 90 per cent) is German-speaking, with small Italian (around 1.5 per cent) and Serbo-Croat (1.2 per cent) minorities. The canton covers an area of 276.1km² (106.6mi²) in the centre of Switzerland, bounded in the north by Lake Lucerne (*Vierwaldstättersee*) and in all other directions by the mountains of the Urner Alps. Framed by Lake Lucerne and striking mountains, the highest points are Mt Rotstöckli (2,901m/9,518ft), on the border with Obwalden, and the Stanserhorn (1,898m/6,227ft), which is accessible via a funicular, built in 1893.

Until the middle of the 20th century, agriculture dominated the economy, and even now 40 per cent of land is still used for farming, employing 10 per cent of the workforce. Today, forestry (forests occupy around a third of the land area), cattle and dairy farming are the most important sectors. Some 60 per cent of the workforce is employed in the service industry (e.g. tourism) and 30 per cent in manufacturing, such as machine construction, medical equipment, optics, electronics and aircraft manufacturing (the largest employer is the airplane maker, Pilatus). Tourism is also a significant contributor, with the canton's lakes and mountains attracting visitors year round. Major resorts include Klewenalp, Stanserhorn, and the region around Bannalp and Bürgenstock. In recent years, Nidwalden has become an increasingly popular place to live and work, due to its low taxes, central location and alluring landscape.

Nidwalden is well connected to other areas of Switzerland, via the A2 motorway (the main north-south route from Basle to Chiasso) and has a direct rail link with Lucerne (25mins) and from there to the rest of Switzerland. The nearest international airport is Zurich (82km/51mi).

## Nidwalden

**Official website:** 🖳 www.nw.ch (German only).

**Other websites:** 🖳 www.stans.ch.

**Tourist office:** Tourismus Stans/ Vierwaldstättersee Tourismus, Bahnhofplatz 4, 6371 Stans (☎ 041-610 88 33, 🖳 www.lakeluzern.ch, ✉ info@ lakeluzern.ch).

## Obwalden

Obwalden (capital Sarnen, pop. 9,500) joined an alliance with Nidwalden, Schwyz and Uri in 1291 – the original four forest cantons (*Vier Waldstätten*) – which was considered the foundation of the Swiss Confederation. At this time Obwalden, along with Nidwalden, formed Unterwalden, which lasted until around 1330. Today, Obwalden and Nidwalden are officially designated 'half-cantons', with just one representative on the Council of States (rather than the two of a 'full' canton). The population is 34,429 (January 2009), of which 4,276 (12 per cent) are foreigners; 80 per cent are Catholic and just 8 per cent Protestant.

Obwalden is situated in the centre of Switzerland – it contains the geographical centre of Switzerland on the Aelggi Alp (1,645m/5,397ft) in the commune of Sachseln – covering an area of 491km²/190mi². The highest elevation is Titlis (3,238m/1,062ft) in

the Urner Alps; the canton includes parts of Lake Lucerne (Vierwaldstättersee) and Lake Sarnen, plus many smaller lakes. The capital, Sarnen, is a peaceful town on the Sarnersee (Lake Sarnen) surrounded by mountains and rolling hills, has experienced steady growth in recent decades, due mainly to its proximity to Lucerne where many locals commute to work.

Small and middle-sized businesses dominate the economy, many of which are specialists in their areas such as miniature engines, synthetics, medical equipment and nanotechnology. Traditional sectors are still important, including forestry and dairy and meat farming, with many organic farms. Tourism is a major sector and employs around a quarter of the population.

The canton's central location in the Swiss Alps meant that it was able to establish itself as a popular winter and summer tourist destination as early as the 19th century. Its main attractions include the Urner Alps, where the resorts of Engelberg, Melchsee-Frutt, Lungern-Schönbüel, Mörliap and Langis are popular among winter sports fans, while in summer, cycling, hiking and climbing are popular pursuits.

In 2007, Obwalden replaced the former degressive cantonal income tax (lower tax rates for higher incomes, which was deemed

illegal) with a flat rate income tax of 1.8 per cent, which is the lowest in the country.

Obwalden is well connected to other areas of Switzerland, via the A8 motorway (Lucerne 20km/12mi, Zurich 66km/41mi) and has a direct rail link with Lucerne (32mins) and from there to the rest of Switzerland. The nearest international airport is Zurich (86km/53mi).

---

### Obwalden

**Official website:** 🖥 www.ow.ch (German only).

**Other websites:** 🖥 www.obwalden.net and www.sarnen.ch (both German only).

**Tourist office:** Sarnen Tourismus, Hofstrasse 2, 6060 Sarnen (☎ 041-666 50 40, 🖥 www.sarnen-tourism.ch/startseite_e. htm, ✉ info@ sarnen-tourism.ch).

---

## St Gallen

The canton of St Gallen (capital St Gallen, pop. 75,000 – variously shown as St. Gall, Saint Gall, Saint Gallen or Sankt Gallen) joined the Swiss Confederation in 1803 and covers an area of 2,026km² (782mi²), with a population of 471,152 (January 2009), of which 101,281 (21.5 per cent) are foreigners and 88 per cent German-speaking; 52 per cent of the population are Catholics and 28 per cent Protestant.

St Gallen is located in the north east of Switzerland, bounded by Lake Constance (*Bodensee*) to the north and the Rhine valley to the east (on the other side of the Rhine are Austria and Liechtenstein). The topography changes from the plains, near the River Rhine and Lake Constance, towards the mountainous areas of the Alps in the south (Appenzell and Glarus Alps). Around a third of the canton is wooded, while nearly half is farmland. The altitude varies from 398m/1,306ft at Lake Constance to 3,248m/10,656ft for the peak of Ringelspitz in the Glarus Alps. The canton includes part of the lakes of Constance, Walensee and Zurich, plus several smaller lakes that are wholly within its borders.

The city of St Gallen is the main urban centre of Eastern Switzerland and is a relaxed, conservative, university city, with a lively modern centre and a beautiful old town. The university of St Gallen (HSG) has the largest business faculty of any Swiss university and is one of the top business schools in Europe. The name and foundation of the city of St Gallen stem from the Irish missionary monk Gallus, who founded a hermitage in around 612 which became a Benedictine monastery in the 8th century. Today the **Convent of St Gall is** a perfect example of a great Carolingian monastery in its original form, and is considered the finest example of Baroque architecture in Switzerland. The Abbey precinct with the cathedral and Abbey Library (containing books dating to the 9th century) was designated a UNESCO World Heritage site in 1983.

Agricultural activity consists predominantly of dairy farming and cattle breeding in the mountainous areas; while in the plains, fruit and wine production are important, but there's also mixed farming. Industries include optical goods, pyrotechnics, chemicals and pharmaceuticals. St Gallen was once important for its textiles and machine-made embroidery, which today is just a cottage industry. Tourism plays an important role, and there are celebrated thermal spas at Bad Ragaz and St Margrethen; the region is also popular with both summer and winter sports enthusiasts. Its location in the four-country corner of Switzerland, Austria, Germany and the Principality of Liechtenstein, make St.

Gallen a convenient base for excursions to Appenzellerland, Säntis and Lake Constance.

St Gallen is well connected to other regions of Switzerland via the A1 motorway (Zurich 75km/46mi), and has direct rail links with Zurich (1hr 6mins), Berne (2hrs 21mins) and Geneva (4hrs 1mins), and internationally to Munich (3hrs 7mins) and Vienna (8hrs 16mins, 1 change). The nearest international airport is Zurich (83km/52mi). St Gallen has its own small airport (St Gallen-Altenrhein) with scheduled flights to Vienna, a local rail (S-Bahn) network and extensive bus services.

---

**St Gallen**

**Official website:** 🖥 www.sg.ch (German only).

**Other websites:** 🖥 www.stadt.sg.ch (German only).

**Tourist office:** St Gallen-Bodensee Tourismus, Bahnhofplatz 1a, 9001 St Gallen (☎ 071-227 37 37, 🖥 www.st.gallen-bodensee.ch/en, ✉ info@st.gallen-bodensee.ch).

---

## Schaffhausen

Schaffhausen (capital Schaffhausen, pop. 34,000) joined the Swiss Confederation in 1501. The largely German-speaking population numbers 75,303 (January 2009), of which 17,012 (23 per cent) are foreigners;

Protestants comprise 50 per cent and Catholics 24 per cent. It's the northernmost canton of Switzerland, bordering Germany (Baden-Württemberg) to the north, east and west (it actually looks as if it was carved out of Germany), and the cantons of St Gallen and Zurich to the south. (Schaffhausen's proximity to Germany had unfortunate results in 1944, when it was mistakenly bombed by the US Air Force, killing around 100 people.) The canton is divided into three parts; the largest includes the capital Schaffhausen, the second-largest contains Ramsen and Stein-am-Rhein to the east (bordering Lake Constance), and the third part in the southwest consists of the small district of Rüdlingen-Buchberg.

The canton covers an area of 298km² (115mi²), most of which lies on a plateau dominated by the Hoher Randen (912m/2,992ft). The Rhine Falls, the largest waterfalls in Europe, lie on the border of the cantons of Schaffhausen and Zurich, while to the west lies Lake Constance (*Bodensee*) covering an area of 571km² (208mi²).

The town of Schaffhausen owes its origins to the Rheinfalls; the settlement arose when shippers needed somewhere to unload and stack their goods when avoiding the rapids that were impassable for ships. It has a pretty old town with fine Baroque houses with oriel windows and richly-decorated façades, which were a status symbol of the rich merchants. The emblem of the town is the Munot fortress, built between 1564 and 1589 to a design by Albrecht Dürer.

The main agricultural activity is viticulture – the canton has some highly-regarded producers of pinot noir (*Blauburgunder* in German) wines, as well as several other varieties. The main industries, however, include the production of machinery and metal goods, watch-making (the world-renowned IWC has its home here), biotechnology, jewellery, textiles, leather goods, glass, cement, paper, chemicals and hydro-electricity (Rheinau). Tourism is also an important contributor to the economy, and the riverside landscape along the Rhine is a popular area for cycling, walking and boating.

Schaffhausen is well connected to other areas of Switzerland, via the A4 motorway (Zurich, 52km/32mi) and to the German *Autobahn* network (Stuttgart 1hr 30mins). The town of Schaffhausen lies on the busy Milan-Zurich-Stuttgart rail route, which is serviced by trains from both the Swiss SBB and the German Deutsche Bahn (Zurich, 39mins). Schaffhausen is also served by regional (S-Bahn) trains from Zurich and Winterthur and has an extensive local bus network. The nearest international airport is Zurich (49km/29mi).

---

### Schaffhausen

**Official website:** 🖥 www.sh.ch (German only).

**Other websites:** 🖥 www.schaffhausen.ch (German only).

**Tourist office:** Schaffhauserland Tourismus, Herrenacker 15, 8201 Schaffhausen (☎ 052-632 40 20, 🖥 www.schaffhauserland.ch/en, ✉ info @schaffhauserland.ch).

---

## Schwyz

Schwyz (capital Schwyz, pop. 14,000) joined an alliance with Obwalden, Nidwalden (subdivisions of the canton of Unterwalden) and Uri in 1291 – the original four forest cantons (*Vier Waldstätten*) – which was considered the foundation of the Swiss Confederation. Switzerland's name in German is derived from the name of the canton and the flag of Switzerland is taken from its coat

of arms. Schwyz has 143,719 inhabitants (January 2009), mostly German-speaking (or Swiss-German!), of which 25,675 (18 per cent) are foreigners; the vast majority of the population is Catholic, with just 13 per cent Protestant.

Schwyz is located in central Switzerland between the Alps in the south, Lake Lucerne in the east and Lake Zurich in the north, covering an area of 908km²/351mi². The highest elevation is the Bös Fulen (2,802m/9,193ft), although the summits of the Rigi massif (Kulm 1,798m/5,899ft, and Scheidegg, 1,665m/5,463ft) are more famous, although not as high. The canton includes parts of the lakes of Zurich and Lucerne and a small part of Lake Zug, plus the entire smaller lakes of Lauerz (Lauerzersee) and Sihl (Sihlsee). Schwyz is comprised of three dominant regions: Talkessel occupies the inner central area of the canton, the Höfe and March regions spread over the outer part of the canton, with Einsiedeln and Ybrig situated in between. The Hölloch cave in Muotathal runs to over 190km (118mi) and is one of the longest caves in the world and the largest in Europe.

The pretty capital town of Schwyz is home to the Forum of Swiss History and important founding documents of the Swiss Confederation. The Museum of the Swiss Charters houses the most important documents of the early Swiss confederacy, including the Confederation's founding document.

In the Middle Ages, the men of Schwyz were highly-prized as mercenary soldiers, and many became wealthy and returned to build the fine townhouses that characterise the old town today.

Agriculture is important in Schwyz, which is famous for its local breed of brown cattle which are renowned throughout Switzerland; other important industries include furniture-making, hydroelectric power plants and some textile production, although only remnants remain of this once important industry. The most famous manufacturer is Victorinox (Ibach-Schwyz) – the name comes from Victoria, the mother of the founder, and the international designation for stainless steel, INOX – makers of the iconic Swiss Army Knife, which celebrated 125 years in 2009.

Tourism is also important, particularly Rigi and its celebrated mountain railways, and the world-famous Benedictine monastery of Einsiedeln (with its 20,000+ volume library), which has been Switzerland's most important pilgrimage cite for over 1,000 years and still attracts over a quarter of a million pilgrims annually. The canton is also a popular winter and summer sports playground – Brunnen on Lake Lucerne, nestling between the Urmiberg and Fronalstock and facing the Rütli and Schillerstein mountains, is an important resort town. The Hölloch (Hell Hole), 190km/118mi, is one of the largest cave systems in the world and the largest in Europe.

Schwyz has among the lowest cantonal tax rates in Switzerland, where Freienbach (on Lake Zurich) in the north of the canton, is noted for the lowest taxes in Switzerland (which has attracted a number of wealthy residents). Schwyz is also the only canton with no inheritance or gift tax, and new companies enjoy tax breaks for up to ten years.

Schwyz is connected to other areas of Switzerland via the A4 motorway, and has direct rail links with Lucerne (46mins), Zug (29mins) and Zurich (53mins). The nearest international airport is Zurich (65km/40mi). The town is also served by a comprehensive bus service.

---

### Schwyz

**Official website:** 🖳 www.sz.ch (German only).

**Other websites:** 🖳 www.schwyz-tourismus.ch (German only), http://flash. swissknifevalley.ch.

**Tourist office:** Info Schwyz Tourismusbüro, Bahnhofstrasse 4, Postfach 655, 6430 Schwyz (☎ 041-810 19 91, 🖳 www.info-schwyz.ch, ✉ mail@ info-schwyz.ch).

---

## Solothurn

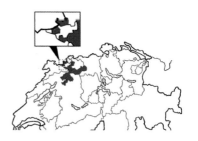

Situated in the northwest of Switzerland, covering an area of 791km²/305mi², Solothurn (capital Solothurn, pop. 15,000) joined the Confederation in 1481. The population of 251,830 (January 2009), 48,321 (19 per cent) of whom are foreigners, is mostly German-speaking. Some 44 per cent of the population are Catholics and 31 per cent Protestants. To the west and south lies the canton of Berne, to the east the canton of Aargau, with the canton of Basle-Land to the north; two districts are enclaves and are situated along the French border (the canton is the most ramified, i.e. branched, of all Swiss cantons). Although the landscape is mostly flat, or what passes for flat in Switzerland, it includes the foothills of the Jura mountains – where the canton's highest point is at Hasenmatt (1,445m/4,741ft) – and the rolling hills of the Schwarzbubenland, and is an area of outstanding natural beauty.

Solothurn, the capital, is one of Switzerland's most beautiful baroque towns, with a wealth of fine Baroque and Renaissance buildings, such as the magnificent St Ursen Cathedral, Besenval Palace, the Jesuit Church, patrician houses, and many gates and towers of the original town walls. From the 16th to 18th centuries, the town was the residence of the French king's ambassador. Olten, which has an equally impressive old town, is the canton's largest town and a major rail hub.

Solothurn has a special affinity to the number 11. It was the 11th canton to become part of the Swiss Confederation; it has 11 churches and chapels, as well as 11 historical fountains and 11 towers. St Ursus cathedral has 11 altars and 11 bells, and the cathedral stairs have levels between every 11 steps. Even the local brewery is named 11 (*Öufi* in Swiss German), and produces a beer with the same name!

Agriculture remains an important sector, but manufacturing and service industries are now more significant. Major industries include watch-making, jewellery, textiles, cement, paper and car parts (the shoe industry used to be important, but collapsed under pressure from cheap foreign imports). There's a nuclear power plant near Gösgen which commenced operation in 1979. Tourism is important and the canton is a popular destination for hikers and cyclists.

Solothurn is well connected to other regions of Switzerland, both by rail and road. The capital has direct rail links with Berne (49mins) and Zurich (53mins), while Olten is Switzerland's main rail hub with direct trains to Basle, Geneva and Zurich. Solothurn is well connected to other regions of Switzerland via motorways A1, A2 and A5. The nearest international airports are Basle (76km/47mi) and Zurich (100km/62mi).

---

### Solothurn

**Official website:** 🖥 www.so.ch (German only).

**Other websites:** 🖥 www.olten.ch (German only).

**Tourist office:** Region Solothurn Tourismus, Hauptgasse 69, 4500 Solothurn (☎ 032-626 46 46, 🖥 www.solothurn-city.ch, ✉ info@solothurn-city.ch).

---

## Thurgau

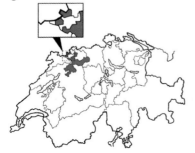

Thurgau (capital Frauenfeld, pop. 22,000) became a member of the Swiss Confederation in 1803 and covers an area of 991km² (383mi²). The population (mainly German-speaking) of 241,811 (January 2009), 49,869 (21 per cent) of whom are foreigners, is 45 per cent Protestant and 36 per cent Catholic.

Thurgau is situated in the northeast of Switzerland, with Lake Constance (*Bodensee*) to the north, bordering Austria and Germany, and the river Rhine to the northwest. To the south lies the canton of St Gallen and to the west the cantons of Schaffhausen and Zurich. It's commonly divided into three hill masses; one stretching along Lake Constance in the north, another further inland between the rivers of Thur and Murg, and the third forming the southern border and merging with the Hörnli mountain in the pre-Alps. The region is characterised by compact farming villages; historic towns, castles and monasteries; unspoilt countryside and woodland, orchards and vineyards; and, of course, the major influence of Lake Constance.

Thurgau is famous for its agricultural produce, notably apples (mainly for the production of cider), pears and other fruit, plus a variety of vegetables; wine is also produced in the Thur valley. The main industries are printing, textiles and handicrafts, with many small and middle-sized businesses concentrated around the capital, Frauenfeld. Among the many products made locally are trains (Stadler Rail), suits (Strellson), sandpaper (Sia), kitchens and radiators (AFG), sewing 'computers' (Bernina), cardboard packaging (Model) and aluminium drinks' bottles (Sigg).

Tourism is also an increasingly important sector; the gentle landscape (no mountains to climb) make the region a favourite among hikers, cyclists (some 900km/560mi of signed routes) and inline-skaters; Lake Constance is a popular venue for watersports or a boat ride over to Germany or Austria, while Connyland at Lipperswil is Switzerland's largest amusement park.

Thurgau is well connected to other areas of Switzerland, via the A1 and A7 motorways and has a direct rail link with Zurich (39mins) – Frauenfeld is also a stop on the Zurich S-Bahn – and a regional train service (Thurbo) connects all the major cantonal towns. The nearest international airport to Frauenfeld is Zurich (45km/28mi – around 30mins).

---

### Thurgau

**Official website:** 🖥 www.tg.ch (German only).

**Other websites:** 🖥 www.frauenfeld.ch, www.thurgau.ch (both German only).

**Tourist office:** Thurgau Tourismus, Egelmoosstrasse 1, 8580 Amriswil (☎ 071-414 11 44, 🖥 www.thurgau-tourismus.ch/en, ✉ info@thurgau-tourismus.ch).

---

## Ticino

Ticino or Regio Insubrica (capital Bellinzona, pop. 17,000) – Tessin in German – joined the Swiss Confederation in 1803 and is the southernmost canton of Switzerland. The 332,736 population (January 2009), of which 84,462 (25 per cent) are foreigners, is mostly Catholic (76 per cent), with a small Protestant minority (7 per cent).

Ticino is the only canton where Italian is the sole official language, spoken by 83 per cent of the population (of the remainder, 8.3 per cent speak German and 1.7 per cent Serbo-Croat). Despite being very similar to standard Italian, Swiss Italian has some variations from the Lombard Italian spoken in northern Italy, mainly due to the presence of French and German from which it assimilates words. Lombard dialects (Ticinese) are still spoken, especially in the valleys, but they aren't used for official purposes.

As a result of its more southerly position, Ticino is one of the warmest cantons in Switzerland, although it's prone to fierce storms and has the highest level of lightning discharge in the whole of Europe.

The canton of Ticino covers an area of 2,812km² (1,086mi²) and is located in the southeast of Switzerland, almost entirely surrounded by Italy, which lies to its east, west and south. To the north lie the cantons of Valais and Uri and to the northeast the canton of Graubünden. Forests cover around a third of the canton, and the lakes of Lugano and Maggiore (officially named Ceresio and Verbano, although these names are rarely used) also make up a considerable part of the total area. The canton is split into two by the Monte Ceneri pass; the northern (more mountainous) part is called *Sopraceneri* and is formed by the two major Swiss valleys (Maggia and Ticino) around lake Maggiore, while the southern part, called *Sottoceneri*, is the region around Lake Lugano.

Tourism is a major industry, thanks in particular to the canton's mild climate which gives it a Mediterranean air. Elegant and sophisticated Locarno (which clocks up the most hours of sunshine in Switzerland) – famous for its international film festival in August – and cosmopolitan Lugano are both popular tourist destinations, particularly in the spring when the camellias are in bloom. Another major attraction is Italianate Bellinzona, the cultural centre of the canton, whose three well-preserved mediaeval castles (Castelgrande, Montebello and Sasso Corbaro) were declared a UNESCO World Heritage site in 2000, as was the peak of Monte San Giorgio in 2003, rising to a height of 1,097m/3,599ft from the shores of the lake opposite Lugano.

The main agricultural production is wine, mostly (red) merlot, while horticulture, milk and cheese production and cattle breeding are also important. Other agricultural produce includes corn (maize), potatoes, tobacco and vegetables. The rivers of the canton are used extensively to generate electricity, while there's considerable light industry concentrated around the main towns. Finance is also an important sector and Ticino is Switzerland's third-largest financial centre after Zurich and Geneva.

Lake and city of Lugano, Ticino

The canton is well connected with the rest of Switzerland, with a number of (road and rail) tunnels through the Gotthard massif, connecting the canton to the rest of Switzerland via the A2 and A13 motorways and the E35 south to Milan. Lugano is on the main European north-south rail route with direct links to Milan and Rome in Italy, as well as Germany via Basle and Zurich (Zurich 2hrs 39mins, Milan 1hr 18mins). The nearest international airports are in Milan: Malpensa (45km/28mi) and Linate (66km/41mi); bus service from Malpensa to Lugano (1hr 15mins) or train from Milan Central (direct service 1hr). Zurich is the closest major international Swiss airport (165km/103mi) and Lugano also has a regional airport.

---

### Ticino

**Official website:** 🖳 www3.ti.ch (Italian only).

**Other websites:** 🖳 www.ascona.ch, www.bellinzona.ch (Italian only), www.locarno.ch (Italian only), www.lugano-tourism.ch/en, www.maggiore.ch, www.ticinohelp.ch.

**Tourist office:** Ticino Turismo, Via Lugano 12, Casella postale 1441, 6501 Bellinzona (☎ 091-825 70 56, 🖳 www.ticino.ch, ✉ info@ticino.ch).

## Uri

Uri (capital Altdorf, pop. 8,500) joined an alliance with Nidwalden, Obwalden and Schwyz in 1291 – the original four forest cantons (*Vier Waldstätten*) – which was considered the foundation of the Swiss Confederation. (In 1291, Nidwalden and Obwalden formed the combined 'region' of Unterwalden.) It's thought that the name *Uri* derives from the old German word Aurochs, meaning wild ox, which is supported by the bull's head that appears on the canton's flag and coat of arms. The mainly German-speaking population is 35,162 (it's one of the least populated cantons), of which 9 per cent (3,217 people) are foreigners, 86 per cent of whom are Catholics and just 6 per cent Protestants.

The legendary William Tell is said to have hailed from Uri – immortalised by Friedrich Schiller in his play 'Wilhelm Tell'.

The canton is situated in central Switzerland, north of the Swiss Alps, covering an area of 1,077km² (416mi²). It encompasses the Reuss river valley stretching from Lake Uri to the Ursern valley at the St Gotthard Pass; Uri's side valleys – Erstfeldertal, Göscheneralptal, Maderanertal, Meiental and Schächental – are particularly attractive. The highest point is the Dammastock

(3,630m/11,909ft), north of the Furka Pass in the Urner Alps, while the Glarus and Lepontine Alps are also partly situated in the canton.

Andermatt in southern Uri serves as a crossroads between southern and northern Switzerland as well as between the east and west of the country. The town is connected by four Alpine passes: the Oberalp Pass (2,044m/6,706ft) to the east, the St Gotthard Pass (2,106m/6,916ft) to the south, the Realp Pass (1,538m/5,046ft) and Furka Pass (2,436m/7,992ft) to the west, in addition to the Göscheneralp Pass (1,783m/5,850ft) to the north.

Although there are a number of farms in Uri, most of the terrain is unsuitable for farming, which isn't a large industry, although forestry is of importance. Hydroelectric power generation is one of the canton's main industries, while others include construction and allied trades, engineering, the electrical industry, rubber and plastics technology. Tourism is also an important source of income and the canton attracts visitors year round, particularly winter and summer sports enthusiasts.

In 2009, the wealthy Egyptian businessman Samih Sawiris began construction of a huge resort in Andermatt, which will comprise six four- and five-star hotels with 850 rooms and apartments, 42 apartment buildings with a total of 490 vacation rentals, 20-30 luxury homes and an 18-hole golf course. The development will include shops, restaurants, bars, a fitness centre, and a concert and event centre. The existing ski resort infrastructure will also be modernised and enlarged. The Urner are hoping the project will create jobs and income in the otherwise relatively poor canton.

Uri is well connected to other areas of Switzerland via the A2 motorway, and has direct rail links with Lucerne (54mins) and Zug (43mins); Zurich is 1 hr 16mins (one change). The nearest international airport is Zurich (92km/57mi). The New Rail Link through the Alps (NRLA) project – usually referred to as the Alp Transit Project (www.alptransit.ch/en) – is building what will be the world's longest railway tunnel (a 57km/35mi) between Erstfeld and Biasca, which is expected to be completed in 2017. It's one of the world's largest construction projects, and includes the extension of two north-south railway lines through Switzerland and three new flat railway tunnels. The

Lötschberg base tunnel section (34.6km/21.5mi) – situated in canton Berne – was completed in 2007 and allows passenger trains to reach speeds of up to 250kph/155mph.

### Uri

**Official website:** 🖥 www.ur.ch (German only).

**Other websites:** 🖥 www.altdorf.ch (German only).

**Tourist office:** Tourist Info Uri, Schützengasse 11, 6460 Altdorf (☎ 041-874 80 00, 🖥 www.uri.info/en, ✉ info@uri.info).

## Valais

The canton of Valais (capital Sion, pop. 29,000), Wallis in German, joined the Swiss Federation in 1815 and is the third-largest canton, covering an area of 5,224km² (2,017mi²). It has a relatively small population of 303,241 (January 2009), of which 60,557 (20 per cent) are foreigners; 81 per cent are Catholics and just 6 per cent Protestants. Valais is predominantly French- and Arpitan-speaking (a French dialect or patois) – spoken by some two-thirds of the population – while German (Walliser dialect) is spoken in the eastern region of Upper Valais.

Valais lies in the southwest of Switzerland, with Italy to the south and France to the southwest. The wide, glacial Rhône valley (the Aletsch Glacier is the longest in the Alps) dominates the area, off which there are many smaller valleys. At the head of the Mattertal valley lies Zermatt, a pretty, car-free village dominated by the Matterhorn (4,478m/14,691ft). In total, 50 mountains in Valais exceed 4,000m (13,123ft), with the highest, Monte Rosa, reaching to 4,638m (15,217ft), including many glaciers. The Roman thermal spa resort of Leukerbad is the country's largest, with no fewer than 65 hot springs.

The capital, Sion (Sitten in German), dates back to Neolithic times, and is known as the wine town – one of the sunniest in Switzerland – and the town with two castles; the Tourbillon Castle ruin and the Valère Fortress towers are the town's major landmarks. Sion was founded in the 4th century, and has a fascinating old town and a truly French atmosphere.

Tourism is the main industry, and the canton is home to many internationally-renowned ski resorts, including Crans-Montana, Saas Fee, Verbier and Zermatt (Saas-Fee and Zermatt, along with Bettmeralp and Riederalp are car-free resorts). Many smaller, lesser-known resorts also attract thousands of skiers and hikers each year and the canton also offers a wealth of thermal spring spas. Apart from tourism, agriculture is important, particularly cattle breeding in the mountains and dairy farming on the plains, while the wine industry is the largest in Switzerland (Chasselas/Fendant whites and Dôle, a blend of Pinot Noir and Gamay, predominate). There are also a large number of orchards and saffron is also grown.

Europe's tallest gravity dam is located at Grande Dixence, and the canton's hydroelectric power plants produce around a quarter of all Switzerland's electricity. The western part of the canton is the most industrial region, where there are many factories and plants, including oil refining, aluminium processing, metal products and chemicals, plus a burgeoning technology park. However, despite its thriving tourist industry, high level of infrastructure and many vineyards, canton Valais remains one of the poorest Swiss cantons.

The people of the Val d'Anniviers (the name means 'seasonal') are the last people in Switzerland to follow a genuinely nomadic lifestyle, although modern ease of transport and economic pressures are making inroads.

Valais is well connected to other areas of Switzerland via the A9 motorway, and Sion has direct rail links with Geneva (1hr 34mins) and Lausanne (1hr), and good connections with Basle, Berne and Zurich (one change). The nearest international airport is Geneva (158km/98mi) and there's also a small regional airport at Sion. Sion also has the largest bus station in Switzerland.

The rail and road networks have benefited from the development of tourism. The two major rail tunnels are the Simplon and Lötschberg, while a new rail tunnel, the Lötschberg Base Tunnel (34.5km/21.4mi) opened in 2007, and is the longest land tunnel in the world (it halved the journey time between Berne and Brig to 50mins). The Great St Bernard road tunnel (Martigny-Val d'Aosta, Italy) is one of the major road crossings in the Alps, while there are a number of other road passes such as the Grimsel Pass. As a result of tourism, there are also numerous mountain railways and cable cars in the canton.

Sanetsch, Valais

### Valais

**Official website:** 💻 www.vs.ch (in French/German only).

**Other websites:** 💻 www.sion.ch (in French/German only), www.zermatt.ch.

**Tourist office:** Valais Tourisme, Rue Pré Fleuri 6, 1950 Sion (☎ 027-327 35 70, 💻 www.valais.ch/en, ✉ info@valais.ch).

## Vaud

Vaud (capital Lausanne, pop. 130,000) – Waadt in German – joined the Swiss Confederation in 1803 and is the fourth-largest canton, with an area of 3,212km² (1,240.2mi²). The population of 688,245 (January 2009), of which 205,928 (30 per cent) are foreigners, is French-speaking and historically was overwhelmingly Protestant (Calvinist), dating from the early years of the Reformation. However, this changed in the 20th century due to immigration from southern Europe, and the population is now fairly evenly split between Protestants (40 per cent) and Catholics (34 per cent).

The canton stretches from Lake Neuchâtel in the north to Lake Geneva in the south, and from the French border in the west to the borders of the cantons of Berne and Fribourg in the east. Vaud is one of only two cantons (the other is Berne) whose territory extends from the Jura to the Alps. The southeast region is mountainous and situated on the north side of the Bernese Alps, where the Diablerets massif (3,210m/10,531ft) is the canton's highest point. This area has several popular ski resorts including Les Diablerets, Leysin and Villars.

The capital, Lausanne, has a magnificent setting, built on three hills, surrounded by vine-covered slopes, with Lake Geneva at its feet and the snow-capped Savoy Alps opposite. The attractive old town is largely car-free and dominated by the cathedral, which is regarded as the country's most impressive early Gothic building. Many consider Lausanne to be Switzerland's most attractive, cosmopolitan, relaxed and exciting city, and the country's equivalent of San Francisco. The neighbouring historic towns of Montreux and Vevey are also world famous, while the shops and museums along the cobbled streets of Morges, Nyon and Rolle are well worth exploring. The resort town of Leysin is renowned for its international schools, and Chateau-d'Oex hosts a celebrated hot-air balloon festival.

Service industries (e.g. finance, telecommunications and tourism) and manufacturing – including packaging, tobacco (Philip Morris have their HQ here) food-processing (e.g. Nestlé in Vevey), watch-making and pharmaceuticals – are the most important sectors; the Vallée de Joux in the Jura is at the heart of the luxury, mechanical watch-making industry. The canton is the second-largest producer of wine (mostly white) in Switzerland, where many vineyards are situated on the steep shores of Lake Geneva. Agriculture is important in the areas away from Lake Geneva, including sugar beet, tobacco and fruit, while cattle breeding and pasture is common in the Alps and Jura mountains. Tourism is important, particularly along Lake Geneva, in towns such as Lausanne, Montreux and Vevey, and the medieval Château de Chillon.

Vaud was the first Swiss canton to grant women the vote in 1959, and foreign nationals have the right to vote in community elections.

The canton is home to several renowned universities and schools, including the University of Lausanne (founded 1537), the Swiss Federal Institute of Technology, the Lausanne Hotel School, the Institut Le Rosey and the American Graduate School of Business. Vaud is also noted for its wide cultural spectrum, including world-famous institutions such as the

Béjart Ballet in Lausanne, the Montreux Jazz Festival, the Théâtre de Vidy and the Swiss Film Archive (Lausanne), plus over 80 museums. Lausanne is also home to many international organisations, notably the International Olympic Committee (IOC) since 1915 – it's officially known as the 'Olympic Capital' – and over 30 other international sports' and other federations.

Like Geneva, Vaud has some of the most expensive real estate in Switzerland and has experienced a housing 'crisis' for the last five years, with a vacancy rate below 0.5 per cent. Property is among the most expensive in the country, both to rent and buy, with prime homes in demand from international executives employed by the numerous multinational companies in the area (and wealthy 'leisured' expats) and by second home owners at the lower end of the market. The cost of living is also among the highest in Switzerland.

Vaud has excellent road, rail and air connections with the rest of Switzerland and internationally and is served by the A1 and A9 motorways (to France and Italy). It has direct rail links with Basle (2hrs 12mins), Berne (1hr 6mins), Geneva (33mins) and Zurich (2hrs 8mins), plus Paris (TGV). The nearest international airport is Geneva (62km/39mi – 40mins) and Lausanne also has a small regional airport, plus local bus, metro (the only one in Switzerland) and trolleybus networks.

---

### Vaud

**Official website:** 🖥 www.vd.ch (French only).

**Other websites:** 🖥 www.vaud.ch/en, www.lausanne.ch.

**Tourist office:** Office du Tourisme du Canton de Vaud, Case postale 164, CH-1006 Lausanne (☎ 021-613 26 26, 🖥 www.lake-geneva-region.ch, ✉ info@lake-geneva-region.ch).

LIBERTÉ
ET
PATRIE

---

## Zug

The canton of Zug (capital Zug, pop. 23,000) – which means train in German, derives from the term fishermen used, 'zuige', meaning to pull (in the fishing nets) – joined the Swiss Confederation in 1352 and is one of the smallest cantons, extending to just 239km² (92mi²). The population of 110,384 (January 2009), of which 25,287 (23 per cent) are foreigners, is mostly German-speaking and Catholic (62 per cent), with a Protestant minority (18 per cent).

Zug is situated in central Switzerland, bordering the cantons of Aargau and Lucerne in the west, Zurich to the north and Schwyz to the west and south. The lakes of Zug and Ägeri comprise a considerable part of the canton's area. Zug is situated on a hilly plateau, where the Wildspitz (1,580m/5,184ft) is the highest point. The lake of Zug is surrounded by some of the most famous mountains in central Switzerland, including Rigi and Pilatus, and on a clear day the peaks of the Bernese Alps are also visible.

The town of Zug has an attractive location on Lake Zug at the foot of the Zugerberg (1,039m/3,408ft), and is noted for its picturesque old town (centred around the Zytturm clock tower), where the most striking old building is the parish church of St Oswald, late 15th century, dedicated to St Oswald, King of Northumbria, England. It's a cosmopolitan town with a wealth of international clubs and a wide range of cultural, leisure and sports attractions.

On the eastern shore of the lake of Ägeri is the site of the famous Battle of Morgaten in 1315, in which the Swiss defeated the powerful Habsburgs.

In the higher regions of the canton, the population is mainly engaged in pastoral pursuits and cattle-breeding. Cham has a well-known condensed milk factory, now owned by Nestlé, while Baar and Zug have a large number of factories. Apiculture (bee-keeping) flourishes in the canton, although the (formerly important) silk-weaving industry has now disappeared. Today's major industries include the manufacture of metal goods, textiles, machinery, electronics and alcoholic beverages (*Kirsch* and cider). Zug is 'home' to a wealth of companies (27,000 – more than one for every inhabitant), although this is mostly for tax reasons – the canton traditionally had one of the country's lowest corporation tax rates at 8.5 per cent – and most are just convenience addresses.

Zug is well connected to other areas of Switzerland, via the A4 and A14 motorways, and has direct rail links with Lucerne (20mins) and Zurich (22mins), while lines running south along Lake Zug join at the Arth-Goldau station of the St. Gotthard railway (Lugano 2hrs 15mins); Zug is also connected to the Zurich S-Bahn network (regional rapid transit trains). The town of Zug has a striking new railway station (2003) featuring a dramatic light display (by James Turrell) at night. The nearest international airport is Zurich (45km/28mi).

Zurich

## Zurich

The canton of Zurich (capital Zurich, pop. 367,000) joined the Confederation in 1351 and has by far the largest population of all Swiss cantons with 1,332,727 inhabitants (January 2009), 23.5 per cent of whom are foreigners; 43 per cent are Protestants and 51 per cent Catholics. The official language is German, although people speak the local Swiss-German dialect called *Züritüütsch*.

The canton covers an area of 1,729km² (668mi²) in the northeast of Switzerland, north of the Alps. It can be roughly divided into the city and lake (most of Lake Zurich is located within the canton), the Unterland in the north, the Oberland in the southeast, the Weinland and Winterthur in the northeast, and the Kronaueramt, southwest of the Albis mountains. The main lakes are Lake Zurich, the Greifensee and the Pfäffikersee, plus many smaller lakes. In the northwest and southeast of the canton there are mountainous areas,

**Zug**

**Official website:** 🖥 www.zug.ch (in German).

**Other websites:** 🖥 www.stadtzug.ch/en.

**Tourist office:** Zug Tourismus, Reisezentrum Zug, Bahnhofplatz, 6304 Zug (☎ 041-723 68 00, 🖥 www.zug-tourismus.ch/en, ✉ tourism@zug.ch).

although they're relatively low-lying by Swiss standards, with the highest point being the Schnebelhorn (1,292m/4,239ft).

The city of Zurich (the unofficial capital of Switzerland) lies on the northern shores of Lake Zurich and is noted for its attractive medieval old town, excellent shopping, wealth of museums and art galleries – notably the Kunsthaus Zurich (Switzerland's leading art gallery), the Rietberg Museum (non-European art, particularly India, China and Africa) and the Swiss National Museum – and the most flamboyant and lively nightlife in Switzerland (the city has long thrown off its staid, boring tag).

Canton Zurich's most popular residential areas include the right shore of the Lake of Zurich (Pfannenstiel region), nicknamed the 'gold coast', the left side of the lake (Zimmelberg region) and the area around Greifensee (Oberland region). In the city of Zurich, the most popular residential areas are the 1st, 2nd, 6th, 7th and 8th districts. The demand for residential property in the Lake Zurich (Zürichsee) region, and good residential areas in the city, such as Zürichberg, is very strong. Property prices in the fashionable locations between Zürichberg and Herrliberg and Kilchberg to Rüschlikon, where demand far outstrips supply, are sky high. Zurich is noted for it high quality of life – it's regularly rated the best in the world in surveys – matched by an equally high cost of living.

Agriculture isn't an important industry in canton Zurich – the economic powerhouse of the Swiss economy – where manufacturing predominates, particularly machinery, along with banking and insurance. Among the many international companies with offices and factories in the greater Zurich area are Cisco Systems, Dow, Ecolab, Google, John Deere, Kraft Foods and Kühne & Nagel. Many companies in the Zurich area are prominent in the fields of life sciences (biotech, MedTech, pharmaceuticals), information and communication technologies (ICT), and micro- and nanotechnology. The greater Zurich area is home to a number of internationally renowned research and education institutes, such as the Swiss Federal Institute of Technology Zurich (*Eidgenössische Technische Hochschule/*ETH Zurich), a science and technology university ranked among the leading universities in the world.

The city of Zurich is the hub of communications in the canton, where the central station (*Hauptbahnhof/HB*) is one of the busiest in Europe (handling almost 1,500 trains a day!), with direct trains to all major Swiss cities (Basle 53mins, Berne 57mins, Geneva 2hrs 43mins, Lausanne 2hrs 8mins) and high-speed trains from France (TGV) and Germany (ICE), with direct connections to many of Europe's major cities. The region is also served by a local rail network (S-Bahn) and the city of Zurich has extensive bus and tram networks. Zurich's Kloten airport (12km/7.5km) is Switzerland's major airport, serving over 125 international destinations. The canton is linked by the A1, A3 and A4 motorways (the A7, A51, A52 and A53 also bisect the canton), with major hubs in Zurich city and Winterthur.

---

### Zurich

**Official website:** 🖳 www.zh.ch (in German only).

**Other websites:** 🖳 www. greaterzuricharea.ch, www.location.zh.ch, www.outandabout.ch, www.stadt-zuerich. ch and www.zurich-airport.com.

**Tourist office:** Zürich Tourismus, Im Hauptbahnhof, 8021 Zurich (☏ 044-215 40 40, 🖳 www.zuerich.com/en, ✉ information@zuerich.com).

---

## CHOOSING THE LOCATION

The most important consideration when buying (or renting) a home is usually its location – or, as the old adage goes, the three most important considerations are location, location and location! A property in a reasonable condition in a popular area is likely to be a better investment than an exceptional property in a less attractive location. There's no point in buying a dream property if it's a 'million' miles from your workplace or the nearest airport or railway station, or it's next door to a motorway or power station.

---

☑ **SURVIVAL TIP**

**The wrong decision regarding location is one of the main causes of disenchantment among foreigners who purchase property abroad.**

---

Where you buy a property will depend on a range of factors, including your preferences, your financial resources and whether you plan to work in Switzerland. If you already have a job in Switzerland, the location of your home will probably be determined by your place of employment. However, if you intend to look for employment or start a business, you must live in an area that allows you the maximum scope. It's unwise to assume that you'll find employment in a particular area. If, on the other hand, you're looking for a holiday or retirement home, you can live virtually anywhere, although accessibility and proximity to shops and other services are crucial. When seeking a permanent home, don't be too influenced by where you've spent an enjoyable holiday or two; a town or area that was fine for a few weeks' holiday, may be far from suitable as a permanent residence.

If you have little idea about where you wish to live, read as much as you can about the different cantons of Switzerland and spend some time looking around your areas and towns of interest. Note also that the climate, lifestyle and cost of living can vary from region to region, and even within a region. Before looking at properties, it's important to have a good idea of the type of property you're seeking and the price (or rent) you wish to pay, and to draw up a shortlist of the areas or towns of interest. If you don't do this, you're likely to be overwhelmed by the number of properties to be viewed. Estate agents usually expect serious buyers to know where they want to buy within a 30 to 40km (20 to 25mi) radius and some even expect clients to narrow it down to specific towns and villages.

The 'best' place to live depends on many factors, including the proximity to your place of work, schools, country or town, shops, public transport, sports facilities, ski resorts (or other attractions), bars and restaurants. There are beautiful areas to choose from throughout Switzerland, most within easy travelling distance of a town or city and an airport. Don't, however, believe the times and distances stated in advertisements and real estate agents' brochures. According to some agents' magical mystery maps, everywhere is handy for an international airport or rail station and close to ski resorts – although this is often true due to Switzerland's compact size!

When looking for a home, bear in mind the travelling times and costs. If you buy a 'remote' country property, the distance to local amenities and services could become a problem, particularly if you plan to retire to Switzerland. If you live in a rural area you'll need to be much more self-sufficient than if you live in a town, and you'll have to use a car for everything, which will add significantly to the cost of living. If you'll be working in Switzerland, obtain a map of the area and decide the maximum distance you wish to travel to work, e.g. by drawing a circle with your workplace in the middle.

If possible, you should visit an area a number of times over a period of a few weeks, both on weekdays and at weekends, in order to get a feel for a neighbourhood (walk, don't just drive around!). A property seen on a balmy summer's day after a delicious lunch and a few glasses of *vino,* may not be nearly so attractive on a subsequent visit *ohne/sans* sunshine and the warm inner glow. If possible, you should also visit an area at different times of the year, e.g. in both summer and winter, as somewhere that's wonderful in summer can be forbidding and inhospitable in winter (or vice versa). If you're planning to buy a winter holiday home, you should be sure to view it in the summer, as snow can hide a multitude of sins. In any case, you should view a property a number of times before deciding to buy it.

If you're unfamiliar with an area and are planning to buy a home, most experts recommend that you rent for a period before deciding to buy (see **Chapter 5**). This is

Solothurn

particularly important if you're planning to buy a permanent or retirement home in an unfamiliar area. Many people change their minds after a period, and it isn't unusual for families to move once or twice before settling down permanently.

Obtain a large scale map of the area where you're looking, which may even show individual buildings, thereby allowing you to mark the places that you've seen. You could do this using a grading system to denote your impressions. If you use a real estate agent, he'll usually drive you around and you can then return later to those that appeal most at your leisure – provided you've marked them on your map!

## CHECKLIST

There are many things to consider regarding the location of a home, including those detailed below – listed in A-Z order, not in order of importance. Bear in mind that you need to take into account the present and future needs of all members of your family.

### Accessibility

Is the proximity to public transport, e.g. an international airport or mainline railway station, or access to a motorway important? Don't believe all you're told about the distance or travelling times to the nearest motorway, airport, railway station, ski resort or town, but check for yourself. Being on a local bus or rail route is also advantageous, particularly when your car is in the garage.

### Amenities

What local health and social services are provided? How far is the nearest hospital with an emergency department? What shopping facilities are there in the neighbourhood? Is there a pharmacy, doctor, post office or train station? How far is it to the nearest town with good shopping facilities, e.g. a supermarket? How would you get there if your car was out of action? Bear in mind that most villages have few shops or facilities, so they aren't a good choice for a retirement home.

### Climate

For most people the climate (see page 17) is one of the most important factors when buying a home in Switzerland, particularly a holiday or retirement home. Bear in mind the climate in both winter and summer, the position of the sun, the average daily sunshine, rainfall and wind conditions. You may also wish to check whether the area is noted for fog, which can make driving hazardous. The orientation or aspect of a building is vital; if you want morning or afternoon sun (or both) you must ensure that balconies, terraces and gardens face south.

### Community

Do you wish to live in an area with many of your fellow countrymen and other expatriates, or as far away from them as possible? If you wish to integrate with the local community, you may wish to choose an area or development with mainly local inhabitants. However, unless you speak fluent French, German or Italian or intend to learn, you should think twice before buying a property in a village. The locals in some villages resent 'outsiders' buying up prime properties, particularly holiday homeowners, although resident foreigners who take the time and trouble to integrate into the local community are usually warmly welcomed. If you're buying a permanent home, it's important to check your prospective neighbours, particularly when buying an apartment. For example, are they noisy, sociable or absent for long periods? Do you think you'll get on with them? Good neighbours are invaluable, particularly when buying a second home.

## Crime

Crime isn't a problem in most of Switzerland, although you may wish to check the local crime rate, particularly in a city. Bear in mind that professional crooks like isolated houses, particularly those packed with expensive furniture and other belongings, which they can strip bare at their leisure. You're much less likely to be a victim of theft if you live in a village, where strangers stand out like sore thumbs.

## Employment

How secure is your job or business and are you likely to move to another area in the near future? Can you find other work in the same area, if necessary? If you may need to move in a few years' time, you should rent rather than buy, or at least buy a property that will be relatively easy to sell without losing money. If applicable, you should also take into account your partner's and children's jobs or job prospects.

## Garden

If you're planning to buy a large country property – admittedly rare and prohibitively expensive in Switzerland – with an extensive garden or plot, bear in mind the high cost and amount of work involved in its upkeep. If it's to be a second home, who will look after the house and garden when you're away? Do you want to spend your holidays mowing the lawn and cutting back the undergrowth?

---

☑ **SURVIVAL TIP**

**Language**

Is the local language (or languages) important? If you're buying a holiday home in Switzerland you may wish to choose an international resort where English is widely spoken.

---

## Natural Disasters

Few areas of Switzerland are susceptible to natural disasters such as floods, storms, forest fires, rock- and landslides, earthquakes and avalanches. Fortunately most of these are rare in Switzerland. Avalanches are, however, common in the Alps, although they rarely result in loss of life, although a number of skiers (who often cause the avalanches) lose their lives each year. Major avalanches that threaten people or destroy villages are rare nowadays – the last 'winter of terror' was 1950-51, when over 250 died in avalanches in the Alps – thanks to better safety measures and an advance warning service.

The Alpine cantons experience some 10,000 avalanches annually, with around 80 per cent occurring between February and April. For centuries, village communes have relied on forests on the mountain slopes for protection from avalanches – a 20- to 30-year-old forest can inhibit or stop small avalanches. Villages, highways, and alpine paths are also protected by costly artificial structures, such as metal barriers, earthen walls, and concrete wedges and enclosures. However, acid rain has caused the illness and destruction of many trees in the mountain areas of Switzerland, and poses a serious threat to their ability to act as barriers to avalanches. In some mountain forests, around 40 per cent of trees have been classified as damaged, sick or dying.

Some areas of Switzerland experience frequent thunderstorms and other violent weather, which can severely damage property. Experts recommend that you safeguard electrical appliances either by installing surge protectors or simply by unplugging everything (including telephone lines and TV antennas, but not refrigerators and deep freezes) before a thunderstorm arrives. However, mobile phones can be used without any danger. Those in danger areas can register free of charge at 🖥 www.wetteralarm.ch to receive weather alarms by email.

Avalanche warnings in Switzerland are based on the recommendations made by the Swiss Institute for Snow and Avalanche Research in Davos.

In the major European floods in August 2005, which hit mainly Romania, Switzerland, Austria and Germany, 62 people lost their lives, including six in Switzerland. However, this was a rare occurrence and Switzerland was unscathed by the devastating central and eastern European floods of 2002. The last serious earthquake to hit Switzerland was in 1356, which destroyed Basle and much of the surrounding area. In the last 800 years there have been over 10,000 'earthquakes' recorded in Switzerland, although only half a dozen have registered more than 6.0 on the Richter scale and damage is rare.

### Noise

Noise can be a problem in some cities and developments. Although you cannot choose your neighbours, you can at least ensure that a property isn't located next to a busy road, railway line, airport, industrial plant, commercial area, discotheque, night club, church, bar or restaurant (where revelries may continue into the early hours). Look out for objectionable properties which may be too close to the one you're considering, and check whether nearby vacant land has been 'zoned' for commercial activities, roads, etc.

Be sure to check planned new roads/ motorways and also whether the property sits atop a railroad tunnel; the law only requires the seller to inform the buyer if the tunnel is less than 30m/98ft below ground, in which case it will be on the house plans. Also check where high-voltage lines run and if any new ones are planned.

In some developments (e.g. apartment blocks), many properties may be second homes and be let short term to boisterous holidaymakers, particularly in mountain resorts. However, Switzerland has strict laws regarding noise and it's unlikely that your peace will be disturbed too often – although you may wish to avoid busy ski resorts unless you're buying a holiday home and will yourself be one of the boisterous holidaymakers!

### Parking

If you're planning to buy in a town or city, is there adequate private or free on-street parking for your family and visitors? Is it safe to park in the street? In some areas it's important to have secure private parking if you value your car. Parking is a problem in towns and cities, where

You can dream...

private garages or parking spaces are rare and can be very expensive to buy, but can usually be rented. Bear in mind that an apartment or townhouse in a town or community development may be some distance from the nearest road or car park. How do you feel about carrying heavy shopping hundreds of metres to your home and possibly up several flights of stairs? Traffic congestion is also a problem in cities and tourist resorts.

### Property Market

Do houses sell well in the area, e.g. in less than six months? Generally, you should avoid neighbourhoods where desirable houses routinely remain on the market for six months or longer (unless the property market is in a severe slump).

### Radon

Radon is a naturally occurring radioactive gas formed underground by the radioactive decay of uranium, which is present in small quantities in rocks and soils, and is particularly prevalent in south-eastern Switzerland (Ticino and Graubünden) and in western Switzerland along the border with France. After surfacing in the open air, radon is quickly diluted to harmless concentrations. However, when it enters an enclosed space, such as a house, it can build up to potentially harmful concentrations. The acceptable limit for radon concentration (known as the 'reference level') is 200 becquerels per cubic metre of air (200Bq/m3). It has been shown that prolonged exposure to concentrations of radon above this level increases the chance of contracting lung cancer, and in some homes in Switzerland there's a cignificant health risk for occupants.

You can have a test carried out to check the level of radon in a building or on a plot. In areas that are particularly at risk, you should contract the services of a surveyor or specialist to carry out tests. There are several websites providing regional radon maps, including 🖳 www.bag.admin.ch/themen/strahlung/00046/01561/index.html?lang=en and www.bre.co.uk/radon/nforum/Appendix2.pdf, both of which are in English.

## Schools

Consider your children's present and future schooling. What is the quality of local schools? Even if your family has no need or plans to use local schools, the value of a home is often influenced by their quality and location, particularly international schools.

## Sports & Leisure Facilities

What is the range and quality of local leisure, sports, community and cultural facilities? What is the proximity to sports facilities such as a swimming pool/lake, golf course, ski resort or waterway? Although properties in or close to popular ski and lake resorts are usually considerably more expensive, they also have the best rental potential. If you're interested in a winter holiday home, which area should you choose? While properties in the more famous ski resorts are relatively expensive, they tend to appreciate faster than properties in other less popular areas, and generally maintain their value in recessions. Bear in mind that the snow line is getting higher due to global warming, and many ski resorts below 2,000m (ca. 6,500ft) may have no snow or poor cover by around 2050.

## Tax Rates

The Swiss income tax rates (see page 180) for both companies and individuals are among the lowest in Europe, despite the fact that taxes are levied by federal, cantonal and community governments. Swiss cantons compete with each other to attract foreign businesses, investment and wealthy individuals, by offering lower corporate tax rates and other incentives. The tax rates in communities also vary.

If you can live in Switzerland, you may wish to opt for a canton and community where the tax burden is lower (see page 184). A number of cantons have reduced their tax rates in recent

years, sparking something of a tax war, including Appenzell-Ausserrhoden, Fribourg, Obwalden, Schaffhausen, Schwyz, Uri, Valais and Zurich. Obwalden replaced a new degressive cantonal income tax (lower tax rates for higher incomes, which was deemed unconstitutional) with a flat rate personal tax rate of 1.8 per cent, which is the lowest in the country. Freienbach in Schwyz is noted as the municipality with the lowest taxes in Switzerland, which has attracted a number of wealthy residents.

There are no federal capital gains on private property, estate, inheritance or gift taxes in Switzerland, but these taxes are levied by most cantons. Capital gains tax is levied by all cantons on property (real estate) but not on other assets, and depends on the amount of profit made and the length of ownership. As with income tax, rates vary from canton to canton. Inheritance and gift taxes also vary from canton to canton (Schwyz is also the only canton with no inheritance or gift tax). See **Chapter 7** for further information.

### Tourism

If you live in a popular tourist area, you'll be inundated with tourists in summer and/or winter. They won't only jam the roads and pack the public transport, but may even occupy your favourite table at your local bar or restaurant (heaven forbid!). Although a property in a popular resort may sound attractive and be ideal for short holidays, it isn't always the best choice for permanent residence. Many resorts are hopelessly crowded in the high season, parking is impossible, services are stretched to breaking point and prices may also be higher. Some people prefer to move to a 'remote' area, or to a town that's more peaceful and relaxed.

On the other hand, getting to and from a remote property can be difficult, particularly in winter when mountain roads may be impassable, or snow chains or a 4WD vehicle necessary. Winter driving is usually no fun on ice and snow and can be treacherous. If you live in a large town or city with good public transport, you can garage your car for the winter and use public transport.

### Town or Country?

Do you wish to be in a town or do you prefer the country? Mountains or lake? Bear in mind that if you buy a property in the country, you'll probably have to tolerate poor public transport (infrequent trains and buses – or even none at all), long travelling distances to a town of any size, solitude and remoteness. You won't be able to pop along to the local café for a coffee, drop into the local bar for a glass of your favourite tipple with the locals, or have a choice of restaurants on your doorstep. In a town or large village, the market will be just around the corner, the doctor and chemist close at hand and, if you need help or run into any problems, your neighbours will be close by.

In the country, you'll be closer to nature, will have more freedom (e.g. to make as much noise as you wish) and possibly complete privacy, e.g. to sunbathe or swim *au naturel*. Living in a remote area in the country will suit nature lovers looking for solitude who don't want to involve themselves in the 'hustle and bustle' of town life (not that there's much of this in Swiss rural villages and towns). If you're after peace and quiet, however, make sure that there isn't a busy road or railway line nearby or a local church within 'donging' distance. Bear in mind that many people who buy a rural home find that the peace of the countryside palls after a time, and they yearn for the more exciting city life. If you've never lived in the country, it's wise to rent before buying.

> ☑ **SURVIVAL TIP**
>
> Although it's cheaper to buy in a 'remote' or unpopular location, it's often much more difficult to find a buyer when you want to sell.

'Bernina Express'

# 3.
# GETTING TO & AROUND SWITZERLAND

**G**etting to Switzerland from most countries is easy, as it's served by air from many of the world's major cities, as well as by direct rail connections throughout Europe; it probably has the best rail services of any European country, being served by France's TGV and Germany's ICE high-speed trains, not to mention the excellent Swiss railways (SBB). Switzerland has three main international airport hubs: Basle (Euroairport), Geneva and Zurich, while a few regional airports (such as Berne) also have a limited number of international flights.

Public transport services (*öffentlicher Verkehr, transport public*) in Switzerland are excellent and provide a frequent, convenient and inexpensive service to every corner of the country. All modes of public transport are highly efficient, integrated, clean, and usually punctual to the minute (among the most reliable clocks in Switzerland are those at railway stations). With some 24,500km (ca. 15,200mi) of fixed transport lines, including trains, trams, trolley-buses, metro (Lausanne), cableways and ferries, Switzerland has the densest public transport network in the world.

It isn't essential to own a car in Switzerland, particularly if you live in or near a large town or city; if you need convincing, see *Switzerland Without a Car* by Anthony Lambert (Bradt). For example, Zurich has one of the world's best public transport systems, which even includes the free loan of bicycles (bicycles, including electric bicycles, can also be rented in many other towns and cities). This is attested to by the high use of public transport by its citizens, which is double that in most other major European cities. However, if you live in a remote village or a town off the main rail and bus routes, you'll find it more convenient or even essential to own a car.

At first sight, Swiss public transport may seem very expensive, but if you take advantage of the often bewildering range of discounts and season tickets available, it provides good value.

## GETTING TO SWITZERLAND

Getting to Switzerland from abroad or getting around Switzerland isn't so important if you're planning to live there permanently and more or less stay put. However, one of the major considerations when buying a holiday home is the cost of getting to and from Switzerland, when you'll need to consider the following:

◆ How long will it take you to get to a home in Switzerland, taking into account journeys to and from airports and railway stations (etc.)?

◆ How frequent are flights or trains at the time(s) of year when you plan to travel?

◆ Are direct flights or trains available?

◆ Is it possible or practical to travel to Switzerland by car?

◆ What is the cost of travel from your home country to the region where you're planning to buy a home in Switzerland?

♦ Are off-season discounts or inexpensive charter flights available?

If a long journey is involved, you should bear in mind that it may take you a day or two to recover, e.g. from jet lag. The travelling time and cost of travel to a home in Switzerland is more important if you're planning to spend frequent long weekends there, rather than a few long stays each year. You should include the price of getting to and from Switzerland in your budget when considering a property purchase, particularly if you're planning to make frequent visits a year.

If you plan to let a property, it will be more popular if it's within easy reach of an airport with a wide range of flights, particularly budget flights, from the UK, for example. Always allow plenty of time to get to and from airports and railway stations in Switzerland, particularly when travelling during peak hours or in inclement weather, when traffic congestion can be a problem.

## Airline Services

Switzerland is well served by airlines, both international and domestic, but no longer has its own international airline – Swiss was taken over by Lufthansa in 2005 (a blow to Swiss air transport and Swiss pride!), although it retains its Swiss identity (🖥 www.swiss.com). Swiss was voted the best short-haul airline by the 2009 *Guardian* and *Observer* Travel Awards and the readers of *Condé Nast Traveller* magazine voted it the second-best short-haul leisure airline in 2009 (it was number one in 2008).

Although standard air fares to and from Switzerland aren't the most competitive in Europe, a range of reduced fares is available. The major Swiss airports are served from the UK by a number of low-cost carriers, including Easyjet (🖥 www.easyjet.com) and Flybe (🖥 www.flybe.com). Geneva is the main gateway for budget flights, while very few budget airlines fly to Zurich.

The introduction of 'no-frills' flights into the Swiss market has been revolutionary and has provided some welcome competition, forcing Swiss and other airlines to reduce their fares. Budget airline fares can be as little as £20 single (e.g. from London), although fares vary considerably depending on the time of day, day of the week and the season. Usually the further you book in advance, the lower the fare. However, bear in mind that budget airlines' advertised prices don't include more than one checked bag, credit card fees and whatever else they can charge extra for.

If you're planning a trip abroad during the school holidays, book well in advance, particularly if you're going to a popular destination.

For details of the airlines serving Switzerland from the UK and US and their contact details, see **Appendix D**.

## Airports

Most major international airlines provide scheduled services to and from Switzerland via one of the three 'Swiss' international gateway airports (*Flughafen, aéroport*) of Basle (EuroAirport), Geneva-Cointrin and Zurich-Kloten. Internationally, Zurich is the most important Swiss airport, although Geneva – due largely to its proximity to France and French ski resorts – has by far the largest number of flights from the UK, with direct flights from 13 UK airports. Berne, the capital of Switzerland, doesn't have an 'official' international airport, although its airport (Bern-Belp) provides a few scheduled international flights and is also served by domestic flights from the major Swiss airports.

Besides the three main airports, there are over 40 smaller regional airports and airfields in Switzerland, including Ambri (TI), Berne (BE), Bex (VD), Birrfeld (AG), Bressaucourt (JU), Buttwil (AG), Dübendorf (ZH), Emmen (LU), Engadin (GR), Grenchen (SO), Gruyere (FR), Langenthal (BE), Lausanne (VD), Lugano (TI), Motiers (NE), Schaenis (SG), Sion (VD), St Gallen-Altenrhein (SG), Triengen (LU) and Yverdon-les-Bains (VD). The regional airports of Berne, Sion and St. Gallen-Altenrhein handle a few international flights, while others handle mainly private and chartered business flights.

You can check-in at the major Swiss airports using self check-in machines, which are also provided at airport railway stations, and there's usually a baggage-drop close to machines with no queues. This also applies to those who check in online. Note that if you book online but don't check in online, you may find yourself bumped off the flight (even if you have a non-refundable confirmed ticket) if you arrive late, e.g. if you're flying with Continental.

The major airports provide bus and rail transport to the nearest city and beyond, and car hire is also available. All major airports have websites (see box), although information isn't always provided in English (see the table below), and most provide useful tourist information, including accommodation options as well as airport information.

The following general information applies to the three major Swiss airports:

♦ Major Swiss airports have wheelchairs and ambulance staff to help disabled travellers, and airlines also publish brochures for disabled travellers.

♦ Long- and short-term parking is available at all major airports, including reserved parking for the disabled.

♦ Both Geneva and Zurich airports have shopping centres open from 8am to 8pm, seven days a week.

♦ A welcome surprise at Swiss airports (particularly Zurich) is an ample supply of luggage trolleys, which also allow you to take your baggage up and down escalators, although they may not be free, e.g. CHF 2 in Geneva.

♦ SBB provides a 'Fly Rail Baggage' service for travellers using Geneva and Zurich airports, whereby you can check-in your baggage (and receive your boarding pass, depending on the airline) at over 50 railway stations and on to your final destination. This also applies to passengers arriving at Geneva and Zurich airports, who can have their baggage forwarded to their destination Swiss rail station and don't need to collect it at the airport and go through customs.

### Basle

Basle EuroAirport (also known as Basle-Mulhouse-Freiburg airport) offers over 50 scheduled daily flights to airports in some 30 countries, including a total of around 20 flights a day to Paris, London and Berlin.

### Flight Information

| Airport | Telephone Number | Website |
| --- | --- | --- |
| Basle-EuroAirport | 061-325 31 11 | www.euroairport.com |
| Berne | 031-960 21 11 | www.alpar.ch (German only) |
| Engadin | 081-851 08 51 | www.engadin-airport.ch |
| Geneva | 022-717 71 11 | www.gva.ch/en |
| Lugano | 091-610 11 11 | www.lugano-airport.ch/en |
| Sion | 027-329 06 00 | www.sionairport.ch |
| St Gallen-Altenrhein | 071-858 51 65 | www.airport-stgallen.com (German only) |
| Zurich | 0900-300 313 | www.zurich-airport.com |

## Access

**Train:** EuroAirport isn't linked directly to the Swiss railway system, but there are connections by public transport to the main railway stations in Basle, from where there are direct trains to other Swiss cities, France, Germany and beyond. The main railway station (*Hauptbahnhof*) serves both SBB and SNCF (French) trains, while the DBB (German) trains use Badischer station near Messe Schweiz.

**Bus:** A bus service (every 15 minutes) to Basle main railway station is provided by the Basel Bus Company (BVB, line 50), taking 20 minutes. Basle hotel guests receive a free Mobility ticket allowing limited free travel on all Basle public transport, including the airport bus service.

**Taxi:** A taxi to Basle costs around CHF 40.

**Road:** Basle EuroAirport is actually situated in France around 5km/3mi (15-20 minutes) from Basle city centre. However, it's unnecessary to go through French customs or immigration to enter or leave Switzerland via Basle airport, as the road between Basle city and Basle airport is fenced in all the way.

**Parking:** There are both long- and short-stay car parks at Basle airport, depending on how long you plan to park.

### Berne

Despite being Switzerland's capital city, Berne's airport (Bern-Belp, 9km SE of the city of Berne) is small, reflecting its role as a secondary regional airport. The only major airlines operating regular scheduled flights are Air France, Lufthansa and Swiss, and these are limited (e.g. Munich, Palma de Mallorca and Paris). Much of the airport's traffic is holiday charter flights. The only direct flight from the UK is operated by Flybe from Southampton.

## Access

**Train:** Bern-Belp airport is situated near the town of Belp and isn't connected directly by rail to the Swiss rail network. You need to take a bus from the airport to Belp or Berne for onward travel by train.

**Bus:** An hourly bus service operates to Berne railway station (line 334) and to Belp and Münsingen (line 160).

**Taxi:** A taxi to Berne city centre costs around CHF 40.

**Parking:** There are various car parks at Berne airport, depending on how long you plan to park, including a 'park, fly & drive' car park (☎ 031-960 22 66), costing from CHF 25 for one day to CHF 56 for a week.

### Geneva

Geneva international airport serves some 12mn passengers a year, but is relatively small in comparison to Zurich, although it has been expanded and modernised in recent years. Its services – and those of the nearby Charter terminal – are stretched to breaking point during the ski season, when it's invaded by thousands of (mostly UK) skiers in transit to nearby ski resorts in France, Italy and Switzerland. Geneva airport is served by over 60 airlines to over 100 destinations, although many flights are seasonal (operated only during the winter ski season). It's a major European hub for the UK airline, Easyjet, not just to the UK (where 13 airports serve Geneva) but throughout Europe.

It's located 4km (2.5mi) northwest of the city centre with direct connections to motorways, buses and trains. The airport's northern limit runs along the Swiss-French border and it can be accessed from both countries; passengers on flights to or from France don't need to go through Swiss customs and immigration

controls, provided they remain in the French sector of the airport.

### Access

**Train:** Geneva airport has a direct rail connection to the main city railway station, taking six minutes. Before passing through customs, a machine dispenses free 80-minute tickets for Geneva Public Transport (Transports Public Genevois), which are valid for both city buses and trains to the Geneva main railway station (*Gare de Cornavin*).

**Bus:** A free bus service is provided to Geneva city (see above).

**Taxi:** A taxi to the city centre costs CHF 20-40 plus a surcharge for baggage. When arriving at the Geneva train station after midnight or leaving Gare-Cornavin before 6am, you can take advantage of a taxibus, which is a shared car service available for a fraction of the price of a taxi.

**Parking:** There are various short- and long-stay car parks (P51 is cheapest, but not the most secure), depending on how long you plan to park. Remember to make a note of the bay and floor where you park (you can get a 'reminder' notice from a dispenser by lifts). There's a valet service for quick arrivals and departures, costing CHF 32 per day or CHF 23 per day for ten days.

### Zurich

Zurich-Kloten airport is by far the largest and most modern Swiss airport (serving over 22mn passengers annually) and is highly rated by international travellers, who consistently rate it one of the best in the world and the most reliable European hub for baggage transport. In 2009, it was voted Europe's leading airport for the sixth year in a row by World Travel Awards for its user-friendliness and general high quality. Zurich serves some 120 destinations in over 70 countries – it's also the home of Swiss airline – and it also handles three-quarters of Swiss airfreight.

### Access

**Train:** Zurich airport has a direct rail connection (every 10 minutes) to Zurich main railway station (*Hauptbahnhof*), taking ten minutes, plus numerous inter-city and regional trains to most of the main towns and cities in Switzerland. Destinations served include Berne, Basle, St. Gallen, Lucerne, Constance, Geneva, Lausanne, Winterthur and Zug, at least every 30 minutes, and Lugano every hour.

**Bus:** Services connect Zurich airport with Zurich city and many destinations in the surrounding region. A bus to Zurich city costs CHF 6. During the winter, a coach service is available from the airport direct to local ski resorts.

**Tram:** The Glattalbahn tram service (no. 10) provides a direct connection between the airport and the surrounding areas, plus the northern suburbs of Zurich, including Irchel, Milchbuck, Zurich-Oerlikon and Glattpark, with up to 8 trams per hour.

**Taxi:** A taxi to Zurich city centre costs around CHF 60 (☎ 0848-850 852).

**Parking:** There are extensive parking facilities at Zurich Airport, both open-air and covered, with varied prices. All parking facilities are open around the clock.

---

**☑ SURVIVAL TIP**

The instability of the airline business means that airlines frequently merge or go bankrupt, which often results in a reduction of services or the disappearance of routes altogether. Budget airlines also frequently change their routes and prices. It isn't, therefore, advisable to invest in a property if you need to rely solely on cheap flights to a local airport.

---

## International Rail Services

Switzerland has the most extensive network of international (EuroCity/EC) rail services in Europe, including direct links with Austria, Belgium, the Czech Republic, Denmark, France, Germany, Italy and the Netherlands. It's also directly connected to France's TGV and Germany's ICE high-speed networks, but Switzerland doesn't have its own high-speed lines or trains (although new lines are reducing journey times). **The Cisalpino direct services between Switzerland and Italy were discontinued in December 2009**

**and the services taken over by the parent companies, SBB and Trenitalia.**

Most of Europe's major cities are connected to Swiss cities by EuroCity trains, which run at least once every hour throughout the week. Restaurant cars are standard on the main EuroCity connections and international trains. Note that although journey times on high-speed routes are much reduced, some international services operate only at night and journeys may involve a change of train. Most international trains to and from Switzerland require a seat reservation, costing around CHF 5.

### TGV Lyria

TGV Lyria (💻 www.tgv-lyria.com) is the service brand used for TGV (*Hochgeschwindigkeitsbahn, Train à Grande Vitesse/TGV*) lines between France and Switzerland, and it's also the corporation that operates the service using SNCF staff in France and SBB staff in Switzerland (the staff change at the border). Up to 17 direct trains are available daily from Paris to Switzerland, with four different TGV Lyria routes going from Paris to the Swiss cities of Geneva, Lausanne, Berne and Zurich via Basle.

Eurostar and TGV trains also provide fast transportation from London (St Pancras) to Switzerland, with a change of trains in Paris. Note that Eurostar trains arrive in Paris' Gare du Nord station, while TGV Lyria trains to Switzerland depart from either Paris Gare de l'Est or Paris Gare de Lyon stations. You need to allow 60-90 minutes to transfer between stations and check in.

The journey time from London to Switzerland is seven to nine hours, including all transfer and waiting times, although departures from London after around 3pm may require an overnight stay in Paris or taking a relatively slow night train. Up to seven TGV Lyria trains run per day directly from Paris Gare de Lyon station to Geneva (Cornavin) in around three and a half hours or four hours to Lausanne. A few TGV Lyria trains per day go directly from Paris Gare de Lyon to the Swiss capital Berne in just under five hours, and from Paris Gare de l'Est to Basle in three and a half hours and Zurich in four and a half hours (changes to regular Swiss trains are often required in Basle).

### ICE

InterCityExpress (ICE – 💻 www.bahn.de/international) is the German high-speed rail network operating in Germany and neighbouring countries, including Switzerland, where ICE trains serve Basle, Berne, Interlaken, Schaffhausen, Spiez and Zurich. In Switzerland a journey on the ICE takes nearly as long as on a domestic train, as trains operate at relatively low speeds (often no more than 160kmh, although the Schaffhausen-Zurich line is faster). There's no surcharge to use ICE trains in Switzerland.

### City Night Line & Motorail

CityNightLine/CNL (💻 www.citynightline.de) was originally a joint project between the German (DB), Austrian (ÖBB) and Swiss (SBB-CFF-FFS) railways that was established

in 1995, but it's now operated solely by the German Deutsche Bahn (DB). CNL serves destinations in Austria (Innsbruck, Salzburg, Vienna), Belgium (Brussels), the Czech Republic (Prague), Denmark (Copenhagen), France (Paris), Germany (most major cities), Italy (Bologna, Bolzano-Bozen, Florence, Milan, Rome, Verona), the Netherlands (Amsterdam, Utrecht) and Switzerland (Basle, Zurich, Brig, Lugano).

CNL non-smoking trains allow you to travel overnight and arrive refreshed – you can choose from a private sleeper cabin (deluxe or economy), a couchette or a seated coach. Sleeper car fares include breakfast, which is served in your compartment, and there's also an on-board restaurant for meals, snacks and drinks.

Eurail Passes are valid on CNL trains, and pass holders pay only a reservation fee for their overnight accommodation. Reservations are compulsory and can be made at railway stations, by phone (☎ +49-1805-141 514) and via the internet (🖥 www.citynightline.de).

Motorail is a European network of special trains, generally overnight, carrying passengers and their cars or motorbikes over distances of up to 1,500km (900mi). Note than many trains operate only in summer. See 🖥 www.seat61.com/Motorail.htm for information

## Driving to Switzerland

Many people prefer to drive to Switzerland, which saves the expense of renting a car on arrival. If you're driving from the UK, bear in mind that it's almost 862km/539mi from Calais to Zurich (taking some eight hours) and only slightly less (827km/517mi) from Calais to Geneva. The distance from all the channel ports to Berne, Geneva and Zurich is shown on the Drive Alive website (🖥 www.drive-alive.co.uk/distance.html). You also need to add the distance/time to get to Calais and the ferry crossing time, not to mention the cost of petrol, ferries and road tolls.

If possible, you should avoid Paris and the Périphérique, where traffic congestion is chronic. A cheaper but longer option avoiding French motorways is via Belgium, Luxembourg, Strasbourg and Mulhouse (or via Germany). However you choose to drive to Switzerland, you should take it easy and make regular rest stops or share the driving if possible.

Bear in mind that you require a Swiss motorway carnet (CHF 40) to use Swiss motorways, available at the Swiss border or in advance from national motoring organisations in Europe.

---

☑ **SURVIVAL TIP**

If you drive to Switzerland, you must ensure that your car insurance covers travel abroad (most do, although you may need to obtain a 'green card'), and you should also have continental breakdown recovery insurance that includes Switzerland.

Due to the high cost of ferries and road tolls and the long travelling times by road between the UK and Switzerland (and from many other countries), you may be better off flying and hiring a car on arrival. If you own a holiday home in Switzerland, you can buy a Swiss-registered car and leave it at your Swiss home.

# GETTING AROUND SWITZERLAND

Getting around Switzerland is simplicity itself, with its excellent public transport system, employing just about every mode of transport known to mankind, and its extensive motorway system. In most cities there's a completely integrated public transport network where one ticket is valid for local trains, trams, buses, metro (Lausanne) and ferries. Any journey by rail, boat or PostBus may be broken without cost or formality, provided your ticket remains valid and doesn't have a time limit.

Free tickets that allow you to travel to a city centre from an airport are available at some airports (e.g. Geneva – dispensing machines are in the baggage claim area), and a rail ticket or hotel booking in some cities includes 'free' travel on local public transport for a period, e.g. 60-80 minutes. In Geneva, anyone staying at a hotel, youth hostel or campsite in Geneva is entitled to a free Geneva Transport Card, which permits the holder to use the entire city public transportation network (bus, train and boat) for the entire duration of their stay, including their departure day. If you're in Switzerland for less than four days, you can purchase day passes for whichever city you visit, which provide unlimited travel on all regional transportation.

For more information about special fares, see **Discounted Tickets** below. There's also a wide range of holiday and visitor tickets in Switzerland (see page 93).

## Domestic Flights

There are domestic flights between all the major Swiss airports, which also serve the regional airports, although fares are high and if you aren't a millionaire or in a great hurry, it's much cheaper to travel by train or drive. Most domestic flights are operated by Swiss (⌨ www.swiss.com) and with the exception of

Zurich-Geneva (45mins), most people travel by train or road between Swiss cities.

## National Rail

The Swiss railway network is one of the most extensive in Europe, with around 5,000km (3,100mi) of track – almost all of it electrified – over 800 stations, some 300 tunnels (totalling 259km/160mi in length) and around 6,000 bridges (totalling 87km/54mi in length). It includes 2,000km (1,240mi) of private lines operated by some 50 'private' companies (they aren't strictly private, as many are run by cantonal governments). The Swiss federal railway company is usually referred to by its initials, which vary according to the local language: SBB (*Schweizerische Bundesbahnen*) in German (and used in this book to refer to Swiss federal railways), CFF (*Chemins de Fer Fédéraux*) in French and FFS (*Ferrovie Federali Svizzere*) in Italian – written as SBB-CFF-FFS on the side of Swiss trains.

Swiss trains run like clockwork and are seldom late, and when you need to make a connection the train is often waiting for you on the next platform.

The SBB, which celebrated its 160th anniversary in 2007, is renowned for its punctuality (although building or maintenance work and bad weather occasionally delay trains), comfort and speed, the only disadvantage being that the speed of some trains doesn't allow you to admire Switzerland's beauty (so if you're sightseeing, take a slow train).

Despite frequent fare increases in recent years to try to reduce SBB's deficit, Swiss trains remain relatively inexpensive if you take advantage of offers, excursion fares, family reductions and holiday package deals (see **Discounted Tickets** below). Over long distances, trains are cheaper than buses. The Swiss are Europe's most frequent train travellers and average around 2,000km (ca. 1,250mi) per year, per head of population. In addition to the SBB, there are many small private railways in Switzerland

The New Rail Link through the Alps/NRLA (*Neue Eisenbahnalpentransversalen/NEAT*) project – usually referred to as the Alp Transit Project (🖳 www.alptransit.ch/en) – is creating what will be the world's longest railway tunnel (57km/35mi) between Erstfeld (UR) and Biasca (TI), which is expected to be completed in 2017. It's one of the world's largest construction projects and includes the extension of two north-south railway lines through Switzerland and three new flat railway tunnels. The first north-south line, the Lötschberg base tunnel section (34.6km/21.5mi) in canton Berne, was completed in 2007 and allows passenger trains to reach speeds of up to 250kph/155mph.

## Types of Trains

Swiss Trains are categorised as local trains (*Regionalzug, train régional*), fast trains (*Schnellzug, train direct*) and international trains. Fast trains include Intercity (IC), which serve the main Swiss cities; fast regional trains, called RegioExpress, operate in some areas, e.g. between St. Gallen and Chur; and S-Bahn (the S is short for *schnell* or fast) suburban trains which operate in many regions, including Zurich. Eurocity (EC) trains (see above under **International Rail Services**) provide services between major Swiss towns and over 200 European cities – most have sleeping cars and cars with seats that convert into berths (*couchettes*), e.g. CityNightLine trains (see above). Most Swiss trains consist of first- and second-class carriages.

A supplement is payable by domestic passengers using EC trains, and bookings (costing CHF 5) are obligatory for international travel. Booking is optional on IC and many domestic fast trains, although it's recommended when travelling during holiday periods or at weekends. Bookings can be made from 24 hours to two months in advance (up to three months for compartments in sleeping cars).

The SBB provides various kinds of carriages on IC trains including a 'silent carriage' where mobile phones, noisy music (with or without headphones) and loud conversation are banned; first class business compartments (identified by a laptop pictogram) equipped with power sockets for laptops, mobile phones and PDAs; and a 'playroom car' for children,

denoted by an illustration of a boy and a girl wearing sunglasses on the outside. Not all of these carriages are provided on all trains, and it's also advisable to book.

Information regarding trains (and tickets) is available from information offices (denoted by a blue letter 'i' in a white circle on a blue background) at major stations or ticket offices at smaller stations.

Information (and seat reservations) about Swiss rail services is also available by telephone (☎ 0900-300 300, CHF 1.19 per minute) or via the internet (🖳 www.sbb.ch).

## Tickets & Fares

Tickets (*Billette, billets*) can be purchased online, via your mobile phone (on some routes) and from ticket offices or ticket machines at most stations. You should buy a ticket before boarding a train, but if you don't get the chance to buy one in advance, it's usually possible to purchase one on mainline trains from the conductor for a surcharge of CHF 5. However, this isn't the case on short-distance local routes, where passengers must have a valid ticket before boarding – look for the 'eye' symbol on the side of the train and departure boards. If you're discovered without a ticket during a random check, there's a heavy fine. Most ticket offices are open from around 6am until 7.30pm (even later at major stations).

Single (*einfach, aller-simple*) and return (*Retour/hin und zurück, aller-retour*) tickets for Swiss destinations can be purchased from touch-screen ticket machines in most stations, which are easy to use and have instructions in several languages, including English (touch the button for the desired language). If you wish to pay with cash, make sure that the machine you choose accepts notes and coins, as some accept only credit cards (machines are clearly marked). All coins except 5 cents are accepted, as well as CHF 10, 20 and 50 notes, but change is returned only up to CHF 20 (and only in coins); if, for example, you use a CHF 50 note to pay for a CHF 20 ticket, you won't receive any change!

Other methods of payment include Euros, REKA cheques, Postcards and credit cards. It's recommended that you use the ticket counter for anything remotely complicated, which will prevent money being wasted on useless tickets, although you can return a ticket purchased in error and obtain a replacement or a refund. Some stations have old-style ticket machines, which aren't touch screen and only accept coins or CHF 20 banknotes.

---

☑ **SURVIVAL TIP**

Bookings (reservations) can be made (for CHF 5) on all IC, ICE, CIS, EC and TGV trains, and are sometimes obligatory. A second-class ticket can be upgraded to first class on payment of the fare difference.

---

### Discounted Tickets

Many season tickets (*Abonnment*) and other discounted tickets are available in Switzerland. These include tickets for families, the young (16-25), senior citizens, commuters and groups of ten or more, as well as 'ski-day', hiking and cycling tickets, and other holiday and excursion tickets. Information is available from the information or ticket office at railway stations (staff usually speak English). A brochure is also available from railway stations describing the various season and discounted tickets available.

### Half-fare Travel Card

The best rail offer in Switzerland is the half-fare travel card (*Halbtax-Abo, abonnement demi-tarif*), a joint venture of Swiss transport operators, costing CHF 150 for one year, CHF 250 for two years or CHF 350 for three years. A half-fare travel card for 16-year-olds (who must usually pay full price for tickets) is available for CHF 92. Over 2mn *Halbtax* cards are sold annually, and entitle holders to half-fare travel on all SBB trains, PostBuses, selected city buses and trams, and many ferries and cable cars – a total network of around 24,500km (15,224mi). Half-fare travel cards are available at all railway stations and many PostBus depots and travel agents, on production of a passport photo and the fee. You must sign your half-fare travel card below your photograph.

Holders of a half-fare travel card may purchase day cards which provide unlimited travel for a whole day on all SBB trains and PostBuses. Day cards cost CHF 64 each for second class (CHF 103 first class) or six day cards for the price of five (CHF 320 2nd class, CHF 515 1st class). Cards don't need to be used on consecutive days and can be used by anyone with a half-fare travel card.

A child's day card is also available for CHF 15 for second class and CHF 30 for first class. As with any other ticket, day cards must be validated before use. Those aged under 25 can purchase a card called 'Track 7' (*Gleis 7/Voie 7*) for CHF 249 (CHF 99 for the Track 7 card and CHF 150 for a one year half-fare card) which provides half-fare travel before 7pm and free travel after 7pm. A monthly travel card is also available to half-fare travel card holders which converts your half-fare travel card into a general season ticket (see below) for one month.

Many Swiss cities and towns sell day cards at much reduced prices (between CHF 30 and 36) to residents. Only a limited number of cards are available per day, and weekend cards (Sat/Sun) are usually sold out quickly, but can be reserved months in advance. Enquire about community day passes (*Gemeinde Tageskarte, cartes journaliéres CFF*) at your community offices or see 🖳 www.tageskarte-gemeinde. ch. Tickets can usually be reserved online and must be picked up and paid for within seven days (they can also be reserved, paid for and collected in person, usually at a town hall or post office). Tickets are pre-dated and are valid for use only on the date stamped on them, and aren't refundable. You don't need a half-fare card to buy day cards, but you must be a community resident (proof required).

### General Season Ticket

The general season ticket (*Generalabonnement – GA, abonnement général – AG*), which is purchased by over 300,000 people each year, provides unlimited travel on all SBB trains, PostBuses and other buses and trams in some 35 cities and towns, plus many private railways and lake steamers. It also includes a 50 per cent reduction on other licensed coach operators, mountain railways and aerial cableways. GA tickets can be extended during a holiday or other 'long' period spent outside Switzerland by depositing them at a rail station and collecting them on your return.

A general season ticket costs CHF 3,100 per year second class (CHF 4,850 first class) if you're aged over 25, CHF 2,250 second class (CHF 3,600 first class) if you're aged between 16 and 25, CHF 2,350 second class (CHF 3,700 first class) if you're a senior citizen, and CHF 2,200 second class (CHF 3,500 first class) if you're disabled. Tickets aren't transferable (outside the listed users) and adults require a passport photo. There are a number of combinations for families – ask ticket office staff for information.

A transferable (impersonal) general season ticket is available for companies and organisations for CHF 5,000 per year second class (CHF 7,900 first class). There's even a general season ticket for dogs, which costs CHF 650 (both first and second class) – no picture required! Although annual season tickets may appear to be expensive, if you do a lot of travelling on public transport, they're a bargain. Transferable general season tickets cannot be extended during absences from Switzerland.

If you have a 15-year old child and purchase a child general season ticket one day before he or she turns 16, the child can travel for a year for CHF1,500 instead of the normal general season ticket price (CHF 2,250) for a 16 year old (a saving of CHF 750).

### Commuter Tickets

If you're a regular train commuter, you can buy a weekly, monthly or annual 'point-to-point' season ticket (*Streckenabonnement, abonnement de parcours*). An annual point-to-point season ticket costs around the same as nine monthly tickets. In some cantons, the rail network is divided into zones, and season tickets are available for a number of zones or the whole network. A photograph is required for an annual season ticket. Multiple journey cards (usually valid for 6 or 12 journeys) can save you time and sometimes money. You can make further savings by combining bus (both PostBuses and local services) and rail journeys. Ask at any railway station.

### Junior Card

A 'junior' card (*Junior-Karte, carte junior*) is valid for one year, and entitles children aged up to 16 to travel free when accompanied by a parent. The parent must have a full-fare or half-fare ticket, but not a commuter ticket. The junior card can be used on all SBB trains, private railways, PostBuses and lake steamers. It can also be used in around 35 towns to purchase city bus and tram day-cards under the same conditions as for trains. Junior cards are available from railway stations (and PostBus depots) for CHF 20 for the first and second children, free for subsequent children.

## Abfahrt Départ Partenza

| Abfahrt | | Gleis | Hinweis |
|---|---|---|---|
| 10.07 IC | Thun Spiez Visp | Brig | 6 |
| 10.07 IR | Burgdorf Langenthal | Olten | 10 |
| 10.08 S5 | Bümpliz Nord Kerzers | Neuchâtel/Murten | 12 Sektor A |
| 10.12 IR | Münchenbuchsee Lyss | Biel/Bienne | 9 |
| 10.12 S44 | Belp Toffen Thurnen Seftigen | Thun | 7 |
| 10.12 S2 | Wankdorf Konolfingen | Langnau | 4 |
| 10.16 S1 | Wankdorf Gümligen | Thun | 3 |
| 10.16 S1 | Bümpliz Süd Niederwangen | Fribourg | 2 |
| 10.19 S51 | Stöckacker Bümpliz Nord | Bern Brünnen | 13 Sektor C |
| 10.20 S2 | Ausserholligen Bümpliz Süd | Laupen | 1 |
| 10.20 S4 | Wankdorf Zollikofen Burgdorf | Affoltern–Weier | 12 Sektor A |
| 10.30 S3 | Wankdorf Zollikofen Lyss | Biel/Bienne | 12 Sektor A |
| 10.32 IC | Zürich HB Winterthur | St. Gallen | 7 |
| 10.32 S3 | Ausserholligen Weissenbühl | Belp | 1 |
| 10.34 IC | Fribourg Lausanne Genève | Genève–Aéroport | 4 |

The card must be signed and dated by the holder.

### *Supersaver Tickets*

One of the best bargains on Swiss railways is Supersaver single tickets, which provide large discounts on selected long-distance routes, e.g. in 2009, Zurich-Lucerne cost CHF 8.20 and Basle-Geneva just CHF 24.20. Book early (up to 14 days before travel) as there are only a limited number of Supersaver tickets per train, and they're only on sale for a limited period (e.g. October to January). Tickets are valid for a specific journey and time and aren't refundable or transferable. For more information and to book tickets, see 🖳 http://sparbillette.sbb.ch.

At the time of writing, Supersaver tickets were only available until 13th January 2010, but if the promotion is successful, SBB will continue with different incentives. SBB also offer Click&Rail Europe low-price online tickets to Austria, Germany and Italy via their website (🖳 http://mct.sbb.ch/mct/en/reiselust/europareisen/europabillettte/clickraileurope.htm).

### *Youth Fares*

Youth fares are available for those aged 16 to 25 (30 for full-time students). Discounts are also available on some international routes.

## Trams & Buses

The main Swiss cities boast efficient public transportation, with trams and buses forming the core of the urban network. The average cost of a single, short journey ticket is around CHF 2.50, which is usually valid for an hour. Depending on the travel required, it may be more economical to purchase a day pass for about CHF 8, a weekly or monthly pass, or a prepaid discount card.

Two separate bus services are provided throughout most of Switzerland; the PostBus service, and city and suburban bus networks. Together they cover most towns and villages in Switzerland. There's also an extensive tram or trolley bus network in all major cities (and a metro in Lausanne). Like Swiss railways, bus companies offer many discounted day, multi-ride and season tickets. There are also international bus services (e.g. Eurolines) to various countries. Combined bus (PostBus and local buses) and train commuter tickets are available from railway stations, offering savings compared with the cost of separate bus and train tickets.

The PostBus service (*Postauto, car postal*), which celebrated its centenary in 2006, covers around 10,450km (6,530mi) of Switzerland's principal roads, and provides regular services to over 1,600 localities on its over 750 routes. Many remote villages are served only by PostBuses, which carry over 100mn passengers a year.

Most towns and cities in Switzerland are served by local bus services. Tickets for both single and multiple journeys must usually be purchased from ticket machines (located at most stops) before boarding. Tickets are also sold at ticket offices, newspaper kiosks, and railway stations near bus and tram stops. Tickets can sometimes be purchased from the driver, but a surcharge may be payable if there was a ticket machine (in operation) at the stop where boarding.

## Driving in Switzerland

Swiss motorways and secondary roads are excellent, and rate among the best in the world.

The total network covers some 71,300km (44,500mi), of which around 1,770km (1,100mi) are motorways. Switzerland is constantly improving its road system, and spends a higher percentage of its motoring tax revenues on its roads than most countries. Every second person in Switzerland owns a car, making it one of the most heavily motorised countries in the world. However, despite the heavy traffic, Switzerland has less fatal accidents (per vehicle) than most other European countries (e.g. fewer than 400 in 2007 – similar to the UK per head of population and kilometres travelled).

Traffic density in the major Swiss cities is fast approaching the choking levels already experienced in many other European countries, although generally there are fewer traffic jams, and parking, although difficult, isn't impossible. During rush hours, from around 6.30 to 9am and 4 to 6.30pm, Mondays to Fridays, the flow of traffic is naturally slower, and any interruptions (e.g. roadworks, breakdowns or accidents) can cause huge traffic jams (*Stau, embouteillage*). Town centres are to be avoided during rush hours, particularly Geneva and Zurich.

You need to pay an annual fee to use Swiss motorways (see **Motorway Tax** on page 222). Motorway travel is generally fast (the speed limit on the motorway is 120kmh/75mph), although it's occasionally slowed to a crawl by road works and the favourite Swiss motor sport of running into the rear of the car in front. Outside rush hours, motoring is usually trouble-free, and driving on secondary roads in country areas is enjoyable. In winter, many mountain passes (see below) are closed due to heavy snowfall from between November and May, and vehicles using pass roads that remain open during winter require snow chains (shown by a sign, which also indicates whether a pass is open or closed). Cars are banned in some mountain resorts.

Although Switzerland has some of the most stringent anti-pollution motoring laws in Europe, traffic pollution is a major concern, particularly in large cities. Nevertheless, it's generally less than in most other western countries.

Information regarding closed passes and tunnels is available from Swiss motoring organisations, the Swiss television teletext road information service, the road conditions telephone service number (☎ 163) and the TCS website (🖳 www.tcs.ch/main/fr/home/verkehrsinfo/paesse_tunnels.html).

Signs on motorways show the local radio frequency on which road and traffic bulletins are broadcast. Emergency SOS telephones are located on mountain passes and motorways at 1.6km (1mi) intervals and every 150m in tunnels, where there are also fire extinguishers. Black arrows on white posts at the roadside show the direction of the nearest SOS telephone. The Swiss Bureau for the Prevention of Accidents publishes safety leaflets for motorists, motorcyclists, cyclists and pedestrians.

Around Swiss cities, it's advisable to use park and ride (P+R) facilities at railway stations and avoid parking costs, traffic jams and the eternal hunt for a parking space in cities. You pay a daily fee of around CHF 5 or a monthly subscription of CHF 110 if you're a commuter. Some P+R tickets include use of local public transport.

Best of all, if you live in a city – where public transport is good, and excellent value for money (especially with an annual season ticket or half-fare travel card (see page 88) – you may not need a car at all! And when you do, you can use CarSharing.

### Winter Driving

Winter driving in Switzerland needn't be a survival course. Most motorists fit winter tyres (*Schneereifen/Winterreifen, pneus neige*), which are compulsory when there's snow on the roads. If you have an accident in the winter and don't have winter tyres fitted to your vehicle, the insurance can refuse to pay, and if you get stuck in snow without winter tyres you'll be fined. In towns, many roads are salted or gritted in winter, although some cantons have cut down on the use of salt due to its corrosive and anti-environmental properties.

It's necessary or even compulsory to fit snow chains (*Schneeketten, chaîne à neige*) on a vehicle's driving wheels in some areas, particularly on mountains roads and passes (see below). When chains are necessary, it's indicated by a road sign; ignore it at your peril. Buy good quality snow chains and practice putting them on and removing them before you get stuck in the snow – even getting the container undone can be a trial with cold numb fingers, let alone fitting them. Studded tyres (spikes) may be used on vehicles up to 3.5 tonnes from 1st November to 31st March. Vehicles with studs are restricted to 80kph (50mph) and aren't permitted to use motorways.

Winter driving courses are held in all areas of Switzerland, where motorists can learn how to drive on snow and ice (don't, however, expect to compete with Scandinavian rally drivers after a day's tuition). The cost is between CHF 300 and 500, and courses usually last a whole day (drivers aged between 18 and 29 usually receive a reduction of CHF 100 at Swiss motoring organisations). It isn't necessary to use your own car, as you can hire (rent) one from the centre (better than wrecking your own). If you use your own car, you can take out special insurance cover for around CHF 15 to 20 a day, which is usually included in the course fee. Contact your canton's motor registration office or Swiss motoring organisations for more information.

The Swiss Conference for Road Traffic Safety (*Schweiz. Konferenz für Sicherheit im Strassenverkehr, Conférence Suisse de sécurité dans le Trafic Routier*) subsidises advanced and special driving courses, e.g. anti-skid courses, for both motorists and motorcyclists throughout Switzerland.

---

☑ **SURVIVAL TIP**

Skis carried on ski roof racks should have their curved front ends facing towards the rear of the car and pointed downwards.

---

Take it easy in winter. In poor road conditions, you'll notice that most Swiss slow down considerably and even habitual tailgaters leave a larger gap than usual between them and the car in front. Even a light snowfall can be treacherous, particularly on an icy road. When road conditions are bad, allow two to three times longer than usual to reach your destination. Most rural roads are lined with two-metre high poles, which mark the edges of the road when there's heavy snow.

### Mountain Passes

Snow chains must be fitted to all vehicles crossing mountain passes in winter (even in summer, freak snow storms can make roads treacherous). Always check in advance whether a pass is open, especially if using a pass means making a detour. A sign on the approach road indicates whether a pass is open (*offen, ouvert*) or closed (*geschlossen, fermé*) and whether chains are necessary.

The following mountain passes are open year round, although opening times may be reduced in winter (e.g. from 7am to 6 or 9pm): Bernina, Brünig, Flüela, Forclaz, Julier, Maloja, Mosses, Ofen (Il Fuorn), Pillon and Simplon. The following passes are open for part of the year: Oberalp, San Bernardino, Susten, Umbrail, St. Gotthard and Splüngen open from May to November; Furka, Great St. Bernhard, Grimsel and Klausen open from May to October; Albula opens from June to November; and Lukmanier is open from April to December.

The Great St. Bernard, St. Gotthard and San Bernardino passes have alternative road tunnels open all year round. There's a toll of from around CHF 30 (depending on your car's wheelbase) to use the Great St. Bernard road tunnel between Bourg St. Pierre and Aosta (Etroubles) in Italy.

The status (open/closed) of Swiss alpine tunnels and passes is given on Swiss television teletext, the road report service (☎ 163) and the TCS website (🖥 www.tcs.ch/main/fr/home/verkehrsinfo/paesse_tunnels.html).

There are also the car transporter trains (*Autoverlad/train auto*) which are popular in the winter months when passes are closed or driving conditions are poor. The most popular are Vereina (🖥 www.rhb.ch/Vereina.83.0.html?&L=4), connecting Klosters and the Engadin (for those headed to St. Moritz), and the Lötschberg (🖥 www.bls.ch/e/autoverlad/autoverlad.php), which takes you from the Bernese Oberland (Kandersteg) to Valais (Goppenstein) in 15 minutes! Trains run on schedules and usually depart every half an hour.

### Car Sharing

One way to save money on motoring in Switzerland is to use car sharing, such as the service offered by Mobility CarSharing (🖥 http://mobility.ch), which allows you to enjoy the benefits of car use without the costs and hassles of ownership – and it's good for the environment as there are fewer cars on the road.

Note that car-sharing, as used here, doesn't mean riding as a passenger in someone else's car or sharing your car with others. It's actually a form of car rental (hire), but unlike traditional car rental, you can 'rent' a car for as short a period as you wish and aren't required to return the car to where you got it from.

Combining Mobility CarSharing with public transport is estimated to save you at least 50 per cent on your annual transport costs, when the full costs of car ownership are taken into account, such as depreciation, maintenance, repairs, insurance, etc.

Mobility has some 2,250 vehicles (there's a choice of ten different vehicle categories, ranging from a two-seater to a transporter) at over 1,150 stations throughout Switzerland, and is designed to combine travel by public transport with car sharing. First-time customers (see subscriptions below) can make a 'Click & Drive' reservation and pay for the rental car by credit card; you then pick up the Mobility-Card and the key to the vehicle at any one of 50 SBB railway stations. Once you have used Click & Drive, you retain the Mobility-Card and can simply log onto the Mobility website to make another booking.

Regular customers can take out a subscription (there are different subscriptions for private and business customers) costing CHF 70, or CHF 40 with a Migros Cumulus card, for a trial subscription of four months. An annual subscription costs CHF 290, or CHF 190 with a general season ticket or a half-fare travel card (see **Discounted Tickets** above). Alternatively, you can become a member of the Mobility Cooperative (CHF 1,000 refundable share certificate plus CHF 250 membership fee), for which you pay no annual fee and benefit from a member's special rate.

Vehicles can be booked round-the-clock online and by phone, and you're charged an hourly and a kilometre rate. Booking online is quick and convenient and allows you to make a single or a series of reservations, enter feedback, change or renew your subscription, pay invoices, create statistics and much more.

## HOLIDAY & VISITORS' TICKETS

Visitors to Switzerland and Swiss residents travelling within Europe can buy a range of holiday and visitors' tickets and passes. These include the Swiss Pass (🖥 www.swisstravelsystem.ch/en), which provides unlimited travel by rail, PostBuses and ships throughout the country, plus buses and trams in almost 40 towns and cities. Among the most interesting trips for train enthusiasts is the Glacier Express, the slowest 'express' in the world (average speed 20mph/12.5mi). It runs from St. Moritz to Zermatt, and negotiates 291 bridges and 91 tunnels during its 7.5-hour journey (the Swiss make holes in both their mountains and their cheese).

Other excursion trains include the first-class Chocolate Train (Montreux to Gruyères and the Cailler-Nestlé chocolate factory at Broc) and the GoldenPass Line/Montreux-Oberland-Bernese (MOB) railway from Montreux to Zweisimmen/Lenk/Lucerne. The first-class MOB trains have panoramic or 'superpanoramic' express carriages and a saloon bar carriage. The Bernina express from Chur to Tirano, in Italy, has the highest (2,253m/7,390ft) railway traverse in the Alps and provides a unique experience. Information about steam train services is published by Switzerland Tourism (ST), including a brochure, *Schweizer Ferien mit Dampf und Nostalgie*.

> ☑ **SURVIVAL TIP**
>
> Note that some visitor's tickets are valid only if your permanent residence is outside Switzerland.

You can also use a Eurailpass (🖳 www.eurail.com) or an InterRail pass in Switzerland, or buy an InterRail One-Country pass that offers travel for three, four, six or eight days in one month within Switzerland. Travellers under the age of 26 receive a discount, and children's tickets are reduced by around 50 per cent (discounts are also offered on *Eurostar* and some Channel ferry routes). Supplements are required for some high-speed services, seat reservations and couchettes. For information, see 🖳 www.raileurope.co.uk/inter-rail.

An excellent book for visitors is *Switzerland: Rail, Road, Lake* by Anthony Lambert (Bradt Publications).

17th century façade, Schaffhausen

Lavaux vineyards, Lake Geneva

# 4.
# FINDING YOUR DREAM HOME

**O**nce you've considered possible locations for a home in Switzerland, you must decide on the type of property that will best suit your requirements, and consider the rental costs or purchase options. When buying or renting a home anywhere, it isn't wise to be in too much of a hurry and to do your homework thoroughly. It's a lucky person who gets his choice absolutely right first time, which is why most experts recommend that you rent before buying (see Chapter 6) unless you're absolutely sure of what you want, how much you wish to pay and where you want to live.

When buying a holiday or retirement home, it's all too easy to fall in love with the beauty and allure of Switzerland and sign a contract without giving it sufficient thought. If you're uncertain, don't allow yourself to be rushed into making a hasty decision, e.g. by fears of an imminent price rise or because someone else is interested in a property. Have a good look around in your chosen region and towns and obtain an accurate assessment of the types of property available, their relative prices and what you can expect to get for your money. However, before doing this, you should make a comprehensive list of what you want (and don't want) from a home, so that you can narrow the field and save time on wild goose chases.

There are plenty of properties for sale or rent in most regions of Switzerland – although there's an acute shortage in a few cantons and cities – and whatever kind of property you're looking for you're likely to have many to choose from. In most areas, properties for sale include modern townhouses and apartments with all mod cons, and a wide choice of detached houses, including chalets.

## BUYING V. RENTING

To buy or to rent? For anyone working in Switzerland it's the perennial question which most expatriates grapple with at some time.

(Obviously if you're a non-resident and are looking for a holiday home or a long-term investment, this question doesn't arise.) Whether buying or renting, finding somewhere suitable to live at a price you can afford – and in an area where you would like to live – is difficult and depends on the region, the type of property you're seeking and the local demand.

Around 63 per cent of households in Switzerland are in rented accommodation, one of the lowest owner-occupancy rates in Europe. However, home ownership is slowly gaining popularity and has increased from 31 per cent in 1990 to 37 per cent in recent years, although it varies from canton to canton (in Geneva only 15 per cent of households are owner-occupiers). Most Swiss are generally happy to rent – even when they can afford to buy – not least because tenants in Switzerland have comprehensive security of tenure.

Property to rent or buy is in huge demand in the major cities (i.e. Basle, Geneva, Lausanne and Zurich) where demand outstrips supply – and property prices and rents are among the highest in the world. Property prices in and around Geneva – where there's an acute shortage of accommodation – have risen by some 70 per cent in the last five years, and the most popular suburbs around Lake Zurich have also seen double-digit increases for a number of years. Rents have also increased sharply in cities such as Lausanne, where they rose by over 4 per cent in 2008 (over twice that of Zurich) and more than double the national average.

> With the rental and buyer's market close to saturation in the major cities, you may be forced to look further afield in the surrounding towns and villages, where rents and property prices are much lower – and thanks to Switzerland's superb trains and motorway network – getting to work won't be a problem.

The east and west of Switzerland and the southern canton of Ticino doesn't have the high population density of northern and central Switzerland and the region around Lake Geneva, and it's generally easier to find affordable property both to rent and buy. However, employment opportunities aren't as plentiful as in the property hotspots. It may be tempting to opt for a low-tax canton such as Zug, which is home to a large number of foreign companies and expatriates; however, Zug has very high housing costs and a dearth of property for sale. (Generally, the lower the local taxes, the higher the rents and real estate prices.)

Also bear in mind that should you decide to buy a home in Switzerland, there's no guarantee that you'll make a profit – even in the long term – and the interest rate won't always be so low. Swiss property prices rose by between 10 and 15 per cent in the late '80s and early '90s, which led the Swiss National Bank to increase interest rates to curb what it saw as runaway house price inflation. This had a severe impact on demand and prices fell by an average of 5 per cent per year between 1993 and 2000, by which time prices were back to their 1987 levels! Since 2000, prices have increased, albeit at a lower rate than in the late '80s and early '90s, thanks to lower interest rates and an increased supply of new apartments.

One of the reasons that the Swiss property market is so stable is that the market is tight, with demand exceeding supply, there's little speculation as non-resident foreigners cannot easily buy property, and banks are conservative in their lending. Switzerland doesn't (usually) experience the huge price inflation seen in many other countries – and consequently doesn't suffer the property crashes either.

The law regarding the purchase of property by foreign residents has also been relaxed in recent years, making it easier for expats to buy property – provided they can afford it. For many expats, particularly families with children and those from countries with a culture of homeownership (such as the UK and USA), buying a home is the obvious choice.

The arguments for and against buying and renting are outlined below.

## Why Buy?

Buying property in Switzerland is an excellent investment, particularly for anyone living there, but should be viewed as a long-term commitment rather than a quick way to turn a profit. If you're a non-resident buying purely for investment, bear in mind that renting may be restricted and you may have to own a property for at least five years before you can sell for a profit. However, property in the top ski resorts is in high demand and short supply, which is driving prices ever higher.

If you're a resident, the advantages of owning a home are obvious: you'll have more security as you cannot be evicted; you'll have a say in the administration, running and use issues; and the costs will be lower than renting. You can redecorate however you wish and make any internal structural changes you like, without asking anyone's permission or having to return the property to its original state when you leave – and you'll have your own washing machine and possibly a garden, and no close neighbours if you buy a detached house.

However, the most compelling reason for buying is that mortgage interest is tax deductible and paying a mortgage is, in many cases, cheaper than renting, with the cost of mortgages in 2009 the lowest for five years. However, although the current low mortgage rates mean that buying is substantially cheaper than renting, when you leave Switzerland you could find it difficult to sell.

The disadvantages include paying a large deposit (usually 20 per cent) plus purchase fees (2.5 to 5 per cent), high running and maintenance costs, and little capital appreciation in the short term – and capital gains tax can also be high in the short term unless the profit is invested in another Swiss property. However, some lenders will provide financing options for the deposit, and changes in pension fund rules in the last few years have meant that it's now possible

for residents to use or pledge their Swiss pension funds (both mandatory and voluntary) to raise the deposit. You will also have less freedom to move house (e.g. if you have noisy neighbours) than if you were renting, will need to deal personally with everything to do with the building and its management, pay for maintenance and repairs, and you could have financial problems if interest rates rise sharply.

The bottom line – at least in the current climate – is that if you're in Switzerland for the long term, have a secure income and spare capital (at least enough for the deposit) that's currently earning a low rate of interest, then buying is a sensible option. However, bear in mind that the interest rate may rise in future years, and that just a 1 per cent increase can increase your repayments dramatically. Many experts believe that you should reckon on average long-term mortgage interest rates of around 5 per cent.

It's often wise for prospective buyers to rent for a period, e.g. six months or a year, which allows you time to become familiar with an area, the type of housing available and the cost, before committing yourself to a purchase.

## Why Rent?

Around 63 per cent of the Swiss population rents, which is generally the best option for those planning to stay in Switzerland for less than say five years, and who don't plan to maintain a home there when they leave. Renting a house or apartment in Switzerland has some advantages over other

countries, such as the high standard of rental accommodation, comprehensive tenants' rights (landlords cannot easily evict tenants) and easy termination of leases. Owning a home in Switzerland is also seen by many Swiss as more of a liability than an asset (the country has the world's highest per capita mortgage debt).

Rents in Switzerland are comparable with other European countries, although there's a huge variation between cantons and, not surprisingly, between the major cities and rural areas. Rent increases must be justified by a landlord's increased costs, and leases tend to be for an indefinite period (open ended); it's rare for a lease to be terminated by the landlord and many people rent the same apartment or house for decades. (Some 20 per cent of housing in Switzerland is owned by institutional investors such as pension funds and insurance companies.)

Many Swiss prefer to rent rather than buy a home, and renting in Switzerland certainly isn't just for the young, the insecure and the poor, which is how it's customarily portrayed in some countries. Although many expats prefer to buy a home – and it usually pays to buy a home in the long term – there are a number of advantages to renting:

♦ it allows you to live in a size or style of property that's out of your price range or in an area where you couldn't possibly afford to buy a home;

♦ it can save you money and leave you better placed to buy a home at a later date, as you can move quickly to buy when the market is favourable;

♦ it gives you time to save a deposit so that you can afford a mortgage and/or can obtain a better mortgage deal;

♦ it can be a more sensible financial option, as there are hidden costs of owning a home, which is a liability as well as an asset;

♦ it allows you to use your capital for a more lucrative venture, such as starting a business or buying a home in another country, where property may be a better investment;

♦ it gives you freedom from DIY and maintenance costs – no hidden expenses;

♦ you can rent a furnished property, which saves you having to spend money on furniture and furnishings;

♦ it provides increased mobility and flexibility, particularly if you don't expect to remain in Switzerland long-term.

There are, of course, also a number of disadvantages to renting, such as:

♦ the difficulty of finding anywhere to rent at a reasonable price – or anywhere at all in Geneva!

♦ possible noisy neighbours (on all sides and above and below if you live in an apartment!), although the Swiss have strict laws about noise levels;

♦ sharing a communal washing machine and drying room (with restricted access) and other communal facilities;

♦ no private garden unless you rent a ground floor apartment or a house (however, an apartment will have a balcony or terrace);

♦ restrictive house rules and regulations (see page 159);

♦ not being able to decorate or improve a property as you would like;

♦ having no equity in the property – rent is 'dead' money;

♦ no indefinite security of tenure.

Always obtain a copy of the house rules (*Hausordnung, règlement d'immeuble*) – and read them – before buying or renting an apartment.

There's also subsidised (social), low-rent housing in Switzerland, which isn't included in the scope of this book. The proportion of subsidised housing varies considerably from canton to canton and is highest in Geneva and Vaud, where free-market rents are very high, with the average being around 2.5 per cent.

## SWISS HOMES

Most Swiss live in (rented) apartments (*Wohnung, appartement*) in and around the major cities, not necessarily out of choice but because the cost of family homes (*Einfamilienhaus, maison individuelle*) is prohibitively expensive due to the high cost of land. The Swiss enjoy a relatively high level of comfort, although modern houses and apartments are usually smaller overall than homes, for example, in the US and have smaller rooms; apartment rooms average around 15m² (160ft²), which is around average for Europe. Owner-occupiers generally live in larger homes (with four or more rooms) than renters, who tend to live in apartments with two or three rooms which are too small to be of interest to most buyers. Large homes with five or six bedrooms are scarce.

In advertisements, the overall built size of an apartment or house is shown in square metres (m²) along with the number of rooms (see table), which includes the living room and each bedroom, but not the kitchen (usually small) and bathrooms/WC. For example, a one-bedroom apartment is shown as *2-Zimmer/2-pièce*, a three-bedroom

| Property Sizes | |
|---|---|
| **Rooms (*Zimmer/Pièce*)** | **Meaning** |
| 1 | studio (one room, usually small with a cooking niche) |
| **1.5 Badezimmer**: | full bathroom and a separate guest WC |
| 1.5 | larger studio, usually with a niche for the bed and a larger area as dining room, living room or kitchen |
| 2 | one-bedroom apartment, i.e. one bedroom and a living room |
| 2.5 | one bedroom, living room and an open dining room |
| 3 | two-bedroom apartment, living room (or living/dining room combined) |
| 3.5 | two-bedroom apartment with an open dining room |
| 4 | three bedrooms, living room/dining room combined |
| 4.5 | three bedrooms with an open dining room |
| 5 | four bedrooms |
| 5.5 | four bedrooms and an open dining room |
| 6 | five bedrooms |

apartment as *4-Zimmer/4-pièce* and a four-bedroom house as *5-Zimmer/5-pièce*. A dining corner or a larger than average living room is indicated in ads as an extra 'half a room', e.g. a *2.5-Zimmer/2.5-pièce* apartment has one bedroom and a larger than average living/dining area. However, in Geneva and some other cantons, the kitchen may count as a room if it's large enough and has an eating area, so always ask the room disposition.

Housing standards are high in Switzerland and among the highest in Europe, particularly when it comes to build quality; and are built to last, using top quality materials and fixtures and fittings. Apartment blocks have at least one and possibly two underground levels; often the first underground level comprises cellars or storage rooms and the lower underground floor the underground parking, but both may be combined on the same level.

An increasing number of houses and apartment developments are 'eco-designed' with low energy requirements and excellent noise and heat insulation, including double- or triple-glazing (*Doppelfensterl Dreifachverglasung, double-vitrage/triple-vitrage*). The windows of traditional houses usually have shutters (*Fensterläden, volets*) while apartments have rolling shutters (*Storen, volets roulants*) made of metal, wood or plastic slats (raised and lowered manually with cords or via an electric motor). The exterior may be made of wood, stone, brick or other (usually fire resistant) materials.

In Alpine and forest regions, people traditionally live in wooden detached chalets with shingled or tiled/slate roofs and carved gables, with corners and roofs often reinforced with stone. Nowadays, traditional chalets may be built from larchwood, which is higher quality and requires far less maintenance than pine; although fewer houses of this type are constructed and newer houses are commonly built of brick or block, even in rural areas. Period houses in cities and historic towns have often been renovated and have modern interiors; many are also protected as historical monuments and command premium prices.

Apartments may have fully fitted kitchens (*Einbauküche, cuisine meublée*) with appliances such as a cooker (*Herd, cuisinière*); usually a ceramic electric hob (*Glaskeramik/plaques vitrocéramique*) and a built in oven and/or steamer oven; built-in fridge/freezer (*Kühlschrank/réfrigérateur, Tiefkühlschrank/congélateur*); possibly a built-in microwave oven (*Microwellenofen, micro-ondes*); and usually a dishwasher (*Gechirrspülmaschine, lave-vaisselle*). Newer apartments are often equipped with a washer/drier (*Waschmaschine/Tumbler, lave-linge/sèche-linge*). As a general rule, apartments and houses in German-speaking regions come with fully equipped kitchens, while those in French-speaking cantons and Ticino are usually 'semi-equipped', e.g. with a cooker but no refrigerator/freezer. The level of furnishings and appliances is usually stated in real estate ads.

New apartments also include state-of-the-art sanitary facilities and cable radio/TV (*Kabelanschluss, télévision câblée*) and phone connections. Unfurnished apartments usually have light fittings only in bathrooms, kitchens and occasionally hallways (most rooms just have bare wires). Fitted wardrobes or closets (*Kleiderschrank, armoire*) in bedrooms are rare, and curtain rails aren't provided unless they're built-in. A number of built-in linen cupboards and a cloakroom unit may be provided.

Apartments may have parquet – common in period homes (e.g. pre-1945) – or wooden floors, and tiles and stone are also fairly common. Wall-to-wall carpet isn't common in modern apartments in Switzerland and isn't associated with quality housing, as it is in the UK and US. Modern apartments usually have under-floor heating.

Kitchens and bathrooms (*Badezimmer, salle de bain*) usually have tiled or stone floors. Bathrooms are usually fitted with a toilet, washbasin and a shower or bath, or a bath with a shower attachment. In 'luxury' homes, bathrooms may contain a bath and a separate enclosed shower and possibly a Jacuzzi or whirlpool bath. Bidets are rare in the German-speaking regions of Switzerland. When there's no separate utility room (*Allzweckraum, buanderie*), the washing machine and dryer may be housed in the main bathroom. Larger apartments (from three bedrooms) usually have a second toilet and may have an en-suite shower or wet room (*Dusche/Nasszelle, salle de douche*) to the main bedroom, in addition to a separate family bathroom.

Apartment blocks usually have a communal laundry room (*Waschküche, buanderie*) with a washing machine and tumble dryer and a separate drying room situated in the basement, if apartments don't have their own washer/driers. In some buildings, the use of washing machines

and driers may be 'free' (although it will be included in your extra charges), while in others you must pay per wash using coins, cards or tokens (usually available from the housekeeper). In some apartment buildings you can wash your clothes whenever machines are free, while in others they have a strict rota system where you aren't permitted to use the laundry unless it's your turn (even if it isn't being used – unless you get permission from the person whose turn it is). Some apartment blocks have outside clothes lines, where tenants may hang their clothes to dry, or drying rooms with clothes lines and a wall-mounted dryer-fan.

In larger, more expensive apartments, a personal washer/drier is provided, which may be located in a utility room. If you wish to buy your own washing machine and wash at your convenience, ensure that you have room to install it in your apartment and an appropriate power point (see **Electricity** on page 247) – and don't forget to ask your landlord for permission if you're renting and need to install a power point or special

old house, Stein-am-Rhein, Schaffhausen

plumbing. Hot water and heating in apartments may be provided by a central system for the whole apartment block and paid for along with other extra charges (*Nebenkosten/NK, charges/frais immobiliers*).

Most apartments have a terrace or balcony (*Terrasse/Balcon, terrasse/balcon*) or a small patio on the ground floor, and some apartment houses have a shared garden or barbecue area. A small storage room or pantry may be provided in an apartment, and a lockable storage room (*Abstellraum, remis*) in the cellar (*Keller, cave*) of the building, which doubles as the mandatory nuclear shelter. Many apartment blocks also have a bicycle storage room (*Veloraum, cellier pour vélos*), and apartment developments may also have a playground (*Spielplatz, cour de récréation*). Luxury apartment blocks may have a communal gymnasium, sauna or indoor heated swimming pool. An apartment doesn't usually include a garage or parking place (*Autostellpatz/ Einstellplatz, parking/place de parking*) in the rent or price, but one can usually be rented or purchased separately, usually in an underground car park (*Tiefgarage, parking souterrain*).

Luxury chalets and apartments often have en-suite bathrooms to all bedrooms; a large lounge with an open (working) fireplace; large balconies and/or terraces with French windows; a cellar, ski room and garage; a swimming pool (which may be shared); a hot tub, Jacuzzi or hammam (Turkish) bath; and panoramic views. If you buy a property off plan or under construction, you can usually choose the appliances, cabinets and counter tops for the kitchen, the bathroom suite(s), and the tiles, floor and wall finishes. Most builders don't finish an apartment until it's sold, so that the new owner can choose these items.

## RESEARCH

The secret of successfully buying or renting a home in Switzerland (or anywhere) is research, research and more research – and knowing what you want and don't want and what you can afford! A successful rental or purchase is much more likely if you thoroughly investigate the various regions, the types of property available, prices and relative values, and the procedure for buying property. The more research you do before committing yourself, the better; this should (if possible) include

advice from those who already own a home in Switzerland, from whom you can usually obtain invaluable information (often based on their own mistakes), as well as by reading publications and visiting property exhibitions.

Finding accommodation in Switzerland isn't the easiest of tasks and requires a lot of patience and perseverance in some regions. It's best to start your search before arriving in Switzerland – or at least do some research so that you know the relative prices and what you're looking for – and if you're bringing your family to Switzerland, it's usually better for them to join you **after** you've found suitable accommodation. Many people take a temporary apartment for a number of months before finding a 'permanent' home.

If you need short-term temporary accommodation, there's a wealth of hotels, bed and breakfast accommodation, holiday apartments and serviced apartments that you can rent. Serviced apartments are fully furnished and equipped, with a kitchen, television/DVD, broadband internet and maid service. They're generally intended for short lets of a few weeks or months, and cost around twice as much as a similar apartment with a long-term tenancy (or around the same as a hotel room). They are, however, ideal for a short period while you look for a longer-term rental. See **Temporary Accommodation** on page 141 for information.

There are a number of books especially written for those planning to live or work in Switzerland (like this one and our sister publication, *Living and Working in Switzerland*, by David Hampshire). You can get a good idea of relative rents and the value of properties from a wealth of websites (see **House Hunting** below and **Appendix C**). Property for sale is also advertised in many newspapers and magazines in Switzerland and abroad (see **Appendix A**) and you can access Swiss newspaper ads online. However, the best resources are real estate websites.

☑ **SURVIVAL TIP**

The cost of investing in a few books or magazines (and other research) is tiny compared with the expense of making a big mistake.

## AVOIDING PROBLEMS

The problems associated with buying and renting property abroad have been highlighted in the last few decades or so, during which the property market in some countries has gone from boom to bust and back again. From a legal point of view, Switzerland is a very safe country in which to rent or buy a home, and both tenants and buyers have a high degree of protection under Swiss law. However, you should take the usual precautions regarding contracts, deposits and obtaining proper title.

Among the most common 'problems' experienced by buyers (although some apply to renters) in Switzerland are:

◆ buying in the wrong area (rent first!);

◆ buying a home that's difficult to resell: a property with broad appeal in a popular area is usually easiest to sell, although it may need to be very special to sell quickly in some areas. A modest, reasonably-priced property is usually likely to be much more sellable than a large expensive home, particularly one requiring extensive maintenance or modernisation.

◆ buying a property that needs renovation and grossly underestimating the cost;

◆ not having a survey done on an old property;

◆ not taking legal advice (see below);

◆ not including the necessary conditional clauses in the contract;

◆ buying a property for business and being too optimistic about the income.

◆ paying too much;

◆ taking on too large a mortgage;

◆ buying a property that's subject to embargoes or an undischarged mortgage, is part of assets of a company, has been sold illegally by a bankrupt builder or company, is subject to claims by relatives or has been sold to more than one buyer. However, all of these are rare in Switzerland and it's possible to check them before signing a contract (if you engage a notary before paying a deposit, he'll also check these).

## Legal Advice

It you're planning to buy property in Switzerland (or anywhere else), it's advisable to obtain expert, independent legal advice. The vast majority of people who buy a home abroad don't obtain independent legal advice, and most of those who experience problems take no precautions whatsoever. Of those who do take legal advice, many do so only after having paid a deposit and signed a contract or, more commonly, after they have run into problems.

---

 **Caution**

Never sign anything, or pay any money, until you've sought legal advice in a language in which you're fluent, from a lawyer who's experienced in Swiss property law.

---

You'll find the relatively small cost (in comparison to the cost of a home) of obtaining legal advice to be excellent value, if only for the peace of mind it affords. Trying to cut corners to save a few francs on legal costs is foolhardy in the extreme when a large sum of money is at stake.

Your lawyer (*Rechtsanwalt, avocat*) will carry out the necessary searches regarding such matters as ownership, debts and rights of way. It isn't wise to use the vendor's lawyer, even if this will save you money, as he's primarily concerned with protecting the interests of the vendor and not the buyer. Your notary will also do his own checks and bring to your attention anything that isn't correct, as will your lender (if you have one), as Swiss banks carry out comprehensive checks on a property before they will lend against it.

These checks include ensuring that the vendor has a registered title; that there are no debts against a property; that the property has all the relevant building licences and that it conforms to local planning conditions; and that any changes (alterations, additions or renovations) have been approved by the local town hall and have planning permission. If a property is owned by several people (e.g. members of a family), all owners must give their consent before it can be sold (see **Conveyancing** on page 131).

Before hiring a lawyer, compare the fees charged by a number of practices and obtain quotations in writing. Always check what's included in the fee and whether it's 'full and binding' or just an estimate. You could employ a lawyer just to check the preliminary contract (see below) before signing it to ensure that it's correct and legal and includes everything necessary, particularly regarding conditional clauses.

You may be able to obtain a list of lawyers who speak your national language and are experienced in handling Swiss property sales, either in Switzerland or in your home country, e.g. British buyers can obtain a list from the Law Society in Britain. Note, however, that if you use a lawyer in your home country, you may have to pay extra fees, as a lawyer in your home country will probably need to use the services of another lawyer in Switzerland.

However, be careful who you engage, as some lawyers are part of the problem rather than the solution (overcharging is also rife)! Don't pick a lawyer at random, but engage one who has been recommended by someone you can trust.

## Professionals

There are professionals speaking English and other languages in most areas of Switzerland, and some expatriate professionals (e.g. architects, builders and surveyors) also practise there. However, don't assume that because you're dealing with a fellow countryman he'll offer you a better deal or do a better job than a Swiss (the contrary may be true). It's wise to check the credentials of professionals you employ, whether Swiss or foreign. In Switzerland, real estate agents aren't licensed, although most are reputable. A building inspector or land surveyor (*Bauinspektor/Landvermesser, expert/arpenteur*) may also be necessary, particularly if you're buying an old property or a property with a large plot of land (see **Inspections & Surveys** on page 128).

The Swiss government has introduced a building surveyor program called IP-Bau-Grobdiagnose, which can be carried out by an expert architect/engineer on an existing building. The inspection costs CHF 1,000-2,000 and consists of a general condition report plus environmental issues such as energy efficiency, but it can also include an estimate of the cost to renovate or modernise a property.

It's never wise to rely solely on advice proffered by those with a financial interest in selling you a property, such as a developer or real estate agent, although their advice may be excellent and totally unbiased.

## Finance

It's recommended to have your finances in place before you start looking for a property and, if you need a mortgage, to obtain a mortgage guarantee certificate from a bank that guarantees you a mortgage at a certain rate subject to a valuation (see **Mortgages** on page 169). Under Swiss law, you can withdraw from a contract and have your deposit returned if you're unable to obtain a mortgage. You'll need to pay a deposit when signing a contract, and must pay fees and taxes (see **Fees** on page 179) of between 2.5 and 5 per cent of the purchase price on completion.

The practice of stating a lower sale price than the actual price on the sales agreement in order to reduce the tax burden isn't common in Switzerland (as in some other countries), although it does occur. By lowering the official sale price, not only is a portion of the conveyance tax avoided but the seller also reduces his capital gains tax on the profit made on the property. This practice is, not surprisingly, strictly illegal and there are severe penalties if you're discovered.

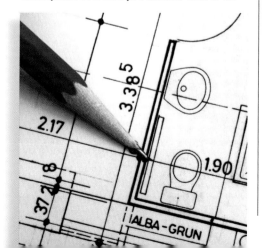

## Buying Off Plan

Many problems and risks can arise when buying off plan (i.c. an unbuilt property) or buying a property on an unfinished development. Because of the problems associated with buying off plan, such as the difficulty in ensuring that you actually get what's stated in the contract and that the developer doesn't go broke (which even happens in Switzerland!), some experts have even advised buyers against buying an unfinished property. However, this isn't practical, because in a seller's market it's essential to buy off plan if you wish to buy a home in a popular development. Although there are many satisfied buyers of off plan property, the process is generally more time-consuming and stressful than buying a resale property.

An off plan property isn't finished until the building is complete in every detail (as confirmed by your own lawyer or architect), communal services have been installed, and all the infrastructure is in place, such as roads, parking areas, external lighting and landscaping (although the landscaping is often completed after the owners move in, for example in the spring if a house was finished in the winter).

A builder must provide buyers who are purchasing off plan, through stage payments, with an insurance policy or banker's guarantee, which protects them against the builder going broke before construction is completed. Developers usually try to sell as many apartments as possible – and collect 'reservation' fees – before starting construction, which can delay the start and completion of a project.

## HOUSE HUNTING

There are many ways of finding homes for sale or rent in Switzerland, including the following:

**The internet:** As in most countries, the internet is the number one resource for property hunters in Switzerland. There are numerous property websites, including 🖥 www.alle-immobilien.ch, www.comparis.ch/immobilien/intro.aspx, www.homegate.ch and www.immoscout24.ch, all with English-language versions, and 🖥 www.anzeiger.ch

(German), www.immoclick.ch, www.immo-net.ch and http://immo.search.ch (the latter three in French/German). Some sites show only their own paid ads (Homegate, Immoclick, Immoscout24), while other collect ads from a number of sites (Alle-immobilien, Anzeiger, Comparis, Immo-search). Many more can be found by typing 'Swiss property' into a search engine such as Google (🖥 www.google.com). A number of banks or bank groups have their own property websites such as the Kantonal Bank (🖥 www.immomarktschweiz.ch).

**Estate agents (see below):** There are numerous real estate agents in Switzerland who sell around half of all Swiss property. The rest are sold by other professionals such as banks (most of which have real estate departments), lawyers, accountants and private individuals.

**Newspapers & magazines:** Property for sale and rent is advertised in many newspapers and magazines in Switzerland and abroad (see **Appendix A**). Most major city newspapers contain property supplements on certain days of the week and they can also be accessed online via 🖥 www.onlinenewspapers.com/switzerl.htm. It may be worthwhile placing an ad under 'Apartments wanted', particularly if you're seeking something out of the ordinary. You can also reply to private ads with a box number.

**Property exhibitions:** There are a number of property shows staged annually in Switzerland, including Lausanne's *Salon Immobilier* in April, which is mainly for buyers in the Vaud and Valais regions, and Zurich's SVIT-Immobilien-Messe (also in April).

> **☑ SURVIVAL TIP**
>
> Note that it's rare to see 'for sale' signs in gardens or in the windows of houses for sale in Switzerland, so you won't be able to drive around an area to see what's for sale, but will need to visit local real estate agents.

## REAL ESTATE AGENTS

Many property sales in Switzerland are handled by real estate agents (*Immobilienhändler, agent immobilier/régie*), although banks, lawyers, building contractors, architects and private individuals also sell homes. An increasing number of owners sell their own homes via websites such as 🖳 www.homegate.ch and www.immoscout24.ch. However, where foreign buyers are concerned, the vast majority of sales are made through agents or developers. It's common for foreigners in many countries, e.g. the UK, to use an agent in their own country who works with a Swiss agent or developer, particularly when buying a new property. The fee charged by agents in Switzerland is usually 2 to 3 per cent, which is paid by the vendor.

A number of Swiss agents and developers also advertise abroad in property magazines and newspapers, and most have websites. Most Swiss agents speak English or have English-speaking staff, particularly those that routinely sell to foreigners. If you want to find an agent in a particular town or area, look under *Liegenschaftvermittlung/ Immobilien, agences immobilières* in the local *Yellow Pages* (*Gelbeseite, pages jaunes*) or you can find one via the internet. Swiss agents don't subscribe to a multiple-listing service and usually have exclusive listings.

Swiss real estate agents – surprisingly – aren't regulated by law or required to be licensed. However, most professionals dealing in real estate are members of the Swiss Real Estate Association/SVIT (Puls 5, Giessereistr. 18, 8005 Zurich, ☎ 044-434 78 82, 🖳 www. svit.ch), the main organisation for real estate agents and property professionals in Switzerland, which has over 2,000 members. The Association adheres to a code of business ethics and runs the SVIT Swiss Real Estate School. It also operates the Swiss Real Estate Tribunal (🖳 www.svit-schiedsgericht. ch/en), which aims to arbitrate in disputes between members and their clients before they escalate.

Agents vary enormously in their efficiency, enthusiasm and professionalism. If an agent shows little interest in finding out exactly what you want, you should look elsewhere.

## Foreign Agents

Many foreign agents deal in property in Switzerland, particularly holiday homes which are often built especially for the foreign market. Agents usually arrange inspection flights to Switzerland and may refund the cost of flights (up to a certain limit) on completion of a sale. Most agents offer rental and management services.

Some overseas agents are members of the Federation of Overseas Property Developers, Agents and Consultants (FOPDAC, c/o NAEA, Arbon House, 6 Tournament Court, Edgehill Drive, Warwick CV34 6LG, UK, ☎ +44-1926-496800, 🖳 www.fopdac.com) and are bound by a code of ethics requiring them to meet local licensing requirements. You can also find an agent through the Association of International Property Professionals (AIPP, 94 New Bond Street, London, W1S 1SJ, ☎ +44-20-7409 7061, 🖳 www.aipp.org.uk), which was established to improve the standards of professionalism in international property sales, which is largely unregulated (members voluntarily agree to follow a professional code of conduct).

There may be advantages in using a foreign agent, particularly an English-speaking one who's experienced in selling to foreign buyers and is familiar with the problems they can encounter, but you should ensure that they're trading legally. If a foreign agent refers clients to a Swiss agent or agents, he may share his commission with the Swiss agent(s) or charge extra for his services – in some cases a great deal extra – therefore you should check what's included (and what isn't) in any prices quoted by foreign agents. When buying, check in advance whether you need to pay commission or any extras on top of the sale price (apart from the normal fees and taxes associated with buying property in Switzerland).

## VIEWING

Before viewing properties to rent or buy, you should have a good idea of the sort of property you want (and what you need),

the area you want to live in – although this may be decided by what's available or what you can afford – and, not least, your budget. It's advisable to draw up a checklist of the most important features you want in a home and its location, such as morning/afternoon sun, views, nearby railway station/motorway access and local amenities; and anything you absolutely don't want, such as tiny cramped rooms, noisy neighbours, a busy road close by and no parking (see the list under **Choosing the Location** on page 71).

You can get a good idea of rents and prices in different areas from websites such as www.homegate.ch and www.immoscout24.ch. Most real estate agents also have extensive websites providing details of properties for sale or rent, although not all properties on their books are included.

Obtain details of as many properties matching your parameters as possible in your chosen area, and make a shortlist of those you wish to view. You will be shown properties personally by agents, and won't be given the keys or be expected to deal with tenants or vendors directly; although if a property is being sold by private treaty you'll usually be dealing with the owner. If you're using a foreign agent, confirm (and reconfirm) that a particular property is still for sale, and the price, before travelling to Switzerland to view it.

You should make an appointment to view properties, as agents don't like people simply turning up unannounced and asking to view properties. If you make an appointment, you should keep it or call and cancel it. If you're on holiday, you can call at agents to see what's on offer, but don't expect an agent to show you any properties without an appointment. If you view properties during a holiday, it's wise to do so at the beginning so that you can return later to inspect any you particularly like a second time.

You should try to view as many properties as possible during the time available, but allow enough time to view each property thoroughly, to travel between properties, and for breaks for sustenance (it's mandatory to have a good lunch in Switzerland). Although it's important to see sufficient properties to form an accurate opinion of price and quality, don't see too many in one day, as it's easy to become confused as to the merits of each property. If you're shown properties that don't meet your requirements, tell the agent immediately. You can help the agent to narrow the field by telling him what's 'wrong' with the properties you reject and what you particularly like about the properties on your short list.

It's wise to make notes of both the good and bad features of properties you like, and take lots of photographs so that you're able to compare them later at your leisure – but keep a record of which photos are of which house! It's also wise to mark each property on a map so that, should you wish to return later at your leisure without the agent (e.g. to check travelling times or check out the neighbourhood), you can find them without getting lost (too often!).

The more a property appeals to you, the more you should look for faults and negative points; if you still like it after stressing the negative points, it must have special appeal!

## COMMUNITY PROPERTIES

In Switzerland, properties with common elements (whether a building, amenities or land) shared with other properties are owned through a system of part-ownership, similar to condominiums in the USA. A community property – called 'ownership by floor' (*Eigentumwohnungen/Stockwerkeigentum, propriété par etage/PPE, co-proprietaire*) in Switzerland – may be an apartment, townhouse or a semi-detached home on a private estate with communal areas and facilities. Over two-thirds of Swiss live in apartments, which are common in cities and mountain resorts. Community properties include most properties that are part of a development. In general, the only homes that aren't community properties are detached houses built on individual plots in public streets or on rural land.

Owners of community properties not only own their homes (plus possibly a garage or garage space and cellar), but also a share of the land and common elements of a building or development, including foyers, hallways, passages, lifts, patios, gardens, roads, and leisure and sports facilities. When you buy a community property, you automatically become a member of the community of owners.

Some 'luxury' developments, particularly those in mountain resorts, offer a range of sports and leisure facilities, including swimming pools, tennis courts, a gymnasium or fitness club, and a restaurant or café. **Note, however, that amenities such as these are rarely found in most apartment blocks in Switzerland.** Many developments have landscaped gardens, a children's playground and good security, although a full-time caretaker is rare.

## Advantages & Disadvantages

The advantages of owning a community property include:

◆ good security;

◆ possibly lower property taxes than detached homes;

◆ a range of community sports and leisure facilities;

◆ community living with lots of social contacts and the companionship of close neighbours;

◆ no garden, lawn or pool maintenance;

◆ properties are often situated in locations where owning a detached home would be prohibitively expensive, e.g. a town centre or popular resort.

The disadvantages of community properties may include:

◆ excessively high community fees;

◆ restrictive rules and regulations;

◆ a confining living and social environment and possible lack of privacy;

◆ noisy neighbours (not a big problem in Switzerland);

◆ limited living and storage space (depending on the size of an apartment);

◆ acrimonious owners' meetings, where management and factions may try to push through unpopular proposals (sometimes using proxy votes).

---

☑ **SURVIVAL TIP**

**If you're planning to live permanently in a community property, you should avoid buying in a development with a high percentage of rental units, i.e. units that aren't owner-occupied, as they may be filled with rowdy holidaymakers, and owners may be unconcerned with the smooth running of the development.**

---

If you're planning to buy a community property, it's important to ensure that it's well managed and that there aren't any outstanding major problems. If there are, you could be liable to contribute towards the cost of repairs, which could run into many thousands of francs.

## Heating

Heating in apartments is usually provided by a central heating system, while houses have their own boilers. Heating in apartment blocks is switched on in October and off in the spring, so if the temperature drops sharply outside this period you'll need an alternative source of heating. You may have two meters, one showing the heat coming into an apartment and one showing the available heat. If the available 'source' heating meter is at zero, the heating system is switched off. You can control the heating in your apartment via a thermostat. If you're away in winter, it's advisable to leave the thermostat on a low setting so that your water pipes don't freeze.

Bear in mind that top floor apartments are both colder in winter and warmer in summer, and may incur extra charges for the use of lifts. On the other hand, they offer more security than ground floor apartments and better views. An apartment that has other apartments above and below it will generally be noisier than a ground or top floor apartment.

## Value & Community Fees

Owners must pay community or extra fees (*Nebenkosten/NK, charges/frais immobiliers*) for the upkeep of communal areas and for communal services, such as heating. Charges are calculated according to each owner's share or value (*Wertquote, quote-part de la valeur*) of a development, which is based on various factors, the most important being the size; other factors include the view, the floor (storey), sun exposure, position in the building, accessibility, floor plan and emissions. The larger your share of a block of flats, the more say (voting rights) you have in the management and running of the property (see **Management** below).

The proportion of the common elements assigned to each apartment owner also depends on the number in the block and is expressed in thousandths, e.g. ten apartments of the same size and characteristics in a block (assuming this was possible) would each own 100/1,000ths of the common elements. Ground floor owners don't usually pay for lifts (elevators), and other owners pay more or less according to the floor they're on (those on the top floor pay the most because they use the lifts most).

General charges are levied for services such as a caretaker, upkeep of the garden and surroundings, and garbage collection. In addition to general charges, there may be special charges for services and equipment such as central heating and hot water, which may be divided according to the share

of the utility allocated to each apartment. An apartment block in a city with a resident concierge/porter will have much higher community fees than one without. Always check the level of general and special charges before buying an apartment.

Fees vary considerably, but are generally around 1 per cent of the cost or value of an apartment, e.g. from around CHF 2,000 per year for a two-bedroom apartment in a modest development up to CHF 5,000 or more for similar accommodation in a luxury development with a range of services and amenities such as a clubhouse, porter, swimming pool and tennis courts.

> ☑ **SURVIVAL TIP**
>
> **High fees aren't necessarily a negative point, assuming you can afford them, as the value of a community property depends to a large extent on how well it's maintained and managed.**

Service charges are billed monthly, and the amount paid is adjusted at the end of the year (which can be a nasty shock) when the annual accounts have been approved and you receive your annual 'extra charges account' (*Nebenkostenabrechung, le décompte annuel des charges*). If you're buying a resale apartment, ask to see a copy of the accounts and bills for previous years and the minutes of the last annual general meeting, as owners may be 'economical with the truth' when stating service charges, particularly if they're high.

See also **Extra Charges** on page 151.

## Maintenance & Repairs

Residents in community properties usually contribute to a renovation or sink fund (*Erneuerungsfonds, fonds de rénovation*), used to finance future repairs and renovation for the common parts of the property. These contributions are considered to be maintenance costs and are tax-deductible in the year they're paid **and** not just later (e.g. 5 or 10 years later) when they're used to pay for repairs. (If you own a house, you should reckon on spending around 1 to 2 per cent of its value per year on maintenance and renovations.)

If necessary, owners can be assessed an extra amount in addition to their community fees to make up any shortfall of funds for maintenance or repairs. Maintenance decisions are by majority vote, therefore if the majority of the owners approve certain maintenance or renovations, then you're obliged to contribute even if you oppose it. This may include, for example, hiring a snow plough to clear a private street in a ski resort; if the majority in the building want snow removal, then you're obliged to contribute whether you agree or not.

You should check the condition of the common areas (including all amenities) in an old building or development and whether any major maintenance or capital expense is planned, for which you could be assessed. You should be wary of 'bargain' apartments in buildings requiring a lot of maintenance work or refurbishment. Under Swiss law, however, disclosure of impending expenditure must be made to prospective buyers before they sign a contract.

## Management

The ownership and management of community properties are regulated by Swiss law, and the rules and regulations for each development are contained in a document produced by the community, a copy of which you should receive. If you don't understand it, you should have it explained or translated. A block of apartments usually has an administrator, who's elected by the owners to manage the property on their behalf. He's responsible for the efficient daily running of the block and the apportioning of charges relating to the building, e.g. management, heating, insurance, repairs and maintenance. The administrator bills individual owners for service charges and management fees.

## Community Meetings

A residents' general meeting must be held at least once a year to approve the budget and discuss other matters of importance, such as capital expenditure and, if necessary, to appoint a new administrator. Owners must be given at least ten days' notice of a meeting, which will include an agenda of items to be discussed such as insurance, maintenance and repairs, management, annual fees, etc.

If isn't compulsory to attend, but if you're unable to attend you can give someone a proxy (written authorisation) to attend and vote for you. Non-residents can give someone in Switzerland a 'permanent' proxy and have communications sent to him.

There are three ways in which decisions can be made, some of which require a simple or qualified majority, while others require a unanimous decision by all owners, as shown below:

1. Simple majority (based on one vote per person):

♦ organising necessary upkeep, for example hiring a gardener;

♦ choosing an administrator;

♦ approving the annual budget;

♦ issuing a house ordinance;

♦ establishing a reserve (sink) fund for renovations, etc.;

♦ agreeing insurance or a change of insurer;

♦ agreeing to a change in owner-part value;

♦ approving routine administration tasks;

◆ giving the administrator the power to represent owners;

◆ closing the meeting.

2. Qualified majority (based on per cent ownership, at least 501/1000 minimum)

◆ changes to the rules;

◆ useful renovation work;

◆ important administrative measures such as hiring an onsite manager or purchasing expensive machinery;

◆ withdrawing the 'use rights' (of community property) from an owner, for example forbidding an owner the use of the communal patio or roof terrace, etc.

3. Absolute majority (unanimous decision)

◆ luxury non-essential construction measures (although a qualified majority suffices if the other owners agree to pay the cost of the whole project);

◆ changes to everyone's quota;

◆ decisions concerning the property;

◆ changes in use rights;

◆ changes in building use (e.g. commercial use).

Any decisions made can be challenged in court and each owner has the right to contest a decision, which must be done within 30 days, otherwise the decision is binding.

### Restrictions

Community property owners are usually bound by certain restrictions on their use of a property and their behaviour, which are included in the house rules. These usually apply to:

◆ noise levels;

◆ the keeping of pets (usually permitted);

◆ exterior decoration and plants (e.g. the placement of shrubs) and care of public areas;

◆ garbage disposal;

◆ the use of swimming pools and other recreational facilities;

◆ resident and visitor parking;

◆ business or professional use;

◆ the hanging of laundry;

◆ renovations;

◆ enclosing a balcony (i.e. creating a sunroom);

◆ erecting fences around a private courtyard/ garden.

Check the regulations and discuss any restrictions with the landlord or agent before buying or renting an apartment or other community property.

## GARAGES & PARKING

The cost of parking is an important consideration when buying or renting a home in Switzerland, particularly if your family has a number of cars. A garage or private parking space isn't usually included in the price when you buy a new apartment or townhouse in Switzerland, although secure parking is usually available for an additional cost, possibly in an underground garage. Modern detached homes usually have a private garage; smaller homes normally have a single garage, while large luxury properties may have garaging for up to four cars.

A parking space in an underground garage usually costs from CHF 30,000-40,000. It may be possible to rent a garage or parking space, although this can be prohibitively expensive in cities. Most rental properties offer the option to rent a parking space or possibly two, and you can usually buy a parking space with a new property.

---

☑ **SURVIVAL TIP**

You should always buy a parking space (two is better!) when buying an apartment – even if you have no car and don't plan to buy one – which will make the property much more attractive when you come to sell, and you can rent it out if you don't need it.

Without a private garage or parking space, parking can be a nightmare, particularly in cities and during the summer in busy resorts or developments. Free, on-street parking can be difficult or impossible to find in cities and large towns, and in any case may be inadvisable for anything but a wreck. A garage or garage space is useful to protect your car from inclement weather such as ice, snow and extreme heat.

If you're buying in a large development, bear in mind that the nearest parking area may be some distance from your home. This may be an important factor, particularly if you aren't up to carrying heavy shopping hundreds of metres and possibly up several flights of stairs.

Winter trotting, St Moritz

Murten, Fribourg

# 5.
# BUYING PROPERTY

**B** uying property in Switzerland is an excellent long-term investment, particularly for anyone resident there, although capital growth is generally relatively low (around 6 per cent annually) by international standards, so you're unlikely to make a killing. A property purchase should be viewed as a long-term commitment rather than a quick way to turn a profit. Non-resident foreign buyers have traditionally been attracted to Switzerland by the country's low taxes and excellent quality of life. The traditional low Swiss interest rates have also helped sustain demand from international buyers, despite the relatively high cost of property.

In recent years Switzerland has experienced a wave of immigration from EU countries, which has considerably increased the demand for housing, particularly apartments, and although there has been an increase in unemployment in the last few years, this has only had a limited effect on the demand for housing. In the major cities (e.g. Basle, Geneva and Zurich), where demand for housing is highest – although mostly for rental properties – there's generally a shortage of homes and the supply is failing to keep pace with demand.

In Geneva, an added problem is the wealth of diplomats and those working for international organisations, who have generous salaries compared to the local market and often have large housing allowances; this drives up the cost of housing at the upper end of the market. The acute shortage of housing in Geneva has forced many Swiss and EU citizens working there to live in France, where property is 20-40 per cent cheaper and there's a lower cost of living (but higher taxes!). This has pushed up housing costs in France – in some areas prices have doubled in recent years – and has inflamed local passions (Swiss citizens haven't required a residence permit to live in France since 2004).

A relatively large number of properties have been built in Switzerland in the last few years, during which there has been a construction boom, which tailed off in 2009 as the recession began to bite. However, the Swiss property market is one of the most stable and balanced in the world, with supply and demand generally evenly matched, although the market for second homes has shown signs of overheating in some parts of the country.

Second and vacation homes are popular in Switzerland and total around 450,000 or roughly one in every nine dwellings. There are some 200,000 vacation homes in tourist areas, with a high concentration in St Moritz, Lenzerheide, Flims/Laax, Arosa, Verbier and Goms – in areas that have focused heavily on tourism, four out of five homes stand empty for a large part of the year (termed 'cold beds'). While the high density of vacation homes generates income, it also has drawbacks for the local population and the countryside, where high demand has led to rocketing prices in some areas and a lack of accommodation for local residents.

Germans comprise around a third of foreign homeowners, followed by Italians, Dutch and British.

There are also some 250,000 second homes in non-tourist areas (many owned by commuters who use them during the week), half of which are situated in the conurbations surrounding the major centres, particularly Basle, Berne, Geneva, Lausanne and Zurich. In recent years, the increase in the percentage of second homes has been particularly noticeable in city centres. Between 1990 and 2000, the figure rose by 130 per cent, while the increase in tourist areas was a relatively low 3 per cent.

Although increasing slowly, home occupier-ownership in Switzerland is only some 40 per cent and the lowest in Europe; this compares with around 45 per cent in Germany, 55 per cent in France, 70 per cent in the UK and Italy, and 80 per cent in Spain and Ireland. Of the fortunate 40 per cent, most never actually own their homes, as the capital on part of the mortgage is never paid off during their lifetimes, only the interest. Historically, most households spend between 30 and 40 per cent of their income on housing costs, although mortgage lending is limited to 30 per cent of income.

This chapter details who may buy property in Switzerland and where, and also explains the purchase procedure, which is relatively straightforward; nevertheless, there can be pitfalls for the unwary. It's wise to employ a lawyer before paying any money or signing a contract and have him check anything you're concerned about regarding a property you're planning to buy (see **Avoiding Problems** on page 104).

# PROPERTY PURCHASE BY FOREIGNERS

The Swiss authorities have long placed restrictions on foreigners buying property in Switzerland, although these have been relaxed in recent years, particularly for EEA nationals. Under the Lex Koller law (1961 – named after the federal councillor who last amended it), there are restrictions on the purchase of real estate by non-EEA foreigners and non-residents, although it's expected to be repealed in future and replaced by a more flexible arrangement which relies on local regulation.

The federal regulations regarding property purchase by foreigners depends on whether the buyer is a resident or non-resident and his nationality. The law varies from canton to canton and a permit may be necessary from the local cantonal authorities before a purchase can be granted. Authorisation is required irrespective of whether a property is already foreign-owned or the legal basis of the acquisition, e.g. purchase, barter, gift, inheritance, legacy, acquisition of assets and liabilities of a business, merger, de-merger, conversion of companies or asset transfer. A property purchase requiring authorisation becomes valid only after a permit has been obtained, although the contracted partners are still bound by the undertaking.

> **Important Note**
>
> Bear in mind that ownership of property in Switzerland doesn't entitle a foreign national to a residence permit.

Questions regarding specific cases must be addressed to the relevant cantonal authorities (see **Appendix A**).

## Swiss Nationals & EEA Residents

Swiss nationals domiciled in Switzerland or abroad, including those with dual nationality, don't require authorisation to buy property in Switzerland, neither do residents of an EEA member state (see page 22) who are resident in Switzerland with a B (annual residence) or C permit (permanent residence), or EEA cross-border commuters with a 'G' permit (*Grenzgängerbewilligung*, *permis frontalier*).

Nationals of other countries who hold a C permit and are domiciled in Switzerland; those working for embassies, consulates and international organisations; or for foreign railway, post and customs administrations based in Switzerland, also don't require authorisation. However, they must be able to prove they have been in Switzerland long enough to qualify for settlement (five or ten years, depending on their nationality).

The Swiss need have little fear that resident foreigners will buy up all their property, as very high property prices mean that most foreigners (and the average Swiss family) can only dream of owning their own home. In fact, many

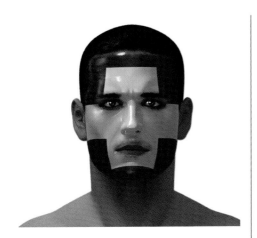

thousands of Swiss live outside Switzerland in what are ostensibly 'second' homes and commute to their jobs in Swiss cities such as Basle, Geneva and Zurich. Working foreign residents and their families comprise around 22 per cent of the Swiss population, but own just a few per cent of Swiss property (although some 5 per cent of Switzerland's total housing is foreign-owned).

Employees of international organisations and members of the diplomatic service enjoy more freedom in purchasing property than most other foreign residents. The regulations outlined here don't apply to these residents, who aren't included in the scope of this book.

## Non-residents

Non-residents include all foreigners domiciled abroad and foreigners domiciled in Switzerland who aren't nationals of an EEA member state and don't hold a C permit (permanent resident). Companies with their registered office abroad or companies with their registered office in Switzerland but which are controlled by persons abroad, i.e. when more than one-third of a company's capital or voting rights are owned by non-residents, are also classified as non-resident.

Those who aren't, in principle, subject to authorisation are considered as non-residents if they wish to acquire property on behalf of persons abroad (called 'fiduciary transactions'). The transfer of property to a trust is also subject to authorisation if any trustees of the beneficiaries qualify as a person abroad.

A non-EEA citizen with a Swiss spouse doesn't qualify to buy property unless he lives in Switzerland and has at least a B permit.

## Primary Residence

Non-EEA foreigners domiciled in Switzerland (in general with a B permit) who don't hold a C permit may purchase a property in their canton of residence without authorisation. They can also purchase building land, provided construction commences within one year. The buyer must buy a property in his own name, must occupy it himself (primary residence) and cannot rent it out, even in part.

The living area may be of any size, but only one property may be purchased. There are no set restrictions on the land area, but it cannot be so large that the purchase (or even part of it) could be regarded as being purely for investment purposes, which generally means the land area must be less than 3,000m² or around three-quarters of an acre. When a purchase exceeds this area, the Land Registry will refer it to the authorisation body to decide whether it's exempt from authorisation.

If a buyer changes his place of domicile, he doesn't need to sell a property and can dispose of it as he sees fit, e.g. he may continue to use it as a secondary or holiday residence or rent it to third parties. He may also purchase another home in his new place of domicile in Switzerland without having to sell the first one.

A non-EEA resident with a B permit who buys a property without the intention of living in it permanently is in violation of the law, especially if he changes his place of domicile for the sole purpose of being able to purchase several properties without authorisation.

## Secondary Residences

An EEA national with a 'G' permit (*Grenzgängerbewilligung*, *permis frontalier*) who commutes cross-border to work in Switzerland, can purchase a secondary residence in the area of his place of work without authorisation. The buyer must occupy the residence himself for as long as he works in the area as a cross-border commuter and cannot rent it out, even in part.

The laws regarding the living area, land area, proceedings, violation of the law, etc. (noted above under **Primary Residence**), also apply to purchases by cross-border EEA commuters. However, the Land Registry won't generally allow a purchase if the land area exceeds 1,000m² or around a quarter of an acre, but will refer the buyer to the appropriate authorisation body.

## Commercial Property

Property that's used for commercial purposes, i.e. permanent business establishments such as manufacturing premises, warehouse facilities, offices, shopping centres, retail premises, hotels, restaurants, workshops and doctors' surgeries, can be acquired without authorisation. It's also immaterial whether the property is used for the buyer's business or rented/leased to a third party for a commercial activity, and it can also be purchased solely as an investment.

This excludes all forms of residential housing with the exception of living accommodation run on a hotel basis, which is considered a permanent business establishment and can be purchased or built without authorisation. In exceptional circumstances, living

accommodation may be acquired without prior authorisation as part of a permanent business establishment when it's necessary for the business, e.g. for a caretaker or technician when their permanent or almost permanent on-site presence is essential.

The purchase of reasonable land reserves, i.e. approximately one-third and in special cases up to half of the total surface area, for expansion in the medium term of an existing or planned business establishment, also doesn't require prior authorisation. This means, however, that around two-thirds of the surface area must be already built upon or should be built upon in the near future, i.e. within a one-year period, and that around one-third can be kept in reserve (undeveloped and unused) for a possible extension in the medium term. If the proportion of undeveloped and unused land exceeds one-third of the total, a ruling must usually be obtained from the appropriate cantonal authorities. Land hoarding, even of land zoned for industrial or commercial rather than residential use, isn't permitted.

## Holiday Homes & Serviced Apartments

A non-resident who requires authorisation to buy property in Switzerland may acquire a holiday home or serviced flat, which must be in an area or town designated (zoned) by the cantonal authorities as a holiday resort. This excludes the major cities of Basle, Geneva and Zurich. Moreover, every authorisation must be deducted from the annual quota assigned to the canton by the federal authorities for holiday homes and serviced flats, except where the seller has already received an authorisation in the past for the acquisition of the property.

Cantons and the municipal tourist authorities can determine their own restrictions. For example, they may decide on a total ban on authorisations for a specific location or permit acquisitions of apartments only, and then only up to a certain quota (see below). Alternatively, they may limit the annual number of authorisations or only permit the purchase of properties that are already foreign-owned.

Grounds for authorisation for the acquisition of holiday apartments or serviced flats are required in the following 17 cantons: Appenzell-Ausserrhoden, Berne, Fribourg, Glarus,

Graubünden, Jura, Lucerne, Neuchâtel, Nidwalden, Obwalden, St Gallen, Schaffhausen (for serviced flats only), Schwyz, Ticino, Uri, Vaud and Valais. Holiday homes cannot be let on an annual basis and, at most, only periodically, and the buyer must be able to use them at any time. Serviced flats (also called time-share apartments or aparthotels), which are half-hotel, half-residential housing, must be made available to the relevant hotel owner for hotel operations, particularly during the high season. This also applies to someone who doesn't require authorisation who purchases a serviced flat from a person abroad.

As a general rule, the floor space, which includes all liveable rooms (such as the kitchen, hall, toilet, indoor swimming pool, sauna and hobby room, stairwell, cellar and attic), and the land area of a property mustn't exceed 200m² (2,152ft²) and 1,000m² (10,764ft²) respectively. However, larger areas may be authorised on proof of additional need up to 250m² (2,691ft²) and 1,500m² (16,146ft²) respectively, and in exceptional cases the limits may be even higher.

Holiday homes and serviced flats may be acquired only by individuals under their own name, and indirect acquisition via a company isn't permitted. If the purchaser of a holiday home or serviced flat, their spouse, registered partner or a child under 18, already owns such a property or secondary property in Switzerland, authorisation may only be granted when the original property is sold before the new purchase is entered in the land register.

Ownership of a holiday home (as a non-resident) entitles you and your immediate family to live for up to six months of the year in Switzerland, although for a maximum of only three months continuously. In some cantons you're obliged to occupy your property for at least three weeks a year and you aren't permitted to let a property full-time, i.e. on an annual basis.

---

**☑ SURVIVAL TIP**

Investors should note that buy-to-let isn't permitted in Switzerland and you cannot usually buy property with the intention of renting (letting) it full-time.

---

## Quotas & Restrictions

There are quotas for foreigners' permits for holiday homes and serviced apartments in the cantons of Appenzell-Ausserrhoden, Berne, Fribourg, Glarus, Graubünden, Jura, Lucerne, Neuchâtel, Nidwalden, Obwalden, St Gallen, Schaffhausen (for serviced flats only), Schwyz, Ticino, Uri, Vaud and Valais. However, around half of all Swiss cities don't allow non-resident foreign nationals to purchase property at all; this includes all the major cities.

The annual quota for the whole of Switzerland is around 1,400 properties and once this quota is filled no further purchases are permitted; however, quotas aren't always filled and cantons that don't fill their quotas can assign their surplus to other cantons, who petition for additional permits. For example, in 2007 the national quota was 1,440 permits, but the actual number issued was 1,832, the extra 392 being unused permits carried over from previous years.

Each canton has slightly different rules and the rules even vary from commune to commune within a canton. Generally speaking, foreigners have the widest choice of properties in French-speaking cantons. The most liberal canton is Vaud, which includes mountain resorts such as Villars, where foreigners can buy virtually any property without any restrictions on resales.

Decisions on permit quotas are taken locally, so the time it takes to purchase a property can vary considerably depending on the canton and community. Waiting times depend on whether the commune has used up its quota, with the average wait one to two years and increasing. (The eastern, German-speaking cantons are less popular with foreign buyers and therefore have relatively short waiting lists.) One way to shorten the wait is to buy from another foreigner, effectively taking over their permit rather than applying for a new one. Alternatively, if you buy off plan, the chances are your permit will have come through by the time the property is built.

Buying a new-build property with a 'licence to enter' agreement is another way of getting to use your property straight away. The normal purchase process means that once you've signed the sales contract on a property, you must then wait for your permit before you're the official owner, which may take a number of years.

For example, in Valais buyers used to be able to take possession of a property while waiting for authorisation, but this is no longer possible, and since 2007 buyers must now wait up to six years for the authorisation (in 2007, Valais had over some 1,300 requests pending). When an authorisation becomes available, the local authority informs the buyer, who must then sign the purchase contract and submit it to the authority within one month. If the purchase contract isn't signed within a month, the guarantee is no longer valid and no authorisation can be granted. In 2007, seven Valais municipalities introduced a moratorium on sales to foreigners.

In some cantons where foreigners are permitted to buy property, resale is possible immediately, although in others a property must be owned for a minimum period before it can be sold, for example five years in Graubünden and Ticino and ten years in Valais. However, sales are permitted in certain circumstances, e.g. in cases of hardship.

---

☑ **SURVIVAL TIP**

Note that the period for which you're required to own a property before selling it, e.g. five years, doesn't commence until your permit to buy the property is issued, which can take up to five years.

---

### Secondary Residence

A foreigner who isn't domiciled in Switzerland may be authorised to acquire a secondary residence (second home) in a place where they have exceptionally close ties deemed 'worthy of protection'. Relationship by blood or marriage with persons in Switzerland and holiday, spa/recuperative, study or other temporary stays, don't constitute close ties worthy of protection. The following cantons have introduced this justification for authorisation: Appenzell-Ausserrhoden, Basle-City, Fribourg, Graubünden, Jura, Lucerne, Neuchâtel, St Gallen, Solothurn, Ticino, Uri, Valais, Vaud and Zurich.

A secondary residence may not be rented to third parties and must be sold within two years if the buyer no longer uses it. Secondary residences may only be acquired by individuals under their own name and not through a company.

The same restrictions as for holiday homes (see above) apply to the land area and net floor area of secondary residences. If the purchaser of a holiday home or serviced flat, their spouse, registered partner or a child under 18, already owns such a property or secondary property in Switzerland, authorisation may only be granted on the condition that the original property is sold before the new purchase is entered in the land register

Cross-border EEA commuters don't require authorisation to acquire a secondary residence in the area of their workplace.

## PROPERTY PRICES

The cost of real estate in Switzerland is generally high, particularly in and around the major cities, where real estate is among the most expensive in the world. However, a slice of the Swiss good life needn't cost the earth, particularly if you're looking for an apartment in a rural area, where property can be surprisingly good value. If you wish to buy a house, it may be better to move to a rural area and commute to work by car or train. Despite the high prices, in most areas there isn't a lot of property for sale, as people seldom move house (it's too expensive) and buyers sometimes spend many months or even years looking for a house or apartment in a particular town or canton.

The cost of 'old' apartments in most areas is usually between CHF 4,000-6,000 per m², with the exception of period (pre-1945) properties in cities such as Geneva and Zurich, when the sky's the limit. You should generally expect to pay CHF 1,000-2,000 more per m² for a new apartment rather than an old one. The cost of new detached houses and luxury apartments is much higher than older properties, e.g. CHF 10,000-15,000 per m² for large properties – and that isn't even in a top resort! The cost of real estate in top resorts and major cities is very expensive; for example you can expect to pay CHF 45,000 per m² for a top-end property on Via Suvretta in St Moritz, one of the world's most exclusive addresses, and property in Zurich's Bahnhofstrasse has been sold for over CHF 250,000 per m².

Always carefully check what's included in the size as it's possible that the vendor or agent may include something such as a balcony, patio, parking space or storage room in the habitable area.

Prices vary considerably with the location – the most important factor – age, number of rooms and size (m²) of a property. New properties tend to command higher prices, not least due to the higher rents that can be obtained. Holiday apartments and chalets are also expensive, not least because there are strict quotas and waiting lists, which allows developers to demand high prices. For a simple studio without any special view, the minimum price is usually around CHF 125,000, while an average two-bedroom apartment costs around CHF 500,000 and a four-bedroom semi-detached or detached house costs at least CHF 800,000, although the latter can cost millions in an expensive region. In some 75 communities, you can expect to pay over CHF 1mn for a new 'standard' apartment with four and a half rooms, i.e. three bedrooms, living room, kitchen and bathroom(s).

The main features that add to the value of an apartment are a lift/elevator (not all apartment blocks have them), a fireplace and views. When buying an apartment, generally the higher the floor the more expensive it is (unless it's number 17, considered by many Swiss to be an unlucky number), as it will have more light, less road noise, better views and be more secure. A parking space or garage isn't usually included in the cost of an apartment and costs between CHF 25,000 and 50,000.

If you're buying a resale property, check the price paid for similar properties in the same area or development in recent months, but bear in mind that the price you pay may have more to do with the seller's circumstances than the price fetched by other properties. Find out how many properties are for sale in a particular development; if there are many on offer you should investigate why, as there could be management or structural problems, or nearby planned infrastructure or developments, such as a new road or a building that will restrict the view. If you're still keen to buy, you can use any negative aspects to drive a hard bargain.

Mortgage facilities are available to residents and non-residents from Swiss banks, but normally for between 60 and 80 per cent of the

Château de Monts, Le Locle, Neuchâtel

| | | Price (CHF) | | |
|---|---|---|---|---|
| **Apartment Price Guide** | | | | |
| No. of bedrooms | Approx. m² | Inexpensive | Moderate | Expensive |
| 0 (studio) | 30-40 | 100-150,000 | 125-175,000 | 150-200,000 |
| 1 | 50-60 | 200-250,000 | 250-350,000 | 350-450,000 |
| 2 | 75-90 | 300-400,000 | 400-550,000 | 550-750,000 |
| 3 | 90-125 | 400-550,000 | 550-650,000 | 650-850,000 |
| 4 | 125-150 | 550-650,000 | 650-750,000 | 750-1mn+ |
| 5 or more | 150+ | 600-700,000 | 700-800,000 | 1mn+ |

purchase price only, although mortgage rates are low. Nevertheless, Switzerland has among the world's highest per-capita indebtedness in the mortgage sector.

The approximate average price for apartments and houses is shown in the table above.

The size (approx. m²) and prices shown in the table are only a guide and are for good quality new or renovated apartments, excluding a garage. Extra large, spacious (*Grosszügig, spacieux*) apartments (with a much larger area than that shown in the table), penthouses and 'luxury' apartments may be much more expensive than the guide prices shown. The table also provides a rough guide to house prices (i.e. excluding apartments), but doesn't include detached houses, houses with a large plot of land, luxury and period houses, and houses situated in the central areas of cities.

Properties classified as 'inexpensive' are generally older, smaller apartments or properties situated in rural or industrial areas, although these prices are around average for most of Switzerland. However, most foreigners live in regions or cities where properties come under the 'moderate' or 'expensive' categories shown in the table. Properties in the expensive bracket are usually situated in the most desirable areas, including the central area of cities. **Note that for apartments in renovated period buildings in major city centres and luxury properties, the sky's the limit!**

The website Comparis (🖳 www.comparis. ch) provides a useful rating which assesses the price-related attractiveness (from very good to insufficient) of an offer price compared

with similar properties in the same or a similar residential area. Criteria include the postcode, liveable area, and, if provided, features such as a balcony, lift (elevator), terrace or fireplace. Note, however, that prices can vary considerably depending on the condition, finish, and fixtures and fittings of a property. The property is then given a rating based on a target price, which is the average price for comparable properties advertised via the internet. The assessment is expressed as a score of from 1 to 6, where one is very expensive and six is very cheap. **You should, however, be wary of a property that's exceptionally cheap, unless it has obvious faults and drawbacks.**

## Price History

Property prices in Switzerland rose by between 10 and 15 per cent in the late '80s and early '90s, which led the Swiss National Bank to increase interest rates to curb what it saw as runaway house price inflation. This had a severe impact on demand and prices fell by an average 6 per cent a year from 1993 to 2000, by which time prices were back to their 1987 levels! Since 2000, prices have increased due to lower interest rates and an increased supply of new apartments, albeit at a lower pace than the late '80s and early '90s. On the other hand, in areas where a glut of apartments has been built, prices are expected to fall.

In recent years, prices have increased by around 5 per cent a year, even when prices have been falling in most countries. (In 2009, prices in Switzerland rose by 7 per cent according to the Knight Frank Global Index, which was only exceeded worldwide by Israel.) However, in some areas where demand outstrips supply, e.g. high-end properties in the Lake Zurich and Lake Geneva regions, prices for detached homes have increased at a rate well above average. Prices in the Lake Geneva region have increased by almost 200 per cent in the last 30 years – 60 per cent in the last five years alone – or by around a third when inflation (i.e. the cost of living increase) is taken into account.

Comparis (⌨ www.comparis.ch) provides a price history feature, whereby you can compare the rent and sale price of properties advertised in the last five years on a map, which may increase your bargaining position. Bear in mind, however, that these are asking prices, not the final price paid.

## Valuations

If you want an accurate market valuation of a property that you're planning to buy (or one you're planning to sell), you should employ a professional appraiser, particularly if you're planning to buy an expensive property or a property with a price that's much higher than the average market value.

The reasons for a property valuation are many and varied and include the following:

♦ the impending sale or purchase of a property;

♦ major renovations are planned or have been carried out;

♦ to increase an existing mortgage;

♦ reassessment of a property's taxable value;

♦ to review the value of your property portfolio;

♦ for an inheritance or anticipated succession.

You can get a good idea of a property's value from a real estate agent or lender, or use a simple appraisal process using a questionnaire from the Swiss Real Estate Information and Training Center (AIZI/CIFI, ⌨ www.iazicifi.ch). The valuation can be done online (in German or French) and costs CHF 290 if you pay by credit card or CHF 344 when paying by invoice. Alternatively, you can print the questionnaire form and send it by mail.

## BUYING OFF PLAN

Many problems can arise when buying off plan and it can be difficult to ensure that you actually get what's stated in the contract. The most common problems associated with buying off plan in many countries include the developer or builder going bust; the build quality or the materials, fixtures and fittings or design being inferior to that stated in the contract (or used in the show house); the facilities included in the development, e.g. landscaped gardens, swimming pool, gym, etc., not being completed on time or not at all; and the property being completed late.

Developers in Switzerland rarely go bust (although they should have a banker's guarantee) and the build quality and materials, fixtures, fittings and design is described in detail in the contract, including serial numbers, so this isn't usually an issue. The main problems are due to 'unexpected' delays in completing a building, as the construction of some off plan properties only starts when a certain number of buyers have paid their deposits. If you pay a deposit and the builder/developer doesn't get his necessary quota, you could find the construction delayed for a long time, or even indefinitely, during which your money is tied up.

The problems associated with buying off plan have even prompted some experts to advise buyers against buying an unfinished property. However, this isn't practical, especially in a seller's market when it's essential to buy off plan if you wish to buy a home in a popular development. However, buying off plan has its risks – even in Switzerland – and the process is generally more time-consuming and stressful than buying a resale property.

A builder is supposed to provide buyers purchasing off plan via stage payments with a banker's guarantee, which protects buyers against the builder going bankrupt before construction is completed.

The single most important factor when buying off plan is the experience and reputation of the developer and/or builder. If a developer doesn't have a long, unblemished track record and cannot provided references, you should carry out a detailed background check, which includes their bankers and insurers, local building authorities, craftsmen and previous customers. You should also investigate the constructor, as the terms 'general contractor' and 'full-service contractor' aren't legally defined in Switzerland.

It's advisable to visit the proposed building site, even if building hasn't commenced, as this will give you a good idea of the locality and the surrounding area – location is, after all, the most important factor when buying property anywhere.

See also **Building Your Own Home** on page 134.

## Pre-sales & Sales' Contracts

When you agree to buy a property off plan, you must usually sign a pre-sales or reservation contract and pay a 'deposit' (or reservation fee) which is usually between CHF 15,000 and 20,000. It's usually stated in the contract that the deposit won't be returned if you change your mind. However, the pre-sales contract is rarely notarised, which means that it isn't legally binding, in which case the deposit should be refunded if you change your mind (although the developer is unlikely to return it voluntarily and you'll probably need to take legal action). You should be wary of a contract that states something like 'the pre-sales contract deposit is lost if the buyer withdraws from this contract' – which you should delete – as it would then be difficult to get your deposit refunded, even if it's illegal to retain the deposit and the pre-sales contract wasn't notarised!

On the other hand, the developer can also withdraw from the contract at any time if the contract isn't notarised. To protect yourself, you should include a clause in the contract that you can withdraw without penalty if the construction doesn't start by the date specified in the contract. What constitutes the 'start' of the development should be specified, e.g. a developer could 'break ground' and then do nothing for a year! The pre-sales and sales' contract should also have a firm completion date. The developer should have a bank guarantee and your deposit should be deposited in an escrow (blocked) account.

The sales contract is usually signed some months after a reservation contract (there is no fixed period) and is always notarised. If a mortgage hasn't been arranged, you may need to present a 'letter of guarantee' from your lender stating that the entire sum is guaranteed (this letter cannot be revoked). When the contract is signed and notarised, the buyer confirms the fixtures and fittings (see

below) required and pays the deposit (less the reservation fee), as specified in the contract.

## Build Quality & Specifications

Most potential problems can be minimised by a good contract and by choosing a development being built by a reliable developer. The contract, which must be in writing, should contain full details of the property to be built (see below), including a copy of the plans and drawings showing its exact location within a development (and that the patio, balcony or roof terrace faces south to maximise sunlight hours!).

---

**☑ SURVIVAL TIP**

The floor plan and technical specifications should be signed by both parties (you receive a signed copy) to ensure that the standard and size of construction is adhered to.

---

Swiss legal regulations and the standards of the Swiss Society of Engineers and Architects (SIA) dictate a high level of quality in Switzerland. Nevertheless, for 'expensive' properties you should demand even more in terms of construction quality, materials and finish. Obviously the size, build quality, and fixtures and fittings are determined very much by the price: you won't usually get a top quality apartment for CHF 500,000 (unless it's in a remote area or tiny!), but you should certainly expect one for CHF 1-1.5mn. Don't be too influenced by the quality of fixtures and fittings in a show home (which aren't common), unless exactly the same quality and specifications are included in the contract.

For every building component and every system, either a specific product or the corresponding budget item should be defined in the specifications. This includes a comprehensive description of all building materials and appliances in the kitchen; the quality standards for finishing the bathrooms, toilets and living areas; and a precise description defining the quality of the doors, windows, window blinds, floors material, etc. Ensure that the contract or building description specifies the insulation standards, for example for exterior insulation, windows and doors (if you're buying an apartment, bear in mind that noise insulation requirements have been raised considerably in recent years). You should ascertain which standards are being used and exactly what it means, and also how the correct implementation will be supervised.

You may wish to check whether you can change the room layout or the colours of, for example, the interior decoration such as walls, tiles and bathroom suites, which is usually one of the advantages of buying off plan. You will need to pay extra to upgrade the tiles, floor coverings, appliances, and fixtures and fittings. Any changes should be agreed in writing with a clear indication of the cost, and be appended to the contract.

The contract should include the following:

♦ whether the property is part of a co-ownership (*Stockwerkeigentum*, *propriété par etage/PPE*) development;

♦ the number of rooms and the total habitable and non-habitable (e.g. patios and balconies) areas in m²;

♦ the materials to be used in the construction and the fixtures and fittings – and in particular the quality, with brand names if applicable. The list of specifications should include the materials used for floors, roofing and pipes, etc; colours of walls, doors, windows and flooring; bathroom fittings; whether fitted wardrobes are installed; and kitchen fittings (if appliances are provided, the brand name and model should be listed).

♦ any installations (service connections) to be provided, such as gas, electricity, air-conditioning, under-floor heating, telephone, internet, music system, central alarm, etc., and the number and location of points (e.g. electricity and telephone outlets);

♦ any amenities to be included in the development such as a swimming pool, gym, etc.

♦ the timetable for construction and the completion date;

♦ the price (including any possible variations or additions), including parking space(s), cellar (usually included in the price of an apartment and doubles as the obligatory nuclear shelter), an extra cellar storage room (may be optional) and any other 'extras';

♦ the payment schedule (see **Stage Payments** below);

♦ the details of penalties for non-completion and the circumstances under which the deposit can be refunded;

♦ the building guarantee.

If there's anything you aren't happy with at any stage you should discuss it with the developer and if you don't receive satisfaction, make a complaint in writing and send it to the developer by registered post.

You should also ask about progress reports. Many developers are lax about providing information on the progress of building work, which can be difficult to obtain unless you visit the site periodically. However, the best developers provide photos – some even have webcams installed so you can watch live progress at the building site – and monthly progress reports by email. In any case, you or your local adviser (e.g. an architect) should make regular checks to ensure that everything is going according to plan, although it's unlikely that you'll be allowed onto the construction site without authorisation (usually it's okay to visit the building site when the roof is on, provided you have permission).

When the property is finished, you should have a meeting on site with the builder or developer to inspect the property's condition and to make a 'snagging' list – also called a hand-over inspection – of anything that needs fixing or completing. A new owner usually has several weeks to inform the builder of discrepancies and months to have things remedied, after which you're covered by the builder's warranty: five years for faults and ten years for hidden faults.

Note that a 'finished' property is a property where the apartment and the apartment building (if applicable) is complete in every detail, communal services have been completed, and **all** the infrastructure is in place such as roads, parking areas, external lighting, water, sewerage, electricity and telephone lines.

## Stage Payments

When a property is purchased off plan, payment is made in stages as building work progresses – usually over a period of 12-18 months. Key stages vary slightly between apartments and chalets, and can vary considerably between developers, although there are legal limits to the sum that can be requested at each stage. Each developer will have his own payment schedule and payments aren't usually negotiable. A typical stage payment schedule is shown in the table below:

| Typical Stage Payment Schedule | |
|---|---|
| **Stage** | **Payment** |
| reservation fee* | 5% |
| signing the contract at the notary | 5% |
| breaking ground | 20% |
| completion of the roof. | 30% |
| kitchen installed or plastering begun | 30% |
| ten days prior to final completion | 10% |

**\* Note:** The reservation fee may be a fixed sum, e.g. CHF 15-20,000, and not a percentage of the price.

If completion isn't planned for at least two years, the deposit may be nominal, e.g. 2.5 per cent. The notary's fees are payable within ten days of the new owner being registered in the land registry.

Generally, when a stage is reached and the buyer receives proof of this or verifies it for himself, then the designated payment is made. However, it's important to ensure that each stage is completed satisfactorily before making payments. If you aren't able to do this yourself, you should engage an independent representative, e.g. an architect, to do it on your behalf.

## BUYING A HOLIDAY HOME

There are a number of special considerations to be taken into account when buying a holiday home in Switzerland. Some real estate agents

Sion, Valais

and developers catering to foreign buyers offer to repay the cost of an inspection trip if you sign a contract within a certain period. However, you shouldn't let this influence you and should inspect properties from a number of developers and agents before deciding to buy. It's also advisable not to be in too much of a hurry to buy on your first inspection trip, unless, of course, you find something that's irresistible at a bargain price.

One advantage of buying off plan from a developer catering for the English-speaking market is that they provide lots of information in English – including a translation of the reservation and purchase contracts – and will hold your hand during the buying process. However, the downside is that their prices can be high compared with the prices of properties available to residents, and they only sell their own portfolio of properties.

Some developers offer a rental guarantee for a number of years plus a number of weeks annual usage, e.g. six, but you should check when you can use a property, as it may not coincide with your family's annual holidays (for example, owners usually cannot use a property over the Christmas holiday period). Some developers may offer a 'leaseback' option, although unlike France, this isn't an official scheme whereby you can legally avoid paying VAT (to encourage the rental of new properties), but simply a sales ploy. You do get a rental guarantee of sorts, but it may be less than you could get elsewhere and you may be restricted to using the property for just a few weeks a year, irrespective of whether it's rented.

If you plan to use a holiday home in the winter, you need to check the snow record and bear in mind that the snow line is getting higher every year in some resorts – you would be wise to look at resorts where the pistes are situated at 2,000m/6,500ft or higher; most resorts use snow cannons to create snow artificially when nature doesn't oblige, but the number of pistes in use may be severely limited. On the other hand, if you plan to use a property in the summer you should note that there's a dramatic change in resorts between the winter and summer seasons, and many bustling winter resorts are very quiet in summer, with many businesses closed and many lifts not operating, although cable cars tend to operate all year round.

Ownership of a holiday home (as a non-resident) entitles you and your family to live for up to six months of the year in Switzerland, although for a maximum of only three months continuously. In some cantons you're obliged to occupy your property for at least three weeks a year and you aren't permitted to let a property full-time, i.e. on an annual basis.

If you can find a property for sale that already has a 'foreigner's permit', you'll be able to take over the permit and thus circumvent the waiting period. However, resale properties with a foreigner's permit are few and far between, and you may have to pay a premium to buy one.

Also bear in mind that in some cantons you're required to own a property for a number of years before you can sell it (to deter speculators), e.g. five or ten years, and this period doesn't commence until your permit to buy the property is issued, which can take up to five years. **It isn't possible in Switzerland to buy a property off plan and sell it on before completion (and without paying the total cost) for a profit, termed a 'back-to-back' sale.**

## Buying a Resale Home

The vast majority of homes for sale in Switzerland are, not surprisingly, 'resale' homes, i.e. any property which has been previously owned and occupied. There are many advantages to buying a modern resale home, compared with a new home (where you're the first occupant), which may include the following:

- an established development with a range of local services and facilities in operation;

- more individual design and style;

- no 'teething troubles';

- savings on the cost of installing water and electricity meters and telephone lines, or the cost of extending these services to the property;

- furniture and other extras included in the price;

- a mature garden and trees.

With a resale property you can see exactly what you'll get for your money, and the previous owners may have made improvements or added extras such as a swimming pool, which may not be fully reflected in the asking price.

Resale properties often represent good value, particularly in resort areas, where many apartments and townhouses are sold fully furnished, although the quality of furnishings varies considerably (from luxurious to junk) and may not be to your taste. 'Luxury' properties and villas, e.g. costing upwards of around CHF 1mn, are rarely sold furnished.

You should consider having a survey done on a resale property, particularly a house, as major problems can even be found in properties less than ten years old, although it's unusual in Switzerland (see below).

## INSPECTIONS & SURVEYS

When you've found a property that you like, you should make a close inspection of its condition. Obviously, the nature of the inspection will depend on whether it's an 'old' property or a modern home. Building standards in Switzerland are generally very high, although you shouldn't assume that an old building is sound, as even relatively new buildings can have serious faults (although rare).

The cost of an inspection or survey is a relatively small price to pay for the peace of mind it affords, although it isn't usually necessary for a modern apartment. Some lenders may insist on a 'survey' on an old building before approving a loan, although this usually consists of a perfunctory valuation to confirm that a property is worth the purchase price.

If a property is pre-1945, a builder or engineer can be employed to check it for soundness, while an architect is usually better qualified to check a modern house. You can also have a full structural survey carried out, although this is rare in Switzerland. However, if you would have a survey carried out if you were buying the same property in your home country, you should have one done in Switzerland. Shop around and compare quotations for a survey.

You may be able to make a satisfactory survey a condition of the preliminary contract, allowing you to withdraw from the purchase and have your deposit returned if serious faults are revealed. However, this isn't usual in Switzerland and a vendor may refuse or insist that you carry out a survey before signing the contract. You may, however, be able to negotiate a satisfactory compromise with the vendor.

### Checks

Always discuss with a surveyor exactly what will be included in a survey and, most importantly, what will be excluded (you may need to pay extra to include certain checks and tests). A general inspection should include the structural condition of buildings (particularly the foundations, roofs, walls and woodwork), plumbing, electricity and heating systems, and anything else you want inspected, such as a swimming pool and its equipment, e.g. filter system or heating.

You should receive a written report on the structural condition of a property, including anything that could become a problem in the future. Some surveyors video their findings in addition to providing a written report. A home inspection can be limited to a few items or even a single system only, such as the wiring or plumbing in an old house. You may also wish to have a property checked for termites and other pests, which are found in some regions, and to have a radon test on a building or land in an area where radon levels are high.

## PURCHASE COSTS

Purchase costs or fees (also called completion costs) incurred when buying property in Switzerland are low compared with most other countries, and vary depending on the canton. They are usually between 2.5 and 5 per cent of the purchase price, e.g. 2.5 per cent in Valais, 3 per cent in Berne and 5 per cent in Vaud. The sale of real estate doesn't incur VAT, although it's payable on materials and labour, e.g. if you're building your own home, and isn't refundable.

In most cantons purchase costs are shared equally by the buyer and seller, although in some cantons (such as Vaud and Neuchâtel), they're borne by the buyer. Parties are, however, free to apportion the costs among themselves however they wish. If applicable, the real estate agent's fee (2–3 per cent) is paid by the vendor. However, if you sign a contract authorising a real estate agent to find you a property, his fee is usually around 2 per cent of the purchase price.

Fees include a transfer tax (Handänderungssteuer, droits de mutation), registration (with the Land Register Authority) and notary fees. Like most fees, transfer tax varies from canton to canton and ranges from 0 to 3.3 per cent of a property's value (it has been abolished in some cantons, e.g. Zurich). It's usually calculated on a sliding (progressive) scale according to the sale price.

Notary's fees are calculated as a percentage of the purchase price of a property and also vary depending on the canton, e.g. 0.1per cent in canton Zurich, 0.25 per cent in Vaud and 0.5-0.7 per cent in Geneva. Notary fees are also dependent on the complexity of the sale (and whether there's a mortgage) and how much work is involved, and are paid by the buyer and seller. If you have a Swiss mortgage, there's usually an additional fee for the mortgage file (Schuldbrief, cedule hypotécaire), e.g. 0.25 per cent of the mortgage amount in Berne. No notary fees are payable by the vendor when he sells.

A list of fees is shown in the table below.

Some lenders insist on a full structural survey on a property, particularly an 'old' property, before they agree to finance a purchase; even when it isn't necessary a survey can be a worthwhile investment when a lot of money is at stake. Life or building (e.g. fire) insurance may also be required as a condition of a mortgage.

If you're buying a new property you may also need to pay for connections to utilities, although these should be included in the price. You also need to take into account removal costs (see **Chapter 8**) and annual running costs (see below), many of which will be payable as soon as you take possession of a property and need to be included in your budget.

| Purchase Costs | | |
|---|---|---|
| **Item** | **Fee** | **Paid by** |
| Transfer tax | 1-3.3% | usually split 50:50 between the buyer/seller, but depends on the canton; in some cantons the buyer pays (there's no transfer tax in AG, GL, SH, UR, ZG and ZH) |
| Mortgage registration fee | 0.25-0.6% | buyer (depends on the loan amount) |
| Notary fees | 0.1-1%* | usually the buyer, but depends on the canton |
| Agent's fees | 2-3%* | vendor (usually a min. of CHF 5,000) |
| * VAT at 7.6 per cent is payable on the notary's and agent's fees. | | |

The practice of stating a lower sale price than the actual price in the contract in order to reduce the tax burden – which is commonplace in many countries – is almost unknown in Switzerland.

## Annual Running Costs

In addition to the fees associated with buying a home, you must also take into account the running costs, which include the following:

◆ property related taxes (see page 184);

◆ building and contents insurance (see page 231);

◆ utilities such as electricity, gas and water (see page 247);

◆ community or co-ownership fees (see page 110) for a community property, which may include the concierge, heating, administration, gardening, snow clearing,etc.

◆ garden and pool maintenance;

◆ management fees if you let your property;

◆ sink fund for maintenance/renovation.

If you have a second home in Switzerland, you can employ a local administration service to handle things such as bill payments, snow clearing, lawn cutting, maintenance, delivery of your car to the airport and other chores.

Annual running costs usually amount to around 1 per cent of the cost of a property, which depend to a large extent on the community or service fees; developments that include a lot of amenities (e.g. swimming pool, gym, etc.) can have very high annual fees.

## THE PURCHASE PROCESS

The process of buying property in Switzerland is straightforward and similar to that in most other European countries, although not the same as in the UK. When you have found a property that you wish to buy, you make an offer which is submitted (e.g. by a real estate agent) to the owner. Once a price is agreed, it's advisable to hire a lawyer to advise you and protect your interests. If you need advice regarding the contract the notary will usually help you – it isn't advisable to use the vendor's

or developer's lawyer, as he'll primarily be looking after their interests, not yours.

**If you require a mortgage (see page 169) to buy the property, this should be arranged in advance.** It isn't possible to include a clause in the contract stating that a purchase is 'subject to mortgage finance'; once signed it's legally binding and the deposit will be forfeited if you're unable to obtain finance and the purchase isn't completed.

Before signing a contract you should also be aware of the legal and tax implications of buying and owning property in Switzerland, and any residence requirements. If you require a permit to buy a property, you should note that it could take a long time to be granted and that during this period your deposit and any other monies paid will be tied up and you won't be able to use the property.

---

### ⚠ Caution

Take care before signing any legal papers in connection with buying property and have your lawyer and lender check all contracts.

---

The legal process of buying property in Switzerland is handled by a local notary (*Notar, notaire*), who's a public official who represents neither the buyer nor seller, but is a municipal or cantonal employee. There's usually no choice of notary (with the exception of a few cantons) as each notary represents an area where he has a monopoly. He is, however, required to protect the interests of both parties. The first step in the process is to sign a contract to buy the property drawn up by the notary, and to pay a deposit, usually 10 per cent of the purchase price (which includes the reservation fee).

The deposit is paid to the notary and will be deposited in his client account. Properties can be purchased individually, in joint names (up to six joint buyers) or in the name of a company when buying a commercial property. It isn't possible for an individual to buy a home in the name of a company. The contract will be in the local language (French, German or Italian), but you can have

canton Zurich, 0.25 per cent in Vaud and 0.5-0.7 per cent in Geneva. You should confirm what the notary's fee will be before signing the contract, which should include the cost for assigning a mortgage and drawing up the mortgage certificate, if applicable.

A notary won't necessarily protect or act in your interests, and you should engage a lawyer to ensure that a purchase is completed to your satisfaction.

The notary must follow a strict code of conduct and have personal liability insurance covering his professional responsibility and any errors he may make. He also has a financial guarantee covering money temporarily in his safekeeping, such as deposits, which are kept in a special client (escrow) account. A notary represents neither the seller nor the buyer (one of his main tasks being to ensure that all state taxes are paid on a sale).

As the notary performs a public service, he's obliged to take a neutral position in the transaction, although he has a duty to inform either party of any unusual provisions in a contract. Don't expect a notary to speak English, although most do, or any language other than the local language (French, German or Italian) or to explain the intricacies of Swiss property law, for which you'll need to engage a lawyer (see **Legal Advice** on page 104).

Conveyancing includes the following:

◆ checking whether the land is registered at the land registry;

◆ verifying the identity of the vendor(s) and buyer(s);

◆ ensuring that all the paperwork is completed and in order, including the civil status questionnaire, the declaration of honour – which states that the buyer doesn't own any other property in Switzerland (if applicable) – and copies of documents such as a passport and/or resident card.

◆ verifying that the property belongs to the seller or that he has legal authority from the owner to sell it;

◆ verifying that the details of the property match those on the registration documents;

it translated into English or have it translated verbally by your lawyer.

If applicable, the agreement is **conditional** on permission for the sale to the foreigner being granted. This is a formality for resident EEA nationals, but can take months or years (e.g. in canton Valais) when a non-resident foreigner is buying a holiday home that isn't already owned by another non-resident foreigner. However, if there are no delays with the paperwork and you don't require permission to buy a property or a mortgage (*Hypotheke, hypothèque*), the whole buying process can be completed in a matter of days!

## Conveyance & Contracts

Conveyance (also commonly referred to as 'conveyancing') is the legal name for processing the legal paperwork involved in buying and selling property, and transferring the deeds of ownership. In Switzerland, conveyance is strictly governed by Swiss law and can be performed only by a notary (*Notar, notaire*), a public official licenced by the canton. In some cantons, e.g. Zurich, notaries belong to the public cantonal services and you aren't free to choose the notary; each transaction is performed by the notary's office responsible for the district where a property is located. However, in Geneva and Vaud, notaries are private practitioners and the buyer can engage any notary.

The notary's fee is a percentage of the purchase price of a property and varies depending on the canton, e.g. 0.1 per cent in

If the buyer doesn't hold a Swiss residence permit (and isn't applying for one) and isn't purchasing a resale property which already has a foreigner permit, the notary cannot sign the deed of sale until he has received authorisation from the Ground Register who's employed on behalf of the canton.

If you're waiting for your residence permit to be approved, in some cantons you can sign a 'promise of sale' *contract* with the vendor, which commits him to sell the property to you at an agreed price by a certain date, i.e. when you expect to have your residence permit. Usually you must pay the vendor a deposit, which is lost if you don't buy the property within the specified time frame, although some cantons don't permit such contracts for non-residents.

The final act of the notary is to arrange the registration of the mortgage and the new ownership of the property with the land register (see **Completion** below).

- ◆ checking that there aren't any restrictions on the transfer of ownership, e.g. an outstanding mortgage larger than the selling price;

- ◆ verifying that there are no pre-emption rights or restrictive covenants over a property, such as rights of way;

- ◆ obtaining a copy of the local planning rules relating to the property;

- ◆ checking that the property isn't in a flood zone;

- ◆ registering the transfer of ownership (and the mortgage if applicable) – see **Completion** on page 133.

A notary in Switzerland isn't responsible for checking planned developments that affect a property or its value (as a lawyer may do in other countries), such as a new railway line or motorway in the vicinity. Obviously a new motorway or railway that disturbs the peace of your home would be something of a disaster; on the other hand, a motorway junction or railway station within a few kilometres may enhance its value. You should either do this yourself or engage a lawyer to make these checks.

Once the deposit has been paid and all the documents completed and returned to the notary, he'll set a date for the signing of the deed of sale (i.e. completion). It isn't necessary to be present in Switzerland to sign the deed of sale (*Kaufvertrag, acte de vente*) and you can give a lawyer in Switzerland or the notary handing the sale a power of attorney (*Vollmacht, procuration*) to act on your behalf.

### Contract Contents

The contract of sale (*Kaufvertrag, acte de vente*) for a property purchase should contain the following:

- ◆ the names of the parties of the contract, i.e. seller(s) and buyer(s);

- ◆ the property description, including priority notices, easements, charges and mortgages on the property;

- ◆ the purchase price, means of payment and payment date(s);

- ◆ the date ownership is to be transferred to the buyer;

- ◆ the completion date, i.e. the date on which legal rights and obligations transfer to the buyer;

- ◆ the arrangements made for paying the fees and taxes incurred, including capital gains tax (immovable property gains tax – see page 184);

- ◆ arrangements made regarding insurance, including existing insurance contracts and property and third party insurance contracts (required by law);

♦ forfeit fees or contractual penalties for late completion or failure to complete;

♦ collateral and interest regarding the deposit, final payment and tax payments;

♦ guarantees for work, products and installations (when faulty);

♦ promised work such as repairs should be listed and described in detail with completion dates for work that's to be done after construction ends (e.g. repairs, etc.);

♦ legal jurisdiction such as which laws apply and what the court of jurisdiction is.

You or your lawyer should obtain an extract from the land registry which provides information about the property and its land area (plot), the owner, notes, charges and mortgages on the property, easements and priority notices. The extract details the rights, charges, obligations and restrictions associated with a property, which may have a major impact on its use and value, and forms an integral part of the contract of sale.

### Conditional Clauses

Notaries generally use standardised contracts which they adopt for each sale. A contract may contain a number of conditional clauses which must be met to ensure the validity of the contract. Conditions usually apply to events out of the control of the vendor or buyer, although almost anything the buyer agrees with the vendor can be included in a contract. If any of the conditions aren't met, the contract can be suspended or declared null and void, and the deposit returned.

However, if you fail to go through with a purchase and aren't covered by a clause in the contract, you'll forfeit your deposit or could even be compelled to go through with the purchase. If items such as carpets, curtains, appliances, furniture or garden ornaments are included in the purchase price, you should have them listed and attached as an addendum to the contract. Any fixtures and fittings present in a property when you view it (and agree to buy it) should be there when you take possession, unless otherwise stated in the contract (see also **Completion** below).

There are numerous possible conditional clauses covering a range of subjects, including:

♦ being able to obtain a mortgage;

♦ being able to obtain a permit to buy the property;

♦ obtaining planning permission, e.g. for renovations;

♦ pre-emption rights or restrictive covenants over a property (such as rights of way);

♦ the sale of another property;

♦ a satisfactory building survey or inspection.

### Completion

When all documents relating to a purchase have been completed and returned to the notary, he sets a date for the completion (or closing), which is the name for the final act in a property purchase. This involves the signing of the deed of sale (*Kaufvertrag, acte de vente*), which is performed at the notary's office, usually in the presence of both parties. It isn't necessary to be present to sign the deed of sale and you can give a power of attorney (*Vollmacht, procuration*) to your lawyer or the notary handing the sale in Switzerland.

If there are no delays with the paperwork and you don't require permission to buy a property or have a mortgage, completion can be performed within a matter of days of viewing a property. However, if you need a foreigner's permit or a residence (B) permit to buy a property – or are buying a property off plan that isn't yet built – completion may be months or even a number of years after the signing of the initial purchase or reservation contract.

---

### ☑ SURVIVAL TIP

When a non-resident is buying a property that doesn't have an existing foreigner's permit – or the buyer requires a residence (B) permit – the notary cannot sign the deed of sale until he has received authorisation from the Ground Register who works on behalf of the canton.

The notary will contact you prior to completion and provide an account for the balance of the purchase price (less the deposit and, if applicable, the amount of any mortgages). He'll also present a bill for his fees and taxes, which must be paid on completion. It's common practice in Switzerland to make the balance payment via an irrevocable banker's draft or letter of credit. This is probably the best method, as you'll have it in your possession (a bank cannot lose it!) and the notary can confirm payment immediately. It also allows you to withhold payment if there's a last-minute problem that cannot be resolved. The payment can also be made directly to the notary's client account prior to completion, although if you do this you must allow sufficient time for the funds to be transferred.

Before the deed of sale is signed, the notary checks that all the conditions contained in the contract have been fulfilled. He will also need to check the parties' identity (e.g. ID cards, residence permits or passports), which includes all parties whose names will be on the deed as co-owners. The notary reads through the deed of sale and both the vendor and buyer must initial each page and sign the last page; the notary then signs the contract and notarises it. If necessary, you should have your lawyer translate the deed of sale verbally. You'll receive several documents, including the ground book extracts certifying that you're the new owner of the property. You'll also receive the keys!

The final act by the notary is to register the deed of sale with the cantonal land register – ownership of real property is officially transferred only when the deed has been registered. If you have a mortgage, this is registered as a charge against the property at the same time. You will also receive an updated excerpt from the land register showing the transfer of ownership.

It isn't a legal requirement that properties are insured against third party risks in Switzerland, although most homeowners (sensibly) have comprehensive building insurance (see page 231). Also bear in mind that you'll need to transfer services (electricity, gas and water) into your name as soon as possible and to make a Swiss will (see page 195) for the property.

## BUILDING YOUR OWN HOME

Building your own home isn't for the faint-hearted and Switzerland is no exception; buying property is very much *caveat emptor* and building a home even more so. There's a huge difference between buying a new build 'turn-key' house from a builder, i.e. a standard house based on an existing design, and building an individual architect-designed house. Building a one-off house from scratch or even carrying out major renovations is fraught with problems and inevitably leads to many minor and major headaches during construction – and a slew of teething problems afterwards. Note that in addition to the land and building costs, you must allow for the cost of extending services such as water, sewerage and electricity, and possibly an access road to the site.

It's unusual in Switzerland to buy a plot of land (see below) or land with a house that can be demolished, and then engage an architect and builder to design and build you an individually-designed home. An easier and more painless way is to buy a plot and house package from a developer, who will then deliver a 'turn-key' property. Swiss builders and

developers have a range of standard designs, although they will generally accommodate almost any interior or exterior variations (for a price), provided they're permitted by local building regulations.

Swiss chalet construction blends traditional Swiss chalet design, with high-tech construction methods and materials, with a choice of modern or traditional interiors. Homes are built to a very high standard and many are eco-friendly developments with minimum energy requirements. A well-known standard is MINERGIE®, a sustainability brand for new and refurbished buildings (see 🖳 www.minergie.ch). The major Swiss banks offer 'Minergie mortgages' with lower interest rates and special conditions to encourage people to build eco-friendly homes (see **Construction Loans** on page 178).

One thing you need to be aware of in Switzerland is that anyone can call themselves an architect, which isn't a 'protected' professional title as it is in many other countries. Therefore before employing anyone you must check their qualifications and have your lawyer scrutinise contracts.

If you decide to go it alone – rather than buy a turn-key package from a developer – and build a house on your own plot of land, you'll need an architect, unless you buy a pre-fabricated house (*Fertighaus, maison préfabriquée* – see 🖳 www.fertighausfuehrer.ch). He won't only design the house of your dreams but will supervise its construction every step of the way (for which he'll charge a fee of around 10 per cent of the construction cost). If you don't have someone to supervise a builder like a hawk, you could have major problems and quality control can go seriously off piste! Only hire an architect who comes highly recommended with excellent references, as some are part of the problem rather than the solution (you may need to supervise your architect!).

If you decide to build your own home, you must ensure that the proposed size and style of house is legal by checking with the local town hall. Don't rely on the builder or developer to do it for you, but check yourself or have your architect or surveyor do it. If a mistake is made, a building may need to be demolished! When you apply for a building permit, the plot must be 'staked out' with poles to mark the boundaries of the planned building and the poles must be as high as the building. The building permit application is then published in the official local paper and anyone can view the plans and lodge an objection, which will delay the building process.

Switzerland has strict building regulations (*Baugesetz, règlements de bâtiment*) which are regulated by the cantons. After building a new house, you must obtain a certificate stating that the building work has been carried out in accordance with the planning application, after which you receive an occupancy permit; you'll also need a professional valuation of your home for insurance purposes.

It's common to finance a building project with a special mortgage which is drawn down in stages as the build progresses, e.g. UBS Building Financing or a UBS Mortgage Overdraft Facility, which allows for flexibility as interest is only payable on the portion of the loan you actually use. A typical payment schedule – which varies depending on the individual project – when building a house is shown in the box below.

| Typical Off Plan Payment Schedule | |
|---|---|
| **Stage** | **Payment** |
| breaking ground/foundations | 30% |
| completion of roof | 30% |
| completion and handover | 30% |
| within 10 days of final completion | 10% |

Some contracts may request a deposit, e.g. 10 per cent, if the builder needs to wait for a permit before he can start building work.

The Swiss construction guarantee is five years for construction defects and ten years for hidden defects.

See also, **Buying Off Plan** on page 123.

## Buying Land

Plots of land for building (*Bauland, terrain à batir*) are scarce and highly sought-after in Switzerland, and the price is accordingly high, often accounting for one-third or more of the total price of a property. You may wish to consider buying a small house or a house in bad repair, demolishing it and building a new house on the plot.

Land costs vary from as low as CHF 100-150 per m² for rural lots without views to CHF 500-600 m² for land with mountain and/or lake views. Premium Lake Geneva and Zurich plots with lake and mountain views are from CHF 850 per m² to many thousands, e.g. CHF 3,000. If you're in doubt about the value of land, it's wise to have it valued by a land surveyor. In any case, you should never buy land before discussing it with your architect and/or builder and obtaining their approval.

Assuming you find a plot that's zoned for building, you need to understand the restrictions, both at the community (*Gemeinde, commune*) and the cantonal level. Communities have a zone use plan, which stipulates what land can be used for and distinguishes between built-up areas or building zones, agricultural zones and protection zones. Councils maintain a plan of all building land in their locality and the name of the owner, which can be inspected by the public. Land outside the building zone cannot be built on and it would be very foolish to build a property illegally in Switzerland (unlike in some other countries, where it's common practice).

You must take the same care when buying land as you would when buying a home. The most important point is to ensure that the land has been approved for building and that the plot is large enough and suitable for the house you plan to build. When a plot has planning permission, the maximum size of building (in square metres) that can be built is usually stated and depends on the density permitted by the local community and possibly also the canton. There may also be restrictions on the type of building you can build; for example, in Kloten near Zurich airport, it's only possible to built flat-roofed houses. If you buy land from an agent, it will usually already have planning permission but, if it doesn't, this should be made a condition of purchase. Always obtain confirmation in writing from the local town hall that land can be built on and has been approved for road access.

Some plots are unsuitable for building, as they're too steep or require prohibitively expensive foundations. Also check that there aren't any high-tension electricity lines, water pipes or rights of way that may restrict building. A plot should have mains electricity and (preferably) a reliable water supply, as the cost of providing services to a property in a remote rural area can be extremely costly. It might also be worthwhile asking the local neighbours whether they have any objections to the house you're planning to build, because if your house blocks their view this could be a serious stumbling block.

☑ **SURVIVAL TIP**

**Builders may have a selection of building plots for sale. Most builders offer package deals, which include the land and the cost of building. However, it isn't always wise to buy the plot from the builder who's going to build your home, and you should shop around and compare separate land and building costs.**

Obtain a receipt showing that the plot is correctly presented in the local property register and check for yourself that the correct planning permission has been obtained (don't simply leave it to the architect or builder). If planning permission is flawed, you may need to pay extra to improve the local infrastructure or, in extreme cases, the property may even have to be demolished!

Berne

# 6.
# RENTING A HOME

For those who associate home ownership with prosperity, it will come as a surprise that the Swiss are surprisingly wedded to renting their homes – and unlike people in some other countries (e.g. France) it isn't common for Swiss to rent in the city where they work and buy a property in the country. Most Swiss are generally content to rent – even when they can afford to buy – not least because tenants in Switzerland have a lot of security and rents are usually reasonable compared to salaries. Nevertheless, the average Swiss family spends around 40 per cent of their income on housing.

In contrast with many other countries, rental units in Switzerland are well-built, often fitted with all modern conveniences, and many developments offer a mix of rental and owner-occupied apartments (there are few rental 'ghettos'). There's little or no difference in quality between rental and owner-occupied units.

Added to which there isn't a lot of property for sale, and very little in areas where most people want to live; buyers in Switzerland need a large deposit, there are few tax advantages and costs are high; and many Swiss consider owning property to be more of a liability than an asset (See **Buying v. Renting** on page 97 for the arguments for and against buying.)

It's now much easier for EEA nationals working in Switzerland to buy property there, although most newcomers still rent for a period, which may be anything from a few months to a number of years – or even permanently. Whether you buy or rent will also depend on how long you're planning to stay, as many people don't consider it worthwhile buying if they're staying for less than five years. Even if you're set on buying, you usually need to rent for a period while looking for something to buy, and it's better not to be too optimistic about finding something suitable quickly, particularly in the major cities. Note also that even if you're

planning to buy and don't need a mortgage, you won't be able to buy property until your Swiss permit is issued.

Don't underestimate the time or difficulty you may have finding a suitable long-term rental in Switzerland!

Finding a suitable rental at a price you can afford – and in an area where you would want to live – is difficult, and depends on the region, the type of property you're seeking and the local demand. If you're seeking a small two- or three-bedroom apartment, it's much easier to find something suitable than if you want a spacious four-bedroom detached house.

Rented accommodation (*Mietwohnung, appartement à louer*) in Switzerland usually consists of an unfurnished apartment, although long-term furnished accommodation is becoming more common in the cities, but it's often very expensive. Unfurnished apartments are available in most areas, although in some regions and major cities accommodation is in short supply and expensive, and the situation has been exacerbated in recent years by the influx of foreign workers (notably Germans in the north and French in the Lake Geneva region) due to the relaxation of work permit regulations.

Rents in most of Switzerland are comparable with other European countries and cities, although there are regional variations. Rents are very high (and among the highest in the world) in Geneva, Lausanne, Zug and Zurich, due to excess demand, an acute shortage of rental accommodation and a vacancy rate of well below 0.5 per cent! There's a particularly acute lack of rental properties in the middle to upper end of the market. The vacancy rate can, however, be slightly misleading, as the turnover of tenants is relatively high in Swiss cities (apparently a third of rental properties in Zurich city change tenants every year!) and apartments become vacant every day, although they're snapped up quickly and therefore make little or no impact on the vacancy rate.

The market in Basle, Geneva, Vaud, Zug and Zurich is distorted by the influx of international employees and company relocations, when incoming companies bring in dozens or even hundreds of employees each year. It can cost up to a million francs to settle a family of four for three to four years, (which may be boosted by temporary housing costs or moving the family twice), therefore companies are willing to pay a premium for good housing that employees can move into immediately. The situation has worked its way down to the bottom and middle of the market, and in some cities it has become virtually impossible for essential workers (such as nurses and police officers) to find anywhere affordable to live.

In Geneva, an added problem is the wealth of diplomats and those working for international organisations, who have generous salaries compared to the local market, coupled with paying no local taxes and large housing allowances, which drives up the cost of housing at the upper end of the market. The acute shortage of housing in Geneva has forced many Swiss and EU citizens working there to live in neighbouring France, where property is 20-40 per cent cheaper and there's a lower cost of living (but higher taxes!). This has had the effect of pushing up housing costs in France – in some areas prices have doubled in recent years – and has inflamed local passions (since 2004, Swiss citizens haven't required a residence permit to live in France).

One of the biggest problems faced by newcomers is finding somewhere to live, and many people stay in temporary accommodation while looking for a long-term rental or somewhere to buy. Some companies have a human resources department to help new arrivals find a place to live or they may hire a relocation company (of which there are hundreds in Switzerland) to do this.

Non-residents are permitted to rent long-term in Switzerland, but they can only live there for a total of six months a year and a maximum of three months continuously.

## RENTING BEFORE BUYING

Even if you're planning to buy a home in Switzerland, it's often prudent to rent for a period to reduce the chances of making an expensive error, particularly in an unfamiliar region. If you're planning to buy a holiday home, you may wish to rent during the worst part of the year (weather-wise) or the period when you plan to live there, especially if you're uncertain about exactly what sort of home you want and where you wish to live. This allows you to become familiar with the region and the weather, and gives you plenty of time to look around for a home at your leisure.

Renting before buying is even more important for those planning to live permanently or establish a business in Switzerland, when it isn't wise to buy a home until you're sure that the business will be a success.

Renting allows you to become familiar not only with the weather but also the amenities and the local people; to meet other foreigners who have made their homes in Switzerland and share their experiences; and, not least, to discover the cost of living for yourself. Renting also 'buys' you time to find your dream home at your leisure. You may even decide to rent a home in Switzerland long-term (or 'permanently'), as it saves tying up your capital and can be surprisingly inexpensive in many regions.

## TEMPORARY ACCOMMODATION

On arrival in Switzerland, you may find it necessary to stay in temporary accommodation for a few weeks or months until you can move into an apartment. Single people can stay in a hostel or find a room to rent in shared accommodation (see page 150), while couples and families can rent self-catering accommodation, a serviced apartment or a flat in an aparthotel. Some hotels also cater for long-term guests and offer reduced weekly or monthly rates.

Switzerland has an abundance of self-catering accommodation, although most is rented short-term only as it's quite expensive (and landlords earn more money renting for short periods), and a lot of it's in resorts rather than the major cities. However, some foreign owners let their homes long-term, particularly outside the peak period, and many Swiss take long vacations, up to a year at a time, and rent out their apartments while they're away.

Renting furnished accommodation is ideal for the short term, as it saves you having to deal with the tricky problem of importing or buying furniture and setting up home, while at the same time grappling with daily life, learning a new language and (possibly) getting to grips with a new job.

An apartment can be cheaper than the cost of a hotel room and you'll have more privacy and freedom, and be able to prepare your own meals. Standards, while generally high, vary considerably, and paying a high price doesn't always guarantee a good location or a well-furnished apartment (most look wonderful in brochures). Most short-term apartments are, however, comfortable and all are spotlessly clean. Apartments are generally well-equipped with bed linen, towels, cooking utensils, crockery and cutlery.

Standards vary but a typical short-term rental is a self-contained apartment with one or two bedrooms (sleeping two to four and possibly including a sofa bed in the living-

room), a living-room/kitchen and family bathroom. Always check whether a property is fully equipped (which should mean whatever you need it to mean) and that it has a telephone, high-speed internet and cable TV, if these things are important to you. Self-catering apartments and houses can be found through a host of agents and through websites such as ▣ www.homegate.ch (holiday rentals), www.immoscout24.ch (click on holiday/rent) and www.interhome.ch.

Another alternative is a serviced apartment or an apartment in an aparthotel (hotel apartment), which are fairly common in Switzerland. These are fully furnished and equipped apartments with a kitchen, television/DVD, broadband internet and optional daily maid service. An apartment may also have a telephone, although it may be cheaper to use a mobile phone. Serviced apartments are generally intended for relatively short lets of a few weeks or months, and can cost up to twice as much as a similar apartment with a long-term tenancy (or around the same as a hotel room). They are, however, ideal for a short period while you look for a long-term rental.

Many companies specialise in serviced apartments, including ▣ www.ae-businesshomes.ch in Basle, Geneva, Zug and Zurich, one of Switzerland's largest furnished housing management companies. Others include ▣ www.glandon-apartments.ch and www.temp-accommodation.ch (various cities); www.adagio-city.co.uk/basel, www.apartments-basel.ch, http://weilamrhein.homecompany.de/en and www.ums.ch in Basle; http://ferney-geneva-apartments.apartotels.com and www.residence-mont-blanc.ch in Geneva; www.oklogements.ch and www.residencedumidi.ch in Lausanne; and www.aas-ag.ch, www.apartments-swiss-star.ch, www.ema-house.ch, www.cityappartements.ch/e and www.pabs.ch in Zurich.

## FINDING RENTAL ACCOMMODATION

Finding a suitable home in Switzerland can be a long and frustrating experience and you should allow plenty of time. If you want to have a long-term rental to move into when you and your family arrive in Switzerland, you'll need to start looking at least a month or two before you plan to arrive and will probably need someone in Switzerland to help, such as a relocation company, real estate agent or your employer (if applicable). Good contacts are priceless when looking for rented accommodation in areas such as Geneva and Vaud.

Before looking for a home you should have a good idea of where you want to live and what you're looking for (see **Chapters 2** and **4**), otherwise you can waste a lot of time on wild goose chases. It's advisable to make your search area as large as possible – which will increase your chances of finding somewhere suitable – and not limit yourself to one town or city neighbourhood.

There are a number of ways to find rental accommodation in Switzerland, including via the internet, the media (newspapers), and real estate and relocation agents, each of which is covered below in detail. You may also find ads for apartment rentals on notice boards in supermarkets, churches, consulates, companies and organisations. However, one of the most effective ways to find somewhere to live in an area where there are very few vacancies (such as Geneva) is through word-of-mouth and contacts, where property rentals often don't come onto the market but are snapped up by friends and colleagues.

Those working in Geneva for an international organisation, Permanent Mission, consulate, non-governmental international organisation (NGO) or an international sports federation, can use the free services of the Geneva Welcome Centre or Centre d'Accueil Genève Internationale (CAGI, 🖳 www.cagi.ch). CAGI offers a wide range of services and assistance to newcomers to help them settle and integrate into the Lake Geneva region, the most important of which is finding a home.

## The Internet

As in most countries, the internet is the number one resource for renters in Switzerland. There are numerous property websites offering rentals, including 🖳 www.alle-immobilien.ch, www.comparis.ch/immobilien/intro.aspx, www.homegate.ch and www.immoscout24.ch, all of which have English-language versions. Foreign-language websites include 🖳 www.anzeiger.ch (German), www.toutimmo.ch (French), and www.immoclick.ch, www.immo-net.ch and http://immo.search.ch (the latter three in French/German). Some sites show

only their own paid ads (Homegate, Immoclick, Immoscout24), while others display ads from a number of sites (Alle-immobilien, Anzeiger, Comparis, Immo-search).

The Homeowners' Association (*Hauseigentümerverband, Association Suisse de propriétaires*) also has a section on its website where you can search for property (🖳 www.hev-immo.ch/hev/home/estate/index.htm), and cantonal banks also have their own website (🖳 www.immomarktschweiz.ch).There are also free classified ads pages such as 🖳 www.anibis.ch (French) and www.xpatxchange.ch.

## The Media

A good source of rental accommodation is local newspapers, when the best days for advertisements are usually Wednesdays, Fridays and Saturdays. Apartments and houses for rent (*Wohnungen zu vermieten, appartements à louer*) are also advertised in free local newspapers, delivered in most areas along with the copious 'junk' mail (Switzerland is a world leader in the production of junk mail). For example, in Geneva there's *GHI Genève* (published on Wednesdays – see 🖳 www.ghi.ch), *Tout l'immobilier* (Mondays, see 🖳 www.toutimmo.ch) and *Tribune de Genève* (daily, plus *Tribune Immo* on Tuesdays and the *Léman Express* supplement on Mondays – see 🖳 www.tdg.ch).

Major Swiss newspapers can also be accessed online via 🖳 www.onlinenewspapers.com/switzerl.htm, www.world-newspapers.com/switzerland.html and www.zeitung.ch. Property ads may appear online before they're published in the printed publication, which will give you a head-start on the competition (who haven't read this book!).

You will find ads under *Kleinanzeigen/ petites annonces* (classifieds section), *Immobilienteil/immeuble* (property) and *Vermietung/location* (flats to rent). Advertisers may be private owners, property managers, rental agents or tenants looking for someone to take over their rental agreement (*Nachmieter gesucht, successeur*). Most advertisements include a telephone number or email address, although some, particularly those for exclusive properties, provide a box number (*Chiffre Nr., chiffre No./sous chiffres*) and you must apply in writing, although it's often a waste of time. If you're seeking something out of the ordinary or extremely rare, it may be worth placing a 'rental wanted' ad (*Mietgesuche, recherche un appartement/une maison*) in a newspaper, although you shouldn't expect to find a home this way.

Apartments and houses for rent are also advertised on company bulletin boards, in company magazines and newspapers, and in official cantonal newspapers. Some communities (*Gemeinde, communes*) publish a list of vacant accommodation and keep an up-to-date list of property vacancies in their area, so it may be worthwhile contacting the communities where you would like to live.

You can also place a 'rental wanted' advertisement on bulletin boards in supermarkets (e.g. Coop, Migros and Spar), churches, consulates, companies, organisations and clubs; many also have newsletters where you can place a wanted ad. Finally, don't forget to ask your friends, relatives and acquaintances to help spread the word, particularly if you're looking in the area where you already live.

## Rental Agents

There are numerous real estate agents in Switzerland who handle the vast majority of rental property (relatively little property is rented privately). Estate agents often have the best accommodation, as most landlords don't want to spend time looking for and liaising with tenants. In most cases, you'll never see the landlord (owner), as the agent handles all administrative tasks.

Most towns have a number of rental and real estate agencies (*Immobilien/makler,*

*agences immobilières*), listed in local telephone directories and *Yellow Pages*. The Swiss search engine ( www.search. ch) displays agents (in A-Z order) with telephone numbers and website links (where they exist), plus a map showing where their office is located. Click on 'Phone Book' (top line) and enter 'real estate' under 'Sector, Occupation' and select the canton. Most agents also have their own websites. You can also find property management agencies throughout Switzerland via the Swiss Real Estate Association (*Schweizerischer Verband der Immobilientreuhändler/Union suisse des professionnels de l'immobilier*, Puls 5, Giessereistr. 18, 8005 Zurich,  44-434 78 82,  www.svit.ch) and  www.die-immobilienmakler.ch.

There are also regional associations of real estate agents, for example in Suisse romande there's Genève Immobilier ( www. geneveimmobilier.ch/gi), the Fédération romande immobilière/FRI ( www.fri.ch) and the Swiss Union of Property Professionals/ USPI ( www.uspi.ch). The FRI and USPI have offices in all French-speaking cantons, e.g.  www.uspi-ge.ch in Geneva and  www.uspi-vd.ch in Vaud.

Agents charge a registration fee of around CHF 50 that's valid for three months. After signing a lease, you must pay an additional fee, which varies from agency to agency, but is usually equivalent to a month's rent. You should avoid 'agents' with only a 900 phone number or who ask for a large fee up front, as they may not be legitimate.

---

☑ **SURVIVAL TIP**

Check what fees you're expected to pay before signing the lease.

---

### Viewing

When you have identified a property that looks suitable you need to contact the agent or landlord to arrange to view it and be prepared to inspect it immediately. However, bear in mind that in major cities (e.g. Geneva and Zurich), adverts can easily attract up to 100 enquiries and it may be a case of 'first come, first served'. It isn't uncommon to arrive at an agent's office to view a property, only to find that it has already been let.

The process differs from agent to agent. Often agents will give you the address and ask you to go have a look at the property from the outside; if you like the building and neighbourhood, they will then arrange a viewing. Some agents will send someone with you to view a property and will drive you there, while others will ask you to arrange a visit with the housekeeper/caretaker or the current tenant, while some will simply give you the keys (of a vacant property) and let you visit on your own. Some landlords may make a list of applicants and have joint viewings or have an open house 'viewing period', during which prospective tenants can view a property.

If you try to arrange appointments to view properties while you're abroad, you may find that agents are unwilling to arrange viewings before you've arrived in the country, which can be frustrating.

## Relocation Agents

If you're fortunate enough to have your move to (or within) Switzerland paid for by your employer, it's likely he'll hire a relocation agent to handle the details. The services provided by relocation agents are many and varied and may include everything from pre-departure planning, packing and shipping your belongings from your existing home, to finding you a home in Switzerland and helping you settle in – and everything in between!

Services generally include orientation tours to check out neighbourhoods and inspect accommodation and schools; obtaining the necessary visas and permits; language and cultural training; education consultation; financial advice; day-to-day

assistance and integration for a non-working partner; assistance with renting or buying a car; a settling-in service (including arranging utilities, TV, telephone and internet services, insurance and registration formalities); and even repatriation assistance when you leave Switzerland.

There are generally three types of relocation consultants in Switzerland: corporate relocation agents (whose clients are usually large companies), commercial property agents and home-search agents, who tend to act for individuals. The larger relocation consultants may provide all three levels of service, while smaller companies have just a few staff and offer a home-search service only. Relocation consultants usually charge a registration (or administration) fee plus a daily fee for their services, which can be quite reasonable, e.g. if they're only engaged to find accommodation, it can cost as little as CHF 2,500, which will include viewing a number of properties that meet your budget and requirements, plus taking care of rental formalities.

The main task of relocation consultants (and home-search companies) is to find you the home of your dreams – or at least the best value for money home that you can afford! This can save buyers considerable time, trouble and money, particularly if you have special or unusual requirements. Having someone on your side who's aware of the local market, locations and pitfalls is a big advantage. Relocation agents are familiar with the local market, know how long a property has been on the market and whether the rent is appropriate, and they may be able to negotiate a lower rent and/or 'improvements' (such as equipment upgrades, redecoration, better contract conditions, etc).

Finding accommodation for single people or couples without children can usually be accomplished in a few weeks in most areas, depending on the city or region, while accommodating families usually takes longer. The time it takes to find accommodation is also seasonal; although not all contracts specify the official moving days, most people move house at the end of March, June or September, while families with school-age children often move after the school year ends. So if you're looking for family accommodation outside the moving dates or summer school holidays, there may be little available. If possible, you should allow at least two months between your initial visit and moving into a rented property.

If you just want to inspect properties for rent in a particular area, you can make appointments to view them with local real estate agents and arrange your own trip to Switzerland. However, you must make **absolutely certain** that agents know exactly what you're looking for and obtain property lists in advance.

There are relocation agents in all parts of the country, most of whom provide the services described below.

### House Moving

The larger relocation companies will arrange the removal of your belongings from your home abroad to Switzerland, including your pets (see page 217).

### House Hunting

This is usually the main service provided by relocation agents, who will find you rented accommodation and/or work with local real estate agents to find you a property to purchase. Services usually include locating a number of properties matching your requirements and specifications, and arranging a visit (or visits) to Switzerland to view them.

### House Negotiations

Consultants usually help and advise with all aspects of home rental, including conducting negotiations on your behalf, checking the lease, liaising during the handover, explaining such things such as the inventory and extra costs, and arranging insurance, utilities and telephone/internet, etc.

### Schools

Consultants can usually provide a special report on local schools (state and private) for families with children, including boarding schools if required.

### Local Information

Consultants usually provide a comprehensive information package for a chosen area or town, including information about employment prospects (if necessary), finance and banking, health services and insurance, local schools (state and private), real estate agents, shopping facilities, public transport, amenities and services, sports and social facilities, and communications.

### Miscellaneous Services

Most consultants provide advice and support (particularly for non-working spouses) before and after a move, orientation visits for spouses, counselling services for domestic and personal problems, help in finding jobs for spouses and even marriage counselling services (moving to another country can put a lot of strain on relationships).

## STANDARDS, FIXTURES & FITTINGS

The standards and fixtures and fittings of rental properties in Switzerland vary from region to region and also according to price. In general, apartments are better equipped in the German-speaking areas of northern and central Switzerland than they're in the French- and Italian-speaking regions. As a general rule, apartments in German-speaking regions come with fully equipped kitchens, while those in French-speaking cantons and Ticino are usually 'semi-equipped', i.e. with a cooker but no fridge/freezer. Unfurnished apartments usually only have light fittings in bathrooms, kitchens and occasionally hallways (most rooms just have bare wires). However, the level of fixtures and fittings and appliances is generally high throughout the country for 'luxury' apartments.

If you don't want to buy furniture you can rent it from a number of companies, including In-Lease (☎ 041-310 73 52, 🖳 www.in-lease.com, ✉ swiss@in-lease.com).

For more information, see **Swiss Homes** on page 100.

## RENTS

The cost of renting an apartment varies considerably according to its size, age, facilities and location. Rents (*Miete, location/loyer*) are high, especially in the major cities, and have risen considerably in the last decade, although in most of Switzerland they're comparable with other European countries. However, it costs twice as much to rent in Geneva as it does in Amsterdam and Brussels, and even Paris and New York are marginally cheaper, with only London exceeding Geneva's average rental costs.

There's a huge variation between cantons and, especially, between the major cities and rural areas. Rents are highest in the Lake Geneva region – where there's an acute shortage of accommodation and rents have outstripped the rest of Switzerland in recent years – and the Lake Zurich area. With the rental market close to saturation in the major cities, you may be forced to look further afield in the surrounding towns and villages, where rents are more reasonable.

There's a perception among some foreigners that they pay more for housing than the Swiss, which was supported by a study published in November 2008 in the Swiss Journal of Economics and Statistics. The difference between rents charged to well-educated Swiss and well-educated foreigners is minimal, with foreigners paying around 2 per cent more on average, but foreigners with a lower level of education can expect to pay up to 7 per cent more in rent than Swiss. However, the real issue is the very tight housing market and the fact that foreigners often need to find somewhere to live at short notice and are therefore at a disadvantage (coupled with the fact that they may not speak the local language).

Rents tend to be from CHF 20-30 per m² (11ft²) per month in the more expensive regions and cities such as Geneva, Lausanne, Zug and Zurich, where a 100m² (1,076ft²) apartment will cost you CHF 2,000-3,000 per month (if you can find one). In less expensive areas you should expect to pay CHF 15-20 per m² (11ft²) per month or between CHF 1,500 and 2,000 for a 100 m² apartment. Luxury property and properties in desirable areas generally cost from CHF 30-40+ per m² per month, which includes many properties in Geneva and Zurich. At the very top end of the market the sky's the limit, with luxury apartments and houses overlooking Lake Geneva or Lake Zurich commanding rents of CHF 5,000-10,000 per month.

The highest cost per square metre tends to be for smaller apartments, because adding on an extra bedroom is relatively inexpensive. It falls sharply for three-room (two-bedroom) apartments, increases for four- and five-room (three- and four-bedroom) apartments, then drops again for six or more rooms on a per square metre basis. An apartment with a patio (*Gartensitzplatz, terrasse*) is usually cheaper than a top floor apartment, which may have a small balcony only. Generally the higher the floor, the higher the cost (you pay for the rarefied air – and the view). Top floor, attic apartments and penthouses (*Dachwohnung, attique*) are the most expensive, and often have an open fireplace (*Cheminée/avec cheminée*), considered a luxury in Switzerland.

The rent (*Miete/loyer*) stated in advertisements is usually the net rent (*Netto Miete/ louer net*) paid to the landlord

each month and doesn't include extra charges (*Nebenkosten/NK, charges/frais annexes*) for services such as garbage disposal, caretaker, heating and water costs, which are extra. Most agents and landlords expect the rent to be paid by standing order each month.

The number of rooms advertised usually excludes the kitchen (except in Geneva), bathrooms and toilets, although the total area (stated in square metres) includes all rooms, excluding exterior areas such as balconies and patios (see **Swiss Homes** on page 100 for further information).

Average rents for unfurnished apartments are shown in the table below.

The size (approx. m²) and rents shown above are only a guide and are for good quality new or renovated apartments, exclusive of extra costs and a garage (see page 112). Those that are classified as 'inexpensive' are generally older, smaller apartments or properties situated in rural or industrial areas, although they are around average rents for much of Switzerland. Nevertheless, most foreigners live in regions or cities where properties come under the 'moderate' or 'expensive' categories shown in the table. Properties in the expensive bracket are usually located in the most desirable areas, including the central area of cities. **Note, however, that for apartments in renovated period buildings in major city centres and for luxury properties, the sky's the limit!**

The website Comparis (🖳 www.comparis.ch) provides a useful rating which assesses the price-related attractiveness (from very good to insufficient) of a rental offer compared with similar properties in the same or a similar residential area. Criteria include the postcode, liveable area, and, if provided, features such as a balcony, lift (elevator), terrace or fireplace. Note, however, that rents can vary considerably depending on the condition, finish, and fixtures and fittings of a property. The property is then given a rating based on a target price, which is the average price for comparable rentals advertised via the internet. The assessment is expressed as a score of from 1 to 6, where one is very expensive and six is very reasonable. You should, however, be wary of a property that's exceptionally cheap, unless it has obvious faults and drawbacks.

Comparis also offers a price development feature (click on a property and then click 'price development at this address' below the rent figures), where you can display a map showing available properties (green dots) and rented units (grey dots). By clicking on a grey dot you can access the archives and see how much rent people have been paying in the area, or, by clicking on the green dot, possibly the actual rent of the property that you're looking at.

To find out how long a property has been on the market, the websites 🖳 www.anzeiger.ch and www.comparis.ch allow you to filter objects by date. Unfortunately, some agents have now caught on to this and now cancel their ads and then upload them again, so that it's no longer evident how long a property has been on the market. However, this feature still provides an indication of how long a property has been on the market – and you can always ask the agent.

## Rent Increases & Reductions

The initial rent can be freely agreed between the landlord and tenant. However, within the

| Monthly Rent (CHF) | | | | |
|---|---|---|---|---|
| No. of bedrooms | Approx. m² | Inexpensive | Moderate | Expensive |
| 0 (studio) | 30-40 | 500-750 | 650-850 | 850-1,200 |
| 1 | 50-60 | 750-1,000 | 1,000-1,300 | 1,400-2,000 |
| 2 | 75-90 | 1,000-1,500 | 1,250-1,750 | 1,750-2,500 |
| 3 | 90-120 | 1,250-2,000 | 1,500-2,000 | 2,000-3,000 |
| 4 | 120-150 | 1,500-2,000 | 2,000-2,500 | 2,750-4,000 |
| 5 or more | 150+ | 2,000-3,000 | 2,500-3,500 | 4,000+ |

for a rent increase to be permitted. If a landlord wants to increase the rent, e.g. after renovation or a mortgage interest rate (*Hypothekarzins/ taux hypothécaires*) increase, he's obliged to complete an official form stating why the increase is justifiable under tenancy law.

If you don't agree with the increase, you can appeal in writing to the arbitration agency/conciliation board of the canton (*Schlichtungsbehörden, autorités de conciliation*) within a period of 30 days. Note that you can also get a reduction in the rent when the mortgage rate decreases significantly (as it did in 2009), although your rent must be linked to the interest rate and this must be stated in your lease. Standard rental agreements either link the rent to the current mortgage rate or to the consumer price index.

If the landlord doesn't voluntarily reduce the rent when there's a mortgage rate decrease, renters seldom petition for a reduction, even if it's their right to do so. A reduction in the rental value of an apartment, e.g. due to major defects or essential renovation work, is also grounds for a temporary reduction of the rent. It's advisable to join the Renters' Association (see **Lease Disputes** on page 155), who will provide you with legal advice regarding your lease (sometimes free of charge!).

It's possible to have a progressive rent clause, whereby the rent increases annually in line with the Swiss Consumer Price Index (inflation), but only for rental agreements that are for a minimum period of five years (usually new builds). If the rental agreement term is for at least three years, the rent can also be increased annually by a fixed formula, as stated in the lease.

If the landlord needs to repair a defect in an apartment and fails to do so, the law allows the tenant to withhold the rent. However, a number of conditions and formalities must be met in order for the rent to be lawfully withheld, and before doing so you should contact the conciliation board for advice. Note that if you delay payment or don't pay the rent without a valid reason, your landlord has the right to terminate the lease after an admonition and evict you at short notice.

If you need any advice or help regarding a lease or have a dispute with your agent or landlord, you can obtain help and advice from

first 30 days of renting a property, a tenant can appeal the rent as abusive; for example if he was forced into agreeing it due to serious personal or family difficulties, due to the conditions of the local residential property market, or the new rent is significantly higher than it was for the previous tenant (you have a right to this information).

In some cantons, e.g. Fribourg, Geneva, Neuchâtel, Nidwalden, Uri, Vaud and Zug, the landlord is obliged to enclose a form informing tenants how to appeal against excessively high initial rents.

The law strongly favours tenants in Switzerland and rent increases are strictly regulated. An increase must be justified in writing and due notice given. The rent may not be increased by more than 5 per cent and typically not more than once every three years. It's easier for a landlord to increase the rent in the case of a fixed-term lease which has come to an end, but even so, if the new rent is significantly higher than the old rent, it runs the risk of being declared abusive.

For a tenancy which is for an indefinite period, several conditions must be met in order the cantonal Rent Association (see **Lease Disputes** on page 155) or from the cantonal arbitration agency/conciliation board.

## SHARED ACCOMMODATION

Finding accommodation in Switzerland that doesn't break the bank is a huge problem for young people, students and low-paid workers such as seasonal workers. For single people (and possibly young couples), the solution may be sharing accommodation (*Wohngemeinschaft, colocation*), which is more common in German-speaking than French-speaking regions. Note that you may find it more difficult to find shared accommodation when the new university term starts (September to November) and students are looking for accommodation.

In recent years, shared-accommodation for those aged 50+ has become more popular; for example, Wohnform50plus on Homegate (💻 www.homegate.ch), where you're required to register (free). Note that this section doesn't appear on the English pages. Homegate also lists shared accommodation for students, which again isn't in English.

It isn't uncommon for people from all walks of life and ages to share accommodation in Switzerland.

The law regarding renting is more complicated with regard to flat-sharing and it's simpler if one person is the tenant and sub-lets to the others, which will need to be agreed with the agent or landlord. It often happens that a tenant sublets an apartment without changing the lease, which means that your name isn't on the lease and you could be 'evicted' if the leaseholder leaves (unless you can take over the lease). It's possible for all sharers to be joint tenants with one tenancy agreement (in which case they're jointly responsible) or to be individual tenants with individual tenancy agreements, although this is unusual in Switzerland.

The main benefit of flat-sharing is that you can afford to live in a bigger and better property in a better area than you could afford on your own, and you'll have a larger choice. Good small one- or two-bedroom properties are usually snapped up quickly, whereas larger properties are often better value and may be easier to find. However, you need to find a landlord who's willing to let to sharers. Sharing a property means either sharing with friends, renting a property yourself and advertising for flatmates, or responding to a 'room to let' advertisement (see below).

Sharing usually involves sharing a kitchen, bathroom, living room and dining room, but

Fribourg

not a bedroom. It also involves sharing all bills (in addition to the rent), including electricity, gas, telephone and internet, and may also include sharing food bills and cooking (by mutual agreement). Some landlords include electricity and gas (plus heating) in the rent. The cleaning and general upkeep of a house or flat is also usually shared (although it's better to employ a cleaner). As always when living with others, there are advantages and disadvantages, and its success depends on the participants' ability to live together in harmony.

Furnished and unfurnished (usual) rooms can be rented in private houses and apartments in most areas of Switzerland for CHF 500 to 1,000 per month, depending on the size, amenities and location, although rents can be much higher for luxury properties and in cities such as Geneva and Zurich. You must usually pay a deposit of up to three months' rent, in addition to one month's rent in advance. Rentals are usually for an unlimited period (*Unbeschränkt, illimité*), which should be stated in ads. If it isn't specified in the rental agreement, the landlord (or the person renting/sub-letting the room) can terminate the contract whenever they like.

The best website for shared housing is ⌨ www.wgzimmer.ch (change the language to English and click on the Swiss flag), mostly students and young professionals; others include ⌨ www.easywg.ch and ⌨ www.anzeiger.ch (German). Students can obtain help from university housing agencies and you can also check the ads on websites such as ⌨ www.student.ch.

---

⚠ **Caution**

If you rent a property with the intention of sharing with others, you should ensure that it's permitted in your lease.

---

## CHARGES OR EXTRA COSTS

Extra costs (*Nebenkosten/NK, charges/frais annexes*) or supplementary charges for services are payable in addition to the monthly rent of an apartment. These usually total around 10 per cent of the rent, although it can be more – usually, the lower the rent the higher the extra costs are as a percentage of the rent. When a property is advertised, it's usually stated whether extra costs are included in the rent (usually a net figure is shown for the rent with extra costs shown separately). If there's no mention of extra costs in a lease (see below) it can be assumed that there aren't any, as when applicable they must be itemised in the lease.

Extra costs are usually paid along with the rent and include an estimated (*pauschal, comptes les frais annexes*) cost for communal expenses such as central heating, electricity, waste collection, water, chimney cleaning, caretaker (*Hauswart, concièrge*), cable television and maintenance. If the cost for a particular item, e.g. for heating, isn't measured individually for each apartment, then it will be split between all tenants in a building according to their apartment size (which isn't a good idea if you aren't a full-time resident). Costs depend on the actual apartment and its location in the building, and are detailed in your lease.

If extra costs are paid in advance (*akonto, par d'acompte*) you'll receive an itemised annual account (*Nebenkostenabrechung, le décompte annuel des charges*), usually in the autumn, when the meters are read and bills rendered. You should be given copies of all annual communal bills for which you're being charged; if you aren't, you should ask for copies. Usually your monthly payments are lower than the actual costs and you'll have a balance to pay, although you'll receive a refund if you've overpaid your fees. If the annual costs are much higher or lower than your monthly payments, they should be adjusted in the following year. If you pay your rent via a bank standing order, refunds will are usually paid directly into your bank account.

Check your account carefully, as it isn't unknown for landlords or management companies to make mistakes. All the charges listed in your rental contract as *Nebenkosten/charges, frais annexes* will appear in your extra costs annual account, which shouldn't include any other charges, such as building repairs, insurance, property tax or public

| Nebenkosten/Frais Annexes – Annual Bill | | |
|---|---|---|
| **English** | **Gorman** | **French** |
| heating costs* | Heizung | chauffage |
| water (cold/warm) | Kalt- und Warmwasser | d'eau (froid/chaud) |
| cable radio/TV | Kabelgebühren radio/TV | cable radio/TV |
| electricity** | Allgemeinstrom | électricité |
| waste water & garbage | Abwassergebühren/ Kehrichtabfuhr | eaux usées/ ramassage des ordures |
| service agreements*** | Serviceabonnemente | Abonnements de service |
| management fee | Verwaltungskosten 3% plus | MWST/charges administrations (3%) |
| staircase cleaning | Treppenhausreinigung | nettoyage |
| management fees | Hauswart | gardien/conciérge |
| snow removal | Schneeräumung | déneigement |
| gardener | Garten und Umbegungspflege | jardinier |

\* includes cleaning and insurance
\*\* for common areas, not your apartment
\*\*\* includes the heating system, washing machine and dryer, boiler and elevator

charges. If you feel the account is incorrect, you can ask the cantonal Rent Association to check it, if you're a member (see **Lease Disputes** on page 155).

## GARAGE OR PARKING SPACE

A garage or parking space (*Parkplatz, parking*) isn't usually included in the rent of an apartment and must usually be rented separately. A single lock-up garage or a parking space in an underground garage is usually available in modern apartment blocks, and costs from CHF 130 to 180 per month and an outside parking space from CHF 50 to 100. Most developments have adequate parking for both tenants and visitors (which is a legal requirement). If an apartment block has no parking spaces, it may be possible to rent one nearby, for example in the underground garage of a hotel or in a private car park. The rent varies considerably and can be anything from CHF 100 to 500+ (e.g. in central Geneva or Zurich) per month.

Most property websites (see **The Internet** on page 243) also contain advertisements for parking space rentals and sales.

You must sign a separate lease for a garage if it isn't rented with your apartment. It's possible to rent a garage for the winter months only, although the lease may need to start and end on fixed dates, for example from 1st October to 1st April (see also **Termination** on page 161). A garage is useful, particularly in winter – unless of course you enjoy trying to find your car among the snow drifts – and it also keeps your car cool in summer.

Free street parking is difficult or impossible to find in most cities and large towns and isn't really an option if you have a valuable car. In many towns, tenants can obtain an annual parking permit *(Parkkarten, abo parkings habitant)* for on-street parking in blue zones (*Blaue Zone, zone bleue*). These also provide limited parking for non-residents, who must have a blue parking disc.

## THE LEASE

When you find a suitable apartment, you need to sign a lease (*Mietvertrag, contrat/ bail à loyer*) with the landlord or agent, which will be either for a fixed term or an indefinite period. If a fixed term is set, the lease expires without any need for notice of termination at the end of the term, but if the parties continue the agreement beyond the expiry of a fixed term lease, it becomes a lease for an indefinite duration.

Most leases are for a minimum of a year but for an indefinite period, with a notice period of three months. If you want to leave without giving notice (or sufficient notice), as noted in your lease, you must find a replacement tenant (see **Lease Termination** on page 161). In general, you sign a lease for between three and five years, with no notice period in the first year, and three months' notice period during each subsequent year. A rental property may only be sub-let by a tenant with the owner's agreement.

A landlord may try to get a tenant to sign a lease for a number of years, e.g. three or five, with a notice period of one year, even after the first year of a lease. In this case the lease may have a progressive rent, for example, the first year's rent is CHF 3,000 per month, the second year is CHF 3,250 francs and the third year is 3,500 francs. This mostly applies to new-build properties. You can have a contract which allows three-month termination throughout the year, or a rental agreement which allows termination at the end of any month excluding December – but it must be in the contract.

It's possible to terminate your lease at short notice, provided you find another tenant who's acceptable to your landlord to take over the lease (see **Subletting** on page 157), although this is difficult unless the property is exceptional and in high demand.

A standard lease form is provided in most cantons, although you should take note of any added or deleted clauses or passages. Your lease should include details of when your rent and extra costs will be increased, if applicable. You must be notified of an unscheduled rent rise (see page 148), e.g. due to a mortgage interest rate increase or an increase in the price index (inflation), by registered post at least three months **plus** ten days in advance, so that you can respond by cancelling your contract if you wish.

Before signing a lease you should check the following:

♦ whether there's a minimum or maximum limit on your tenancy period – this is usually negotiable;

♦ on which dates the lease can be terminated;

♦ what deposit is required (maximum three months' rent – see page 172);

♦ how many people may live in the apartment and whether you can sublet or share;

♦ what laundry facilities are provided and when they're available;

♦ if cable television is available and what channels;

♦ if satellite television is available or whether it's possible to install an aerial;

♦ whether the telephone line is connected and how many points there are;

♦ if pets are allowed (you can be evicted if you keep a pet against your landlord's wishes);

♦ when the rent and extra costs are to be reviewed or increased;

♦ what the parking facilities are (particularly covered parking, in winter) and the cost, which may be covered in a separate agreement;

♦ what the house rules are (see page 159);

♦ any unusual rules or restrictions;

♦ whether there's a lift or a goods lift for furniture (some cantons' regulations require

lifts in all new buildings with four or more floors).

If you rent a house (rather than an apartment), it's even more important to check the rules and regulations for tenants, because you can be responsible for the following if they're included in the lease:

◆ the gardens and grounds;

◆ the heating system maintenance, insulation, ordering fuel, etc.;

◆ maintenance of the water supply;

◆ heating-system maintenance, such as chimney-sweeping twice a year, which is compulsory for oil- and wood-burning systems (your landlord may pay for this);

Specific legal terms and conditions apply to renting a house or apartment as a 'family home', i.e. the primary residence of a married couple or family. In this case, both partners must sign the lease, and matters such as termination or a change in the terms are only valid if both partners sign. If a landlord wants to terminate a lease, notification must be made to both spouses separately. The landlord must be informed if a single tenant gets married, a couple are divorced or additional people wish to share an apartment. If you're sharing a home, you should have your name added to the lease, otherwise you have no legal rights. If a couple wish to terminate a lease, both must sign the termination letter.

## Lease Details

The lease contains details about the apartment, in addition to the rights and obligations of the tenant and landlord, and usually contains the following details:

◆ the landlord's name or his representative and the name(s) of the tenant(s) signing the lease;

◆ a description of the property to be rented, including whether a store room, garage parking space or anything else is included;

◆ the rental period and whether it's fixed or indefinite;

◆ the net rent plus extra costs if they aren't included in the rent (a list of the extra charges must be provided);

◆ when and how the rent is to be paid;

◆ the deposit (maximum of three month's rent) and the interest to be paid (see page 172);

◆ the notice period and when notice can be given;

◆ The conditions under which the rent can be increased, i.e. mortgage rate index and/or consumer price index;

◆ a list of the keys provided and the number;

◆ whether smoking or pets are permitted;

◆ what (if any) insurance a tenant requires;

◆ the general conditions (*Allgemeine Bedingungen, conditions générales*) and the house rules (*Hausordnung, règlement d'immeuble*) – see page 159.

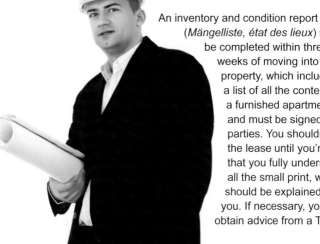

An inventory and condition report (*Mängelliste, état des lieux*) must be completed within three weeks of moving into a property, which includes a list of all the contents in a furnished apartment, and must be signed by all parties. You shouldn't sign the lease until you're sure that you fully understand all the small print, which should be explained to you. If necessary, you can obtain advice from a Tenants

Association (see **Lease Disputes** below). Note that if you back out of an agreement before signing a lease that has been drawn up for you, an agent is entitled to demand reimbursement of his administrative expenses (unless the lease has changed in any way from that agreed verbally).

## Documentation

Most properties are let through agents who manage properties for the owners, and the documentation required varies, but includes some or all of the following:

◆ a completed application form;

◆ a copy of your residence permit and passport or ID card;

◆ a copy of your employment contract and/or salary certificate, issued and signed by the employer (or copies of salary receipts for the last three months);

◆ character references (which will be taken up);

◆ a bank reference (you may also be subject to a credit check);

◆ a police record from your previous country;

◆ students and others with low or no regular income may need a Swiss guarantor to co-sign their lease.

If you're moving house within Switzerland (rather than coming from abroad), you'll need a declaration (*Auszug aus dem Betreibungsregister, extrait du registre des poursuites/attestation de non-poursuite*) from the Debt Collection Office at the town hall where you're registered, stating that you haven't been prosecuted for non-payment of debts and haven't defaulted on your debts.

When applying for properties, it's advisable to apply for a property where the rent doesn't exceed one-third of your salary or the combined salaries of a couple (if it does, you'll be refused), but which also isn't too inexpensive – otherwise an agent or landlord may prefer to rent to someone who couldn't afford more expensive accommodation. Similarly, if you're a single person or a couple with no children and you're applying for a 'large' property (4 rooms or more), the agent

or landlord may prefer to let it to a family with children.

In an area where good rental properties are difficult to find, such as Geneva and Zurich, it may be worthwhile attaching a personal letter to your application, plus a CV and photo, which may make a good impression on the landlord or agent. It's also important to submit references, for example from your supervisor or other people in a position of authority, plus a previous landlord, even if it's in English (but have it translated). Note that the decision of landlords or agents can take weeks. The agent and/or landlord will sift through all the applications and decide who will make the 'best' tenant; anything you can provide that will make your application stand out may get your file on the top of the pile!

## Lease Disputes

There are communal and cantonal conciliation boards for tenancy matters in all cantons, which advise tenants and landlords regarding accepted practice and the law. In the event of a dispute over a tenancy agreement (rent reduction, rent increase, unreasonable extra charges, etc.), the conciliation board (*Schlichtungsbehörden/Mietämter, autorités de conciliation*) tries to reach an amicable settlement. In some cases, such as the termination or extension of a lease and the use of rental deposits, they're able to make a ruling. You can find your local conciliation board via the 'Rent Law' website (⌨ www.mietrecht.ch – click on '*Schlichtungsbehörde*' from the menu and enter the postcode or name of your town in the box).

The conciliation board, whose services may be free of charge, provides information and advice to both tenants and landlords and can also issue you with any forms you need. The conciliation boards consist of representatives from tenants' and landlords' associations and are chaired by an independent chairperson.

The Swiss tenants' association acts in the interests of tenants, although you need to be a member of your local cantonal Tenants

Association (membership costs vary, but are around CHF 95 per year in Zurich). Associations provide 'free' initial legal advice to members and will check and answer questions regarding leases, and mediate in disputes between tenants and agents/landlords. Non-members can call their hotline (☎ 0900-900 800, CHF 3.70 per minute) for advice.

To find your local cantonal representative for German-speaking cantons, visit 🖳 www.mieterverband.ch and click on the canton flag. For French-speaking cantons, see the Association Suisse des locataires website (🖳 www.asloca.ch) and for Ticino, contact the Associazione Svizzera Inquilini (🖳 www.asi-infoalloggio.ch). Note that all websites are in the local language and none are in English, although if you telephone your local branch they may be able to answer a query in English.

Information can also be obtained from the Federal Office of Housing (Bundesamt für Wohnungswesen/BWO, Office fédéral du logement/OFL, Storchengasse 6, 2540 Granges, ☎ 32-654 91 11, 🖳 www.bwo.admin.ch), who publish a brochure (available in 11 languages) explaining rental procedures in Switzerland.

## Insurance, Maintenance & Repairs

It's usually optional for a tenant to take out home contents insurance to cover fire, water and theft, except in the cantons of Basle, Fribourg, Glarus, Jura, Nidwalden, Solothurn and Vaud, where fire insurance is compulsory. Some lease agreements require the tenant to have contents insurance (see page 233) and it's also recommended that tenants have personal liability insurance (see page 234), but it isn't compulsory (except for dogs and cars).

If you wish to change anything in an apartment such as paint walls, replace carpets, etc., you must obtain written permission from the agent or landlord. You need to have a name plaque on your mailbox (by the building's main entrance) and next to your door bell, which your landlord or agent may order for you or tell you where to obtain (there's a fee of around CHF 30).

If you rent an apartment or house with a working fireplace, it must be swept once a year if you use it – the chimney sweep may leave

a reminder in your mailbox about a week or so before doing his rounds. If you're renting a house, the heating installation must also be maintained, although this is something the owner or agent will organise (usually they have a service contract). The boiler must be descaled regularly (approximately every five years) and the furnace should be checked annually.

If you have oil heating, you should check the oil level in late summer or early autumn and have the tank filled if it's less than a quarter full. This can be done at any time, but oil prices are higher in winter. Take care not to let the tank run empty, as it may be expensive if the heating system needs to be shut down and restarted. If you plan to be away during the winter, you should leave your heating on at around 15°C (59°F) to prevent the pipes freezing. Outdoor water pipes should be drained and isolated from the main supply to prevent freezing.

If you're renting a house, you should ensure that you know exactly what you're responsible for and how surfaces (etc.) should be cared for, e.g. floors, kitchen worktops and tiles. The maintenance of a garden or terrace is usually the responsibility of the tenant, unless otherwise stated in the lease, although this doesn't include the pruning of trees. You may also be responsible for clearing the gutters and down-pipes of leaves and other debris. If the premises aren't well maintained, the owner is entitled to have the work done professionally and send you the invoice.

Minor repairs or cleaning must usually be taken care of and paid for by the tenant, e.g. the replacement of an extractor hood filter, a baking tray or shower attachment, or the unblocking of drains (unless it happens immediately after you take possession). If you have caused the problem or damage, then you must pay at least part of the cost, but if you aren't responsible, the landlord must pay. You aren't required to replace damaged or broken items at the 'new' price, but at the current value of the item less 'wear and tear'. If you have private liability insurance (see page 234), it may pay for accidental damage caused to a rented apartment, although glass may be excluded.

---

**☑ SURVIVAL TIP**

In the case of severe damage to a property, e.g. a tree falls and damages the roof, the agent or landlord should be informed immediately; if he fails to take action, you should notify him again in writing by registered post. If part of a property is unusable due to maintenance or renovation work, you can ask for a rent reduction.

---

## Subletting

Subletting is usually permitted, but is subject to certain conditions. A tenant who wants to sublet all or part of an apartment must obtain written consent from the agent or landlord, stating the terms and conditions of the sublease. For example, if you decide to let a room in an apartment (see **Shared Accommodation** on page 150) to a third party, you must usually obtain permission.

If you wish to terminate your lease (*Mietvertrag Kündigung, résiliation anticipée*) – see **Lease Termination** on page 161 – outside the official dates, at short notice or in the first

year of a lease, you must find a replacement tenant who's acceptable to your landlord. Your landlord can insist that you provide him with the names of three suitable replacement tenants, although he isn't obliged to accept one of them. You can place a 'tenant wanted' (*Nachmieter gesucht, cherche successor*) advertisement on a property website or in a local publication (see **Finding Rental Accommodation** on page 142), although you should bear in mind that it's difficult to find someone to take over a lease.

If you don't find a replacement tenant before you move out, you're liable for the rent until the next official moving date or until a new tenant is found, if earlier. If you find a suitable replacement tenant and the landlord or agent accepts him, when the new tenant signs a lease you're no longer responsible for the property. Bear in mind that the contract for the parking space or garage may be separate and must be also be terminated.

Taking over a lease can be a good deal, although the vacating tenant may ask you to purchase his furniture and kitchen appliances, which may be a better option than buying everything new, provided it's reasonably priced, in good condition and is what you need. However, you shouldn't pay the outgoing tenant a cent until you have signed the lease.

## DEPOSITS

A security deposit (*Kaution, caution*) equal to one to three months' rent (more than three months' is illegal) must be paid when renting a property. The deposit must be put into an interest-bearing account (*Mietkautionskonto, compte de garantie de loyer*), which is protected from unauthorised access by both parties; neither the landlord nor the tenant can withdraw the money without the other's consent. The account can be opened by either the tenant, landlord or his agent in the tenant's name, on completion of an 'Application for Rental Deposit Savings Account' form.

The deposit is repaid with interest when you leave, less any outstanding costs, e.g. for damages or cleaning (see **Lease Termination** on page 161). The owner must present the tenant with a final invoice and the tenant must agree to the amount, after which the deposit is repaid, usually within a few weeks. If any necessary repairs must be paid for by the tenant, the deposit may be used to pay for them, but only with the tenant's agreement. If a tenant doesn't agree, a landlord must get a court ruling for repairs to be paid for out of the deposit. In this case, the deposit can be blocked for a maximum of one year after the lease expires, after which the tenant is free to withdraw the deposit if the owner hasn't made any claims against it. The arbitration board (*Schlichtungsbehörden, autorités de conciliation*) can hear any dispute between the owner and tenant regarding a deposit.

Not everyone can afford to pay a huge rental deposit or wishes to 'freeze' three month's rent in an account paying very low interest. Fortunately, there's a solution. There are rental deposit companies in Switzerland such as Swiss Caution (🖳 www.swisscaution.ch/en), who pay the deposit on your behalf, in return for which you pay a small flat-rate premium in the first year and a small percentage of the deposit amount in subsequent years of a tenancy. Generally, this is a better solution than paying a deposit which is tied up for an unlimited period, but you must be either a Swiss citizen or a have a B or C resident's permit to qualify.

> ☑ **SURVIVAL TIP**
>
> **If you plan to use a rental deposit company, be aware that there are bogus companies.**

## INVENTORY & CONDITION REPORT

One of the most important tasks on moving into a new rental property is to complete an inventory and report on its condition (*Mängelliste, état des lieux*), which must be completed and checked in the presence of the landlord or agent. There's a handover at the start of the lease (*Übergabeprotokoll, état des lieux d'entrée*) and at the end of the lease when you leave (*Abgabeprotokoll, etat des lieux de sortie).* This includes the condition of fixtures and fittings, the cleanliness and state of

the decoration (paintwork, plaster, floors, walls, etc.), and anything missing or in need of repair.

If you're renting a furnished apartment, the inventory will include all furnishings and equipment down to the last teaspoon. The apartment should be spotless when you move in, as this is certainly what your landlord will expect when you move out – see **Lease Termination** on page 161.

The inventory form is provided by your landlord, and must be completed, signed and returned within 14-21 days of occupying your apartment. If you're taking over an apartment from the previous tenant, the landlord may arrange for the hand-over to be done when you're both present, so that any problems can be sorted out on the spot. The inspection list should be as accurate and detailed as possible, as it's accepted as proof of any faults and deficiencies that existed when you moved in. If any problem isn't listed, you can be held responsible when you vacate the property. When the participants agree on the contents of the inspection list, it's signed by all parties, who each receive a copy.

You should inspect the apartment carefully over the first few days and check that all the equipment and electrical and plumbing installations are operating correctly. If you discover any problems, you should add them to the signed inventory report and return it to the landlord or agent within the time required (usually three weeks). The landlord or agent must counter-sign it and return a copy to you for your records.

Bear in mind that if you agree to take over or buy anything from the previous tenant, e.g. you agree to buy or accept a fitted carpet, you'll have to dispose of it at your expense when moving out if the next tenant doesn't want it.

Note the reading on your meters (electricity, gas and water) and check that you aren't overcharged on your first bill. Most Swiss landlords are honest and won't try to cheat you, but it's better to be safe than sorry.

## KEYS

You usually receive three keys to an apartment or house and two keys for the post box. You must ensure that you receive all the keys stated in the lease or inventory and the correct

number – and check that they work! Note that with some locks, you need to pull up the handle to lock or unlock a door. Your house key may also fit your garage door (and everything else) or you may receive a garage remote control, although the doors to underground garages are usually opened with a key.

If you require extra keys you must pay for them. The locks fitted to most apartments and houses are usually of a high security type; keys have individual numbers and copies cannot be cut at a local hardware store. If you require additional keys you must ask your landlord or agent, who'll arrange for copies to be made and sent to you (along with the bill).

If you lock yourself out of your apartment (or car), there's usually a local locksmith on call day and night to help. Ask the telephone operator (☎ 1811) for the number. This service is, however, very expensive and it may be much cheaper to break a window to gain entry to your apartment (unless you live on the 14th floor!). Whatever you do, don't call the locksmith out at night or at weekends – it could bankrupt you (stay with a friend). Your landlord or agent will have a copy of your house keys, but isn't permitted to enter the premises without your permission.

If you vacate your apartment for an extended period, it may be obligatory to notify your caretaker (*Hauswart/concierge*) and leave a key with him or with a neighbour in case of emergencies. If you don't have all the copies of your keys when you vacate an apartment, the barrel of a lock for which you've lost a key may need to be changed at your expense; if it's a 'pass' key for the main entrance to your building (and possibly the cellar, garage and laundry room), you could be charged for changing all the locks in the building and providing new keys for all the owners/tenants!

Most house keys are security keys and coded, and anyone finding a key can drop it in a post box and the post office will send it to the company that made it. They in turn will return the key to you (or the landlord) along with a payment slip for CHF 25 to cover their costs and the finder's fee (they pay the finder a reward, if known).

If you're a habitual key loser, there are a number of companies that provide a key-return service, such as 🖳 www.keyfinder.ch. For CHF 6 per year (five-year contract CHF 30) they'll provide you with a coded tag which you attach to your key-ring. A message on the tag asks anyone finding the keys to drop them in the nearest post box. Return rates of over 90 per cent are claimed, including keys lost outside Switzerland.

## HOUSE RULES

All apartment blocks have house rules (*Hausordnung*, *règlement d'immeuble*) – which apply whether you're an owner or tenant – some of which may be dictated by your local community and enforceable by law, particularly those regarding noise and siesta periods. You should receive a copy on moving into your apartment; if you don't understand them, you should have them translated.

House rules generally include the following (basically, anything that isn't compulsory is strictly forbidden!):

◆ Entrances, landings, stairwells, corridors and fire escape routes must be kept free of obstructions. It's forbidden to place object in stairwells. No leaving footwear or personal belongings such as children's toys in public areas or outside your door in the stair well.

◆ The building and its surrounds must be kept clean and tidy at all times.

◆ A noise curfew between 10pm and 6am (times may vary). The Swiss generally take this very seriously, as most go to bed early and rise at the crack of dawn. They may hammer on your door, walls, floor or ceiling, or even call the police if you play music or hold a noisy party after 10pm. It may be forbidden to play a musical instrument for more than two hours a day.

♦ If you have a party you must warn your neighbours, but don't be surprised if it results in complaints about too much noise – even inviting your neighbours to a party doesn't always do the trick, as they've been known to call the police and complain about the noise as soon as they're back in their own apartments! Some apartment blocks have a party room.

Limmat River, Zurich

♦ Absolutely no loud noise, e.g. drilling, banging in nails or playing loud music, on Sundays and public holidays. Sunday is a day of rest, when working is forbidden by law.

♦ A siesta (*Mittagsruhe*, *sieste*), e.g. from noon to 1 or 2pm, during which time you mustn't make any loud noise. This is to allow young children and pensioners (and exhausted writers) an undisturbed afternoon nap.

♦ Small house pets such as birds in cages, guinea pigs and fish can usually be kept without permission, but written permission is usually required to keep cats, dogs, parrots or reptiles. If pets are allowed, it's forbidden to let them run wild in public areas (e.g. playgrounds) and owners must clean up after them.

♦ No smoking on stairs, in lifts or in other communal areas and rooms – some landlords will only rent to non-smokers;

♦ No installations (e.g. satellite dishes, flags, signposts, etc.) in communal rooms, on balconies or patios, or on the outside of the building without the written permission of the management.

♦ Flower boxes on balconies and window boxes must be secure. It's necessary to take care when watering and ensure that water doesn't drip onto the wall or the neighbours' windows, balconies or vehicles.

♦ Rubbish must be put in the rubbish containers provided and separated for recycling where possible. It's forbidden to put toxic substances and large objects in rubbish containers.

♦ Children are required to use play areas and are forbidden to play in cellars, on grass areas, in underground car parks or in other communal areas. Parents are required to tidy play areas after their children, e.g. put away toys.

♦ It may be forbidden to barbecue with charcoal on balconies.

♦ Hanging net curtains at your windows is compulsory in some apartments;

♦ Airing bedding, i.e. hanging it from windows, may be permitted only at certain times, which may be dictated by cantonal law;

♦ It's forbidden to park in the courtyard, on a path or on the grass. It's also prohibited to wash a car or motorcycle (unless there's a area set aside for this) or do any repairs on the property. Drivers must drive slowly when entering the car park or parking.

♦ Bicycles must be stored in the bicycle rack or in the bicycle room.

♦ Sunblinds must be rolled in at night and during rain and storms.

♦ Windows in the cellar, stairwells and roof must be kept closed during the cold winter months.

♦ If a roster exists for the use of the laundry room, you're only permitted to use it during your allotted times. Usually a laundry room can be used only between 7am and 9pm, Mondays to Saturdays. It's forbidden to use it on Sundays and national holidays. Machines must be cleaned after use.

♦ No toilet flushing between 10pm and 6am; a request for gentlemen to 'please sit down when using the toilet between these hours' was even displayed in an expensive apartment block in Zurich (presumably with *very* thin walls).

♦ Airing a few times a day (two windows open on opposite sides to create a through draft), particularly in winter, for around five minutes (unless your apartment has an automatic air circulation system). When not airing, windows must be closed in winter and can be left in the semi-open position only during the summer months.

♦ The building entrance door and other entrance doors (e.g. cellar and garage entrances) must be kept locked between 10pm and 6am.

♦ Any damage to an apartment or the communal areas of the building must be reported to your landlord or the management ASAP.

You should take the house rules seriously, as repeated transgressions (e.g. making too much noise) can lead to a police fine or even eviction. (Your Swiss neighbours will usually be happy to point out any transgression of house rules!) Most of the above regulations are listed in the house rules of most apartment blocks.

If disputes between neighbours cannot be resolved between tenants or owners (e.g. complaints regarding noise or untidiness), tenants can call on the caretaker (*Hausmeister, concierge*) or house management (*Hausverwaltung, régie*) to mediate or make a decision. Together, the caretaker and management are responsible for the day-to-day running and organising repairs.

## LEASE TERMINATION

You must generally give a minimum of three months' notice by registered letter (*Einschreiben Brief, lettre recommandée*) when you wish to terminate (*Kündigung, résiliation*) the lease of an apartment, which cannot usually be done in the first year of a lease. This applies to most contracts in Switzerland. Notice letters must be signed by both the husband and wife, where applicable (if a landlord wants to terminate a lease, he must notify both spouses separately), and you must receive confirmation from the landlord that he has received and accepted your termination.

> ☑ **SURVIVAL TIP**
>
> Bear in mind that if you have a contract for the lease of a parking space or garage, this must be terminated separately,

The lease may usually be terminated only on the official dates listed in your lease, e.g. the end of March, June or September in canton Zurich, which applies to both parties. If it isn't terminated by either party, a lease is normally automatically extended for a further period, as stated in your lease. However, a landlord isn't permitted to terminate a lease without good reason and must use an official form provided by the cantonal authorities. Good reasons include the landlord requiring the property for his own family's use or when a property has been sold, in which case the new owners can effect an extraordinary termination of the tenancy under certain conditions.

The legally or contractually agreed periods of notice and due dates must be complied with and at least three months notice given. Tenants are entitled to be notified of the reason for the termination and a termination that isn't made in good faith can be contested before a conciliation board within 30 days. If a termination constitutes hardship for the tenant, e.g. financial or family difficulties or homelessness, an extension of the term of the tenancy can be applied for at the conciliation board.

A lease can be terminated with 30 days notice by the tenant if the landlord has failed to remedy any serious defects within a reasonable period of time. Similarly, the landlord can terminate the lease with 30 days notice if the tenant hasn't paid the rent, has seriously neglected or damaged the property, has used the property unlawfully (for example, to produce illegal drugs!), or has been officially warned for some other matter, such as persistent noise, and has failed to comply.

If you wish to terminate your lease outside the official dates, at short notice or in the first year of a lease, you must find a replacement tenant who's acceptable to your landlord (see **Subletting** on page 157). If you're given notice to vacate a property, you can find out about your rights and options from the cantonal Mieterverband (see **Lease Disputes** on page 155).

## Cleaning & Redecoration

You're expected to leave your apartment spotlessly clean – as it was when you took it over – and the return of your deposit in full depends on this. Your landlord may even don white gloves to check that the oven is clean! One method of avoiding any problems is to employ professional cleaners, which most people consider well worth the money. You can find ads in local newspapers and *Yellow Pages* under 'Removal cleaning' (*Umzugsreinigung, nettoyage pour remise d'appartement*) or can look on the internet. Professional cleaning can be expensive, for example CHF 1,000 or more, depending on the size of your apartment. Charges vary from company to company, so shop around and don't pay the bill until the apartment has been cleaned to your landlord's satisfaction. You should have a 'handover acceptance guarantee' from the cleaning company.

Book well in advance as cleaning companies can be very busy, particularly around popular house moving dates.

The cleaning of your apartment should include everything, including carpets (professional cleaning), floors, walls, paintwork, windows, oven, cupboards, bath/WC, lampshades, refrigerator, dishwasher, blinds, pipes and radiators, in all rooms; plus the garage, patio, balcony, storeroom, attic and basement, and the decalcification of taps (faucets). A cleaning company contract should include all the above. Also bear in mind the following points:

♦ any stains or scratches on floors (e.g. parquet floors, which must also be polished), paintwork and walls must be repaired. They may require painting, papering or sanding. However, you shouldn't try to erase parquet floor scratches (usually the entire room has to be done) as a certain amount of wear and tear is acceptable.

♦ any holes made in walls for pictures, mirrors and other fittings must be filled.

♦ the garden and house surrounds must be in good order, e.g. no weeds on your patio or balcony.

♦ any alterations or improvements made to the property must be sold to the next tenant or 'given' to the landlord. However, the landlord may insist on professional alterations or restoration, usually stated in your lease, and not do-it-yourself.

♦ fixtures or fittings that are easily removed and which weren't part of the original inventory, e.g. light fittings, must be removed.

Your agent or landlord will inspect the property just before you vacate it and will expect it to be in the same state of cleanliness and repair as it was when you took it over. A new inventory and condition report (*Mängelliste/Abgabeprotokoll, état des lieux de sortie*) will be completed (see page 158) and compared with the one completed when you took over the property. The landlord will also collect the keys (see page 158).

You must pay for any damage to fixtures and fittings and you may also be required to redecorate the apartment, depending on its condition when you moved in, how long you've lived there and the terms of your lease. Redecoration usually includes filling any holes in walls and repainting them, erasing excessive marks on wooden floors (resanding/polishing), carpet cleaning, and repainting woodwork. Necessary repairs or replacements may depend on the length of your tenancy; if you're a long-term tenant certain things may be overlooked, e.g.

'normal' wear and tear, although this is open to interpretation.

You will receive a copy of the inventory and condition report, which you and your landlord must sign, which verifies that the apartment is in an acceptable condition – or as otherwise noted – and that no further claims can be made.

You may wish to make a note of your electricity, water and gas meter readings and ensure that the telephone is disconnected. Finally, if applicable, ensure that your deposit is repaid with interest. Any deductions from your deposit should be accompanied by an itemised list of all work completed and a copy of the receipts.

Nyon Castle, Vaud

# 7.
# MONEY MATTERS

One of the most important aspects of buying a home in Switzerland and living there (even for relatively brief periods) is finance, which includes everything from transferring and changing money to mortgages and taxes. The good news is that Switzerland is one of the lowest taxed countries in the world – for both direct and indirect taxes – and has very low inflation. The bad news is that it also has one of the highest costs of living, particularly in the major cities.

---

**⚠ Important Note**

The information in this chapter is based on the market in late 2009. Bear in mind, however, that due to the banking crisis in the last few years, the situation regarding mortgages is very fluid and likely to change at short notice. Before making any large financial transactions you should always obtain advice from your accountant or bank.

---

If you're planning to invest in a property in Switzerland financed with imported funds, it's important to consider both the present and possible future exchange rates. On the other hand, if you live and work in Switzerland and are paid in Swiss francs, this may affect your financial commitments abroad. If your income is received in a currency other than Swiss francs, it can be exposed to risks beyond your control when you live in Switzerland, particularly regarding inflation and exchange rate fluctuations.

If you own a home in Switzerland, you can employ a Swiss accountant or tax adviser to look after your financial affairs there and declare and pay your local taxes. You can also have a representative receive your bank statements, ensure that your bank is paying your standing orders (e.g. for utilities) and that you have sufficient funds to pay them. If you let a home in Switzerland through a Swiss company, they may perform the above tasks as part of their services.

If you plan to live in Switzerland, whether temporarily or permanently, you must ensure that your income is (and will remain) sufficient to live on – 'leisured foreigners' must provide proof – bearing in mind devaluations, rises in the cost of living, and unforeseen expenses such as medical bills or anything else that may reduce your income. You can obtain an assessment of your tax liability from a cantonal tax office.

## SWISS CURRENCY

The unit of Swiss currency is the Swiss franc (*Frank, franc*), one of the strongest and most stable currencies in the world, backed up by low inflation of well below 1 per cent and a central bank interest rate of just 0.25 per cent (since 12th March 2009). The Swiss franc is divided into 100 cents (*Rappen, centime*) and Swiss coins are minted in values of 5, 10, 20 and 50 cents and 1, 2 and 5 francs. Banknotes are printed in denominations of 10, 20, 50, 100, 200 and 1,000 francs. High-tech banknotes with a wide range of security features have been introduced in recent years and are allegedly 'virtually impossible' to counterfeit. The new notes contain five visible safety features, plus a second level detectable by special equipment and a third level known only to the central bank.

The Swiss franc is usually written CHF (the official international abbreviation), as used in this book. When writing figures in Switzerland, a quotation mark (') is used to separate units of millions, thousands and hundreds, and a comma (,) to denote cents, e.g. 1'500'485,34 is one million, five hundred thousand, four hundred and eighty five francs and 34 cents – a nice healthy bank balance! Values below one franc are written as a percentage of a franc rather than in cents, e.g. 0,75 is seventy-five cents (note that in this book they're written in the standard English format, with a point instead of a comma, e.g. CHF 0.75).

In the last few years the Swiss franc has been a major beneficiary of the worldwide economic meltdown – being traditionally seen as a refuge in times of turmoil – during which it gained in value against most major currencies.

## IMPORTING & EXPORTING MONEY

Switzerland has no currency restrictions and you may import or export as much money as you wish, in any currency. The Swiss franc exchange rate (*Wechselkurs, taux de change*) against most European and major international currencies is listed in banks and daily newspapers and on websites such as 🖳 www.xe.com.

If you plan to send a large amount of money to Switzerland for a business transaction or to buy property, you should ensure that you receive the commercial rate of exchange rather than the tourist rate. Shop around! There are many companies that specialise in foreign exchange, particularly large sums of money, such as Currencies Direct (🖳 www.currenciesdirect.com), HiFX (🖳 www.hifx.co.uk) and Moneycorp (🖳 www.moneycorp.com).

## BANKS

If there's one place in Switzerland where you can be sure of a warm welcome, it's a Swiss bank (unless you plan to rob it!). It will probably come as no surprise that there are lots of banks in Switzerland, although many have closed in recent years or been swallowed up by the major banks. Switzerland is one of the most 'over-banked' countries in the world and in addition to the two

major banks (UBS, Switzerland's largest bank, and Crédit Suisse), which have branches in most towns, there are many smaller regional, canton, loan and savings banks, plus private (mainly portfolio management) and foreign banks.

If you do a lot of travelling abroad, you may find that the comprehensive range of services provided by the major Swiss banks is more suited to your needs than those of smaller banks. The major banks are more likely to have staff who speak English and other foreign languages, and they can provide statements and other documentation in English and other non-Swiss languages. The major Swiss banks also offer 24-hour banking via ATMs and the internet, although this applies to most banks nowadays.

In a small country town or village, there's usually a branch of one of the local banks (e.g. Raiffeisenbank, Banque Raiffeisen) and a post office, but not a branch of a major bank. Local banks usually provide a more personal service, may offer cheaper loans and mortgages than the major banks, and (in most cantons) provide a guarantee for deposits. Many Swiss prefer using local cantonal banks.

### General Information

The following points apply to most Swiss banks:

♦ All bills can be paid through your bank. Simply send the payment forms to your bank with a completed payment advice form (provided by banks on request) or drop them in your bank's post box, and your bank will make a payment order (*Zahlungsauftrag, ordre de paiement*). This method of payment is free and has the advantage that your payments (or the total payment) are recorded on your monthly bank statement. Alternatively you can pay your bills at a post office or via the bank machines provided (e.g. UBS Multimat machines) in branch lobbies.

♦ Internet banking is provided by most Swiss banks and is usually free.

♦ Buying stocks and bonds in Switzerland is normally done through a bank and not through a stockbroker. Most banks post the latest Swiss share prices in all branches and some have computer enquiry systems where information is displayed on a screen. Swissquote (🖳 www.swissquote.ch) is the leader in online trading in Switzerland.

◆ You can open a foreign currency account with any Swiss bank. However, if you receive a transfer from abroad, make sure that it's deposited in the correct account – it could be deposited in a foreign currency account, even if you don't have one!

◆ All correspondence from the major Swiss banks can be requested in English and certain other non-Swiss languages, in addition to French, German and Italian.Note that banks charge postage for each item sent to you, e.g. CHF 1 or 0.85, depending on whether you choose 'A' or 'B' class post.

◆ Many banks offer extra interest to students or youths aged, for example, from 16 to 20. This costs the banks very little as most students are broke, but all banks know that you need to 'get 'em while they're young', as few people change banks (which is why some banks offer to open a savings account for your new baby with a free deposit of CHF 25 or 50!).

◆ An account holder can create a joint account by giving his spouse (or anyone else) signatory authority. A joint account can be for two or more people.

◆ At the end of the year (or more frequently, depending on your bank) you'll receive a statement listing all bank charges, interest paid or earned and the taxes, e.g. federal withholding tax (see page 192), deducted during the previous year. If you're a Swiss taxpayer, you should keep this in a safe place as when you complete your income tax return you can reclaim the withholding tax and any interest paid is tax deductible.

◆ The charge for standing orders from a salary account is around CHF 15 a year. Standing orders are paid automatically, provided there are sufficient funds in your account to cover them. If you have insufficient funds in your account, your bank may not pay your standing order payments (*Dauerauftrag*, *ordre permanent*) and may not inform you of this.

◆ If an American citizen wishes to hold US securities in a Swiss account, he must sign a form stating that either the Swiss bank is allowed to inform the IRS about the account or that on the sale of the securities a withholding tax of 31 per cent of the profits or capital gains will be levied. All other account holders must sign a statement to the effect that they aren't American citizens and have no tax liabilities in the US.

All major Swiss banks produce numerous free brochures and booklets (many in English) describing their services and containing interesting and useful information. The major banks also publish newsletters in English and other foreign languages, which are sent free to customers.

## Opening Hours

Normal bank opening hours are from 8 or 9am to 4.30 or 5pm Mondays to Fridays, with continuous service during the lunch period in cities and large towns. Most banks are open late, e.g. until 5.30 or 6.30pm, on one day a week, depending on the bank and its location. In cities, a few banks have extended opening hours during the week and are open on Saturdays from around 9am to 4pm. In large shopping centres (*Einkaufszentrum, centre commercial*) most banks are open until 5pm on Saturdays and major banks are also open on Saturdays in many tourist areas.

There are no general opening hours for 'village' banks, which may be closed on Monday mornings and Wednesday afternoons and open on Saturday mornings. They usually close for lunch, which may extend from 11.45am until 2pm, but often remain open until 5.30pm, Mondays to Fridays. Banks at Swiss airports and major SBB stations are open from around 6.30 or 7am until 6.30pm (10.30pm at major airports).

In major cities there are 24-hour automated banking centres, where you can purchase foreign currencies, change foreign currency into Swiss francs, buy travellers' cheques and

gold, change Swiss banknotes and coins, and rent safety deposit boxes. You can also obtain 24-hour telephone customer advice, stock market and general banking information via computer terminals. These services are provided in addition to the usual automatic banking facilities, such as cash withdrawals, deposits and checking account balances.

## Opening a Bank Account

One of your first acts in Switzerland should be to open a bank account. Simply go to the bank of your choice and tell them you're living or working in Switzerland and wish to open a private (*Privatkonto, compte personnel*) or current account (*kontkorrent, compte currante*). Some companies have a preferential arrangement with a particular bank, which may offer lower bank charges for employees. Current accounts in Swiss francs and foreign currencies are available to all residents.

Banks offer a range of other accounts, including a variety of savings accounts providing higher interest rates than a salary or current account. Migros bank (💻 www.migrosbank.ch), owned by Switzerland's largest supermarket chain, usually pays higher interest than most other banks.

After opening an account, if you'll be working in Switzerland, don't forget to give the account details to your employer (or you won't be paid). Your salary is normally paid by your employer directly into your bank account. Your monthly salary statement is sent to your home address or given to you at work.

Bank statements are usually issued monthly (optionally daily, weekly or quarterly); interest is paid on deposits and an overdraft facility is usually available. With a salary account, as well as a monthly or quarterly statement, you receive confirmation of payment of standing orders and a credit advice for deposits other than your salary. Bank charges are levied annually, plus postal and other charges. Note

that if you ask your bank to retain your post for collection, fees can be astronomical. You don't receive a cheque book with any account, but an account 'debit' card containing your encoded account information.

There are considerable differences in bank fees, for example UBS and Crédit Suisse are the most expensive for accounts with relatively small balances, although if the balance averages over CHF 10,000 fees are reduced. Some banks charge fees only if you don't maintain a minimum balance. If you have less than CHF 10,000 in your UBS account, you pay CHF 0.30 for payments to another Swiss bank and CHF 5 for payments to banks outside Switzerland. Smaller banks, such as cantonal banks, Migros and Coop bank, usually have lower fees.

If you pay a cheque drawn on a non-Swiss bank into a Swiss bank account, it may take weeks to be cleared and can be very expensive.

## Paying Bills

In contrast with many other countries, cheques drawn on bank accounts aren't the most important everyday means of payment in Switzerland (in fact cheques are hardly ever used in Switzerland due to the high fees imposed by banks). Most people pay their bills via the post office giro service, online (via e-banking) or via machines in bank branches which look like ATMs (ask for a demo).

An orange or red giro payment form (*Einzahlungsschein, bulletin de versement*) is usually included with every bill you receive by mail. The payment date (*Fällig am . . ./Zahlbar bis . . ., payable le . . ./échéance . . .*) is usually stated on the bill accompanying the giro payment form, or the number of days within

which you must pay the bill. Payment is usually due immediately or within 10, 30 or 60 days. Some creditors offer a discount for prompt payment of bills or payment in cash. If it's a regular bill (e.g. rent or utility) you can give your bank a permanent bank payment (standing) order.

Payment forms produced by a computer include all the necessary details including your name and address, the payee's name and account number, and the amount due. If it's a non-computerised form you'll need to enter these details. If you're paying in person at a post office, post office payment forms must be completed in blue or black ink and in BLOCK CAPITALS. If you make a mistake you must complete a new form as you aren't permitted to make corrections. If you're paying via your bank (e-banking/bank business machines or a permanent payment order) then it doesn't matter if you make a mistake as you can correct it.

The left hand stub of the payment form is your receipt and is stamped by the post office clerk and returned to you when you pay bills at a post office.

## MORTGAGES

Switzerland has a large and sophisticated mortgage (*Hypotheke, hypothèque*) market, which is the cornerstone of its flourishing banking system. The country's unique mortgage system features the highest per capita mortgage indebtedness in the world, interest rates which almost never vary more than 2 to 3 per cent, and the highest withholding tax rate (see page 187) of any country.

The major mortgage lenders in Switzerland are the large national banks and the cantonal banks, although mortgages are also provided by regional, cooperative and savings banks (all Swiss banks are generally allowed to grant mortgages). The high level of foreign deposits in Switzerland, coupled with a high rate of domestic savings and the small population, results in a high rate of per capita mortgage indebtedness. Because of the vast mortgage debt, the mortgage rate is the leading interest rate indicator in Switzerland, and it has traditionally been kept low thanks to the huge capital inflows into the country and interest rate cartels maintained by Swiss banks.

There's also a direct link between the mortgage interest rate and inflation, where the rate of inflation is increased markedly by minor mortgage rate increases which have a direct affect on rents, which are in turn included in the Consumer Price Index (CPI) used to calculate inflation. Rising interest rates push up rental rates, which then exert upward pressure on wages, which are also tied to the CPI, leading to what is commonly referred to as the 'price-wage spiral'. Therefore, the mortgage rate isn't just a leading interest rate indicator, but is of major political importance, as it directly involves most Swiss and foreign residents, whether they're property owners, tenants or savers (the Swiss are the world's biggest savers).

Swiss regulations determine that rents for residential and business premises are dependent upon a reference interest rate (currently 3 per cent) set by the Swiss National Bank. The reference rate is based on the volume-weighted average interest rate of Swiss franc-denominated domestic mortgages held by banks in Switzerland, and is published quarterly. If the newly published reference rate doesn't correspond to the rate for variable-rate mortgages previously used for rental agreements, a landlord or tenant is entitled to call for the rent to be increased or decreased, as applicable.

### Tax Benefits

Buying property in Switzerland needs to be planned carefully in order to take full advantage of the tax benefits. Property is treated as an asset which is subject to both wealth and income tax, and its imputed rental value (*Eigenmietwert/valeur locative*) – estimated by cantonal or federal officials – must be declared as taxable income. However, the deemed rental value can be offset against mortgage interest payments which are tax-deductible, which is why it's standard practice to take out a large mortgage in Switzerland, even if it isn't essential, solely in order to offset the additional income tax which homeowners must pay. For the same reason, mortgage debt isn't usually paid down as it simply doesn't make any financial sense, which is particularly true for homeowners in the higher tax brackets. Mortgage interest can generally be offset against any rental income earned on a property, which also minimises the amount of tax payable.

---

### ☑ SURVIVAL TIP

There are several initiatives afoot to abolish the imputed rental value (*Eigenmietwert/valeur locative*) along with the deductions for mortgage interest, which are particularly onerous for retirees with little income and no mortgage.

---

Mortgages in Switzerland can be repaid either directly (direct amortisation) or indirectly (indirect amortisation). With direct repayment the loan amount decreases with every mortgage repayment, which reduces the mortgage debt and, in turn, the interest charges. However, the tax-deductible amount is also reduced and your income tax burden increases as the tax deductions reduce. With indirect repayment, the mortgage debt remains the same for the whole of the term and instead of making mortgage repayments directly to your mortgage account, you pay contributions into a 3rd Pillar pension account (see **Pension Mortgages** on page 179). These contributions aren't used to pay off the mortgage debt until the 3rd Pillar account is closed, which has considerable tax advantages.

Instead of investing in a 3rd Pillar, you can also invest in a life insurance policy which attracts a special low rate of tax.

## Swiss Mortgages

Swiss banks generally grant mortgages of up to 80 per cent (sometimes more) of the current market value of a property, which means that you must usually pay a minimum 20 per cent deposit from your own resources (see **Deposits** below). The larger the deposit, the lower your monthly mortgage payments, although repayments cannot usually be more than one-third of your gross salary.

A Swiss mortgage is usually made up of a first and, if necessary, a second mortgage. The first mortgage is usually 66 per cent of the property's value and the second mortgage the balance of the amount borrowed up to 80 per cent of the value or 80 per cent loan-to-value (LTV). In the example shown below (under **Status & Affordability**), the balance of the mortgage is CHF 70,000 (or 14 per cent of the property's market value), which is the second mortgage. The minimum loan amount is usually CHF 50,000-200,000, depending on the type of mortgage chosen.

There's no mandatory amortisation of the first mortgage, which is interest only and isn't paid until maturity, usually between the age of 60 and 70. The second mortgage, which covers the balance of the loan has an interest rate around 0.75 per cent higher than the first mortgage, because of its secondary claim on the collateral. This must usually be paid off (amortised) by the age of 60, with a minimum 1 per cent of the loan amount repayable each year (usually payable quarterly). The length of the first mortgage term can be anywhere between 5 and 50 years up to the age of 70.

Swiss mortgages of between 50 and 65 per cent of the sale price are also available to residents buying second or holiday homes in Switzerland and to **non-residents**. The LTV depends on the lender and the canton; when buying off plan, the developer may have an arrangement with a particular lender whereby a higher LTV (up to 80 per cent) is offered when a bank is appointed as the sole lender for a development.

If you can provide acceptable collateral (security), other than the property that you're buying, you'll qualify for a larger mortgage. Interest rates (see below) are higher for holiday homes, second homes, and industrial and commercial buildings, both for residents and non-residents.

## Interest Rates

Swiss mortgages are available to both residents and non-residents and traditionally have enjoyed among the lowest interest rates in the world; the base rate set by the Swiss National Bank fell to just 0.25 per cent in March 2009, an historic low. Swiss variable mortgage rates in 2010 were from just 2.5 per cent and in the last ten years have never been higher than 4.5 per cent. There's relatively little difference between fixed and variable rate mortgages in Switzerland, with variable rates starting at around 2.5 per cent and fixed rates varying from 1.25 per cent (one-year fix) to between 3 and 3.7 per cent for a ten-year fixed rate mortgage.

The low rates in 2009 for fixed-rate mortgages made them much more attractive to buyers and they were chosen by the vast majority of buyers. There are also combined fixed and variable rate mortgages, where part of the mortgage loan has a fixed rate of interest and part a variable rate of interest. Note that a 1 per cent increase in the mortgage rate – for example from 3 to 4 per cent – will result in a one-third increase in your monthly mortgage payments!

Mortgages designated in Swiss francs have long been a favourite for international property purchases, although they're risky for anyone whose income isn't in Swiss francs. If the currency in which you earn your income is devalued against the Swiss franc, your mortgage payments can rise dramatically (as many people found to their cost in the last few years).

Before taking out a mortgage you should obtain offers from at least three banks; however, bear in mind that it isn't uncommon for banks to make a better offer than the advertised or market rate. One quick way to compare mortgages is by using a comparison tool such as that provided by Comparis (🖥 www.comparis.ch/hypotheken/default.aspx, ☎ 44-360 52 61). This allows you to compare variable and fixed-rate offers (over 1-15 year) in a particular canton at a glance and indicates the current 'top offer' (but not the lender!). For a fee of CHF 290 you can make a detailed mortgage request online via the Comparis Mortgage Market, which is sent anonymously to various banks and insurance companies. The fee is refunded by Comparis if you receive no offers or by the lender if you conclude a mortgage agreement. Other websites, such 🖥 www.homegate.ch, offer a similar service.

It's advisable to arrange a mortgage in principle before committing to a purchase or even looking at properties. This will allow you to confirm how much you can borrow so that you don't waste time looking at properties that you cannot afford. Even if you haven't found a property that you wish to buy, you can establish what you can afford to pay and obtain an 'approval in principle' based on your current financial situation.

## Status & Affordability

In order to obtain a Swiss mortgage, it's necessary to prove your income and status to prospective lenders (non-status loans without proof of income aren't offered in Switzerland). A lender will also want to know that the property you're planning to purchase is adequate in terms of security and that you can reasonably be expected to meet the mortgage repayments. As a general rule, a Swiss lender will check all your current liabilities including mortgage or rental obligations, credit card debts, personal loans, maintenance payments, extra costs (household bills), etc. If you're already a Swiss resident, a lender may check whether you have any debts with the Swiss Debt Enforcement Office (*Betreibungsamt, office des poursuites*).

Lenders also make an annual allowance for the ancillary or incidental expenses associated with owning a home, such as extra costs (charges), utilities and property maintenance, which is usually calculated as 1 per cent of the property valuation. These are largely the same as those paid by a tenant, although owner-occupiers incur additional costs such as building insurance, maintenance and repairs. The total of all your liabilities shouldn't exceed one-third of your gross income in order to qualify for a Swiss mortgage, although some lenders allow a little leeway.

You will need to prove your income by providing a copy of your current salary verification (*Lohnausweis/certificat de salaire*), a copy of your last tax return including attachments, and a current 'debt collection' report (not older than three months), available from your municipal debt inforcement office. Some lenders will take the potential rental income from the property that you're planning to purchase into account, therefore you'll need to shop around if this is important. A life insurance policy could be requested by a lender, depending on their credit policy; Swiss banks sometimes also require insurance for personal loans.

The table below shows the costs for a married couple aged 40 buying a home in Zurich (8004), valued at CHF 500,000 with a 10-year fixed rate mortgage.

The example shown in the box is based on actual interest rates offered at the time this book went to press. Because the couple – or main wage earner – is aged 40, the second mortgage must re repaid over 20 years, i.e. by age 60. Some banks calculate the affordability using an average mortgage rate over the last 20 years, e.g. 5 per cent for the first mortgage and 5.75 per cent for the second mortgage, which are much higher than the current rates available. **Note that the above costs don't take into account the income tax benefit of having a mortgage.**

Many websites (e.g. 🖥 www.comparis.ch, www.homegate.ch, https://entry.credit-suisse.ch and www.ubs.com) contain a mortgage calculator, where you can obtain an estimate of the cost of buying a property and how much you can afford to borrow.

A table showing the annual payments for mortgages from CHF 500,000 to 2mn is shown in the table opposite.

## Deposit

The deposit can be paid in cash or with certain assets that can be pledged as security, although only a limited range of assets are acceptable for non-residents, e.g. foreign life policies and properties aren't accepted, but time deposits held by foreign institutions are. Swiss residents can

| Annual Mortgage Costs | |
|---|---|
| **Item** | **Amount (CHF)** |
| Purchase price | 500,000 |
| Deposit (20%) | 100,000 |
| Borrowing (80%) | 400,000 |
| Costs: | |
| - interest 1st mortgage (CHF 330,000/66% @ 3.6%) | 11,880 |
| - interest 2nd mortgage (CHF 70,000/14% @ 4.35%) | 3,045 |
| - ancillary costs (1% of the purchase price) | 5,000 |
| - Amortisation of 2nd mortgage at 5% (paid over 20 years) | 3,500 |
| **Annual Costs** | **23,425*** |
| (Monthly costs | 1,952) |

In the above example, the couple would need a joint gross income of 3 x 23,425 = CHF 70,275. In order to buy a property costing CHF 1mn (i.e. double the above purchase cost), the couple would need a CHF 200,000 deposit and an income of approx. CHF 135,774. Note, however, that a bank doesn't always take into consideration the salary of a spouse, e,g, a young wife who may stop work to have children.

also pledge their Swiss pension funds (2nd/3rd pillar – see page 174) and insurance policies with a surrender value.

The simplest way for Swiss residents to raise the deposit – and the most tax efficient option – is to pledge their 2nd/3rd pillar pension funds (see below). Contributions to this are tax-free as are profits on the investment/interest. You also aren't required to have the full deposit or amount required in your pension fund, as a bank will usually accept the commitment as security. However, the lender will insist on risk insurance to cover the sum, the amount of which decreases as your 3rd pillar fund increases.

### Using a Swiss Pension as Deposit Security

If you're a Swiss resident and working in Switzerland, you can use the capital from your company or occupational pension fund (2nd pillar) and/or private pension fund (3rd pillar) as collateral for the deposit to fund or build a primary residence, but not to buy a second or holiday home. You can acquire the property as sole or joint owner, buy the freehold to an apartment in a larger building, invest in the property to increase or maintain its value, or buy a share in a housing association.

This is a tax-privileged way to finance owner-occupied residential property; you use your accrued pension capital as a deposit, or, instead of paying off your mortgage directly, you can make indirect repayments to a 3rd pillar account or life insurance policy, which has considerable tax benefits (see **Tax Benefits** on page 169).

The advance withdrawal or pledge of occupational retirement funds is governed by

## Mortgage Calculation Table

| Price (Sfr.) | Deposit (20%) | Loan (80%) | Mortgage Sum* Mort. 1 (66%) | Mort. 2 (Bal.) | Annual Interest* Mort. 1 (3.6%) | Mort. 2 (4.35%) | Ancillary Costs | Annual Amort. (1%) | Total Charges | Monthly Costs (5%) | Minimum Annual Income |
|---|---|---|---|---|---|---|---|---|---|---|---|
| 500,000 | 100,000 | 400,000 | 330,000 | 70,000 | 11,880 | 3,045 | 5,000 | 3,500 | 23,425 | 2,020 | 70,275 |
| 750,000 | 150,000 | 600,000 | 495,000 | 105,000 | 17,820 | 4,567 | 7,500 | 5,250 | 35,137 | 2,928 | 105,411 |
| 1mn | 200,000 | 800,000 | 660,000 | 140,000 | 23,760 | 6,090 | 10,000 | 7,000 | 46,850 | 3,904 | 140,550 |
| 1.5mn | 300,000 | 1.2mn | 990,000 | 210,000 | 35,640 | 9,135 | 15,000 | 10,500 | 70,275 | 5,856 | 210,825 |
| 2mn | 400,000 | 1.6mn | 1.32m | 280,000 | 47,520 | 12,180 | 20,000 | 14,000 | 93,700 | 7,808 | 281,100 |

* Mortgage 1 (Mort. 1) is equal to 66% of the sum borrowed; the balance is mortgage 2 (Mort. 2).

N.B. All examples are for a couple 40 year of age, 10-year fixed rate mortgage. Second mortgage repaid over 20 years.

Swiss Federal Law to encourage the use of vested pension accruals for home ownership. Ask your employer for an up-to-date pension fund statement which will show your pension entitlement, which will be required by your lender. Both the Federal Social Insurance Office (🖳 www.bsv.admin.ch) and the insurance institutions involved can provide independent advice about pledging your pension for the deposit on a home.

### 2nd Pillar: Company or Occupational Pension

You can opt to withdraw money from your 2nd pillar pension fund or to pledge it as security; pledging it as security is by far the better option – shop around for a bank that will accept your 2nd pillar as security. If you choose (or are forced) to withdraw the money from your fund, tax – which varies depending on the canton – is due immediately and the advance cannot be offset against income tax. Lump-sum payments from pension funds are declared separately from other income and are taxed at a reduced rate at the federal, cantonal and communal level.

---

**☑ SURVIVAL TIP**

If you repay the capital into your 2nd pillar fund at a later date, the tax is refunded, albeit without interest. Note, however, that if you sell your home without buying another owner-occupier (principal) home in Switzerland, you must repay the capital you received into your 2nd pillar fund, and the payment isn't deductible from taxable income for the purposes of federal income tax. You can, however, reclaim the tax paid (without interest) by proving that you have repaid the sum in question.

---

If you pledge your 2nd pillar fund to obtain a mortgage, you'll either be granted a reduction on the interest on your second mortgage or be permitted to borrow more than 80 per cent of the market value of the property. The pledge has no impact on the down payment and serves only to help you borrow additional capital. For example if you need CHF 200,000 for a 20 per cent deposit on a CHF 1mn property, but only have CHF 100,000 in cash, you can pledge CHF 100,000 from your 2nd pillar fund (assuming you have enough) to make up your 20 per cent deposit. Note, however, that this generally leads to higher annual mortgage repayments and you must take out risk insurance against death and disability.

If you pledge your retirement assets and take out risk insurance, you can obtain an interest-bearing loan, usually 90 per cent of your pension entitlement. In return, the bank will undertake to pay off the loan in instalments after a given period, so that you have access to your total, unpledged retirement assets when you reach retirement age. The interest which you pay on the loan can also be deducted from your taxable income.

### 3rd Pillar: Private Pension

Savings held in a 3rd pillar account and/or safekeeping account can also be used as a deposit for the purchase or construction of a home that you're going to live in as your main residence. You can also make partial withdrawals every five years. Payouts are taxed differently according to the canton and capital is generally taxed separately from other income and subject to a reduced rate. A number of websites (e.g. 🖳 www.credit-suisse.com) have calculators where you can calculate the tax on lump-sum withdrawals from your 3rd pillar fund.

## Refinancing

If you already own your home and your mortgage is about to expire, you aren't required to refinance or extend your mortgage with the same bank, or under the same terms and conditions, but can shop around and check deals offered by other lenders. You can forward fix your mortgage with some lenders up to two years in advance, which may allow you to take advantage of low interest rates. It isn't necessary to replace your whole mortgage at the same time if your mortgage is in tranches, and you can replace each tranche when the term expires.

You can also refinance your mortgage with your existing lender, although there may be a penalty or fee for changing to a more favourable product – just because you signed up for the wrong mortgage at the wrong time, it doesn't mean that you're stuck with it until the end of the term. For example, if you have a variable mortgage you can usually switch to a fixed rate mortgage, although there's usually a fee.

You may find it advantageous to change your main bank and transfer your savings accounts, as some lenders offer attractive deals to get your business. For example UBS, offers new customers a 50:50 mortgage, where you get a reduction of 0.5 per cent off the standard interest rate when you transfer the balance on your current or custody (e.g. savings) account to them. The reduction applies to the whole mortgage for a period of three years, provided the balance in your current account is equivalent to at least half the mortgage sum.

You can compare mortgage offers online using the websites listed under **Interest Rates** above.

It may pay you to switch your mortgage to another product or lender, even when it involves paying an early repayment penalty. However, before doing this you should do your sums carefully and take advice from an independent mortgage broker or analyst.

## Types of Mortgages

Swiss borrowers can choose from a wide range of mortgages, the most common of which have a fixed or variable interest rate or a combination. The main types of mortgages offered by Swiss banks are:

♦ **Fixed rate mortgage:** the mortgage interest rate is fixed for a number of years or for the entire term, up to a maximum of 10 or 15 years depending on the lender; it offers maximum protection against rising interest rates and is the best strategy when interest rates are low (see also **Fixed Rate Mortgages** on page 176);

♦ **Variable rate mortgage:** the mortgage is subject to interest rate fluctuations; you benefit from falling interest rates but if interest rates rise your payments can rise sharply (see also **Variable Rate Mortgages** on page 177);

♦ **Combined rate mortgage:** a fixed and variable rate mortgage in one, where part of the mortgage has a fixed interest rate and is protected against interest rate increases and the other part has a variable rate of interest (see also **Combined Rate Mortgages** on page 177);

Banks also offer a wide range of other mortgages, including special offers for first-time buyers and families, plans for those building a home or buying off plan, and specialist money market mortgages, many of which are listed below.

♦ **50:50 mortgage:** a mortgage where you get a reduction of 0.5 per cent off the standard interest rate on the whole mortgage for a period of three years, provided the balance on your current or custody (savings) account balance is equivalent to at least half of the amount of the mortgage. This is offered to new customers only.

♦ **8 for 6 mortgage:** a mortgage where you receive an 8-year fixed-rate mortgage at the rate of a 6-year fixed-rate mortgage. Your gain is twofold: you secure a current low interest rate over the long term and at the same time lock in today's preferential interest rates.

### Building Loans

A special loan or mortgage for those who are buying off plan or building their own home – usually termed a building or construction loan – which can also be used for major renovations and extending (or remodelling) a home, where the loan is drawn in tranches as the building progresses. See also **Building Loans** on page 178.

◆ **Eco/Minergie mortgage:** the lender rewards your commitment to sustainable construction and renovation of buildings according to the Minergie standard and the use of solar technology.

◆ **Family mortgage:** a mortgage with more favourable interest conditions for families with children under 18 years of age, which are offered by a number of lenders under various names.

◆ **Flex or Flexible mortgage:** a mortgage where interest rate movements are kept within a predefined band (with both a floor and ceiling), thus protecting you from sharp rises in interest rates. Interest rates are revised every three months and hedging costs are included in the interest rate. The costs are based on the low LIBOR rate for three-month money (see also **Money market/LIBOR mortgage** below).

◆ **Forward (fix) mortgage:** If financing isn't required for some months or even years in the future, many lenders allow you to arrange a mortgage in advance. For example, you may which to arrange a mortgage for when your current fixed-rate mortgage expires or you're building a home and will require finance. You can usually protect the interest rate of your fixed-rate mortgage up to two years in advance, for which a special premium is payable.

◆ **Graduated mortgage:** a mortgage where Interest repayments are distributed according to a certain formula over a fixed period. This is aimed at new buyers (see also **Start-up bonus mortgage** below) who may wish to make lower repayments at the beginning and gradually increase them over time, e.g. as their income increases.

◆ **Money market/LIBOR mortgage:** A mortgage with a variable interest rate over a duration, e.g. one to five years, agreed in advance. The interest rate is revised every three to six months according to the corresponding LIBOR (London Interbank Offered Rate) index. Depending on the provider, a money market mortgage cannot be terminated before the expiry date or only against payment of a penalty for premature termination. Money market mortgages usually have a cap/ceiling and/or a floor, whereby the interest rate cannot exceed a certain maximum (ceiling) or go below a certain minimum rate (floor). A specialist mortgage product for those who follow developments on the money and capital markets.

◆ **Rollover mortgage:** a mortgage which combines a fixed mortgage with a money market mortgage.

◆ **Start-up bonus (or Low-start) mortgage**: a fixed-rate mortgage for first-time buyers with favourable conditions – such as a 0.5 per cent interest rate reduction on half the loan amount for half the agreed term (which applies to both the first and second mortgages). These are offered by most lenders, although the name varies. Some lenders also offer similar conditions for new customers wishing to refinance a mortgage.

◆ **Portfolio mortgage:** a portfolio mortgage (a similar mortgage from Credit Suisse is called a 'Flex Rollover mortgage') is a fixed rate mortgage which is split into tranches with different maturity dates, also called a fixed mix. This limits the risk due to an increase in interest rates and means that you can avoid having to renew all your financing at one time, which could coincide with an unfavourable interest-rate environment. There's usually a minimum loan of around CHF 100,000. However, you need to be aware that this locks you into the lender and makes it more difficult to refinance your mortgage with another lender at a better rate. If you cancel any mortgage tranche before the end of its fixed rate period, you must pay a penalty! **It's advisable to seek independent financial advice (not from the bank trying to sell you a portfolio mortgage) before taking it out.**

### Fixed Rate Mortgages

A fixed rate mortgage is where the interest rate is fixed for a number of years or the entire term, although there's usually a maximum period of 10 or 15 years. It's ideal for those with a fixed income who need to know exactly how much their mortgage will cost over a number of years, as it offers protection against rising interest rates. However, bear in mind that if you take out a long-term fixed rate mortgage when interest rates are falling, then you'll find yourself paying more than necessary. In 2009, when interest rates were at rock bottom, over 90 per cent of mortgages in Switzerland were at a fixed rate. You can also forward fix your mortgage rate, e.g. up to two years prior to payment, which allows you to take advantage of low rates and plan your mortgage costs in advance. There's usually a minimum loan of around CHF 100,000.

The longer the fixed rate period the higher the interest rate – typical rates for one to ten year fixed-rate mortgages in early 2010 are shown in the box below.

### Sample Fixed-Rate Mortgage Interest Rates 2010

| Term (Years) | Interest Rate* (%) |
|---|---|
| 1 | 1.85 |
| 2 | 1.87 |
| 3 | 2.22 |
| 4 | 2.49 |
| 5 | 2.75 |
| 6 | 2.96 |
| 7 | 3.13 |
| 8 | 3.27 |
| 9 | 3.39 |
| 10 | 3.50 |

* Actual rates quoted by UBS in January 2010.

It's possible to terminate a fixed rate mortgage early, but it can be expensive as there are penalties for early termination. Penalty payments are usually based on the remaining duration of the original agreement or on the difference in interest, i.e. the interest payable over the remaining years of the mortgage.

### Variable Rate Mortgages

Variable rate mortgages – also called adjustable-rate, dynamic, flex or flexible mortgages – are where the mortgage interest rate fluctuates with the bank rate set by the Swiss National Bank. You benefit from falling interest rates but if interest rates rise your payments can rise sharply. Interest rates for variable rate mortgages are lower than for fixed mortgages, but you don't have the security of knowing what you'll be paying for a number of years. There's usually a minimum loan of around CHF 100,000.

Note that if the mortgage rate increases by 1 per cent, e.g. from 3 per cent to 4 per cent, your mortgage repayment will increase by a third!

However, when interest rates increase, most lenders will allow you to switch to a fixed rate mortgage, although it may take three to six months, and some banks impose a fee.

### Combined Rate Mortgages

A combined rate mortgage is a combination of a fixed and variable rate mortgage, where part of the loan has a fixed interest rate and is protected against interest rate increases, and the other part has a variable rate of interest, thus allowing for both security and flexibility. The mortgage is usually in two tranches (but can be more), e.g. a term of two to ten years (fixed tranche) and three years (variable tranche). A typical

variation is half fixed rate and half variable rate or two-thirds fixed and one-third variable, with each tranche having a different maturity date.

## Building Loans

Most lenders offer special mortgages for buyers who are buying off plan or building their own home – usually termed a building or construction loan – which can also be used for major renovations and extending (or remodelling) a home. There are various types of construction loans, which may include:

♦ A classic construction loan in the form of a current account loan, which is consolidated into a mortgage once the construction phase has been completed.

♦ A construction loan with fixed consolidation dates in the form of a current account loan, which is converted into a forward fix mortgage (part or the total credit amount) before or until the start of construction with a term beyond the completion of the building work.

♦ A construction loan with partial consolidation in the form of a current account loan, where part of the loan is converted into a mortgage prior to the completion of the construction phase, with a term extending beyond the planned completion of the building work.

With a new building, the mortgage is paid in tranches into a special construction loan account, as detailed in the contract schedule agreed with your builder or developer. The payment structure may vary depending on the location of the property, as regulations vary from canton to canton. You only pay interest on the actual amount borrowed until the building is completed and the full loan is drawn down. For examples of payment schedules, see **Stage Payments** on page 126.

The major Swiss banks also offer special Eco or 'MINERGIE® mortgages' with special rates and conditions to reward a borrower's commitment to sustainable construction or renovation of a building according to the Minergie standard and the use of solar technology (see **Building Your Own Home** on page 134). Benefits include extended financing (5 per cent of the market value), a longer amortisation period (e.g. five years) for the second mortgage, a lower imputed affordability calculation (with ancillary costs of 0.75 per cent of the total investment cost rather than 1 per cent) and Minergie certification costs up to a maximum sum, e.g. CHF 3,500.

Some lenders offer a mortgage overdraft facility to mortgage holders, which is a fixed credit limit, e.g. from CHF 25,000 to 200,000 depending on the market value of your home (up to around CHF 1.5mn) and your equity. The combined total of your mortgage and the overdraft facility cannot exceed 80 per cent of the market value of your home, minus any funds derived from pension schemes (e.g. pillars 2 and 3a) used to finance your mortgage.

This can be used to make renovations, extend your home or simply improve your cash flow. You are free to decide when you want to take advantage of the overdraft facility and you only pay interest on the amount used. You determine when you want to use or pay back the money available and benefit from a low interest rate.

Note that in some cantons, interest on building loans is counted as capital expenditure and therefore isn't deductible for income tax purposes. This applies in at the federal level in cantons Appenzell-Innerrhoden, Basle-City, Fribourg, Geneva, Glarus, Jura, Lucerne, Neuchâtel, Obwalden, Uri and Vaud. If the property is sold,

capital expenditure is deducted from the sales price to calculate the capital gain. In other cantons, i.e. Aargau, Appenzell-Ausserrhoden, Nidwalden, Valais and Zurich, interest on building loans can be deducted from taxable income as debit interest, while in Berne, Basle-Land, Graubünden and Schwyz you can choose whether to deduct building loan interest from income or offset it against capital expenditure when you sell.

## Pension Mortgages

There are various types of pension mortgages offered by lenders, which allow you to save for your retirement and also protect your home in the event of financial difficulties. A pension mortgage combines three different elements: financing, pension provision (a private 3rd pillar mortgage) and insurance. Many lenders also offer a lower interest rate, e.g. 0.25 per cent, for pension mortgages, which helps you to build up your pension fund. A pension mortgage also offers attractive tax advantages, as your payments to your 3rd pillar fund are tax deductible.

---

### ☑ SURVIVAL TIP

The maximum pension mortgage is usually around CHF 500,000 and it cannot be combined with other mortgage offers, such as a start-up bonus mortgage or construction loans.

---

With a pension mortgage, the mortgage is set up as interest only and the loan is paid off through the use of a 3rd pillar private pension, usually an endowment insurance policy, although special bank deposit accounts can also be used. This is called indirect amortisation, which is the latest 'buzz word' for mortgages in Switzerland.

Your 3rd pillar fund can not only boost your mortgage deposit, but it can also make your mortgage repayments more tax-efficient by reducing your income tax or withholding tax liability. In the case of indirect repayments, your instalments aren't paid to the bank but go into your 3rd pillar fund. The entire repayment is only made to the bank upon closure of your

3rd pillar retirement account, e.g. if you leave Switzerland or retire. You benefit from indirect repayments in the following three ways:

♦ your mortgage debt remains unchanged over the term, during which you can declare the full mortgage debt and offset the interest due against your income tax bill;

♦ you receive (tax-free) interest on your 3rd pillar retirement account for the repayment contributions you make;

♦ you can deduct the statutory maximum 3rd pillar contributions from your taxable income.

The downside is that pension mortgages have high initial set-up fees (which can take many years to recover) and the tax advantages may also be too insignificant for lower wage earners to benefit from them. Swiss banks also often have an exclusive arrangement with one insurance company (which they may own!), so you should compare products from many companies on the basis of both costs and performance.

If you don't have a pension mortgage and are planning a partial or full repayment of your mortgage, it may be worthwhile converting your mortgage to a pension mortgage and utilising your 3rd pillar pension fund contributions to reduce your income tax, rather than paying off your mortgage.

If you're considering a pension mortgage, you should have the figures (provided by lenders) checked by an independent financial adviser before signing any paperwork, as getting the best financing package could save you tens of thousands of francs in the long term.

## Mortgage Fees

There are various fees associated with mortgages. All lenders charge an arrangement fee for establishing a loan, usually around 1 per cent of the loan amount, although you may be able to negotiate a reduction depending on the lender and the mortgage sum. There's also a mortgage registration fee, which varies depending on the canton and the loan amount.

See **Purchase Costs** on page 129.

## Insurance Cover

Buying your own home is a big step and has long-term financial implications, therefore it's important to insure your family (and your mortgage repayments) against unforeseen events such as the incapacity to work due to an accident or extended illness, unemployment or death. Insurance is particularly important if only one person in the household is the breadwinner or if part of the property purchase is financed through early withdrawals from your pension fund.

Mortgage insurance cover is solely term life insurance, where the insured sum reduces the amount of your mortgage and thus lowers your housing costs in the case of an insured event. Your beneficiaries can usually choose between constant or variable capital payment upon your death.

Most lenders, particularly the major banks, have a preferred insurance company and may only offer or accept insurance from these companies. Theoretically this means that you pay lower or more 'attractive' premiums but in reality you may pay higher premiums than you would on the open market. Premiums may be guaranteed or fixed for a number of years and usually no medical examination is required.

Some lenders may insist on certain borrowers having life insurance and it's also mandatory with certain mortgage products, such as a pension mortgage. For example, life insurance must be taken out as part of a restricted retirement account 3a or an unrestricted retirement account 3b.

---

☑ **SURVIVAL TIP**

In addition to life and employment protection insurance, you'll also need buildings insurance (see page 231), which usually includes fire, water damage, property owner's liability and household insurance. The cost of insurance is included in your ancillary costs.

---

## INCOME TAX

Switzerland has no uniform system of taxation and income tax (*Einkommenssteuer*, *impôt sur le revenu*) is levied by the federal government (direct federal tax), cantons and communities.

The Swiss confederation and the 26 sovereign cantons all have their own laws for the collection of taxes, as do the 2,750 municipalities. This means that taxes can vary considerably from canton to canton and to a lesser extent from community to community, and you can reduce your tax bill by comparing the rates in a number of cantons and communities.

The rate of income tax levied in Switzerland varies between around 20 and 40 per cent (the total tax burden is around 30 per cent of GDP), which is good news for many foreigners, particularly those from most other European countries, although (overall) Swiss taxes are higher than the US.

In general, Swiss income tax rates are progressive and different rates usually apply for single and married taxpayers, as the income of a husband and wife is aggregated. Cantons (including municipalities) play by far the most significant role in the tax system, collecting some 70 per cent of all tax revenues, while the federal government levies the rest. For the most part, spending decisions are made at the level at which taxes are levied and there's no disconnect between tax sovereignty and the spending authority.

Cantonal tax rates vary considerably. Usually, the tariff mentioned in the cantonal tax act results only in so-called 'basic rates', which are subject to cantonal and municipal multipliers. Church taxes are levied in the same way.

The canton of Obwalden introduced a regressive system of income tax in 2006, whereby the more you earned the less income tax you paid! However, this was declared unconstitutional and was replaced by a flat rate for individual taxpayers.

There are many websites providing Swiss tax information, as well as tax comparisons between cantons or towns within a canton. The Federal Department of Finance (🖥 www.estv. admin.ch) has an online tax calculator for each canton, while the website Comparis (🖥 www. comparis.ch) provides canton and community tax comparisons and even has a facility to calculate the tax levied on foreigners who pay direct income tax (*Quellensteuer/impôt à la source*).

### Liability

An individual is resident in Switzerland if the centre of his vital interests is there (and in the applicable canton/municipality respectively), which includes key factors such as where a person has a permanent home, where his family lives and where his most important personal and economic contacts are. If you're domiciled or resident in Switzerland, you're liable for income tax on your worldwide income, subject to unilateral exceptions (e.g. foreign real estate) and tax treaty provisions (see below). You're considered resident in Switzerland if any of the following apply:

♦ you work in Switzerland for a minimum of 30 days or have a Swiss work permit;

♦ you carry on a business in Switzerland;

♦ you live in Switzerland for over 180 days a year, although if you remain in the same abode for 90 days a year you're considered to be a resident for tax purposes.

With the exception of the 'fiscal deal' method of taxation, Switzerland doesn't discriminate between Swiss residents and foreign employees of 'offshore' operations for the purposes of personal income tax. In any case, the Swiss authorities consider the various kinds of tax-privileged company as legitimate tax planning structures, which are available to both Swiss nationals and foreigners alike, and not as 'offshore' operations in the traditional sense of the word.

Some people who are domiciled abroad may have a limited Swiss tax liability and be required to pay tax as a result of their economic ties to Switzerland, e.g. real estate, business premises, etc. In addition, legal entities (limited companies, cooperatives, associations, foundations, etc.) with their registered offices or de facto management in Switzerland must pay tax there.

## Double Taxation Treaties

Switzerland has double taxation agreements with around 70 countries, some of which cover only tax on income while others also cover net-worth (wealth) tax. Despite the name, double-taxation treaties are to prevent your paying double taxes, and **not** to ensure that you pay twice! Under double taxation treaties, certain categories of people are exempt from paying Swiss tax. If part of your income is taxed abroad in a country with a double

taxation treaty with Switzerland, you won't have to pay Swiss tax on that income. Tax treaties don't affect the fiscal privileges of members of diplomatic missions or consular posts provided by the general rules of international law or special agreements.

The treaties apply to persons (an individual or a legal entity) who are residents of one or both of the contracting states. In general, residents of Switzerland taxed under the lump-sum tax system (see page 190) also fall into the personal scope of application of Swiss treaties, as they're considered to be residents. There's an exception in the treaties with Austria, Belgium, Canada, Germany, Italy, Norway and the USA. Under these treaties, Swiss residents subject to tax under the lump-sum system are only considered as residents when all their income from source in these contracting states is subject to ordinary taxation in Switzerland (the so-called modified lump-sum system). In addition, under the treaty with France, French nationals resident in Switzerland who are taxed only on the basis of the rental value of their home residence, aren't treated as residents by France.

The conventions with France, Italy, Austria and Germany provide special rules with respect to border commuters, i.e. persons who reside in those countries and commute daily to their workplaces in Switzerland, who are taxed in their country of residence.

Citizens of most countries (the US is the main exception) are exempt from paying taxes in their home country when they spend a minimum period abroad, e.g. one year. It's your responsibility to familiarise yourself with the latest tax procedures in your home country or country of domicile. If you're in doubt about your tax liability in your home country, contact your embassy or consulate in Switzerland.

For further information, contact the Swiss Federal Tax Office (International Fiscal Law and Double-Taxation Matters, Eigerstrasse 65, CH-3003 Berne, ☏ 031-322 71 06, ▭ www.estv.admin.ch).

## Taxable Income

Swiss tax laws apply a rather broad concept of income which includes salaries and wages, and any other income derived for any activity performed in an employed or self-employed occupation. This includes secondary income derived from special services; commissions, allowances; seniority and anniversary gifts; gratuities; bonuses; tips and other wage- or salary-related remuneration; and benefits. Income from employment includes income from employment in the public or private sector; associated supplementary income; benefits in kind; and employees' share option schemes. It also includes income from movable and immovable property, retirement income, compensations, etc. All types of income are pooled and taxed together, with the exception of capital gains on immovable property.

The income of spouses who are legally married, and living together as husband and wife, is combined. Alimony payments are deductible for the payer and taxable for the recipient. The rental value of owner-occupied dwellings is also added to your taxable income (see **Property-related Income Tax** on page 184). The income of minor children is added to the income of the person who exercises parental care over them, except when a child obtains income from gainful employment, when it's taxed separately.

Recurring and non-recurring income of any kind is deemed income for tax purposes, including capital gains (see page 193), although capital gains made by residents on immoveable property in Switzerland are generally tax-exempt. Federal and cantonal tax regulations may differ in their treatment of exemptions, allowances and personal deductions; however, most cantons apply the same general principles in determining gross income. The concept of taxable income is broad and includes the following categories of income:

◆ earned income, i.e. income derived from any lucrative activity, including employment (salaries), professional and business income;

◆ investment income;

◆ compensatory income such as social security payments;

◆ income form other sources (sundry income).

Income from the above categories is usually combined and taxed at one rate, although annuities, pensions and other retirement income, usually benefit from more favourable tax treatment. Income from real estate comprises the deemed rental value of a principal (owner-occupied) home owned by a taxpayer.

Certain kinds of income aren't subject to income tax, including inheritance, bequests, gifts or matrimonial property allocations; proceeds from capital insurance; subsidies paid from private or public sources; compensation

for mental or physical pain suffered; and supplementary payments from retirement, survivors and disability insurance. Maintenance payments and other support finance to family members are tax-free (e.g. payments from the assets of a foundation), but alimonies are taxable. Most cantons also impose inheritance and gift taxes (see page 193).

## Tax Breakdown

Swiss income tax consists of the following taxes:

♦ **Federal tax** (*Direkte Bundessteuer, impôt fédéral direct*) is levied at rates between 0.77 and 11.5 per cent, depending on your income and comprising around 20 per cent of your total tax bill. It's assessed differently from cantonal and community taxes and entered on a separate tax form, sent with your community and cantonal tax forms. The deductions allowed against federal tax, based on your net annual salary, aren't the same as those for cantonal and community taxes.

♦ **Cantonal & community taxes** (*Staatssteuer/Kantonssteuer, impôt cantonale* and *Gemeindesteuer, impôt communal*) comprise by far the major part of your total tax bill. Generally, the richer the community, the lower its tax rate. You can compare the tax rate levied by cantons and communities on the Federal Department of Finance website (🖵 www. estv.admin.ch).

♦ **Fire service tax** (*Feuerwehrsteuer, taxe d'exemption au service de feu*) is paid by all male community residents who aren't active members of the local fire service. It may be calculated as a percentage of your basic tax value (see **Tax Calculation** on page 189) or may be a fixed sum (e.g. CHF 100 per year), depending on your canton. If you join the local fire department or you're aged over 44, you're exempt from paying fire service tax.

♦ **Church tax** (*Kirchensteuer, impôt écclésiastique*) is imposed in accordance with community income tax and is calculated as a percentage of your basic tax value. It's payable by all those who pay direct tax, but can be reclaimed by those who aren't registered as members of an official Swiss religion, e.g. the Reformed Church, the Roman Catholic Church and the Old Catholic (Protestant) Church. The amount payable varies from community to community depending on your canton and church, and may be up to 20 per cent of your basic tax value (or over CHF 1,000 a year for those earning CHF 100,000 per annum). For more information, see page 224.

## Federal Tax

Federal income tax is payable on incomes above CHF 16,900 for a single person and CHF 29,200 for a married couple, and is capped at 11.5 per cent (under the Swiss constitution) when income exceeds CHF 712,500 for singles and CHF 843,600 for married couples. The rates apply to married couples living together and also to widowed, separated, divorced or single persons living with children who are minors or studying full-time. An unmarried couple living together are taxed as single taxpayers.

| Swiss Federal Tax 2009 | | | | |
|---|---|---|---|---|
| Taxable Income (CHF) | Single Taxpayers Tax | % | Married Taxpayers Tax | % |
| 50,000 | 496.05 | 1.00 | 254 | 0.5 |
| 75,000 | 1,347.75 | | 996 | |
| 100,000 | 3140.75 | 3.14 | 2,171 | 2.17 |
| 120,000 | 4,900.75 | | 3,520 | |
| 150,000 | 8,044.55 | 5.36 | 6,846 | 4.56 |
| 180,000 | 11,648.15 | | 10,746 | |
| 200,000 | 14,288.15 | 7.14 | 13,346 | 6.67 |
| 300,000 | 27,488.15 | | 26,346 | |
| 400,000 | 40.688.15 | | 39,346 | |
| 500,000 | 53.888.15 | 10.78 | 52,346 | 10.47 |
| 750,000 | 86,250.00 | 11.5 | 84,846 | |
| 1,000,000 | 115,000.00 | 1.5 | 115,000 | 11.5 |

## Cantonal & Community Tax

The cantons not only set their own tax rates and tax brackets, but also have their own filing requirements, deduction provisions, and frameworks of rules to set and change tax laws. At the local level the 2,750 municipalities (*Gemeinde, commune*) also enjoy various degrees of sovereignty, depending on their respective canton's constitution. Canton and community taxes together comprise around 80 per cent of your income tax liability.

Tax rates are progressive – the more you earn the more tax you pay – apart from canton Obwalden which has a flat rate of tax of 1.8 per cent (the lowest in Switzerland). How progressive the system is also depends on the canton and varies according to whether you're married and how many children you have, as well as your community and religion. Married couples and their children under 18 are assessed jointly. A divorced or legally separated person is assessed separately.

Tax rates vary considerably between cantons and communities, with the income tax burden varying by a multiple of five between the lowest- and highest-taxed cantons. For example, a family with two children living in canton Zug and paying withholding tax on an income of CHF 100,000 could pay just 3.5 per cent income tax, while the same family in canton Geneva would pay over 17.25 per cent. The marginal tax rate in the top tax bracket in Zug is only 11.5 percent, while in Geneva it's almost 30 per cent. Other cantons fall somewhere between these extremes, with the lowest taxed cantons including Zug, Schwyz, Zurich, Valais, Ticino and Uri, and the highest Geneva, Basle-City, Neuchâtel, Jura, Vaud and St Gallen.

Note also that taxes can also vary considerably between communities, with the difference in some cantons, e.g. Schwyz, being as high as 100 per cent! However, this is an extreme example, although the difference between municipal tax in most cantons can still be a not insignificant, 10-40 per cent. Generally, the lower the average tax rate in a canton, the larger the difference between communities.

| Cantonal & Community Taxes 2009 | | | |
| --- | --- | --- | --- |
| Canton | Annual Income (CHF)/Tax Payable | | |
| | 50,000 | 100,000 | 200,000 |
| Basle | 3,850 | 16,016 | 50,527 |
| Berne | 3,532 | 14,637 | 48,171 |
| Fribourg | 3,624 | 14,775 | 48,685 |
| Geneva | 832 | 12,589 | 47,878 |
| Ticino | 1,357 | 10,912 | 44,283 |
| Zug | 1,207 | 7,210 | 29,263 |
| Zurich | 2,396 | 10,702 | 39,536 |

The tax (2009) examples in the table above are for a married couple without children.

In recent years many cantons have competed to offer lower taxes to incoming companies and wealthy individuals. As a result, the cantonal tax system has come under attack from the European Commission, which argues that the Swiss tax regime which allows cantonal governments to set their own tax rates to attract companies and individuals breaches the 1972 trade agreement between Switzerland and the EU by distorting trade and competition.

## Property-related Income Tax

Both the federal government and the cantons levy taxes on income from real estate, whether it's the actual rental income or an imputed (also termed deemed, hypothetical or notional) rental value (*Eigenmietwert, valeur locative*) when property is owner-occupied. Therefore initially a distinction must be made between a property that's rented and one that's owner-occupied. Property income includes, rent, lease payments, ground rent and payment for usufruct rights, which are taxable as income in some cantons.

The imputed rental value tax is intended to make for a fairer system, as renters cannot usually deduct their rent from their taxable income, unlike the interest on mortgages. However, a limited deduction of rent is permitted in the cantons of Basle-Land, Vaud and Zug, as imputed rental values are low in these cantons, e.g. in canton Zug you can deduct 20 per cent of your rent up to a maximum annual income of CHF 52,000.

If you're a non-resident or a resident who owns a second home in another canton, you must pay tax on any income from your second home plus wealth tax on that home (see below), but this won't influence your tax situation in the canton where you have your permanent home.

There are several initiatives afoot to abolish the imputed rental value along with the deductions for mortgage interest, which are particularly onerous for retirees with little income and no mortgage.

Rental income is subject to income tax (among the highest in the world for non-resident landlords) minus loan interest, administrative expenses and maintenance, i.e. value-maintaining expenses, but not value-enhancing investments. Maintenance includes garden maintenance, repairs, and essential painting, plumbing, joinery, etc. The replacement of household appliances (dishwashers, fridge/freezers, ovens, washing machines, etc.) is also partially allowed, as are property insurance premiums, road maintenance, sewerage charges, management fees and property taxes. This list isn't a comprehensive list as the deductions and rules vary according to the canton. Practically all energy-saving investments (exterior and roof insulation, installation of double glazing, etc.) can be offset against income tax, as can expenditure for sustainable heating systems (heat pumps, heating elements, solar heating, etc.), even when they have a value-enhancing effect.

In most cantons (Geneva is an exception) you can claim the actual costs of maintenance or renovations, or a flat-rate deduction, e.g. 10 or 20 per cent of the rental income value, depending on the canton and the property's age. You can reduce your tax liability further by carrying out several small renovations in the same year if the total cost is higher than the flat-rate deduction. Larger-scale renovation work, on the other hand, is better spread over several years in order to benefit from the individual deductions over a longer period. Switching between actual and flat-rate deductions from year to year is permitted at the federal level and by most cantons (the exceptions are Geneva, Graubünden, Lucerne, Neuchâtel, Solothurn, Ticino and Uri).

If you own a holiday apartment that's rented, then the occupants are liable to pay tourist or visitor's tax (*Kurtaxe, taxe de séjour*) in most resorts, which is around CHF 2 to 3 per night, depending on the resort and the time of year. Long-term tenants may be able to pay a one-off annual fee, e.g. the equivalent of 30 overnight stays, when someone living in a holiday apartment with an overnight tax rate of CHF 2.50 would pay CHF 2.50 x 30 = CHF 75. The annual sum is non-transferable and applies to each resident spending 30 days or more in the property during the tourist business year.

Previously, buyers of 'newly acquired and well-kept' property weren't permitted to claim for maintenance for the first five years following the purchase (under the Dumont ruling), which applied at both the federal level and in most

cantons. However, a recent Supreme Court ruling declared that maintenance costs **can** be claimed during the first five years provided: it cannot be delayed; it doesn't lead to an increase in rental or leasing income; it doesn't include major structural work which results in a change of use; and the cost of repairs to maintain the property in its current condition. In other words, the cost of maintaining 'newly acquired and well-kept' properties is tax deductible provided it covers regular maintenance work.

Contributions to a renovation or sink fund (*Erneuerungsfonds, fonds de rénovation*) for a community property, used to pay for future repairs to the common parts of a property, are considered to be maintenance costs and are tax-deductible in the year they're paid – **not just years later when they're used to pay for repairs.**

Ensure that you retain any receipts for value-adding investments as the cost can be offset against capital gains tax (see page 193) when you sell the property. The costs of renovation are added to the original investment costs and serve to reduce the capital gain, which in turn reduces the tax payable.

When your children leave home and you have a number of rooms which aren't in use for long periods, you can claim a reduction in the rental income value of you home (equivalent to the percentage of the total living area that isn't in use). To qualify, the rooms mustn't be used as guest rooms, second homes or holiday accommodation. The claim for under-utilisation is valid at the federal level and in cantons Graubünden, Solothurn, Schaffhausen, Schwyz, Thurgau, Uri, Zug and Zurich.

In the case of an owner-occupied home, a hypothetical rental income is calculated by the local municipal council, called the fiscal value, which may be significantly below the market value (e.g. 60 per cent), particularly for older properties. The calculation varies according to the canton and is usually one of the following:

♦ cantonal assessment, where the rental income value comprises a percentage of the taxable value of a property;

♦ an individual valuation procedure according to its size or comparative rent;

♦ a special valuation for villas, holiday homes, etc.

Direct federal taxation is calculated using the taxable value determined by the cantons, although in Aargau, Berne, Basle-Land, Solothurn, Schwyz, Thurgau, Vaud and Zug, a supplement is charged for direct federal taxation.

However, as with actual rental income, mortgage interest payments, administrative expenses and maintenance costs are tax deductible. If you pay your mortgage through direct amortisation, the mortgage interest will decrease annually and the tax savings will reduce. For example, a couple buying a home valued at CHF 650,000 with a total mortgage (first and second mortgages) of around CHF 500,000, and repaying mortgage interest each year of around CHF 5,000, will save around CHF 50,000 in taxes over 20 years through direct amortisation. Note that debit interest is limited to the total of gross property income plus CHF 50,000, which can be deducted from income for both cantonal and federal tax purposes.

| Debit Interest Tax Relief | |
|---|---|
| **Item** | **Sum (CHF)** |
| Interest income and dividends | 7,500 |
| Rental income value | 30,000 |
| Rental income | 32,500 |
| Total investment income | 70,000 |
| Supplement | +50,000 |
| | 120,000 |
| Total debit interest | -150,000 |
| Non-deductible debit interest | 30,000 |

rate than the Swiss. There are the following exceptions:

♦ anyone married to a Swiss citizen;

♦ those who own property in Switzerland;

♦ those who work in Switzerland but live in a neighbouring country (e.g. Austria, France, Germany or Switzerland), pay the bulk of their income and other taxes in the country where they're resident. However, they may still pay some income tax in Switzerland.

If you pay direct tax, you should be aware of anything that entitles you to a refund such as mortgage interest. You should write to your canton's tax authorities requesting a reduction of your tax liability if you have interest expenses such as credit cards, car loans, mortgages or child support payments, whether in Switzerland or another country (a letter documenting the expenses and requesting a refund will suffice). Most cantons require the letter to be received by 31st March of the year following the tax year for which you're claiming.

Some cantons don't require foreigners to pay direct income tax when their gross income is above a certain amount, e.g. CHF 120,000 per year, or when their cantons of residence and employment are different. However, foreigners without a C permit must pay direct income tax in most cantons irrespective of their income level, but those earning above CHF 120,000 per year can apply for an ordinary assessment and any tax withheld is credited against their final tax liability.

You're always subject to tax in your canton of residence and not your canton of employment if they're different; this is a constant source of conflict between some cantons, e.g. Geneva and Vaud, as thousands of residents of Vaud work in Geneva but pay no taxes there. The income of non-resident (Swiss or foreign) employees who are employed only for a short period in Switzerland or who are cross-border commuters, are subject to direct income tax. The Swiss income of non-resident entertainers (such as actors, musicians and public performers), athletes and lecturers, is also taxed at source.

Some cantons offer tax breaks (concessions) to expatriates such as tax deductions for relocation costs, travel costs (to your home

On the other hand, if you pay your mortgage through indirect amortisation, your payments will remain constant, as will your tax savings (see **Tax Benefits** on page 169 and **Pension Mortgages** on page 179). By making regular payments into a retirement account (3rd pillar), you benefit from an attractive, tax-free return, while building up your personal pension. At the same time you can deduct your mortgage payments in full from your income, while the interest payable on your mortgage remains high (as the mortgage sum doesn't reduce), which in turn provides you with the maximum tax deduction.

## Withholding & Direct Income Tax

All foreigners are subject to direct income tax (*Quellensteuer, impôt à la source*), unlike the Swiss and permanent residents (those holding a C Permit), who pay their tax in arrears under a system of self-declaration.

When a foreigner obtains a C permit after five or ten years, he automatically ceases to pay direct income tax and must complete an annual income tax return and pay tax annually.

Withholding income tax is deducted from salaries each month by employers and generally settles your income tax liability, which may result in foreigners paying a higher tax

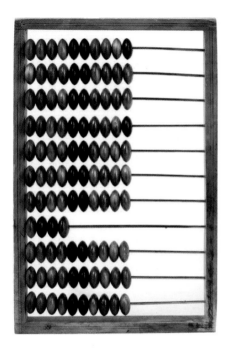

country and back), schooling for children and even housing costs in Switzerland. There are conditions such as the length of stay and the position held and few expatriates qualify, but it might be worth checking with your canton's tax office.

Foreigners paying direct income tax aren't required to file a tax return, although it's advisable (and may be necessary) if your gross earnings exceed CHF 120,000 per year and/or you have considerable assets (such as property and investments), either in Switzerland or abroad.

In addition to Swiss taxes, you may be liable for taxes in your home country. Citizens of most countries are exempt from paying taxes in their home country when they spend a minimum period abroad, e.g. one year, although US nationals remain subject to US income tax while living abroad (lucky people!).

It's your responsibility to familiarise yourself with the tax laws in your home country or country of domicile (as well as Switzerland). If you're in doubt about your tax liability in your home country, contact your nearest embassy or consulate in Switzerland. US citizens can obtain a copy of the *Tax Guide for US Citizens and Resident Aliens* from American Consulates or from 🖥 www.irs. gov/publications/p54/index.html.

### Tax Deductions

In general, all expenses related to taxable income are deductible, including employment expenses. The following list is a rough guide to the deductions you can make from your gross salary when calculating your taxable income; note that deductions are different for federal and cantonal/community taxes.

♦ obligatory insurance contributions such as federal old age and survivor's insurance, disability insurance, accident insurance, health insurance, unemployment insurance and contributions to a company pension fund. Most obligatory insurance contributions are deducted from your gross salary by your employer.

♦ premiums for optional insurance such as life insurance, a private pension, accident insurance and sickness insurance, up to a maximum amount;

♦ business and travel expenses, e.g. car expenses (including travel from your home to your place of work), entertainment (if not paid or reimbursed by your employer), essential tools and special clothing, and board and lodging;

♦ interest on mortgages, loans and overdrafts;

♦ medical expenses for your family that aren't reimbursed by an insurance policy and which total 5 per cent or more of your annual income (in some cantons all medical expenses are deductible);

♦ alimony payments;

♦ study costs (employment-related training, education and books) if they aren't reimbursed by your employer;

♦ donations to recognised charities up to a maximum amount.

Standard allowances are permitted for many items, without proof of expenditure, above which claims must be verified by invoices, etc. Personal allowances vary according to your circumstances, e.g. single, married, divorced or widowed, and the number of children or dependants that you have. Allowances vary from canton to canton.

Self-employed taxpayers may also carry-forward losses (in general for seven years), but there's no 'carry-back' to previous tax years in Switzerland.

## Tax Calculation

Your cantonal/community income tax assessment is based on a 'basic tax value' (*ordentliche Steuer/einfache Steuer, impôt de base*), calculated from your taxable income after all deductions have been made. The basic tax value is derived from tables produced by cantons and is different for single and married people. A simple example of a tax calculation for federal and cantonal/community taxes is shown below:

| Example of Tax Calculation for Federal and Cantonal/Community Taxes | |
| --- | --- |
| **Item** | **Sum (CHF)** |
| Net annual salary | 100,000 |
| Deductions | (12,000) |
| | |
| **Taxable income** | 88,000 |
| | |
| **Basic tax value** | 6,000 |
| | |
| **Tax Calculation:** | |
| Cantonal tax (120% of basic tax value) | 7,200 |
| Community tax rate (120% of basic tax value) | 7,200 |
| Parish church tax (20% of basic tax value) | 1,200 |
| Community fire tax | 100 |
| | |
| **Total Canton/Community Tax** | 15,700 |

## Income Tax Return

If you don't pay direct income tax, you must complete an income tax return annually. Note that in some cantons, foreigners with a B permit paying direct income tax and earning above a certain amount, e.g. CHF 120,000 a year, must complete a tax return. The forms are sent to you by your community tax office, e.g. in January, and must usually be completed and returned by 31st March. If necessary, you can ask for a delay in completing the return, which should be a formality as it takes months to process them all.

It's advisable to contact a tax accountant (*Steuerberater, conseil fiscal/fiduciaire*), your local tax office (*Steueramt, service des contributions*) or your bank for help in completing your tax return. Apart from language problems and the tax knowledge necessary, a pile of forms must be completed. For most people it simply isn't worth the effort doing it themselves, particularly as a tax accountant may charge 'only' a few hundred francs to complete a simple return. If you need information regarding your tax return or with any correspondence from your local tax office, it's best to go in person rather than to telephone. Take someone with you if you don't speak the local language.

Taxable income includes your total income from all sources and all net assets worldwide, excluding property. If part of your income is taxed abroad in a country with a double-taxation treaty with Switzerland, you won't be required to pay Swiss tax on it. However, your Swiss tax rate (basic tax value) may be assessed on your total worldwide income, including the portion on which you've already paid tax.

Income derived from property outside Switzerland is exempt from Swiss tax, but may be taxed abroad. For information, contact the Swiss Federal Tax Office (International Fiscal Law and Double-Taxation Matters, Eigerstrasse 65, CH-3003 Berne, ☎ 031-322 7106, 🖳 www.estv. admin.ch).

If you pay direct income tax, you can request a tax review (by completing an income tax return) if you think that you've paid too much tax. Note, however, that there's the possibility that instead of giving you a rebate, the tax authorities may 'invite' you to pay additional tax.

Anyone can lodge an appeal against their tax assessment. If your tax status changes in the first year after completing a tax return, e.g. due to the birth of a child, marriage or a large change in your income, you can ask to have an intermediate assessment instead of waiting until the end of the tax period. If your spouse starts working, an intermediate assessment is obligatory. Tax for a period of less than one year is assessed on a pro rata basis.

All Swiss taxes must be paid when changing cantons or before leaving Switzerland.

## Tax Bill

Income tax for Swiss nationals, foreigners with a C permit and others who aren't eligible to pay direct income tax is paid annually. Most cantons have now switched to a system whereby tax is based on the income of the preceding year and an assessment is made annually. If you have no income record in Switzerland, you receive a provisional assessment until a full tax year has passed, when the difference between what you've paid and your actual tax bill is payable (or, if you've paid too much, refunded).

The Swiss don't call it a tax demand, but an 'invitation to pay' – if you decline the invitation, they lock you up! Only joking! In Switzerland, tax evasion is a civil NOT a criminal offence.

Your tax bill (*Steuerrechnung*, *prélèvement fiscale*) usually comes in two parts: one for federal tax and one for canton and community taxes.

### Federal Tax Bill

Federal tax bills are payable annually by 1st March. If you don't pay your bill by the due date, you can be charged interest

on any outstanding sum. In practice it may be possible to pay your tax bill, or part of it, a month or two late without paying interest (but don't count on it). If you aren't going to be able to pay your tax bill on time, it's advisable to inform your community tax office (so they won't think that you've absconded).

### Canton & Community Tax Bill

You usually receive your canton and community tax bill for the current year a few weeks after filing your tax return, although the dates tax is due can be different for federal, cantonal and community taxes. In some cantons, tax is due before the end of the current tax year and it's up to you to estimate the amount in order to pay it on time. When you pay late, interest of around 5 per cent is charged. If you pay a bill early, the tax office pays you interest, which is usually higher than if you'd left the money in a savings account (and the interest isn't taxable!). Payment slips for advance payments are available from tax offices.

If you prefer to pay your tax bill monthly or quarterly, inform your tax office and they will send you the appropriate payment advices. If you receive a late assessment and bill for tax, you may be given an extra month or two to pay it, in which case your tax bill may consist of various parts, payable at different times.

## Lump-sum Taxation

Retired or non-employed foreigners resident in Switzerland may be able to choose to be taxed on a lump-sum basis (*Pauschalbesteuerung*, *forfait fiscal*) or 'fiscal deal', whereby tax assessment (at both the federal and cantonal/municipal levels) is made according to your 'lifestyle'. Tax isn't based on your actual income but on your rental payments (or the rental value of your home), and has no relation to your real income, assets or wealth, which you aren't even asked to declare.

The fiscal deal is often criticised as a privilege for wealthy foreigners seeking to avoid taxation in their own countries, which, of course, it is! However, the number of people who benefit from it is relatively small – around 0.25 per cent of the foreign population or less than 4,000 people.

The lump-sum method is restricted to foreign residents who haven't been engaged in any substantial economic activity in Switzerland for the last ten years; they must be retired and undertake no professional activity or employment in Switzerland or abroad, but can 'oversee' their investments. To qualify you must officially spend a minimum of 180 days a year in Switzerland. Note that certain Swiss tax treaties only apply if the income derived from a partner state is subject to ordinary Swiss income taxes. If treaty protection is important in such a case, the taxpayer may opt for a modified lump-sum taxation which includes such income.

The overall tax rate depends on your town and canton of residence; there are huge variations between cantons and sometimes towns (some cantons, such as Zurich, have voted to abolish lump-sum taxation and others, such as Zug, may follow suit). Most cantons have an unofficial minimum for the level of taxable income before they will grant a residence permit, although if you're flexible regarding the choice of canton the sum can be reasonable. It's highest in the cantons of Geneva and Vaud, where assessment is based on five times the annual (theoretical) rental of your accommodation (including a garage) or between 3 and 7 per cent of a property's value. Generally you should have a taxable income of a minimum of CHF 150,000 a year to be eligible or net wealth of at least CHF 2mn. You can usually obtain a ruling before moving to Switzerland, so that you'll know exactly how much tax you'll have to pay before deciding on the move.

The rates of tax payable under the lump sum scheme are the same as would apply normally, but the advantage is – of course – the fictitiously low proportion of your income on which you're assessed. You aren't required to declare your actual income or assets. Assuming your circumstances don't change, such as moving to a larger, more expensive home, you pay the same amount of tax each year (indexed for inflation). You can choose to give up your lump-sum taxation at any time and revert to the regular tax system.

To give an example of how the fiscal deal works, if you're planning to rent a home for CHF 4,000 per month, the annual rent would be 12 x 4,000 = CHF 48,000. let's assume that your taxable income is calculated at five times the

annual rent, i.e. 5 x 48,000 = CHF 240,000. You annual tax bill would therefore be approximately 30 per cent of CHF 240,000, which is CHF 72,000. If you buy a home in Switzerland for CHF 3mn, the rental value is calculated using a variable capitalisation rate (which decrease as the home increases in value) which is subject to negotiation. Assuming that the rate is say 2.5 per cent, this makes the annual rental value 3mn x 2.5 per cent = CHF 75,000. Your taxable income would be five times the imputed annual rent, i.e. 5 x 75,000 = CHF 375,000, on which your annual tax bill would be approximately 30 per cent (CHF 112,500).

A comparison of regular income tax and lump-sum taxation is shown in the table below (for a person living in a CHF 3mn home in Switzerland with other assets totalling CHF 17mn):

### Example of Lump-sum Taxation

| Item | Sum (CHF) |
|---|---|
| Pension income | 200,000 |
| Dividend & interest income | 500,000 |
| Swiss real estate income | 50,000 |
| **Total (actual) Income:** | **750,000** |
| **Ordinary Taxation:** | |
| Swiss Income Tax (30%) | 225,000 |
| New Wealth Tax (on CHF 20mn At 0.75%) | 150,000 |
| **Total Swiss Taxes** | **375,000** |
| **Lump-sum Taxation:** | |
| Fiscal deal income | 250,000 |
| **Lump-sum Tax (30%)*** | **75,000** |
| **Saving** | **300,000** |

* Effective tax rate on actual income = 10%

To give an example of how the fiscal deal works, if you're planning to rent a home for CHF 4,000 per month, the annual rent would be 12 x 4,000 = CHF 48,000. let's assume that your taxable income is calculated at five times the

There are companies in Switzerland which specialise in helping wealthy foreigners to become Swiss residents and pay tax under the fiscal deal system. They will calculate the tax payable in different cantons, and, when you have decided where you want to live, negotiate your taxable income with the authorities and help you obtain residence permits.

# FEDERAL WITHHOLDING TAX

A federal withholding tax (*Verrechnungssteuer*, *impôt anticipé*) of 35 per cent – the highest in the world – is deducted directly from investment income, which includes all interest on bank balances in Switzerland. The banks thus act as fiscal agents of the federal government, deducting withholding tax and paying it to the tax authorities, which is a powerful tool for fighting domestic tax evasion. This tax is automatically deducted by banks from the interest on deposits, but is reclaimable by individuals who pay Swiss income tax, provided they declare their assets. You may, however, be liable for wealth tax on your assets (see below).

If you pay direct income tax, federal withholding tax can be reclaimed for the preceding three years via a form available from your community office. If you declare and pay tax annually, a claim should be made on your income tax return. You can choose to have federal withholding tax repaid in cash or into a bank account or deducted from your next tax bill, when you'll be paid interest on the amount due.

# WEALTH TAX

A wealth or net-worth tax (*Vermögenssteuer*, *impôt sur la fortune*) is levied on assets by all cantons and municipalities, but not at the federal level. Assets are valued at market value and those up to a certain threshold (from around CHF 50,000 to 200,000 depending on the canton) are tax-exempt. Assets include property, including your owner-occupied home, although you can deduct the amount of your mortgage, which is usually higher than the tax value.

The taxable value of your home is based on the value entered in the land register, known as the fiscal value, which is usually some 60 per cent of its market value (it cannot exceed the market value of a property). Check your tax assessment carefully – it's usually only

adjusted after major structural changes or renovations have been made – as it has a major influence on the level of rental income value. If you think your property is over-valued, you can have it valued independently.

> The net-worth tax base includes almost every type of asset held by individuals, including immoveable property, intangible personal property, securities, the cash redemption value of life insurance policies, investments in proprietorships or partnerships, and other beneficial interests. Wealth tax is also calculated on assets that don't yield an income.

Beneficial, not legal, ownership is used for the allocation of assets liable to wealth tax, which means that property under usufruct (i.e. from which you benefit – such as a field you farm or a home you use – but don't legally own) or under a fiduciary relationship is included in the tax base of the beneficiary. Usufruct of moveable and immoveable property is taxed at the end of the usufruct. Certain assets (personal and household effects, etc.) are exempt from taxation.

Resident Swiss taxpayers, who have an unlimited tax obligation, pay the cantonal wealth tax on all their assets, except immovable property in (and assets attributable to) a canton other than the one where they're resident or property in another country. If you own assets in several cantons, the assets located in a particular canton, less a proportional part of your liabilities, are subject to taxation by that canton. Generally intangible property is considered to be located at the residence of the taxpayer. Taxpayers with a limited Swiss tax obligation pay tax on immoveable property within the canton where it's situated and on assets belonging to a permanent home within that canton.

Personal debts, mortgages, bank loans and overdrafts are deductible from the taxable base, as well as certain personal deductions and allowances, depending on the canton. A 'fixed' deduction of between CHF 5,000 and 10,000 may also be allowed. The wealth tax rate is progressive in most cantons and varies from 0.18 (Nidwalden) to 1 per cent (Geneva) of the net value for assets valued at up to CHF 250,000. For taxable wealth of CHF 1mn, the tax rate varies from 0.172 per cent (Nidwalden) to 0.697 per cent (canton of Fribourg). Where applicable, wealth tax is paid with your cantonal and community taxes.

## CAPITAL GAINS TAX

There's no federal capital gains tax (CGT) in Switzerland on property or at any level for moveable assets such as shares, securities, art works, etc., unless they were business transactions. However, there's a cantonal real estate gains tax (*Grundstückgewinnsteuer; impôt sur les gains immobiliers*) in all cantons, applicable to both residents and non-residents.

If an owner-occupied principal home is sold and the revenue from the sale is used within an limited period (e.g. one to five years, depending on the canton) to buy or build a replacement property for immediate occupation (known as a replacement acquisition), capital gains tax is deferred. However, if you only reinvest a portion of the gain, the portion that isn't reinvested is taxed, but provided you live in the replacement home the tax remains deferred and the retention period for both properties is calculated as an aggregate total. Depending on the canton, the deferred real property gains tax is reduced or eliminated altogether, e.g. after 20 years in the canton of Zurich, when you sell the replacement property. However, if you move into rented property or move abroad, the deferred tax becomes due.

Real estate transfers based on gifts, inheritances, legacy, separation or divorce settlements, and changes of ownership due to a compulsory sale or forced execution, are usually exempt from CGT. Any tax due is usually taxed separately and isn't based on income or assets. It's calculated on the difference between the cost of a property and the sale price, less the purchase and sale fees and the cost of any improvements (remodelling), i.e. the cost of value-adding enhancements. If the sales proceeds are greater than the total investment cost, the different is subject to CGT.

The rules regarding capital gains tax on property vary from canton to canton, including the way in which it's calculated, the deductions and the tax rates. However, in all cantons the tax payable depends on the length of ownership; the longer you own a property the lower the amount of tax payable. Some cantons calculate the tax due using full years while other calculate it in months, therefore it's worth timing a sale with this in mind. CGT is banded and decreases each year of ownership according to the canton, e.g. from 30 per cent in year one, 9 per cent after ten years, down to 1 per cent after 25 years. For information about local rates, contact your local cantonal tax authority (see **Appendix A**).

## INHERITANCE & GIFT TAX

There are no federal estate, inheritance (*Erbschaftsteuer, taxe successorale*) or gift taxes in Switzerland, but these taxes are levied by most cantons – the exceptions being Lucerne, which has no gift tax, and Schwyz which levies neither. In the cantons of Graubünden and Solothurn a tax on the estate (*Nachlasssteuer, taxe sur l'héritage*) is levied in addition or instead of the inheritance tax. In addition to inheritance tax, some cantons (e.g. Neuchâtel and Solothurn) also levy death duties on the non-apportioned property of the deceased. The canton of Graubünden levies only a death duty, although communes may also levy inheritance tax.

Communities are also entitled to levy inheritance and gift taxes in a few cantons, e.g. Lucerne, although in most cases the communities share in the revenue from the cantonal tax.

Note that even if you have no tax to pay in Switzerland, if you're a non-resident you may have to pay inheritance tax in your home country (Switzerland has double taxation treaties, which apply to inheritance tax with some countries, including the UK and USA).

The canton that has the right to levy inheritance and gift tax is the canton in which the beneficiary was last domiciled, with the exception of immoveable property (real estate) which is taxed where it's situated. Taxes on donations of moveable property are levied by the canton in which the donor had his domicile at the time of the donation. With inheritance, the market value of the estate at the time of the testator's death serves as the basis for assessment, while with donations (gifts), the tax due is based on the market value at the time of the transfer.

Tax rates vary from canton to canton – and are usually the same for inheritance and gift taxes – and are low compared with those in many other western European countries. However, rates vary considerably depending on the relationship of the beneficiary to the deceased or donor and the value of the bequest or gift. Generally, relatives (particularly the spouse and children) of the deceased pay lower rates of inheritance tax than non-related beneficiaries. For example, in many cantons the spouse and children of a deceased person who was a resident taxpayer are exempt from inheritance tax, and in some cantons, for example Basle-City and Berne, only unrelated beneficiaries are taxed. In eight cantons, estates and gifts to direct ascendants, i.e. parents, are also tax-exempt.

The most important variation between the cantons is the treatment of descendants and the applicable tax rates. Only eight cantons tax inheritances or gifts transferred to direct descendants (children): Appenzell-Innerrhoden, Berne, Lucerne (no gift tax and no inheritance tax at the cantonal level, although it's applies in around three-quarters of communities), Graubünden, Jura, Neuchâtel, Solothurn and Vaud. Jura also taxes inheritances between spouses.

Where applicable, inter-spousal gifts and an inheritance by a surviving spouse are frequently exempt or taxed at very low rates, e.g. up to 6 per cent, whereas gifts and inheritances to unrelated persons attract rates ranging from 20 to 40 per cent. The taxable base is usually the market value of assets with special provisions for securities and real property. After determining the applicable rate based on the value of the bequest or gift, the amount is subject to a multiplier according to the relationship between the donor and the recipient (see below).

Upon the death of a Swiss resident, an inventory is taken of the estate which serves as the basis for the inheritance tax assessment. The assessment of gift tax is based on a tax return, which must usually be filed by the donor.

Given the complexity of inheritance tax rules and the wide differences between rates in different cantons, you're advised to take advice from a tax professional, preferably one with knowledge of the inheritance tax laws of all the countries involved.

## Inheritance & Gift Tax Example: Zurich

Inheritance and gifts left to spouses and direct descendants are exempt in the canton of Zurich, where the following allowances are also granted:

♦ CHF 200,000 for parents;

♦ CHF 15,000 for fiancés, siblings, grandparents, stepchildren, godchildren, foster children and home helps employed for at least ten years;

◆ CHF 50,000 for the partner of the deceased or the donor if a couple have lived together for at least five years in the same household and none of the above deductions apply;

◆ CHF 30,000 for dependent persons who have a permanent or partial occupational disability.

| Zurich Inheritance & Gift Tax Rates | |
|---|---|
| **Tax Base (CHF)** | **Tax Rate** |
| Up to 30,000 | 2% |
| 20,001-90,000 | 3% |
| 90,001-180,000 | 4% |
| 180,001-360,000 | 5% |
| 360,001-840,000 | 6% |
| 840,001-1.5mn | 7% |

If the taxable inheritance exceeds CHF 1.5mn, a flat rate of 6 per cent applies to the whole amount. A multiplier, which varies according to the relationship of the deceased and the beneficiary, is then applied to the calculated tax, as shown in the table below:

| Inheritance & Gift Tax Multiplier | |
|---|---|
| **Relationship** | **Multiplier** |
| Parents | 1 |
| Grandparent, stepchildren | 2 |
| Siblings | 3 |
| Step-parents | 4 |
| Uncles, aunts and descendants of siblings | 5 |
| Others | 6 |

For example, a brother is left CHF 300,000 by his sister, which is taxed at 5 per cent = CHF 15,000. This is then subject to a multiplier of three (siblings) = 15,000 x 3 = CHF 45,000 (making the effective tax rate 15 per cent).

## WILLS

It's an unfortunate fact of life that you're unable to take all those lovely Swiss francs with you when you make your final bow. All adults should therefore make a will (*Testament, testament*), irrespective of how large or small their assets. In general, all valid wills made in accordance with the law of the place of execution are recognised in Switzerland, both under the Hague convention, to which Switzerland is a signatory, and under the Swiss Private International Law Act 1987. Experts advise that you make a Swiss will for property situated in Switzerland, which can be registered with a local notary, and a separate will for each country where you own property.

If you live in Switzerland and wish your will to be interpreted under Swiss law, you can state this and that you've abandoned your previous domicile. If you don't want your estate to be subject to Swiss law, you're usually eligible to state in your will that it's to be interpreted under the law of another country. This depends on your and your spouse's nationality and your ties with that country. A foreigner who also holds Swiss nationality **must** make his will under Swiss law if he's resident in Switzerland. If your estate comes under Swiss law, your dependants may be subject to Swiss inheritance laws.

Swiss law is restrictive regarding the distribution of property and the identity of heirs, and the estate is divided according to the number of children, who may receive the lion's share of the spoils. You may not be too concerned about this, but your other dependants might be!

In order to avoid being subject to Swiss inheritance tax (see above) and inheritance laws, you must establish your domicile in another country. Note, however, that foreigners living in Switzerland with a C permit are usually considered under Swiss federal and private international law to be domiciled in Switzerland. Take advice from an expert before establishing or changing your domicile to Switzerland or any other country.

Making a will in Switzerland is simple: it must be hand-written, state your full name, and be dated and signed. No witnesses are required. However, to ensure that the contents of your will comply with Swiss law, it's advisable to obtain legal advice.

Keep a copy of your will(s) in a safe place and another copy with your solicitor or the executor of your estate. Don't leave your will in a safe deposit box, which in the event of your death will be sealed for a period under Swiss law. You should store information regarding bank accounts and insurance policies with your will(s) – but don't forget to tell someone where they are!

If you die while working in Switzerland and have more than five years' service, your salary is usually paid for an extra month or two (maybe the Swiss – who all go to heaven – have access to ATMs there?).

## COST OF LIVING

No doubt you would like to know how far your Swiss francs are likely to stretch and how much money (if any) you'll have left after paying your bills. First the good news. As you're probably aware, Switzerland has one of the world's highest standards of living, its per capita income and purchasing power is among the highest in the world, and managerial and executive salaries are among the highest in Europe.

'It's no use trying to hide the fact: Switzerland is one of the most expensive countries in the world. According to an AC Nielsen Euro-Barometer study conducted in 2005, a Swiss household pays, for example, 26 per cent more than a French household and 63 per cent more than a Spanish household to fill the same shopping basket.' (from ☐ www.swissemigration.ch)

On the other hand, some 12.5 per cent of the population (almost a million people) live below the official poverty line, which is calculated as a net monthly income of CHF 2,480 for a single person and CHF 4,600 for a family with two children. Switzerland also has relatively low taxes and a low inflation rate. The inflation rate at the beginning of 2008 was 0.7 per cent, which rose to 2.6 per cent by the end of the year, but by late 2009 it had fallen to almost zero, thanks to the recession.

The bad news is that Switzerland has one of the highest costs of living in the world,

particularly the cities of Geneva and Zurich. The average price of many goods and services in Switzerland is up to 40 per cent higher than in EU countries and up to 60 per cent higher than in the US. According to the European Statistical Department, rental costs in Switzerland (including heating and electricity) are around 70 per cent higher than the EU average, food 50 per cent more expensive and meat almost 100 per cent dearer (now you know why Swiss salaries are so high!). However, prices of many goods and services (e.g. most retail goods, government-fixed prices such as hospital, postal and railway charges, insurance premiums and credit costs) are monitored and controlled by the office of the Price Controller to prevent unjustifiable price increases.

In the Mercer 2009 Cost of Living Survey (☐ www.mercer.com/costofliving), Geneva was ranked the 4th most expensive city in the world and Zurich 6th – up from 8th and 9th respectively in 2008. Selected other rankings were: Tokyo (1st), Moscow (3rd), Hong Kong (5th), Copenhagen (7th), New York City (8th), Milan (11th), Paris (13th), Oslo (14th), London (16th), Rome (18th), Los Angeles (23rd), Dublin (25th), Amsterdam (29th), White Plains (31st), San Francisco (34th), Madrid (37th), Honolulu (41st, equal with Brussels), Miami (45th), Munich (47th) and Chicago (50th). (The fundamental flaw with all cost of living surveys is that they convert local prices into $US, which means that any changes are as much the result of currency fluctuations as price inflation.)

In the 2009 Union Bank of Switzerland (UBS) iPod index – which calculates the hours of work needed to buy an iPod Nano – Zurich was the world's 2nd most expensive city and Geneva 6th. Residents of Geneva and Zurich tend to pay around 20 per cent more on average for products, services and accommodation than people in other Western European cities. The International Geneva Welcome Centre estimates that a family of four living in Geneva needs a monthly net income of at least CHF 7,000 just to maintain a modest standard of living.

As food and especially meat is so much more expensive than in most EU countries and North America (Switzerland's food prices are

exceeded worldwide only by Japan's), your food bill will almost certainly be higher; the actual difference will depend on what you eat, where you lived before coming to Switzerland and whether you refrain from buying imported food. Around CHF 1,000 should feed two adults for a month in most areas, excluding frequent dining out, fillet steak, caviar and alcohol (living in Switzerland provides an excellent incentive to cut down on all those expensive, rich foods).

Your cost of living in Switzerland will depend very much on where and how you live. The inhabitants of canton Appenzell-Innerrhoden enjoy the highest levels of disposable income after tax and fixed costs such as housing, followed by those of Obwalden, Glarus, Thurgau and Appenzell-Ausserrhoden. Geneva residents were the worst off, followed by Basle-City, Vaud, Basle-Country and Zurich.

However, despite the high cost of food and housing, the cost of living in Switzerland needn't be astronomical. If you shop wisely, compare prices and services before buying, and don't live too extravagantly, you may be pleasantly surprised at (relatively) how little you can live on. In high rent areas (such as Geneva), you can save money by renting an apartment in an unfashionable suburb or a rural area – or even in a neighbouring country – and commuting further to work.

You can also save on motoring, as petrol (gas) in Switzerland is cheaper than in neighbouring countries. The price of cars is around average for Europe but running a car (including depreciation) is relatively expensive; according to the Swiss Touring Club it costs around CHF 11,000 a year to drive a medium-sized car 15,000km. Leasing a car may save you money, as will running a diesel car. Even better, if you live in a city – where public transport is good and excellent value for money (especially with an annual pass or half-fare card – see **Chapter 3**) – you may not need a car at all!

If you live near a border you can also make savings on food and many other goods by doing you weekly shopping and buying 'big ticket' items abroad (see page 240). You can also save money by comparing prices using a comparison website such as Comparis (💻 www.comparis.ch), where you can compare the cost of housing (to rent and buy), mortgages, insurance, cars (purchase and lease), telephone (mobile and fixed), the internet and consumer electronics.

## VALUE ADDED TAX

Goods and services in Switzerland are subject to value added tax (*Mehrwertsteuer/MWSt*,

| Swiss VAT Rates | |
|---|---|
| **Rate** | **Applicability** |
| **2.4% (reduced)** | food and drinks (excluding alcoholic drinks and cooked meals); meat; cereals; plants, seeds and flowers; some basic farming supplies; mains water; medicines; books, newspapers, magazines and other printed matter; and radio and television services. |
| **3.6% (hotel rate)** | hotel and other accommodation; |
| **7.6% (standard rate)** | all goods and services not listed above. |

taxe sur la valeur ajoutée/TVA) at rates of 2.4 to 7.6 per cent (increasing to 8 per cent from January 2011) – the lowest in Europe; the average in EU countries is over 15 per cent. Certain products and services are exempt from VAT, including real estate sales and rentals, postal services, healthcare, social security/ services, educational services, sport and cultural activities, insurance, current-account (money and capital market) transactions and exports.

VAT applies to other goods and services at the rates shown in the table above.

Most prices in Switzerland are quoted inclusive of VAT. Companies and sole traders (the self-employed) must register and add VAT to their bills when their annual turnover exceeds CHF 75,000. Smaller companies with an annual turnover of up to CHF 250,000 are exempt if their tax burden is less than CHF 4,000. Companies subject to VAT can deduct VAT paid at earlier stages in the economic process. To reduce the administrative burden, companies with a turnover not exceeding CHF 3mn and an annual tax liability of less than CHF 60,000 can settle on the basis of fixed rates, known as the net-tax rate.

# PENSION SYSTEM

Switzerland has a three-part social security **pension system** for all employees, called the 'three-pillar' system (Drei-Säulen-Konzept, système des trois piliers). It consists of:

1. Compulsory federal old age and survivors' insurance and disability insurance, which is the Swiss federal social security **(state) pension** scheme;

2. Compulsory private **company pension** funds for employees;

3. Voluntary tax-deductible **private pension** savings and life insurance.

The aim of the federal social security system is to guarantee employees at least a subsistence income on retirement or in case of disability. To receive a full state pension you must contribute for the maximum number of years, which is 44. A full state pension and a company pension bring your pension to around 60 per cent of your final salary. The 3rd pillar (private pension) below is intended to make your pension up to around 80 per cent of your final salary.

## Private Pension

The federal and company pension schemes (see above) are equal to a maximum of 60 per cent of earnings (for those who have worked in Switzerland their whole working life!). To supplement these and bring your pension closer to your final salary, you can contribute to a private pension fund (Alterssparheft, caisse privée de prévoyance-vieillesse) and receive tax relief on your contributions (up to a limited amount). This is the third part of the Swiss social security system, called 'pillar three' (Selbstvorsorge, épargne personelle).

If you're a member of a company pension fund, you may pay up to 8 per cent of the maximum average 'pensionable' salary, which is CHF 6,566 a year (2009), tax-free into a private pension fund or a special bank account. If you aren't a member of a company pension fund, you may save up to 20 per cent of your annual net income tax-free, or a maximum of CHF 32,832 per year.

The interest and investment income is tax-free for the term of the savings plan.

You can receive the benefits of a private pension scheme up to five years before the Swiss retirement age of 65 (men) or 64 (women), when the amount withdrawn is taxed separately from other income and at a reduced rate. A private pension can also be redeemed in the following circumstances:

♦ if you become an invalid;

♦ if you leave Switzerland permanently;

♦ if you become self-employed (after being an employee);

♦ if you join another pension scheme;

♦ if you purchase a (first) residence or repay a mortgage.

The interest paid by banks on private pension savings in Switzerland is very low, although there are no bank charges or taxes. You may find it worth comparing the interest on a private pension fund in Switzerland with that paid in other countries. However, you should take care which currency you choose, as your savings could be considerably reduced if the currency is devalued (and you may have to pay tax on the interest).

# 8.
# MOVING HOUSE

**M**oving to Switzerland or buying a holiday home there may be the culmination of your dreams, but it can also be a highly stressful experience. However, it's possible to limit the strain on your mental and physical health by careful planning and preparation. When moving house there are many things to be considered and a 'million' people to be informed. The information and checklists contained in this chapter are designed to make the task easier and help prevent a nervous breakdown – provided you don't leave everything to the last minute!

Moving house is an ideal opportunity to be ruthless and throw out all your old furniture, clothes and other belongings that you haven't used in years. This is a good time to have a (car) boot or garage/yard sale, which not only gets rid of all the junk but may also bring in a tidy sum. It also allows you to reassess your lifestyle, particularly when moving to a new country.

---

### ▲ Important Note

The information contained in this chapter assumes that you're moving to Switzerland from another country. If you're moving within Switzerland, the people you need to inform are detailed in our sister publication *Living and Working In Switzerland*, but you'll also find much of the information and the checklists in this chapter helpful.

---

## SHIPPING YOUR BELONGINGS

After finding a home it usually takes just a few weeks to have your belongings shipped from within Europe – from anywhere else it varies considerably, e.g. from four to six weeks from North America. If you're flexible about the date, it's cheaper to have your move done as a part load, rather than an individual delivery. After considering the costs, you may decide to ship only selected items of furniture and personal effects, and buy new furniture in Switzerland.

If you're moving to Switzerland from within Europe and only have personal belongings and a few items of furniture to transport, it's possible to ship your belongings to Switzerland yourself. In this case you'll need to check the customs requirements in all the countries you must pass through. Most removal companies sell packing boxes in numerous sizes and rent or sell removal equipment (e.g. trolleys and straps) for those who feel up to doing their own packing.

If you're taking pets with you, you may need to ask your vet to tranquillise them, as many pets are frightened (even more than people) by the chaos and stress of moving house.

See also **Customs** on page 222.

## Choosing a Shipping Company

You should obtain at least three written quotations before choosing a removal (house moving) company, as costs can vary considerably. It's advisable to use a removal company that's a member of an organisation such as the Federation of International Furniture Removers (FIDI, 🖥 www.fidi.com) or the Overseas Moving Network International (OMNI, 🖥 www.omnimoving.com). Members have an 'insurance' scheme that provides a guarantee: if a member company fails to fulfil its commitments to a customer, the removal will be completed at the agreed price by another company or your money will be refunded.

When choosing a removal company, you should be wary of a company whose quotation is much lower than others, as some removal companies will promise anything to get a contract and then try to increase the cost later for 'extras'. Always use an established removal company with a good reputation. Check that a company uses its own vans and staff, as some companies use sub-contractors. For international house moves it's best to use a company that specialises in international removals.

Make a list of everything to be shipped and give a copy to the removal company. Don't include anything illegal (e.g. guns, bombs, drugs or pornography) with your belongings, as customs checks can be rigorous and penalties severe. Don't forget to include everything, such as the contents of your garage, garden, attic, loft, cellar, annexe and workshop, as quotations can increase dramatically (and disproportionately) if you increase the load later.

Most major companies provide a variety of levels of service which may include a standard move (load and unload only), fragile packing, full packing service and a combined service, e.g. packing and unload but not unpack. They may also provide storage services. A company may give a rough quote over the phone or a website, which will give you a good idea of the final cost, but they should send a representative to your home to provide a detailed quotation after assessing the volume of your home's contents.

Companies base quotes on the number of hours they expect loading and unloading to take, the amount of fuel required, driving time and extras such as packing, laying covers for carpets, navigation of difficult stairs, using winches to access upper floors, etc. If there are access problems or parking restrictions for a large truck (the ground must also be firm enough to support a

heavy vehicle) at either end, you should warn the remover as this is likely to influence the quotation (otherwise the bill will need to be adjusted later).

Check whether a quote includes packing and packaging, as these are optional extras with some companies and part of the standard service with others. A company may provide different packing services such as packing only breakables or packing everything, while others won't pack anything, but will provide packing materials (sometimes they don't even do this). Check whether the quote includes insurance and tax (e.g. VAT).

Always try to negotiate on the price, as you may be surprised at the reduction you can get, simply by asking.

## Insurance

It's highly recommended that you insure your belongings when moving house. Most people take out the insurance offered by their mover, which is specially designed to cover the risks involved in moving house. However, it isn't advisable to insure with a removal company that carries its own insurance (some do), as they may fight every penny of a claim. Insurance premiums are usually 1 to 2 per cent of the declared value of your goods, depending on the type of cover chosen. Find out what is covered and ask them to provide a list of exclusions, which is easier than trying to wade through the small print. Make sure that they have insurance for injuries to their staff during the move, as you don't want to be sued when one of the removal men falls down the stairs (most companies have insurance for injuries to staff).

Most insurance policies cover for 'all-risks' on a replacement value basis, although you may be able to choose between replacement basis ('new for old') or indemnity basis ('like for like' with an allowance for age, wear and tear). Bear in mind that china, glass and other breakables are usually only included in an 'all-risks' policy when they're packed by the removal company. Insurers may also pay only for the loss or damage to goods packed by a customer if there's the total loss of a consignment.

If there are any breakages or damaged items, they should be noted and listed before you sign the delivery bill, although it's obviously impractical to check everything on delivery. If you need to make a claim, be sure to read the small print, as some companies require clients to make a claim within a few days, although 7 or 14 is usual. Send a claim by registered post. Some insurance companies apply an 'excess' of around 1 per cent of the total shipment value when assessing claims. This means that if your shipment is valued at £50,000, claims must be over £500.

It's prudent to make a photographic record of valuables for insurance purposes. You may also wish to photocopy your important documents and keep the originals in a safe deposit box when you get to Switzerland (for official use, only originals or certified copies are acceptable). If you're taking valuables with you personally, you may wish to ensure that they're covered by your home contents or travel insurance while in transit.

Make sure that the insurance covers your belongings for their true value and check the policy small print for exclusions.

## Packing

Most companies will pack your belongings and provide packing cases and special containers. It can, however, be very expensive, although it's worthwhile if you have a lot of valuable glass or ceramics. Ask a company how they will pack fragile and valuable items, and whether the cost of packing cases, materials and insurance (see above) is included in the quotation. If you're doing your own packing (as most people do), most shipping companies will provide packing crates and boxes, but you may have to pay for them. You will also need a number of rolls of strong tape and possibly a trolley to move boxes after you've packed them. Some items such as books, which should only be packed in small boxes, are very heavy.

If money is no object, the best advice is probably to leave it all to the professionals, particularly as anything you pack yourself won't be covered by insurance. However, most people choose to pack small items,

leaving the removers to deal with (and protect as necessary) larger items of furniture. Take care to pack small, valuable items (such as jewellery) separately and carry them with you – in any case, valuables aren't covered by standard insurance policies. If you have any questions about how to handle pets, fish, plants, antiques, fine art, wine cellars or anything else of particular importance or value, discuss it with your removal company well in advance. See also **Doing Your Own Packing** below.

## Storage

If you're unable to ship your belongings directly to your new home, you may need to put them into storage for a period. It's advisable to use your removal company to store your goods, which will minimise the number of people handling them and also reduce the cost. Most removal companies have their own storage facilities and some allow a free storage period before shipment, e.g. 14 days. Storage costs are based on volume and there may also be handling fees. You may have no access to your belongings while they're in storage, so take care not to pack anything that you may need before you move into your new home.

When leaving items in storage for a long period, you should ensure that they're adequately protected against temperature changes, damp and humidity. Warehouses are rarely heated, and in winter the temperature is much lower than in a centrally-heated home. Bear in mind that items can be damaged by mould or mildew if they're left in storage for a long time.

 **Caution**

If you need to put your household effects into storage, it's imperative to have them fully insured as warehouses have been known to burn down! Note also that some warehouses have no fire alarms, sprinklers or fire-fighting equipment. It's better to be safe than sorry!

## Bookings

The first thing you'll need to do – on which everything else will hinge – is to decide your moving day and book a removal company. It's advisable to book a removal company well in advance for the best price – preferably a few months ahead. If you book at short notice you may not be able to make a booking on the day that you want and may need to pay more, particularly as a company will be aware that your options are limited and may increase its rates. At the very least, it may not be willing to negotiate a discount.

If possible, avoid peak holiday periods, public holidays (or the week in which bank holidays fall) and school half-term holidays; if you want to save money you'll need to book well in advance if you plan to move during a peak period. Friday is the most popular day of the week for house moves, although if you have any problems you may not be able to contact anyone over the weekend. Bear in mind when moving home, everything that can go wrong often does; therefore you should allow plenty of time and try not to arrange your move from your old home on the same day as the new owner is moving in. That's just asking for fate to intervene!

### Instructions

Give the removal company an itinerary for moving day with approximate arrival times, and provide them with a map and directions to your new home. It you aren't going to be at your new home when they arrive, you must arrange for someone to be there to meet them. Give them a local (preferably) or mobile phone number (or two, in case your phone packs up at the last minute, you forget to recharge it or a pay-as-you-go phone runs out of money). This could be the number of a friend in Switzerland who can contact you or who you can get in touch with. You should attach a floor plan of your new house and a colour-coded guide for the carton labels, so that the movers know where to put things (this is standard practice with some movers).

If there are access or parking restrictions for a large truck (the ground must also be firm enough to support a heavy vehicle) at either house, you should warn the remover, as the cost can increase significantly if access or parking is restricted or there are any other obstructions that cause the job to take longer than would otherwise be expected.

If necessary, arrange with the local council around a week in advance to suspend parking restrictions or get the police to cone off a parking area. If you don't have access for a large vehicle (some are the size of a double-decker bus), your removal company may be able to use a smaller vehicle. If access to upper floors is restricted by narrow doorways, difficult or spiral staircases, lack of lifts, etc., the shippers will need to arrange for furniture to be hoisted on a pulley or 'lift' and be taken in through an upstairs window or balcony, which will incur extra costs.

If your household and personal effects are sent unaccompanied, the receiving freight company will send you a customs form to be completed and signed. In addition, they will require a photocopy of your residence permit, a copy of the personal details' pages of your passport and proof of accommodation, e.g. a copy of a rental or purchase contract.

## DOING YOUR OWN PACKING

If you're using a removal company but doing your own packing, there may still be certain items that you cannot deal with or would prefer the experts to handle. If you have any questions about how to deal with pets, plants, tropical fish, antiques, chandeliers, fine art, wine cellars or anything else of particular importance or value, discuss it with your removal company.

Take care to pack small, valuable items (such as jewellery) separately and carry them yourself, as they're usually excluded from liability by insurance companies. Note also that anything you pack yourself won't be covered by the removal insurance policy. Check that your home contents insurance covers your belongings in transit and insure your possessions from the day of arrival in your new home.

---

☑ **SURVIVAL TIP**

Take care not to pack anything that you'll need on moving day (see Survival Rations on page 207) or pack them last and mark the box prominently.

## Packing Materials

Most shipping companies provide packing crates and boxes, but you may have to pay for them. Start collecting packing materials if your removals company isn't providing them. You can obtain free boxes from supermarkets and other stores, although it may be better to obtain stronger boxes from your removal company. Note that you'll need lots of small boxes for books and other heavy items.

You will also need a few rolls of strong plastic tape (with a dispenser), coloured marker pens, coloured tie labels or tape, bubble wrap and tissue paper for delicate items, corrugated cardboard or thick foam sheeting (for packing mirrors and paintings), and a plentiful supply of plastic bags and newspapers. If you have a shredder, you can use it to convert newspapers into extra packing material for bulky/fragile items or you can use crumpled newspapers. You may also need some old blankets or sheets to protect large delicate items such as mirrors and light fittings.

## Start Early

Start packing early – for example at least a few weeks before you're due to move. It's surprising how long it can take to pack, particularly if you only have free time in the evenings and at weekends. If two people are packing you'll need to allow at least three full days (or two weekends) to pack the contents of an average 4-bedroom house. Get your children to help pack their own belongings, but check that they're doing it correctly. Two weeks before you move, you should have finished sorting your cupboards, loft, garage, cellar, etc., and have discarded, sold or given away anything that you don't plan to take, e.g. to friends, charity shops or a recycling centre.

## Packing Boxes

Ensure that your boxes and other containers are strong enough (they will be if the removal company provided them) to permit stacking in the van without damaging the contents. Don't over-fill boxes (all boxes should be sealed and flat) and don't fill large boxes with heavy items such as books, as they will be too heavy to lift. You may need to pad the bottom of boxes with extra sheets of cardboard. You can pack the bottom half of large boxes with books and other heavy items and fill them with lighter items; don't pack heavy items (such as iron pans) with delicate items (such as porcelain). Make sure that you have plenty of boxes – too many is far better than too few!

You can fill empty spaces in boxes with crumpled newspapers. Label boxes clearly (see below) with their contents and colour coding (corresponding to the appropriate room in your new home) and secure them with heavy duty plastic tape.

## Fragile Items

Pack fragile items in tissue or bubble wrap with plenty of padding, and mark boxes 'FRAGILE' or 'GLASS' in large red letters (you can also buy special tape). Paintings and mirrors should be securely wrapped in corrugated cardboard or foam sheeting (available from removal companies) and have their corners protected – you can buy ready-made cardboard corner protectors and picture boxes. Extra care must be taken with valuable paintings. Wrap the legs on chairs and tables to prevent damage. Remove bulbs from lamps and other items, and wrap plugs to prevent them from damaging lamp bases. Large pieces of silver should be wrapped in acid-free tissue paper, especially if they're going into storage, which prevents them from becoming tarnished. If you have any really fragile or valuable items, you

should transport them personally, if at all possible.

## Marking Boxes & Items

Make a floor plan of your new home and where you want your belongings to be stacked by the removers by 'colour-coding' each room in your new home. You can then mark boxes and items with a broad-felt-tipped coloured pen, labels or tape, so movers can readily identify where to put them.

Don't forget to give your removers a copy of the floor plan and colour-coding, along with a map and instructions on how to find your home. If you're really organised you can number each box and keep a reference sheet with what each box contains. Mark boxes on the top and the side(s), as the top of a box will be obscured when it's stacked. Tie coloured labels to items that aren't boxed or mark them with coloured tape or sticky labels.

## Special Items

When it comes to packing, certain items may need special consideration or handling – your moving company will advise you. These may include:

♦ **Self-assembled furniture:** This usually needs to be dismantled before you can move it and you may need to arrange with the supplier or a specialist to do this (a removal company may also do it). If possible, move small items in one piece, although this won't be possible with large items of furniture such as wardrobes and sideboards.

♦ **Kitchen appliances:** Cookers, washing machines, refrigerators, freezers and dishwashers should all be disconnected before moving day. The drums of washing machines must be secured with the proper brackets (obtainable from the vendor or a local agent) to avoid damage. Refrigerators and freezers should be washed with detergent and dried thoroughly to avoid unpleasant odours, and if they're going into storage you should wedge the doors open to allow air to circulate and tape them in place.

♦ **Fixtures & soft furnishings:** Curtains, blinds and fixed items such as shelves and lamp fittings need to be taken down before moving day and cleaned – soft furnishings should be washed or dry-cleaned.

♦ **Clothing:** Clothing on hangers can be transported in special wardrobe cartons available from removal companies. Clothing in chests of drawers may be able to be left in situ, although if in doubt pack them separately (the drawers may need to be removed to lighten the load). Note that if drawers are removed from a chest of drawers, they should be numbered.

♦ **Computers, audio & DVD equipment:** This is best moved in its original packaging. Items should be secured for transit in accordance with the manufacturer's instructions.

♦ **Foodstuffs:** It's unusual to ship foodstuffs when doing an international move and it may even be illegal. If you want to transport any foodstuffs to Switzerland, they must not be perishable and must be in unopened containers such as tins or other sealed containers. If you're planning to ship food in bulk, e.g. a year's supply of your favourite baked beans or curry paste, you should check the regulations with Swiss customs. Any cartons that contain liquids, such as bottles of wine (subject to import tax!), should be labelled as 'Liquids'.

♦ **Flammable items:** Note that your removal company won't be insured to transport flammable substances, tins of paint, creosote, paraffin, matches, gas bottles or similar items. Any dangerous, acidic or flammable items must usually be specially transported.

♦ **Fragile items:** Easily breakable items such as glass should be carefully packed and be prominently marked as 'Fragile' or 'Glass'.

---

**☑ SURVIVAL TIP**

Pack things together that you'll need in the same room when they're unpacked – don't be tempted to randomly throw things belonging in different rooms into boxes!

---

## SURVIVAL RATIONS

You should pack any items separately that you may need on moving day or that you'll need before unpacking your boxes. If you're travelling to Switzerland from within Europe by road, you can take these with you. Otherwise, have them stored somewhere in your new home where you can find them quickly on arrival. These items ('survival rations') may include some or all of the following:

### Essentials

You should obviously take the following items with you personally:

♦ Passports, residence and customs' documents;

♦ Keys for your new home;

♦ Directions to your new home and a local map;

♦ Removal contract (in case of queries);

♦ Mobile phone (or two – and battery chargers), address book (with numbers of real estate agent, removal company, solicitor, vendor, your buyer, neighbours, utility companies, etc.);

♦ Notepad, pen/pencil;

♦ Medication (headache pills!) and first-aid kit;

♦ Wallet/handbag with cash (foreign currency), credit/debit cards, etc;

♦ Driving licence, car registration and insurance papers (if driving to Switzerland);

♦ Briefcase with copies/originals of important documents.

## Tools & Equipment

The following items should be to hand after your arrival and should be loaded last (in a specially marked box) so that they're the first things to be off-loaded:

♦ Vacuum cleaner;

♦ Broom, dustpan/brush and mop;

♦ Cleaning materials (unopened containers only);

♦ Light-bulbs, plugs and lots of Swiss plug adapters;

♦ Self-sealing universal plugs (for sinks and bath);

♦ Tool kit with an adjustable spanner, large and small (electrical) screwdrivers, hammer, picture hooks, tape measure and pen knife;

♦ torches (flashlights) and candles;

♦ Camera or camera phone (you may wish to take pictures of your old and/or new homes).

### Basics

The following 'essentials' should be packed in specially marked boxes, so that you can easily find them on arrival (they will be particularly useful if you arrive late in the day). They should also be loaded last so that they're among the first things to be off-loaded.

♦ Small TV (with remote control – if it will work in Switzerland) and/or computer (to pacify children!);

♦ Radio/CD player and CDs;

♦ Laptop computer;

♦ Electric kettle, saucepan(s), frying pan, teapot, cups/mugs, tin opener, can and bottle opener, corkscrew and a sharp knife;

♦ Tableware, dishes, glasses, cutlery, can opener, corkscrew, napkins and paper towels. Alternatively, plastic or disposable cups, plates and cutlery;

♦ Washing-up liquid, dishcloth and rubber gloves;

♦ Toilet paper, tissues and wipes;

♦ Toiletries (soap, toothpaste, shampoo, deodorant, etc.);

- Make-up bag;

- Change of clothes, bed clothes and slippers for all the family;

- Nappies and toys;

- Bed linen, duvets and towels;

- Tinned/packet foods and drinks;

- Hot-water bottles and a portable heater (that will work in Switzerland) if the house has been empty for some time (although in winter you should ensure that the heating has been turned on).

## Provisions

You can take these with you if travelling by road, otherwise you can buy them on arrival:

- Tea, coffee, milk (long-life or powder), sugar (sweeteners), biscuits, soft drinks, bottled water, beer and wine;

- Breakfast cereals, snack food (fruit, crisps, cheese, bread, etc.), prepared meals for lunch/dinner and tinned food;

- Pet food, bowls and litter;

- Baby food;

- Bottle of bubbly to drink when the removal men have gone!

☑ **SURVIVAL TIP**

It may be easier and more pleasant to treat yourself to a meal in a local restaurant on your first evening in your new home, rather than cook a meal.

## COUNTDOWN TO MOVING DAY

As soon as you know your exact moving date – ideally at least four weeks in advance – you should begin to plan your removal. The key to a smooth move is to consider all aspects well in advance and make a schedule of when jobs need to be done – and stick to it! You also need to allow for Murphy (fate) to throw a spanner in the works at the last moment!

The way to ensure a trouble-free move is to make a number of checklists of jobs to be done before moving day, split into periods of from a few months before the move to the actual moving day itself. These checklists relate solely to the task of moving your family and belongings from one home to another. They don't include other activities involved in the buying or selling process, therefore you should bear in mind that there will be many other things going on that could affect your schedule. To help you plan your move, the jobs to be completed before moving day have been divided into the timeframes shown below.

- A few months before moving;

- Four weeks before moving;

- Two weeks before moving;

- One week before moving;

- Three days before moving;

- The day before moving;

- Moving day;

- On arrival;

- After moving.

Note that the checklists below are only a guide and you may prefer to do some things earlier or later than indicated. The most important thing is that you have them on your list!

## A Few Months Before Moving

There are a number of things you need to plan well in advance of a move to Switzerland, which include the following:

- Check that your and your family's passports are valid, and check whether you need a visa to live or work in Switzerland.

- Obtain the necessary customs forms and start to complete them. This may be taken care of by your moving company, but you need to check, both with them and with customs.

- Give notice to your employer, if applicable. If you're self-employed, you'll need to wind down (or sell) your business and notify your clients.

- If you live in rented accommodation you must give your landlord notice, as required by your rental contract. This also applies if you have a separate contract for a garage or other rented property, e.g. a holiday home. Arrange a date with your landlord for the handover and repayment of your deposit. If you own a home abroad, you may need or wish to sell or rent it.

♦ Book a removal company to ship your personal belongings to Switzerland. Payment may need to be by credit or debit card in advance if you're moving abroad. Arrange to sell anything you aren't taking with you, e.g. house, car and furniture.

♦ Inform your children's current schools as far in advance as possible of their leaving date, or warn them that you'll be moving; it may be necessary to give a term's notice. This also applies to colleges, universities and local educational institutions where any members of your family are studying. Obtain a copy of any relevant school reports or records from schools, and arrange to visit schools in Switzerland and enrol your children in schools in your new community.

♦ Contact companies and organisations from whom you need to get a refund, such as the tax authorities, insurance companies, local community (property taxes), utility companies, pension company, etc. Contact companies well in advance as they may be slow to respond (and even slower to pay!).

♦ You may wish to have health and dental check-ups before leaving for Switzerland. Obtain a copy of your health and dental records, and a statement from your health insurance company stating your present level of cover.

♦ Arrange alternative accommodation if required in the period between vacating your current home and taking up residence in a new home in Switzerland. If you need hotel or self-catering accommodation, you should book well in advance, particularly if you're moving during the summer months.

♦ If you're renting an apartment or house in Switzerland, confirm that the contract has been signed and is valid.

♦ Arrange for any inoculations, microchips, permits or quarantine (as necessary) for any pets you're taking with you to Switzerland. If they will be travelling with you, they may need to be sedated – ask your vet for advice. See also **Pets** on page 26.

♦ Terminate any loan, lease or hire purchase (credit) contracts and pay any outstanding bills (allow plenty of time, as some companies are slow to respond).

♦ If you're from outside the EU, you should obtain an international driving licence; nationals of some countries may also need a translation of their foreign driving licence. (Foreign residents can usually drive in Switzerland for a year with a foreign driving licence, after which they must exchange it for a Swiss one. However, people from certain countries need to take a Swiss driving test.)

## Four Weeks Before Moving

There are many things you need to do well in advance of a move. Some of the following tasks can be left until one or two weeks before your move, but you should at least be aware of them and make sure that they're on your 'jobs to do' list:

♦ Do anything not yet done from the **Some Months Before Moving** list above.

♦ Reconfirm your moving date with the removal company. Arrange for a delivery (or to collect) packing boxes from your

removal company if you'll be doing your own packing.

♦ Inform your insurance companies (for example health, car, house contents and private liability); banks, post office, stockbroker and other financial institutions; credit card and hire purchase (credit) companies; lawyer; accountant, and local businesses where you have accounts;

♦ Inform your family doctor, dentist and other health practitioners, and obtain copies of your health and dental records.

♦ Inform all regular correspondents, subscriptions, social and sports clubs, professional and trade journals, and friends and relatives. Give or send them your new address and telephone number. Free address cards may be available from your local post office. Arrange to have your mail redirected by the post office.

♦ Check whether you're entitled to a rebate on your road tax, car and other insurance. Obtain an official letter from your motor insurance company stating your no-claims bonus.

♦ Notify your existing insurance companies, for example private health, car (see above), buildings and home contents. You should insure your new home from the day you move in (or when you become the legal owner) and may need to arrange other insurance, such as health and travel, before leaving for Switzerland.

♦ You may wish to arrange for a few friends to help you move or pack, which you'll need to organise well in advance, particularly if they need to take time off work.

♦ If you require a residents' parking permit or special permission from the council or police for the removal vehicle to park outside your current home, you may need to make an application for a permit to reserve a parking space. This may also need to be done in Switzerland (check with your shipping company and real estate agent in Switzerland).

♦ Arrange for a friend or neighbour to look after your pets on moving day or book them into a kennel/cattery. If they will be travelling with you they may need to be sedated – ask your vet for advice. You'll need to make prior arrangements to ship your pets to Switzerland (see **Pets** on page 26).

♦ In necessary, arrange for a babysitter or friend to look after your children on the day of the move.

♦ Contact any relevant government agencies (health, social security, pensions, tax authorities, etc.) in your home country and inform them that you're moving to Switzerland.

♦ Contact your telephone (fixed and mobile), internet, and cable or satellite TV companies and terminate any contracts.

♦ If you're taking a foreign-registered car to Switzerland, you're only permitted to drive it there for six months, after which you must re-register it in Switzerland or export it.

♦ If you're taking any appliances (which must be able to be legally used in Switzerland) or anything requiring specialist removal and installation, arrange for someone to disconnect or remove them. Some removal companies will do this or will arrange for someone to do it. If you need to buy new fitted carpets or curtains for your new home, arrange someone to take measurements and order them well in advance. It obviously pays to have carpets laid in a new home before you install your furniture.

♦ If you're taking carpets and curtains with you, you may wish to take the opportunity to have them professionally cleaned.

♦ Make arrangements for the cleaning of your old home or for furniture disassembling and assembling if you won't be doing it yourself. You may also wish to arrange for your new home to be professionally cleaned after the seller has moved out (if you're renting a home in

Switzerland, the previous tenant should have left it spotless).

♦ Start running down food stocks, particularly frozen foods. If your fridge and freezer are going into storage, they will need to be thoroughly cleaned and dried in order to prevent mould developing (store them with their doors ajar).

♦ Start sorting through your belongings in cupboards, loft, garden shed, workshop, garage, annexe, etc. and discard, sell or give away anything you don't plan to take with you. Investigate local car boot sales (or Ebay) and charity shops.

♦ Make a list of all the major items that you're taking with you for insurance purposes, including the cost, date and place of purchase.

♦ If applicable, arrange to have the telephone connected in your new Swiss home (☏ 0800-800 800) or get your agent to do it for you. If it's a new apartment, you may need to arrange for telephone sockets to be installed.

♦ Confirm that your children have been enrolled in their new schools in Switzerland.

♦ Go through all your papers and make a copy of important documents – store the originals and copies separately in a secure place, such as a safe. The originals will need to be taken with you to Switzerland. These may include birth certificates; driving licences; marriage certificate, divorce papers or death certificate (if a widow or widower); educational diplomas and professional certificates; employment references and curricula vitae; school records and student ID cards; medical and dental records; bank account and credit card details; insurance policies; and receipts for valuables.

♦ Arrange a leaving party for your friends, relatives and neighbours (you can also use this as an excuse to dispose of anything you don't want to take with you).

♦ Check that the apartment or house that you're buying or renting will be professionally cleaned. If you're renting, it should be spotless; but if you're buying, the vendor is under no obligation to clean the property and you may need to arrange this yourself. Check with the agent or previous owner.

## Two Weeks Before Moving

By now you should have finished sorting your cupboards, loft, garage, cellar, etc. and have discarded, sold or given away anything you don't plan to take with you. You should also have accumulated packing materials ready to start packing items that you won't need in the next few weeks. Other jobs to do in the next week include:

♦ Do anything not yet done from the **Four Weeks Before Moving** list above.

♦ Start packing anything you won't need until after your move.

♦ If you have arranged for anyone to help you on moving day or with packing a few days earlier, confirm the arrangement and that they will be available.

♦ Cut the lawns short so that you won't have to do them again. Drain any fuel from garden equipment such as lawnmowers, clean your BBQ, and ensure that all outdoor equipment is clean enough to transport.

♦ Make arrangements with gas, electricity and water companies to read meters. Although most companies officially require only a few days notice, it's advisable to contact them one or two weeks in advance and confirm the meter reading appointment (if applicable) a few days before.

♦ If you haven't already done so, start running down the contents of your freezer. This is necessary if you need to defrost it – either to clean and leave, or to take it with you.

♦ Sort through your kitchen cupboards and start packing any equipment, tinned food, crockery and cutlery that you won't need before you go. Dispose of anything you don't want.

♦ Make a backup copy (or two) of any important data on your computer to a portable hard disk drive, DVDs or a flash drive. After making a backup, check that you can read the backup files – there's nothing worse than a backup file that you cannot read!

---

### ⚠ Caution

Bear in mind that computer hardware doesn't always travel well, and the last thing you want to find is that you've lost vital data due to a hard disk crash and you don't have a backup!

◆ Contact banks, building societies, post office, credit union, stores and other institutions where you have accounts. You may wish to keep at least one local account open to pay bills (etc.) and also retain a credit/debit card until you have replaced it in Switzerland. If you have a safety deposit box or documents in safe keeping at your bank, you'll need to collect them and make alternative arrangements. Arrange for any direct debits or standing orders for your old home to be cancelled at the appropriate time.

◆ Contact credit, charge and store card companies and give them your new address and bank account details (if applicable). Also notify your card protection insurance company if you have one.

◆ Contact insurance companies such as health, pets, travel, income protection, third party liability, life, car, etc.

◆ Give your new address to your private pension companies, accountant, solicitor, and professional or regulatory bodies.

◆ Contact hire purchase and loan companies, and local businesses where you have accounts.

◆ Ask your removal company about protection for floors and carpets on moving day. They should be able to provide special self-adhesive floor protection or tell you where you can buy it.

◆ Inform your family doctor, dentist, optician and other health practitioners that you're moving to Switzerland. If you have regular prescriptions, ensure that you have sufficient medicines to last until you've registered with a new doctor. If you're undergoing a course of treatment, notify a new doctor as soon as possible and arrange to continue treatment in Switzerland.

◆ Notify private clinics or health practitioners such as a chiropodist, chiropractor, optometrist, osteopath, physiotherapist, etc.

◆ Obtain a letter from your children's school principal(s) regarding their status (year, standard, etc.) and exam results.

◆ Contact anyone necessary to tell them that you're moving. These may include your accountant, alarm company (home), babysitter, car breakdown service, car washer, catalogue shopping companies, charities, cleaner, chiropodist, football pools coupon collector, frequent flyer schemes, gardener, gym or leisure centre, hairdresser, library, masseur, milkman, national savings/premium bonds, newsagent, nursery or playgroup, online shopping accounts (e.g. Amazon or Ebay), pension provider, religious organisations, store cards, trade unions, tutors, vet, website hosting companies and window cleaner. It's unnecessary to give everyone your new address, but it will save time to have a 'change of address' notice printed to distribute to your family, friends and those listed above – this can also be done via email.

◆ Arrange for the electricity, gas and water to be turned on (usually they will have been left on) when you arrive, and have the heating switched on if necessary. You may need to get your agent or a friend in Switzerland to arrange this.

## One Week Before Moving

One week before moving, you should have completed most of your packing and should only have minor items to pack, such as clothes and essentials that you're taking with you.

◆ Do anything not yet done from the **Two Weeks Before Moving** list above.

◆ Check that you haven't forgotten anything that you didn't agree to leave such as

bathroom cabinets, shelving, mirrors, pictures and light fittings. If you haven't already done so, now is a good time to dismantle any furniture that cannot be moved in one piece (keep all the nuts and bolts in a labelled bag).

---

**☑ SURVIVAL TIP**

Have your mail redirected at the local post office. A post office usually requires at least one week's notice or five working days. If you don't want your mail redirected to Switzerland (which may be unreliable and is expensive) you can have it redirected to a friend or relative in your current country who can inform you of anything urgent by phone, or scan mail and send it to you via email.

---

♦ Contact the local authority and inform them of the day you're moving. You may be entitled to a refund of part of your council tax.

♦ Arrange to drop off your house keys with your real estate agent.

♦ Give the kitchen a thorough spring clean.

♦ Start finalising your 'survival rations' (see above).

♦ Check (again) that the removers have all the instructions and information necessary – including maps and instructions about how to find your old and new homes and a colour-coded floor plan of your new home – and confirm the moving date and time.

♦ If applicable, apply to the local council to suspend a parking bay (or two) or get the police to cone off a parking area outside your house on moving day.

♦ Obtain your pets' records from your vet.

♦ Give friends, relatives and business associates the address and telephone number of your new home or, if you're moving into temporary accommodation, an address (plus email) and telephone number (mobile?) where you can be contacted.

♦ Return any library books and DVDs or anything borrowed.

♦ Give your new address to all regular correspondents such as newspaper and magazine subscriptions, book clubs, social and sports clubs, and professional and trade journals. You can do this earlier, but it's advisable not to do so before the exchange of sales contracts or the rental agreement is signed, as your purchase or rental could fall through.

♦ If you operate a business from home, arrange for the printing of new headed notepaper and business cards.

♦ Collect any dry cleaning, repairs or anything on loan.

♦ Make sure that you've got a telephone number on the removal day where you can be contacted by the removers, your spouse or partner, and anyone else who may need to contact you urgently. This could be your own or a borrowed mobile phone, or that of a friend who can relay messages.

♦ If you have a large amount of rubbish or things to be recycled or taken to a dump, arrange for someone to collect them.

♦ If someone is moving into your old home the same day you're moving out, co-ordinate your move with them.

## Three Days Before Moving

By now you'll be wondering whether you'll ever get everything done in time, although you should be well on track if you've been following these guidelines!

♦ Do anything not yet done from the **One Week Before Moving** list above.

♦ Finish off cleaning the kitchen. Clear out the freezer, defrost the fridge and freezer and give them a thorough clean (make sure that they're dry).

♦ Complete odd jobs such as finding and labelling spare keys, throwing away any junk you aren't taking with you, getting rid of sacks of rubbish, recycling bottles and newspapers, etc.

♦ Finish packing and labelling boxes and check that they're labelled correctly.

♦ Start cleaning the rest of the house.

◆ Confirm that meters will be read by utility companies before or soon after you move.

◆ Do last minute laundry and pack any clothes you won't need until after your move.

◆ Cancel any regular deliveries, e.g. milk, newspapers and magazines, and pay any outstanding bills.

◆ If you're renting a home, arrange the handover and inventory/condition report with the landlord or agent and the handover of the keys – or what to do with the keys on moving day.

## The Day Before Moving

By now you should be almost finished, and sitting around enjoying a well-earned rest, rather than running around like a headless chicken!

◆ Do anything not yet done from the **Three Days Before Moving** list above.

◆ Confirm that there's a parking area for the removal vehicle or hire van.

◆ Confirm the arrangement for your children and pets if they're being looked after by friends or relatives.

◆ Provide the removal company with any last minute instructions regarding how to find your home from the nearest motorway or main road and how you can be contacted if they get lost.

◆ Make sure that you have all your survival rations (see page 207) – if not, you may have to dash out and do a quick shop.

◆ Pack any remaining things that you've wanted to leave out until the last minute.

◆ Take down and pack the curtains and blinds, if they aren't being left for the new owner.

◆ Check that you have the keys for your new home, or when and where you can collect them.

◆ Finish cleaning the house.

◆ Disconnect the power and water from your washing machine and fit transit bolts if necessary.

◆ Disconnect your TV aerial or satellite dish if you're taking them with you.

◆ Note the readings on your gas, electricity and water meters.

◆ Have a final check over your home to see whether you've forgotten anything.

◆ Withdraw some cash from the bank to cover emergencies and out-of-pocket expenses.

◆ Get a good night's sleep – but don't forget to set the alarm (or two) if you're making an unusually early start!

## Moving Out

There are certain unwritten rules when moving out of a property:

◆ Don't remove door handles, light-bulbs or light fittings, fireplaces, fitted cupboards or anything planted in the garden or cemented down, unless it was specifically excluded in the purchase contract.

◆ Leave a property in the condition in which the buyer first saw it, but cleared of items that weren't included in the purchase price or weren't purchased separately by the new owner.

◆ Do as you would be done by – clean the property and dispose of all rubbish and unwanted belongings.

◆ Don't forget to take everything with you, as the new owner could claim that any items you leave behind are his, and they could be difficult to recover.

## Moving Day

Hurrah – it's moving day at last! If you have forgotten to do anything from the above lists, it's now too late! However, before you break open the champagne you have a long, exhausting day ahead of you, where anything and everything can go wrong.

The following list assumes that you'll be there to supervise the move at both ends. If this isn't the case, you must ensure that someone will be at the collection and delivery addresses to supervise the loading and unloading, otherwise everything could end up in the wrong place!

◆ Cover the floors and carpets to protect them from water, dirt, heavy boots, etc. The covering must lie flat and be slip resistant. You can buy special self-adhesive floor protection. Plastic sheets and paper aren't suitable.

◆ Show the removal team's foreman around the house and give him any final instructions regarding the removal or packing of any special items.

◆ Ensure that the movers have the floor plan and colour-coded guide of your new home so that they know where to put items.

◆ Take the children and pets to their carers for the day or, if they're staying with you, set aside a room with food, drinks, toys, books and laptop computer.

◆ Provide ample tea, coffee, soft drinks and biscuits/snacks for everyone!

◆ Pack up your toiletries and make a last check of bathroom cabinets.

◆ Check that wardrobes and cupboards are empty.

◆ Strip the beds and put the bedding in plastic bags; you may want to take this with you for use on arrival if you'll be travelling by road to Switzerland.

◆ Make sure that the movers haven't packed anything which was included in the sale of your home (these should be prominently marked);

◆ Check that all the rooms are empty and the lights switched off.

◆ Switch off the fridge (and leave the door ajar) and boiler, and disconnect any appliances that you're leaving. Ensure that the water, gas and electricity supplies are turned off at the mains.

◆ Empty rubbish bins and leave rubbish bags for collection.

◆ Close and lock all windows and doors. Leave all keys to internal doors, windows, garage, shed and other outbuildings (which should be clearly labelled).

◆ Once the van is loaded, check the complete house, garden and outbuildings with the foreman to ensure that all items to be moved have been loaded.

◆ Say goodbye to your old home, wipe away the tears and drive off into the sunset (taking one last backward glance in the mirror!).

◆ Drop the front door keys off at your solicitor or real estate agent.

## On Arrival

On arrival at your new home you'll need to do the following, or arrange for someone to do them for you:

◆ Unload your survival rations (if travelling to Switzerland by car) and organise the children and pets. Pets should be kept in a quiet room from which they cannot escape.

◆ Install lamp fittings and light bulbs before it gets dark, otherwise the property may have no lighting.

◆ Make sure that you've protected the flooring where it will get a lot of use from the removers, particularly if it's a wet day.

◆ Ensure that everything is unloaded and stored in the appropriate rooms in your new home (and unpacked by the removers if applicable).

◆ Because it's usually impossible to complete unpacking and putting everything into its proper place in one day (or half a day), you should concentrate on the rooms that are most important for daily life, such as the bedroom(s), bathroom(s) and kitchen.

◆ Once you're satisfied that everything has been delivered (check them off against your inventory) and positioned in the appropriate place, you'll be asked to acknowledge this by signing the delivery sheet. If you find that anything is damaged or missing later, contact the removal company immediately and make a claim.

◆ Have something to eat and drink (not forgetting to offer the removers a drink – but not alcohol).

◆ Make the beds with the bed linen that you've brought with you (if applicable).

◆ Plug in your fixed-line phone (if you have a Swiss phone) and any appliances (e.g. fridge/freezer) that were left by the previous owners.

## After Moving In

In the few days following your move, you'll need (or may wish) to do the following; some things will have been done already:

◆ One of the most important tasks to perform after moving into a new home in Switzerland is to make an inventory of the fixtures and fittings, and, if applicable, the furniture and furnishings. When moving into a rental property, it's necessary to complete an inventory (*Hauszustand/Mängelliste, état des lieux*) of the contents and a report on their condition (see page 158).

◆ Make a note of the meter readings, and check that you aren't overcharged on your first utility bills.

◆ Check that the owner or management has changed the name plates for your letterbox and doorbell (or arranged to have them fitted). Empty the mailbox and take any mail addressed to the previous owner to a post office.

◆ Open a bank account if you haven't already done so.

◆ Arrange for an internet service if you haven't already done so, or check it's working and that you can send and receive emails. If you don't have an internet service, you'll need to find a local library or business office where you can check your email.

◆ Arrange for all household bills (utilities, cable TV, internet, etc.) to be transferred to your name, and for all regular bills to be paid by standing order.

◆ Register with your local community within eight days of taking up residence (see **Registration** on page 223);

◆ Arrange health, household and any other insurance necessary, if not done previously. You can do this by contacting a local independent insurance broker.

◆ You may also wish to have an alarm system installed or have the general security checked, e.g. are there locks on the windows?

◆ Get extra house keys cut if required.

◆ Contact the local council offices and tourist office (etc.) to obtain information about local amenities, sports facilities, clubs, educational establishments, etc.

◆ Make courtesy calls on your neighbours. This is particularly important in villages and rural areas if you want to become part of the local community.

◆ If you have oil or gas-fired central heating, you may need to order a delivery of oil or have the gas installation checked.

◆ Check with your local town hall regarding regulations about such things as rubbish collection, recycling and parking.

◆ Check that you've given everyone necessary your new address, email address and telephone number(s). You may wish to have stationery or business cards printed with your new address.

◆ Make sure that you're receiving your post if it's being forwarded to Switzerland.

◆ If you need to store any items in Switzerland, either permanently or temporarily, there are storage companies in all major cities, e.g. Zebra Box, 🖥 www.zebrabox.com/en.

◆ Organise your house-warming party and invite your neighbours!

## PREPARING YOUR NEW HOME

If you're lucky, you'll have some time between taking over a new home and actually moving in. This will give you time to get your new home ready and to have any necessary work done before you move in. After you move in, it takes a while to get settled, and the last thing you want is the disruption caused by renovation, repairs or redecoration going on around you.

☑ **SURVIVAL TIP**

**Cleaning**

Whether you hire a professional cleaning firm or do it yourself, an empty house is far easier to clean than a full one. If you're renting, the property should already have been professionally cleaned, but there are no rules when buying a home.

### Decoration

Doing any decorating before you move in means that you don't have to worry about rearranging rooms, putting dust covers on everything, getting paint spots on the carpet (if you're changing the carpets, do it after you've decorated) and living with the smell of wet paint.

### Renovation & Repairs

Sometimes you must make some repairs to satisfy your lender, or maybe your survey revealed a few nasty surprises that you want to get fixed. If you buy an old house it could need rewiring, new plumbing or eradication of damp. When a property is empty it's an ideal opportunity to get this work out of the way without having to live on a building site.

### Improvements

Whether it's installing a new shower room, refurbishing the kitchen or installing new windows, the best time to get work done is before you move into a new home. Even relatively straightforward jobs such as sanding floorboards, laying carpets or getting the existing carpets professionally cleaned, are far simpler when you can entirely remove the contents of a room.

## CHILDREN

Moving with young children can be highly stressful. Many parents find that it's best to get a relative or friend to look after them on moving day or allow older children to stay with friends. Failing this you should try to keep them occupied and out of the way by providing diversions in your survival rations (see page 207) such as a computer, TV, books, games and toys. You can invite some of their friends to stay once you're settled in, which will give them something to look forward to and help them feel less isolated. You should also suggest that they write, email or phone their friends if visiting them is difficult.

## PETS

Cats and dogs become very attached to their familiar territory, so you should give them extra care and attention before and during a move. It may be possible to arrange for a friend or neighbour to look after them on moving day or arrange for them to go into a kennel/cattery for a few days. If they will be travelling with you, they may need to be sedated, as many pets are unsettled by the loss of their familiar surroundings and may run off and hide. On moving day it's best to keep them indoors in a quiet room, well away from the hustle and bustle of workmen.

Small animals such as guinea pigs, hamsters and rabbits are best transported in well-ventilated 'chew-proof' containers made of metal or rigid plastic. Give them plenty of bedding and a little food and provide lots of water in a non-spill container. Budgies travel best in a well-ventilated box with subdued lighting, which has a calming effect. If a budgie is travelling in its cage, make sure that you remove any articles that could become dislodged. Keep a bird as quiet as possible during the trip – covering part of the cage with a cloth or blanket may help, but ensure that there's good ventilation.

Fish should be transported in clean, strong, polythene bags part-filled with tank water – not tap water. Make sure that you seal the bags properly and leave a good air pocket above the water. Gently place the bags into a polystyrene container (available from fish importers and aquatic specialists) and label the containers with their contents and the words 'THIS WAY UP'.

Many animals don't like travelling by car and can suffer from travel sickness, panic attacks and anxiety. To prevent travel sickness, it's advisable not to feed pets for 12 hours prior to a journey. If you know that your pet suffers from travel sickness, ask your veterinary surgeon about anti-sickness pills and ensure that the car is well ventilated. Dogs need frequent stops for exercise, watering and toilet breaks. Ideally, your dog should travel in a holding cage, but make sure that it's a suitable size.

Don't leave dogs alone in a car during hot weather as the temperature can rise very quickly and they can die from heat exhaustion. If you have to leave them for a short period, leave a window open and make sure that the car is parked in the shade. Cats may take a little while to adjust to their new surroundings. Give your cat a fresh litter tray, its favourite food and lots of attention. Let it rest quietly at least overnight, then when things have settled down let it explore the rest of the house. After a few days or so, you can let your cat out (on a lead ideally) for a short period to let it get its bearings. Give a cat only part of its normal feed just before it goes out alone for the first time, which will encourage it to come back to its new home.

Dogs adapt quicker to new surroundings, although they still need to be left in a quiet room with food and water to recover from the journey. Take dogs on lots of walks on a lead to introduce them to their new surroundings. Fish need to be settled into their new home straight away. You should treat them as if they were new fish, de-chlorinating the water in the tank and ensuring that both the water in the tank and in the bags in which they were transported is at room temperature.

Each year many animals are lost when their owners move house. Make sure that your cats and dogs have a microchip implanted (compatible with the Swiss system if it's done before arrival) as soon as possible after arrival and register them with ANIS. Contact a veterinary surgeon for information. If a dog is over six months of age, it must be licensed (see **Pets** on page 26) by your local community.

Stockalper Palace, Brig, Valais

Ouchy Marina, Lausanne

# 9.
# ARRIVAL

**S**witzerland is a signatory to the Schengen agreement, an open-border policy between 25 European countries. Switzerland officially became a member on 12th December 2008, when all land border controls between Switzerland and the other 24 member countries were removed (air border controls were removed in March 2009).

Other Schengen members are Austria, Belgium, the Czech Republic, Denmark, Estonia, Finland, France, Germany, Greece, Hungary, Iceland, Italy, Latvia, Lithuania, Luxembourg, Malta, the Netherlands, Norway, Poland, Portugal, Slovakia, Slovenia, Spain and Sweden. Bulgaria, Liechtenstein and Romania are planning to implement the agreement later. The United Kingdom and Ireland aren't members, but are signatories to the Schengen police and judicial cooperation treaty.

So-called third-world citizens who aren't on the Schengen visa-free list (see 🖳 http://switzerland.visahq.com/requirements) can obtain a Schengen Visa (🖳 www.schengenvisa.cc) costing CHF 60, which allows them to travel freely between all Schengen member countries. Under the Schengen agreement, immigration checks and passport controls take place when you first arrive in a member country from outside the Schengen area, after which you can travel freely between member countries. A Schengen visa allows the holder to travel freely within Schengen countries for a maximum of 90 days in a six-month period.

Schengen visa holders aren't permitted to live permanently or work in Europe (short business trips aren't considered to be employment). Foreigners who intend to take up employment or self-employed activity in Switzerland (or any Schengen country) may require a visa, even if they're listed on the Schengen visa-free list.

Third-world nationals who are resident in Switzerland (or another Schengen country) can travel freely to all Schengen member countries without a visa, simply by showing their Swiss residence permit and passport (or other valid travel document). New third-world nationals resident in Switzerland receive a Schengen ID card (existing third-world residents receive one when their paper residence permit expires).

On arrival in Switzerland to take up employment or residence, there are a number of formalities that must be completed. These are described in this chapter, where you'll also find suggestions for finding local help and information, and useful checklists.

## BORDER CONTROL

On arrival in Switzerland, present your passport, Schengen visa and – if applicable – your 'assurance of a residence permit' (*Zusicherung der Aufenthaltsbewilligung, assurance d'autorisation de séjour et de travail*) document to the immigration authorities at the frontier or airport. If you're driving, you may need to arrive at the border control during 'business' hours. For a list of all Swiss Federal Customs offices, locations and opening hours, see 🖳 www.ezv.admin.ch (under Services/List of Offices). If you have an entry visa it will be cancelled by the immigration official. Ask the immigration official to stamp your 'assurance of a residence permit' document to verify your date of entry. This isn't obligatory but, in the words of the Federal Office of Public Health, 'is strongly recommended'.

Foreigners from certain countries, planning to work in Switzerland, may be required to have a health check (usually consisting only of an X-ray) within 72 hours in order to detect contagious diseases. The health check is no longer required for nationals of EEA countries, Australia, Canada, New Zealand and the US. Where applicable, the health check is carried out by a Swiss doctor of your choice, and you receive a stamp in your passport confirming that it has been completed.

## Customs

When you enter Switzerland to take up residence, household or personal effects that have been used for at least six months can be imported without incurring duty or VAT. A complete list of the items being imported must be provided at the time of entry, together with a request for duty-free import (a form is provided). VAT (7.6 per cent) must be paid on any articles you've used for less than six months; itemised invoices should be provided. If your Swiss home is a second home, you must usually pay VAT on all imports except clothes and other exempt items (you may be granted an exemption if your home country grants reciprocal rights to Swiss nationals). You will also require the following:

♦ an inventory of all goods to be imported. Articles which don't fulfil the conditions for duty-free charges should be itemised at the end of the list as 'goods for normal customs clearance'.

♦ your Swiss residence permit or assurance of a residence permit;

♦ the official foreign registration certificate for cars, motorcycles, motorboats and aeroplanes, as well as the sales receipt if available;

♦ a contract for the lease or purchase of a property or other proof of accommodation;

♦ a photocopy of the passports of everyone taking up residence in Switzerland;

♦ a completed form 18.44 (declaration/ application for clearance of household effects), available from the Federal Administration (Bundesverwaltung) website (🖳 www.ezv. admin.ch – follow links to *Dienstleistungen*,

*Publikationen und Formulare bestellen*, and *Übersiedlungs - und Erbschaftsgut*; the form includes instructions in English).

---

### ☑ SURVIVAL TIP

If you import a car duty-free and sell it in Switzerland within one year of your arrival, you're required to inform the customs authorities at the location where it was imported and pay import taxes, which are calculated on the age, value and sale price.

---

If you plan to enter Switzerland with a foreign-registered car and household effects (for example on a trailer), it's advisable to enter via a major frontier post, as smaller posts may not be equipped to deal with you unless they're informed of your arrival in advance.

Note also the following:

♦ Switzerland has no currency restrictions – the Swiss love all money!

♦ A licence is required to import guns and ammunition.

♦ There are restrictions on the type and quantity of plants and bulbs that may be imported.

Information regarding the importation of pets on page 26 and duty-free allowances (e.g. alcohol and tobacco) on page 241. Information about Swiss customs regulations is contained in a leaflet entitled *Customs Regulations for Travellers Domiciled Abroad*, available from customs offices, Switzerland Tourism offices or the Head Customs Office, (Eidgenössische Zollverwaltung/EZV, Administration fédérale des douanes/AFD, Monbijoustr. 40, CH-3003 Berne, ☎ 031-322 65 11, 🖳 www.zoll.admin.ch). The Head Customs Office also provides information regarding the importation of special items.

## MOTORWAY TAX

On entering Switzerland you may be asked whether you plan to use Swiss motorways, particularly if you enter via Basle, and if you answer yes, you must pay an annual motorway tax of CHF 40 on the spot. This tax is payable in addition to Swiss road tax and is applicable to all motor vehicles (including motorcycles) under 3.5 tonnes using Swiss motorways, whether Swiss or foreign-registered.

On payment of the tax, you're given a sticker (*vignette*) which must be affixed to your windscreen on the left hand side (top or bottom) or centre top. The *vignette* isn't transferable between vehicles and tears to pieces if you attempt to remove it (unless you know how!). If you have a trailer or caravan, it requires an additional *vignette*. Vehicles weighing over 3.5 tonnes are subject to a 'heavy vehicles' tax which is payable daily, monthly or annually (a 10-day pass is available for those who visit Switzerland frequently for periods of one or two days).

If you don't buy a *vignette* and are subsequently stopped by the police on a motorway, you're fined CHF 100 and must also pay the road tax on the spot. It is, of course, possible to drive around Switzerland without using motorways, but (very) time consuming (and pointless). The motorway tax is a small price to pay for the convenience of using some of the finest roads in Europe, particularly when you consider that there are no road tolls in Switzerland. To put it into perspective, the annual Swiss motorway tax is about the same price as around one day's motoring on French, Italian or Spanish motorways!

The *vignette* is valid for a calendar year, with a month's overlap at each end, e.g. 1st December 2009 to 31st January 2011 (although if you buy one in November, you must buy another in December for the following year).

It can be purchased in advance (although it's unnecessary) at Switzerland Tourism offices or from automobile associations throughout Europe. In Switzerland it's sold at border crossings, customs offices, post offices, garages, service stations and cantonal motor registries.

## REGISTRATION

Within eight days of arrival in Switzerland and before starting work, you (and your family) must register (*anmelden, s'annoncer*) with the local community (*Gemeinde, commune*) where you're living, even if you're in temporary accommodation, e.g. a hotel. This is done at your local community office (*Gemeindehaus, maison communale*) in country areas or an area office (*Kreisbüro, bureau d'arrondissement*) in cities. Cities and large towns often have an ominous-sounding 'residents' control' department (*Einwohnerkontrolle, contrôle des habitants*).

Switzerland has strict regulations regarding registration for a number of good reasons, the most important of which is that most residents pay taxes levied by their local community from their date of registration. Another is that each new resident foreign worker is deducted from a canton's annual permit quota. In any case, you must register in order to obtain a residence permit. If applicable, you must have a health check (see **Border Control** above) before you can register. Registration is obligatory for all residents, both foreigners and Swiss nationals.

At your community registration office you'll be asked to produce the following (as applicable):

♦ passports (containing the border health check stamp, if applicable) for all family members;

♦ 'assurance of a residence permit' document, which will be retained by your community registration office;

♦ a property lease or purchase contract;

♦ proof of health insurance;

♦ a contract of employment;

♦ a marriage certificate or divorce papers;

♦ birth certificates for each member of your family;

♦ two passport-size photographs (black and white or colour) for each member of your family aged up to 18 years (family members over 18 must present their own documents).

It's useful to have a supply of passport-size photos for all members of your family, for example for school ID cards, train and bus season tickets, ski passes and Swiss driving licences. Photographs are available from machines at most railway stations and in town centres.

You must complete a form that may include (vital) information such as your mother's and father's Christian names, and (for men) your mother's and wife's maiden names or (for women) your husband's mother's maiden name (make sure he knows this!). If you're divorced, separated or widowed, you should state this on the registration form, as you may be entitled to a small tax concession. You're also asked to state your religion (see **Church Tax** below). Annual B permit applicants receive their permits within a few weeks via their employer or community.

If you're moving to a new community or leaving Switzerland permanently, you must de-register (*Abmeldeung, déclaration de départ*) in your present community up to eight days before your departure, and register in your new community within eight days of taking up residence (if applicable).

If you're a B permit holder and live and work in different cantons, your residence permit won't be renewed by your canton of residence until your permission to work has been approved by the canton where you're employed.

## Church Tax

When you arrive in Switzerland and register in your local community (see **Registration** above) you must complete a form asking you to state your religion. All communities in Switzerland levy a church tax (*Kirchensteuer, impôt ecclésiastique*) on members of the three main Swiss churches: Catholic, Old Catholic (Protestant) and Reformed. (Now you know why Swiss churches are in such excellent repair.) If you enter 'Protestant', for example, you're registered as a member of the relevant church and must pay church tax. Members of other religions such as the Church of England, Methodists and Baptists, should clearly indicate their religion on the application. If you aren't a member of any church, just enter 'NONE' as your religion. This is legal and will ensure that you're able to reclaim any church tax deducted from your salary (see below).

Most foreigners pay direct income tax (*Quellensteuer, impôt à la source*) and in most cantons church tax is deducted at source from your gross salary, often without your knowledge or permission. It doesn't appear on your pay slip or your annual salary statement (*Lohnausweis, certificat de salaire*) and many foreigners are unaware that they pay it.

> **☑ SURVIVAL TIP**
>
> **If you pay direct income tax, in some cantons you automatically pay church tax, even if you're registered as an atheist.**

If you aren't registered as a member of an official Swiss church, you can reclaim your church tax every one to three years, via a form available from your community or by writing a letter to the relevant tax office. Enter your personal particulars and bank account information and attach a copy of your salary statement (*Lohnausweis, certificat de salaire*) for the period in question. Send the form to your canton's tax office (*Steueramt, Service des contributions*), the address of which is printed on the form. You will be advised by letter when your money (excluding interest!) has been credited to your account, usually after six to eight weeks.

If you're wrongly registered as a member of a taxable religion, you can have your records officially changed and reclaim any tax paid, although you can reclaim church tax for a limited period only, for example the last three years. The procedure depends on the canton where you live and the religion under which you're registered. If you do this, you cannot get married

to do so in case of an emergency (when the embassy can contact you).

## FINDING HELP

One of the biggest difficulties facing new homeowners in Switzerland is how and where to obtain help with day-to-day problems. However, in addition to the comprehensive information provided herein, you'll also require detailed local information. How successful you are at finding help will depend on your employer (if you work), the town or area where you live, your nationality, language proficiency and sex (women are better served than men through numerous women's clubs).

There's an abundance of general local information available in the Swiss national languages (French, German and Italian), although it usually isn't intended for foreigners and their particular needs; but little in English and other foreign languages. You may find that friends and colleagues can help, as they're often able to proffer advice based on their own experiences and mistakes, but it may be irrelevant to your circumstances and needs.

### Local Community

Your community is usually an excellent source of reliable information, but you'll probably need to speak the local language to benefit from it. Some companies may have a department (e.g. human resources) or staff whose task is to help newcomers settle in, or they may use a relocation company. Unfortunately, many employers in Switzerland seem totally unaware of (or uninterested in) the problems and difficulties faced by their foreign employees.

In some cities, e.g. Geneva and Zurich, there are free advice centres for foreigners, and the city of Zug (🖥 www.stadtzug.ch) provides not only an expat section in English, but supported the launch of the private website 🖥 www. thezugpost.ch, which provides local daily news in English, with the goal of integrating the expat community into daily life.

### Women's Clubs

If a woman lives in or near a major town, she's able to turn to many English-speaking women's clubs and organisations for help. The single foreign male (who, naturally, cannot possibly

or buried by this church (without paying a huge fee) and it may affect your children's religious status; for example, they may no longer receive religious instruction at school. Nevertheless, there are plenty of other churches only too happy to have you as a tax-free member, e.g. Anglicans, Baptists, Methodists, Pentecostals, the Salvation Army and many others, not to mention any number of religious sects. If you don't reclaim wrongly paid church tax, the three churches divide the spoils among themselves – the interest alone must be worth a Pope's ransom.

The amount of tax payable depends on your salary (church tax is calculated as a percentage of your basic tax value – see page 182), your community (parish), your canton tax rates and your religion, and can amount to several thousand francs a year if you earn a high salary.

### Embassy Registration

Nationals of some countries are required to register with their local embassy or consulate as soon as possible after arrival in Switzerland. Even if registration isn't mandatory, it's wise have any problems) must usually fend for himself, although there are men's expatriate clubs in some cities and mixed social clubs throughout the country.

## *FAWCO*

Among the best sources of information and help for women are the Swiss branches of the Federation of American Women's Clubs Overseas (FAWCO, 🖥 www.fawco.org) with branches in Berne, Basle, Geneva, Lausanne and Zurich. FAWCO clubs provide comprehensive information in English about both local matters and topics of more general interest. They can provide detailed information about all aspects of living in Switzerland, including accommodation costs, school profiles, names of English-speaking doctors and dentists, shopping information and much more.

FAWCO clubs produce data sheets and booklets containing a wealth of valuable local information, and they also run libraries open to non-members. FAWCO publications can be purchased directly from FAWCO clubs or from local bookshops. Clubs organise a variety of social events, plus many day and evening classes, ranging from local cooking to language classes.

The main disadvantage for many foreigners is that FAWCO clubs have quotas for non-American members (i.e. anyone who isn't an American citizen, married to an American or the daughter or mother of a member). The rules vary slightly from club to club, although in general members must speak fluent English and have strong links with the US, e.g. through study, work or a husband who works for a US company or the US government. Anyone can, however, subscribe to their newsletters.

FAWCO runs excellent orientation programmes for newcomers to Switzerland, open to both men and women, including non-members. Courses are usually held once a year and consist of a series of meetings over a period of weeks, usually during the day (which can be a problem if you're working). Places are limited, so apply early. Course participants receive a comprehensive resource book, which may be available to non-participants for a fee. FAWCO clubs are non-profit, charitable organisations and are staffed by volunteers.

## AngloPhone Information Service

A good source of information for both newcomers and long-term residents is the AngloPhone Information Service, PO Box 2024, CH-1227 Carouge (☎ 0900-576 444 – CHF 3.12 a minute, Monday-Friday from 9-12am and 2-7pm, 🖥 www.anglophone.ch). AngloPhone can provide information about virtually anything, including finding help in emergencies, classes (in English), activities, professionals and their services (such as tax advisers, accountants and lawyers), leisure and entertainment, sports activities and facilities, shopping, clubs and associations, and myriad other subjects.

---

☑ **SURVIVAL TIP**

AngloPhone staff will attempt to answer questions on almost any subject, whether it's related to Switzerland or not.

---

Anglophone will try to find English-speaking tradesmen and professionals for those who don't speak the local language. They also provide a message service, e.g. for family, friends, business associates and club members and publish a magazine, *Swiss Style*, containing information for both residents and tourists (available free from over 600 distribution points throughout Switzerland or on subscription).

## Other Sources

In addition to the above, there are numerous social clubs and other organisations for foreigners in Switzerland, whose members can help you find your way around. Many embassies and consulates provide information, particularly about clubs for their nationals, and many businesses (e.g. Swiss banks) produce booklets and leaflets containing useful information. Bookshops may stock useful publications, and Swiss English-language periodicals provide useful information and contacts. Local tourist and information offices can also be of assistance.

# CHECKLISTS

## Before Arrival

The following checklist contains a summary of the tasks that should (if possible) be completed before your arrival in Switzerland:

- obtain a visa, if necessary, for you and all your family members (see page 22). Obviously this must be done before your arrival in Switzerland.

- you may wish to visit Switzerland to compare communities and schools, and arrange schooling for your children (see **Choosing the Location** on page 72).

- find temporary or permanent accommodation (see **Chapter 6**) and arrange for shipment of your personal effects to Switzerland (see **Chapter 8**).

- arrange health insurance for yourself and your family (see page 32). This is essential if you don't have a private insurance policy and won't be covered automatically by your Swiss employer.

- open a bank account in Switzerland and transfer funds (many people can open an account with the major Swiss banks from abroad, although US citizens may have difficulties since the US government's crackdown on tax evasion). It's best to obtain some Swiss francs before your arrival in Switzerland, which will save you having to spend time changing money on arrival. See **Chapter 7**.

- Collect and update all your family's personal records including medical, dental, schools, insurance (e.g. car insurance), professional and employment (including job references). See also the list below.

- obtain an international driving permit, if necessary.

certified copies, official translations and numerous passport-size photographs (students should take at least a dozen).

## After Arrival

The following checklist contains a summary of tasks to be completed on or after arrival in Switzerland (if not done before):

- on arrival at the Swiss border or airport, give your permit approval document and passport to the official for date stamping.

- if you're importing a car, you may need to complete a form for temporary importation. If you don't own a car, you may wish to rent one for a week or two until you buy one locally.

- visit a health clinic within 72 hours for a health check (if necessary, you'll be informed when you arrive at the border or airport).

- open a bank account (see page 168) and give the details to your employer in order to get paid.

- register at your community registration office within eight days of arrival (see above).

- register with your local embassy or consulate (see above).

- obtain a Schengen visa, if necessary (see page 221).

- arrange schooling for your children.

- arrange whatever insurance is necessary for your home, car and your family (see **Chapter 10**).

Don't forget to bring all your family's official documents with you, including birth certificates, driving licences, marriage certificate, divorce papers or death certificate (if a widow or widower), educational diplomas, professional certificates, job references, school records and student ID cards, employment references, medical and dental records, bank account and credit card details, insurance policies and receipts for any valuables. You also need the documents necessary to obtain a residence permit, plus

# 10.

# MISCELLANEOUS

This chapter contains miscellaneous, but nevertheless important, information for homeowners in Switzerland, including crime, insurance, public holidays, shopping, telecommunications, television and radio, utilities and waste disposal/recycling.

## CRIME

Switzerland is a very safe country in which to live or visit and has a very low crime rate – one of the lowest, if not the lowest, in the world. Violent crimes such as assault, mugging and rape are fortunately rare in Switzerland and you can safely walk anywhere, day or night. Gun crime rates are so low that statistics aren't even kept. Over half of all crimes in Switzerland are committed by foreigners (particularly violent crime and drug offences) and Swiss prisons contain a high proportion of foreigners, although most are non-residents who come to Switzerland especially to commit crimes.

Negligence is the cause of many thefts, with mopeds and bicycles being the main target. The Swiss are too trusting for their own good and often leave doors, windows and even safes open for their friendly neighbourhood thief (if you're a crook, you shouldn't be reading this). Don't leave cash, cheques, credit cards, passports, jewellery and other valuables lying around or even hidden in your home (the crooks know all the hiding places). Good locks help but may not keep the professionals out (they drill them out). It's better to keep your valuables in a safety deposit box and ensure that you have adequate home contents insurance (see below). Remember to lock your car and put any valuables in the boot or out of sight, particularly when parking overnight in a public place, and look after your expensive skis and other belongings in ski resorts.

Most modern apartment blocks in Switzerland are fitted with an intercom system, allowing residents to speak to callers before giving them access to the building. In addition, most apartment doors have a spy-hole so that you can check a visitor's identity before opening the door, and many homes also have armoured doors with high security locking systems which help prevent burglaries.

There are pickpockets in major cities and tourist centres, so don't walk around with your wallet or purse on display and men shouldn't keep their wallet in their back trouser pocket. Some theft insurance doesn't cover pickpocket thefts, only robbery with violence (so tell your insurance company that you were robbed at gun point!).

### Home Security

Security is important when buying a home in Switzerland, particularly if it will be vacant for long periods. Obtain advice from the local police, security companies and neighbours. Bear in mind, however, that no matter how good your security, a property is rarely impregnable, so you shouldn't leave valuables in an unattended home unless they're kept in a safe.

If you keep a lot of valuables in your home, such as antiques, jewellery or a valuable art collection, your insurance company may insist on extra security measures (such as a monitored alarm system) or that valuables are stored in a safe or safety deposit box, particularly when a property is left unattended for long periods.

Most thieves are opportunists looking for money, jewellery and items that can be easily resold, such as laptop computers, mobile phones and cameras. They target both apartments and villas, and affluent and non-affluent areas equally. In the majority of cases, the burglar is in-and-out of a home in a matter of minutes, usually breaking and entering through a door (patio or balcony doors are a weak point) or window. Police recommend that external doors have a steel frame, particularly

in border areas such as Basle and Geneva. However, if you aren't a homeowner, you may be disinclined to pay for a security door if your landlord isn't willing to contribute.

If you live in a house, you may wish to have a security alarm fitted, which is usually the best way to deter thieves and may also reduce your household insurance (see below). It should include all external doors and windows, internal infra-red security beams, and may also include a coded entry keypad (which can be frequently changed and is useful for guests if you let a home) and 24-hour monitoring (with some systems it's possible to monitor properties remotely from another country). With a monitored system, when a sensor (e.g. smoke or forced entry) detects an emergency or a panic button is pushed, a signal is sent automatically to a 24-hour monitoring station. The duty monitor will telephone to check whether it's a genuine alarm and, if he cannot contact you, will send someone to investigate.

You can deter thieves by ensuring that your house is well lit and not conspicuously unoccupied. External security 'motion detector' lights (that switch on automatically when someone approaches); random timed switches for internal lights, radios and televisions; dummy security cameras; and tapes that play barking dogs (etc.) triggered by a light or heat detector, may all help to deter burglars. It's advisable to inform your neighbours when you're away from home for an extended period and arrange for someone to clear the (junk) mail from your mail box and check your home periodically.

You can fit UPVC (toughened clear plastic) security windows and doors, which can survive an attack with a sledge-hammer without damage, and external steel security blinds (which can be electrically operated), although these are expensive. A dog can be useful to deter intruders, although he should be kept inside where he cannot easily be given poisoned food. Irrespective of whether you actually have a dog, a warning sign with a picture of a fierce dog may act as a deterrent. Bear in mind that prevention is better than cure, as stolen property is rarely recovered.

Remote holiday homes are particularly vulnerable to thieves. No matter how secure your door and window locks, a thief can usually obtain entry if he's sufficiently determined, often by simply smashing a window or even breaking in through the roof or knocking a hole in a wall! In isolated areas, thieves can strip a house bare at their leisure, and an unmonitored alarm won't be a deterrent if there's no-one around to hear it. If you have a holiday home in Switzerland, it isn't wise to leave anything of great value (monetary or sentimental) there.

If you vacate your home for long periods, you may wish to notify your caretaker or landlord. When closing up a property for an extended period, e.g. over the winter, you should ensure that everything is switched off and that it's secure. If you have a robbery, you should report it immediately to your local police station, where you must make a statement; you'll receive a copy, which is required by your insurance company if you make a claim.

Another important aspect of home security is ensuring that you have early warning of a fire, which is easily accomplished by installing smoke detectors. Battery-operated smoke detectors cost from around CHF 50 (or less than half this, abroad) and should be tested periodically to ensure that the batteries aren't exhausted (some emit a beep when the batteries are low). You can also fit an electric-powered gas detector that activates an alarm when a gas leak is detected.

There are specialist home security companies in Switzerland who will inspect your home and offer free advice on security, although you should shop around and obtain at least two quotations before having any work done.

# INSURANCE

An important aspect of owning a home in Switzerland is insurance, not only for your home and its contents, but also health insurance for your family when living in or visiting Switzerland. It's vital to ensure that you have sufficient insurance, when visiting your home abroad, which includes travel insurance, building and contents insurance and health insurance, as well as car insurance (including breakdown insurance) and third party liability insurance.

If you live in Switzerland permanently, you'll require additional insurance. It's unnecessary to spend half your income insuring yourself against every eventuality, from the common cold to being sued for your last cent, although it's important to insure against any event that could precipitate a major financial disaster, such as a serious accident or your house being burned to the ground or demolished by a storm. The cost of being uninsured or under-insured can be astronomical.

> ☑ **SURVIVAL TIP**
>
> In all matters regarding insurance, you're responsible for ensuring that you and your family are legally insured. The law in Switzerland may differ from that in your home country or your previous country of residence, and you should never assume that it's the same.

While most policies have what looks like a fixed term, e.g. three years, they're still renewed automatically by another year if you don't give the company notice three months before the end of the term. It's advisable to choose a policy with as short a contract period as possible, e.g. an annual policy with an automatic extension, or one that can be terminated annually, which will allow you to switch to a better/cheaper policy when possible.

You can compare the cost of insurance via websites such as Comparis (🖥 www.comparis. ch). See also **Health Insurance** on page 32.

## Building Insurance

When buying a home, you're usually responsible for insuring it as soon as you become the official owner, which is usually before you move in. Building insurance (*Gebäudeversicherung, assurance immobilière*), also referred to as fire and elementary damage insurance, is obligatory in all but four cantons: Appenzell-Innerrhoden, Geneva, Ticino and Valais. In all cantons except for Appenzell-Innerrhoden, Obwalden, Schwyz and Uri (where you'll need to find a private insurance company), the canton has a monopoly on building insurance, i.e. you must insure your home with the canton insurance office. The advantage is that the premiums are quite reasonable and everyone pays the same rate based on an index system (see below).

Building insurance includes cover for loss or damage caused by fire (including fire, explosion, smoke damage and lightning strike); damage from natural events such as storms, flood, hail, avalanche, snow, rockfalls and mud slides; damage caused by crashing airplanes or helicopters; television implosion; and oil tank leakage. Insurance companies also offer optional cover, for example outbuildings and trees and shrubs damaged maliciously or by storms. Canton Zurich is the only canton where earthquake insurance is obligatory and is included in building insurance, although there's an on-going debate as to whether this should be mandatory throughout Switzerland. (N.B. There isn't a greater risk of earthquakes in canton Zurich than elsewhere in Switzerland.)

Water leakage from pipes isn't covered by building insurance and it's advisable to have separate building water insurance. If furniture and belongings are damaged by water leakage, your household contents insurance will cover the damage, but if the leakage damages, for example, wooden floors and wallpaper, then it won't be covered by the building insurance but would come under the building water insurance. However, water damage caused by floods and storms is covered.

Water damage caused by an indoor fountain or aquarium, a burst waterbed or an overflowing bathtub generally isn't covered by building insurance, and you should check with your insurance agent whether they cover these. Damage from rain or snow that enters via a damaged roof or open window also isn't covered by building insurance. Building water insurance also covers the drying costs after flooding. Some insurance companies don't include cleaning up as the result of a claim (for example if a house burns down), therefore you should check with your insurer whether this is covered.

> ☑ **SURVIVAL TIP**
>
> The cost of building insurance depends on the value of the property; for example, if your home is valued at CHF 550,000, then you can expect to pay between CHF 400 and CHF 600 per year for building insurance from a private insurer, and much less if you insure with a cantonal insurance office: e.g. in canton Zurich, insurance costs (2010) 32¢ for every CHF 1,000 insured. Therefore, to insure a CHF 550,000 home in Zurich would cost CHF 176 a year.

If you buy an apartment or townhouse (*Eigentumswohnung/Reihenhaus, apartement/ maison de ville*), the homeowners' association will take out homeowners' liability insurance, the cost of which is divided among the owners. A policy for an average apartment building with, say, six apartments, would cost each owner around CHF 150 per year. The homeowners' association will also take out building insurance, although it's still advisable to have your own private liability coverage (see below).

Building insurance should be reviewed each year to ensure that a policy still provides the cover required and that there isn't a better or cheaper option elsewhere. If you arrange your own building insurance, it must meet the level of cover required by your lender. The amount for which your home should be insured isn't the current market value, but the cost of rebuilding it if it's destroyed. This varies according to the type of property and the area. Building insurance doesn't, however, cover structural faults that existed when you took out the policy, which is why it's important to have a full structural survey done before buying a house.

Most insurers provide index-linked building insurance. It is, however, your responsibility to ensure that your level of cover is adequate, particularly if you carry out renovations or extensions which substantially increase the value of your home. If your level of cover is too low, an insurance company is within its rights to reduce the amount it pays out when a claim is made, in which case you may find you cannot afford to have your house rebuilt or repaired, should disaster strike.

If you need to make emergency repairs, e.g. to weather-proof a roof after a storm or other natural disaster, most insurance companies allow work up to a certain limit (e.g. CHF 5,000) to be carried out without an estimate or approval from the insurance company, but check first. Most insurance companies provide emergency telephone numbers for policyholders who require urgent advice. If you let your house (or part of it) or you intend leaving it unoccupied for a period of 30 days or longer, you should inform your insurance company as your insurance could be suspended or you may have to pay a higher premium.

Construction time insurance (see below) and building insurance are included in the same policy; the construction time insurance covers the period when the house is being built and the building insurance thereafter.

## Builders' Insurance

If you're having a home built, the builder or developer should have builders' liability insurance (*Bauherrenhaftpflicht, assurance responsabilité civile du maître d'ouvrage*), which is comprehensive liability insurance that covers damage to third parties during building; for example, cracks in nearby houses caused by excavations. You should verify that the builder/developer has builders' insurance. Builders' insurance terminates on the day that the completed house is handed over to the new owner, although any damage that occurred during the construction period is still covered.

If you plan to renovate your apartment, you should check whether your building liability insurance covers any damage which occurs during renovations. For example, water damage caused by a damaged pipe or a crack in the wall of your neighbour's apartment. Some policies include CHF 100,000 coverage for renovation. If you aren't covered, it would be wise to take out construction insurance (see below), as building liability insurance won't be sufficient if any major problems arise.

It's also recommended that the builder/developer has construction insurance (*Bauwesenversicherung, assurance tous risques chantier*), which covers damage relating to the construction itself, such as extra costs as a result of construction site accidents (for example, a cement floor collapsing) plus theft from the construction site. It also covers natural disasters such as mudslides, or scaffolding collapsing and damaging the building.

A third insurance during the construction period is the so-called construction time insurance (*Bauzeitversicherung, assurance des travaux en cours*), which covers damage to the new building such as fire or natural disasters, for example a storm causing a wall to collapse. Construction time insurance and building insurance is the same insurance; when the construction period is finished it automatically becomes building insurance. It's obligatory in all but four cantons (Appenzell-Innerrhoden, Geneva, Ticino and Valais) and can be arranged with the cantonal insurance office in all cantons except Appenzell-Innerrhoden, Obwalden, Schwyz and Uri, where you'll need to find a private provider. It covers almost anything that can happen on a construction site, from explosions caused by a spark from a welding machine to clothes catching fire on drying ovens.

If you purchase a finished home package – even if it's still to be constructed (i.e. you buy off plan) – you don't need to be concerned about builders' liability insurance and construction insurance as they're the

responsibility of the builder/developer. You only need verify that the builder/developer is properly insured if you're building your own home.

## Household Insurance

In most cantons it's mandatory to take out household insurance (*Hausratsversicherung/Haushaltversicherung, assurance ménage*) covering your belongings against hazards such as fire, flood, gas explosion and theft. Rental contracts usually require that renters have house contents and liability insurance, but even when it isn't mandatory, both are highly recommended. Most people take out household insurance together with private liability insurance (*Privathaftpflichtversicherung, assurance responsibilité civile*) – see below. Together these cost around CHF 300-350 a year for a couple with a two-bedroom apartment and no children. House contents insurance is inexpensive, at around CHF 200 per year for cover totalling some CHF 75,000, plus an extra CHF 20 for each additional CHF 10,000 of cover.

Most house contents insurance policies cover the cost of replacing items at their replacement cost ('new for old') and not their second-hand value (except bicycles, skis and

snowboards, although you can include 'new for old' cover for these items for a small additional fee). House contents insurance doesn't include accidental damage caused by you or members of your family to your belongings. It may also exclude accidental damage to fixtures or fittings (e.g. baths, wash basins, electrical fittings and apparatus), which can be covered by a private liability insurance policy (see below). A supplement may be payable to cover special window glass, which is expensive to replace.

> Most policies include cover for personal items when used outside the home, such as bicycles, laptops, cameras and mobile phones, up to a certain value.

Take care that you don't under-insure your house contents and that you periodically reassess their value and adjust your insurance premium accordingly. Alternatively, you can arrange to have your insurance cover automatically increased annually by a fixed percentage or amount by your insurance company. If you make a claim and the assessor discovers that you're under-insured, the amount due will be reduced by the percentage by which you're under-insured. For example, if you're insured for CHF 50,000 and you're found to be under-insured by 20 per cent, your claim totalling CHF 5,000 is reduced to CHF 4,000. You should keep a record and receipts for all major possessions.

Insurance companies will provide you with a free estimate based on the number of rooms in your home, the number of occupants and whether you have expensive possessions or worthless junk (like struggling authors!). Don't forget to mention any particularly valuable items, e.g. the family jewels or an antique collection. House contents insurance can be combined with private liability insurance (see below).

### Holiday Homes

Premiums are generally higher for holiday homes, due to their high vulnerability (particularly to burglaries), and are usually based on the number of days each year that a property is occupied and the interval between periods of occupancy. Cover for theft, storm, flood and malicious damage may be suspended when a property is left empty for more than three weeks at a time. It's possible to negotiate cover for periods of absence for a hefty surcharge, although valuable items are usually excluded.

If you're absent from your property for long periods, e.g. more than 60 days a year, you may also be required to pay an excess on a claim arising from an occurrence that takes place during your absence (and theft may be excluded). You should read the small print in policies. Where applicable, it's important to ensure that a policy specifies a holiday home and not a principal (owner-occupied) home. Always carefully check that the details listed in a policy are correct, otherwise your policy could be void.

### Claims

If you wish to make a claim, you must usually inform your insurance company in writing (by registered letter) within two to five days of an incident or 24 hours in the case of theft. Thefts should also be reported to the local police within 24 hours, as the police statement, of which you receive a copy for your insurance company, usually constitutes irrefutable evidence of your claim. Check whether you're covered for damage or theft that occurs while you're away from the property, and are therefore unable to inform your insurance company immediately.

## Private Liability Insurance

It's customary in Switzerland to have private liability insurance (*Privathaftpflichtversicherung*, *assurance responsibilité civile*), for both tenants and owners. Cover should include material damage, health treatment and compensation, including salary loss, and a pension for the bereaved or compensation for a disability. To take an everyday example, if your soap slips out of your hand and jumps out of the window while you're taking a shower, and your neighbour slips on it and breaks his neck, he (or his widow) will sue you for millions of francs (joke – see box). With liability insurance, you can shower in blissful security (but watch that soap!).

The American habit of suing people for $millions at the drop of a hat is fortunately almost unheard of in Switzerland, although for peace of mind (and your wallet) it's advisable to have liability insurance.

If you flood or set fire to your rented apartment, your landlord will claim against your liability insurance (if you don't have insurance, the authorities will lock you up and throw away the key). The cost is around CHF 100-125 per year for cover of CHF 5m, which is the recommended cover. For some claims or policies, you may be required to pay an excess, e.g. the first CHF 100 to 200 of a claim.

Private liability insurance is usually combined with house contents insurance (see above) – which may provide a discount – and covers all members of a family, including damage or accidents caused by your children and pets (for example if your dog or child bites someone). However, where damage is due to severe negligence, benefits may be reduced. Check whether it covers you against accidental damage to your apartment's fixtures and fittings. Some sports accidents aren't covered by private liability insurance; for example, if you accidentally strike your opponent with your squash racket, he cannot claim against your liability insurance to have his teeth fixed (but he can claim against his accident insurance).

You may require additional liability insurance if you keep wild animals, work from home, provide services or are self-employed, or participate in certain sports or pursuits such as horse riding. An insurance company or broker should discuss all the options with you before you take out a policy.

## Holiday & Travel Insurance

Holiday and travel insurance (*Reiseversicherung, assurance voyage*) are recommended for anyone who doesn't wish to risk having their holiday or travel ruined by financial problems, or to arrive home broke. As you probably know, anything can and often does go wrong with a holiday, sometimes before you even get started (particularly when you don't have insurance!). The following information applies equally to residents and non-residents, whether you're travelling to, from or within Switzerland. Nobody should visit

Switzerland without travel and health (see page 32) insurance.

Travel insurance is available from many sources, including travel agents, insurance companies and brokers, banks, motoring organisations and transport companies (airline, rail and bus). You can also buy 24-hour accident and flight insurance at major airports, although it's expensive and doesn't offer the best cover. A peculiarly Swiss product is the protection letter (*Schutzbrief, livret*), a comprehensive travel insurance policy, available from Swiss motoring organisations. It covers most travel and holiday emergencies and is valid irrespective of the mode of transport used.

Before taking out travel insurance, you should carefully consider the range and level of cover you require, and compare policies.

Short-term holiday and travel insurance policies may include cover for holiday cancellation or interruption; missed flights and departure delay at both the start and end of a holiday (a common occurrence); delayed, lost or damaged baggage; lost belongings and money; medical expenses and accidents (including evacuation home); personal liability and legal expenses; and default or bankruptcy, e.g. a tour operator or airline going bust. Travel insurance usually excludes high-risk sports such as skiing and jet-skiing.

If you belong to a Swiss health fund or health insurance scheme, you're usually covered for health treatment worldwide for up to twice the cost of similar treatment in Switzerland, and if you work in Switzerland you'll also be covered for accidents. Note, however, that this may not include helicopter evacuation by REGA (🖥 www.rega.ch), the Swiss air rescue service, although this is covered by Swiss third party car insurance and accident insurance (which all Swiss employees have).

Always check any exclusion clauses in contracts by obtaining a copy of the full policy document, as all relevant information won't be included in an insurance leaflet. High risk sports and pursuits should be specifically covered and listed in a policy (there's usually an additional premium). Special winter sports policies are available and more expensive than normal holiday insurance ('dangerous' sports are excluded from most standard policies). Third party liability cover should be CHF 5mn in North America and CHF 2.5mn in the rest of the world. However, this doesn't usually cover you when you're driving a car or other mechanically-propelled vehicle.

## PUBLIC HOLIDAYS

If you're making a house-hunting trip to Switzerland, you may wish to avoid public holidays (*Feiertage, jours fériés*), which may vary from canton to canton, depending on whether the predominant local religion is Catholic or Protestant. The following dates or days are public holidays in most Swiss cantons; those marked with an asterisk are Swiss national holidays.

There are also half-day public holidays in some cantons, e.g. Zurich, and Catholic cantons have more religious holidays. For a list of holidays by canton, see 🖥 www. feiertagskalender.ch (choose English, Switzerland and the canton).

If a public holiday falls on a weekend, there's no substitute weekday holiday unless the number of public holidays in a particular year falls below a minimum number. When a holiday falls on a Thursday or a Tuesday, many employees take the Friday or Monday (respectively) off to make a long weekend. Many Swiss companies close down during Christmas and New Year, e.g. from midday or 4pm on 24th December until 2nd or 3rd January.

## SHOPPING

Switzerland isn't one of the world's great shopping countries, unless, of course, you're a multi-millionaire and never need to look at the price tag. The prices of some goods and services can be up to 50 per cent higher than in many EU countries, which makes shopping in Switzerland's neighbouring countries rewarding. There's generally no bargaining in Switzerland, although if you plan to spend a lot of money in some stores you may be able to

| Swiss Public Holidays | |
|---|---|
| **Date** | **Holiday** |
| *1st January | New Year's Day (*Neujahr, Jour de l'An*) |
| 2nd January | St. Berchtold's Day (*Berchtoldstag, le 2 janvier*) |
| *March or April | Good Friday (*Karfreitag, Vendredi Saint*) |
| | Easter Monday (*Ostermontag, Lundi de Pâques*) |
| 1st May | May Day (*Tag der Arbeit, Fête du Travail*) |
| May | Ascension Day (*Auffahrt, Ascension*) – Thursday 40 days after Easter |
| *June | Whitsuntide (*Pfingsten, Pfingstmontag, Pentecôte*) – Sunday and Monday, ten days after Ascension |
| *1st August | Swiss National Day (*Bundesfeiertag, Fête nationale*) |
| *25th December | Christmas Day (*Weihnachtstag, Noël*) |
| *26th December | Boxing Day (*Stefanstag, le 26 décembre*) |

get a discount, for example when furnishing a home.

Sales and prices of most goods in Switzerland are strictly regulated, and prices for many goods are fixed to protect small shop owners. However, in recent years discount supermarkets, such as the German Aldi and Lidl chains, have become established in Switzerland with literally hundreds of stores, leading to price wars with the Coop and Migros, who have responded by dropping their prices and introducing 'Budget' (Migros) and 'Bon Prix' (Coop) product ranges.

There are, however, a few times of the year when 'poor' foreigners can afford to shop for 'luxuries': during the summer and winter sales. Most shops hold sales (*Sonderverkauf/ Ausverkauf*, *soldes*) in January and July, when goods are often available at bargain prices; if you plan to have a shopping spree, it's definitely worth waiting for the sales. You can compare the cost of some goods, such as consumer electronics, on websites such as Comparis (🖥 www.comparis.ch). See also **Cost of Living** on page 196.

To help reduce the high cost of living in Switzerland, if you live near a border you can make savings on food and many other goods by doing your weekly food shopping and buying 'big ticket' items abroad (see **Shopping Abroad** on page 240).

For those who aren't used to buying goods in metric measures or clothes in continental sizes, lists of comparative sizes, weights and measures are included in **Appendix D**.

Note that shopping bags aren't free in Switzerland, where paper shopping bags cost CHF 0.30 each – many stores, such as the Coop and Migros, sell hard-wearing, long-life bags for around CHF 2.50. To avoid paying for bags or being caught short, most Swiss carry a bag with them at all times.

## Shopping Hours

Shopping hours in Switzerland are usually from around 8 or 9am to 6.30 or 6.45pm, Tuesdays to Fridays, and from 8am to between 4 and 6pm on Saturdays. On Mondays, many shops close in the morning and open from between 1 and 2pm until around 6.30 or 6.45pm, although some are closed all day. Many towns have late night shopping until 8 or 9pm on Wednesday,

Thursday or Friday (in Zurich, many shops stay open until 8pm from Mondays to Fridays), and many shopping centres also have extended shopping hours. In smaller towns, all shops and businesses close for lunch, e.g. from noon until 2pm.

Local shops, for example those situated in villages, close for a half or full day a week (usually Monday) and may close earlier on a Saturday, e.g. 2pm. It's customary for certain businesses to be closed on the same day; for example, most hairdressers (*Friseur, coiffeur*) are closed on Mondays. Shops generally close at 4 or 5pm the day before a public holiday, even when it's a late shopping day.

All shops are closed on Sundays except bakeries, some of which open from around 10am to noon. However, stores are permitted to open on six Sundays or official holidays a year, and stores are often open on a few Sundays in the run up to Christmas. Geneva and Zurich airports have shopping centres open from 8am to 8pm daily, and some motorway (*Autobahn, autoroute*) shopping centres are open every day of the year, with the exception of Christmas Day. In and around most main railway stations (*Hauptbahnhof, gare centrale*) in the main cities, you can find shops with extended opening times (e.g. 7am to 10pm), including Sundays and public holidays.

In recent years, Migros and Coop have added mini-markets to their petrol stations – open seven days a week – where you can also buy fresh bread. Grocery stores near border crossings are usually open on Sundays, and shops in many tourist resorts (including the 'tourist' areas of some major cities) are open on Sundays and public holidays throughout the season. Migros and Coop do home deliveries throughout Switzerland, although you need an internet connection to place an order.

## Furniture & Furnishings

Furniture (*Möbel, meubles*) is generally quite expensive in Switzerland compared with many other European countries. There is, however, a huge choice and the quality is invariably good. Exclusive modern and traditional furniture is available everywhere from a wide range of

speciality home stores, although not everyone can afford the exclusive prices. At the upper end of the market is Roche Bobois (🖥 www. roche-bobois.com), with stores in Fribourg, Geneva, Lausanne and Zurich, selling designer furniture and soft furnishings, and Möbel Pfister (🖥 www.pfister.ch) with 20 stores, offering a huge choice with a wide quality and price range.

Ikea (🖥 www.ikea.com/ch) sells good quality, modern furniture for home assembly plus home furnishings, and has seven stores in Switzerland: Basle/Pratteln, Berne/ Lyssach, Lausanne/Aubonne, Lugano, St. Gallen, Zurich/Dietlikon and Zurich/ Spreitenbach. Fly (🖥 www.fly.ch), owned by Manor, is an inexpensive but fashionable chain with 20 stores selling furniture and home accessories, while Conforama (🖥 www.conforama.ch) has 13 stores selling furniture, home accessories, appliances and consumer electronics. Two reasonably-priced national chains are Micasa (🖥 www. micasa.ch), part of the Migros group, which offers good value furniture (especially quality leather suites), and Manor (🖥 www.manor. ch), which is good for home furnishing and appliances. More upmarket is Interio (🖥 www.interio.ch), owned by Migros, specialising in modern designer furniture and accessories, with eight main stores (plus many smaller shops), and Globus (🖥 www. globus.ch – 14 stores, owned by Migros), which is excellent for top quality home furnishings and household goods.

Note that you cannot buy furniture 'off the shelf' in most stores, particularly large items, and delivery can take four to eight weeks.

Otto's (🖥 www.ottos.ch) is a discount chain store that also sells furniture – their inventory depends on what they can buy that's surplus, over-stock, in liquidation, etc., as they buy cheap and sell cheap. They also have a food section with many international items. Otto's have almost 100 stores in Switzerland, of which 60 carry furniture. Lipo (🖥 www.lipo-moebel.com) is another discount store selling surplus, over-stock and liquidation items, including furniture and furnishings. It has 13 stores in Switzerland (11 in northern Switzerland).

A rare exception to fixed prices in Switzerland is when you're buying a large quantity of furniture. Don't be reticent about asking for a discount, as many stores will give you a 10 to 20 per cent discount. If you need to buy furniture in a hurry, bear in mind that delivery can take four to eight weeks (even from Ikea), depending on the manufacturer and supplier. Most shops don't keep much furniture in stock, and usually it's ordered direct from the manufacturer who may also deliver it to your home.

If you live near the border, shopping across the border for furniture is an option worth considering. You can also order furniture from catalogues, e.g. from France and Italy. If you're buying a holiday home, some developers will furnish it for you, either by accompanying you to local furniture stores or choosing from catalogues. It's also possible to rent furniture from a number of companies, such as In-Lease (☎ 041-310 73 52, 🖥 www.in-lease.com, ✉ swiss@in-lease.com).

## Household Goods & Appliances

There are numerous stores selling home appliances and household goods in Switzerland, including many of those listed above (under **Furniture & Furnishings**). Among the best are Fust (🖥 www.fust.ch), owned by the Coop, which has over 140 stores throughout the country selling cookers, washing machines, dryers, refrigerators, freezers, televisions and vacuum cleaners, Conforama (🖥 www.conforama.ch), Globus (🖥 www.globus.ch), Micasa (🖥 www.micasa. ch) and Manor (🖥 www.manor.ch).

Large appliances such as cookers and refrigerators are usually provided in rented accommodation, although not always in French-speaking areas. Dishwashers are sometimes installed and private washing machines are rare in cheaper apartments. The standard width of kitchen appliances in Switzerland is 5cm less than across the rest of Europe (to reduce foreign competition!) and consequently domestic prices for dishwashers, washing machines and dryers are much higher than the European average. If you can tailor your kitchen to accommodate foreign appliances, you can save a lot of money by buying them abroad.

> ### ☑ SURVIVAL TIP
>
> **Check the latest Swiss safety regulations before shipping white goods to Switzerland or buying them abroad, as they may need expensive modifications.**

If you already own small household appliances, it's worthwhile bringing them to Switzerland, as usually all that's required is a change of plug (but check first). If you're coming from a country with a 110/115V electricity supply, e.g. the US, then you'll need a lot of expensive transformers. Don't bring a TV to Switzerland without checking its compatibility first, as TVs from the UK and the US won't work. Smaller appliances such as vacuum cleaners, grills, toasters and electric irons aren't expensive in Switzerland and are of excellent quality. Note that the Swiss generally take their lighting fixtures with them when moving home, therefore you'll need to buy these (and possibly hire an electrician to install them) in addition to buying lamps and shades.

If you need kitchen measuring equipment and cannot cope with decimal measures, you need to bring your own measuring scales, jugs, cups and thermometers. Foreign pillow sizes, e.g. British and American, aren't the same as Swiss sizes, and the Swiss use duvets and not blankets to keep warm in winter (besides central heating).

## DIY

There are vast DIY (do-it-yourself) stores and garden centres in all regions of Switzerland, selling everything for the home handyman, including DIY supplies, furniture, bathrooms, kitchens, decorating supplies and lighting, plus services such as tool rental and wood-cutting. The largest chains include Jumbo (🖥 www. jumbo.ch), which has 40 stores throughout the country selling bicycle accessories and children's toys in addition to those items listed above, and the ubiquitous Migros (🖥 www. migros.ch) Do It+Garden stores, selling floorings, paints, wallpapers, soft furnishings, tools, garden equipment and plants.

Other major DIY chains include the Coop (🖥 www.coop.ch) Bau+Hobby, which has 20 stores in Switzerland; OBI (🖥 www.obich.ch), a German franchise (run by Migros), with ten stores in Switzerland (and over 450 throughout Europe); and Hornbach (🖥 www.hornbach. com) with four DIY megastores in Biel/Bienne (Berne), Etoy (Vaud), Littau (Lucerne) and Villeneuve (Vaud), selling tiles, flooring, tools, wallpaper, paint, bathroom fittings and garden products.

The cost of some DIY materials and tools are relatively expensive in Switzerland and you may be able to save money by buying them abroad.

## Second-hand Bargains

Switzerland has an active second-hand (*gebraucht, occasion*) market, particularly in antiques, motor cars, gold and gem stones, although asking prices are generally higher than in other countries. There's a local second-hand furniture and junk store (*Brockenhaus, broccante*) in most towns, which may also have a Salvation Army (*Heilsarmee, armée du salut*) shop. These usually have restricted opening hours. Second-hand clothes shops are also popular. The Seefeld district in Zurich has numerous factory shops offering designer clothes at a fraction of the original price, and shops offering clothes of humbler (and cheaper) pedigree are available in many areas.

---

☑ **SURVIVAL TIP**

You can find bargain and second-hand goods via the internet at Glocals (🖥 www.glocals. com/classifieds/goods-for-sale), mainly for the Geneva region, Fundgrueb's Local website (🖥 www.local.ch) and the ubiquitous eBay (🖥 www.ebay.ch), although the Swiss prefer Ricardo (🖥 www.ricardo.ch).

---

There are special weekly newspapers in some areas devoted to bargain hunters, for example *Fundgrueb* (🖥 market.local.ch) and *Inserate-Markt* (🖥 www.inserate-markt.ch) in German-speaking areas, and *Aux Trouvailles* (🖥 www.auxtrouvailles.ch) in French-speaking areas. Advertising is usually free, as advertisements are financed by newspaper

sales, although you must buy a copy in order to place an advertisement. *Fundgrueb* also have a list of Swiss flea markets and fairs on their website (🖥 http://market.local.ch/de/m/fleamarkets).

The classified advertisements in local newspapers and adverts on shopping centre, supermarket and company bulletin boards, may also prove fruitful. Many expatriate clubs and large companies publish monthly magazines or newsletters containing small ads, where everything from furniture to household apparatus and cars are advertised for sale. Sales are held in many towns and villages, e.g. for children's clothes and toys, usually in the spring and autumn.

## Shopping Abroad

Shopping abroad makes a pleasant change from all those boring Swiss shops full of diamond necklaces, fur coats, gold watches and *haute couture* fashions. It can also save you a lot of money and makes an enjoyable day out for the family. Don't forget your passports or identity cards, car documents, dog's vaccination documents and Euros. Most shops in border towns gladly accept Swiss francs, but usually at a lower exchange rate than a bank.

Many foreigners and Swiss, particularly those living in border areas (e.g. Basle, Geneva and Lugano), take advantage of the generally lower prices outside Switzerland and do their weekly shopping abroad. Almost half the residents of Geneva – almost 40 per cent of whom are foreigners – regularly do the bulk of their shopping in France (don't forget to take some bags, as they no longer provide free paper or plastic bags), and overall around one-third of Swiss residents regularly shop abroad. Germany, France and Italy all have a lower cost of living than Switzerland (although salaries are also much lower).

A combination of lower prices, a favourable exchange rate and low Swiss VAT, mean that savings can be made on many items, although savings on foodstuffs (and wine) aren't as high as they were before Aldi and Lidl entered the Swiss market. You can still save money when shopping abroad, although how much you save depends very much on where you shop and what you buy.

Note that in all countries except Germany there are minimum purchase levels, below which you're unable to reclaim local VAT.

The best buys in Germany include electrical, electronic and photographic equipment; household appliances; computers and software; DVDs; optical goods and services; furniture; sporting goods; car parts, servicing and accessories; alcohol; and meat products. Buying a car abroad, e.g. in Germany or Italy, can also yield huge savings.

On weekdays, shopping hours are much the same as in Switzerland, except on Wednesdays, when shops usually close at 1pm. In many German towns bordering Switzerland, most shops are open until 6pm on Saturdays especially to cater for the influx of shoppers from Switzerland. Note, however, that prices may be slightly higher in border towns than in larger inland German cities.

Of course, not everything is cheaper abroad and it's wise to compare prices and quality before buying. Bear in mind that if you buy goods that are faulty or need repair, you may have to return them to the place of purchase, which could be a hassle with customs paperwork. Shops in border areas will often deliver goods to you in Switzerland, in which case you won't pay local VAT, but will be charged Swiss VAT – and they may even deliver free of charge.

## Duty-free Allowances

Swiss customs regulations allow duty-free purchases up to CHF 300 per person, per day, with the following restrictions:

♦ 1l/kg of butter and cream;

♦ 4l/kg of oil, fat and margarine;

♦ 5l/kg of milk, cheese, yoghurt and other dairy products;

♦ 2.5kg of eggs;

♦ 20kg of vegetables;

♦ 20kg of fruit (excluding oranges);

♦ 3l of fruit juice;

♦ 2.5kg of potatoes and potato products (including crisps!);

♦ 20kg of cereals, flour and flour-based products (bread, cakes etc);

♦ 3.5kg of meat and meat products such as sausages and poultry. This may include a maximum of just 500g of fresh or frozen meat (beef, pork, lamb, veal, goat, horse, donkey and mule!). On no account may you exceed the limit on meat imports.

Those aged over 17 may also import the following:

♦ 2l of wine or champagne under 15° proof and one litre of alcohol over 15° proof – if you import more than one litre, duty on the excess amount is likely to equal or exceed its cost;

♦ 200 cigarettes **or** 50 cigars **or** 250g of pipe tobacco (double for visitors domiciled outside Europe).

There are regulations prohibiting the importation of meats from certain countries, and occasional restrictions on the import of some meats due to an outbreak of swine fever or foot and mouth disease. If you're in doubt, check with the Federal Veterinary Office (Schwarzenburgstr. 155, CH-3003 Berne, ☎ 031-323 30 33, 🖥 www.bvet.admin.ch). At the Swiss border you must declare what you've purchased and, if asked, produce receipts to verify the place of origin and the price paid. When you exceed the permitted tax-free limit, you're liable to pay VAT (see page 197) on all your purchases, including the duty-free allowance. Customs duty on goods imported above the duty-free allowance is calculated by weight, depending on the category of goods, which is payable in addition to VAT. Swiss customs officials are usually reasonable and flexible and unless you're a big-time smuggler, will treat you fairly.

For further information, see the Swiss Federal Customs Administration website (🖥 www.ezv.admin.ch/zollinfo_privat – change the language to English and click on 'food').

Never attempt to import illegal goods and don't agree to bring a parcel into Switzerland, or to deliver a parcel in another country, without knowing exactly what it contains. It could contain illegal drugs.

## TELECOMMUNICATIONS

Among the various reasons for Switzerland's economic success are the many unfair advantages it has over other countries, one of which is that its telephones always work. The country has one of the highest numbers of telephones per head of population in the world and nearly every household has a telephone. However, the number of fixed-line phones has fallen in recent years, during which the number of mobile phones has increased sharply.

The Swiss telecommunications market has been open to competition since 1st January 1998, when the state-owned Telecom PTT was privatised and became Swisscom, although it still owns and maintains the telephone infrastructure. Switzerland's mobile phone system, previously operated by Swisscom, has also been opened to competition with the entry of Orange and Sunrise into the market, and there are also 'dozens' of internet providers in the country. As a consequence of deregulation, call costs have tumbled in the last decade.

### Phone Installation & Registration

One of the first things you should do when you have found somewhere to live is to sign up for a telephone and internet service (plus cable TV if applicable). You can usually get telephone, internet and cable TV services from the same provider (see below), which may save you money. Check with the owner or agent which cable company serves your apartment, if applicable. You can compare service providers via Comparis (🖥 www.comparis.ch).

If you move into an old apartment, i.e. any apartment where you aren't the first occupant, a telephone line will usually have been installed. A new apartment may have telephone outlets only in the living room and the master bedroom, but usually there will be no telephone sockets (which need to be installed by an electrician) and the line will need to be connected. If you want additional outlets in other rooms, you'll need to have them installed.

Foreigners without a B, C, G or diplomat's permit (see **Chapter 3**) must pay a deposit of CHF 300 before they can have a telephone line connected. The deposit is returned with interest when you leave the country or obtain a qualifying permit, or may be repaid after one to two years if you pay your bills regularly.

To have a telephone line connected, contact your nearest Swisscom office (or ☎ 0800-800 800) or a local electrician, who can organise everything including setting up the internet. Line connection (CHF 43) is usually quick, and takes an average of around two days.

### Choosing a Phone Company

After registering with Swisscom (☎ 0800-800 800, 🖥 www.swisscom.com), you can sign up to one of Swisscom's packages or choose an alternative service provider. Other phone companies include Abalon (☎ 041-747 17 00, 🖥 www.abalonag.com), Cablecom (☎ 0800-668 866, 🖥 www.cablecom.ch), EconoPhone (☎ 0800-188 188, 🖥 www.econophone.ch), Orange (☎ 0800-700 700, 🖥 www.orange.ch), Sunrise (☎ 0800-707 707, 🖥 www.sunrise.ch), Tele2 (☎ 0800-242 424, 🖥 www.tele2.ch), recently purchased by Sunrise, and Vtx Datacomm (☎ 0800-883 883, 🖥 www.vtxnet.ch). (Orange and Sunrise are merging in 2010.) There are also smaller companies operating in certain cantons or cities, and direct call (previously call-back) companies offering low-cost international calls.

Swisscom retains part of its monopoly because irrespective of which phone company you use, you must still pay them a line rental fee; CHF 25.25 per month for an analog line (EconomyLINE) or CHF 43 for an ISDN line (MultiLINE). The only way to avoid paying this fee is to choose Cablecom (☎ 0800-660 800, 🖥 www.cablecom.ch), which has its own cable network, although it isn't available in all areas.

## Emergency Numbers

The following national emergency numbers (*Notfallnummern, numéros d'appel en cas d'urgence*) are listed on page one of all telephone directories.

The above telephone numbers are staffed or provide recorded information 24 hours a day, and can be dialled directly from anywhere within Switzerland. Recorded information is given in the local language (French, German or Italian); CHF 0.50 is required to dial an emergency number from a coin payphone, but is returned.

You can also find local emergency numbers via local.ch, e.g. 🖥 www.local.ch/en/Zuerich/tel.html, for Zurich.

## The Internet

The Swiss are among the world's most avid internet users. According to the OECD, some 75 per cent of Swiss households have internet access, over half with broadband (via ADSL/DSL and cable). There are some 150 internet service providers (ISPs) to choose from in Switzerland, so getting online is easy. Although many people still have dial-up internet, most people who have the option choose a broadband connection (often via cable), which isn't only faster but allows you to surf the net and make phone calls on the same line simultaneously.

Broadband fees vary with the provider and the usage, but you can expect to pay around CHF 50 per month for unlimited access and download speeds of up to 100mpbs (which is 12.5mb per second). A subscription typically

| Emergency Telephone Numbers | |
|---|---|
| **Tel. Number** | **Service** |
| 117/112 | **Police** (*Polizeinotruf, police secours*) 112 is the international emergency number |
| 118/112 | **Fire** (*Feuermeldestelle, feu centrale d'alarme*) 112 is the international emergency number |
| 140 | **Emergency road service** (*Strassenhilfe, secours routiers*) |
| 143 | **Samaritans** (*Die dargebotene Hand, La Main Tendue*); CHF 0.20 per call |
| 144 | **Ambulance** (*Sanitätsnotruf, appel sanitaire d'urgence*) |
| 145 | **Poison emergency service** (*Vergiftungsnotfall, intoxication en cas d'urgence*); CHF 0.08/0.04 per minute |
| 147 | **Telephone support for children & youths** (*Telefonhilfe für Kinder und Jugendliche, ligne d'aide aux enfants et aux jeunes*) |
| 1414 | **Helicopter rescue** (REGA – *Rettung mit Helikopter, sauvetage par hélicoptère*); CHF 0.20 per call |
| 1415 | **Air Glacier** (helicopter rescue in the Alps) |

includes a number of email addresses. There may be other initial charges such as connection fees or modem/router costs – it pays to shop around, which you can do via Comparis (🖳 www.comparis.ch). The minimum contract length is usually one year.

Popular providers include Bluewin (☏ 0844-844 884, 🖳 www.bluewin.ch), Econophone (☏ 0800-188 188, 🖳 www.econophone.ch), Green (☏ 056-460 23 23, 🖳 www.green.ch), Orange (☏ 0800-700 700, 🖳 www.orange.ch), Sunrise (☏ 0800-707 707, 🖳 www.sunrise.ch) and Tele2 (☏ 0800-242 424, 🖳 www.tele2.ch), the last three of which provide English web pages.

Cable internet access accounts for around a third of broadband subscriptions. Prices vary, for example CHF 0.33 per MB or CHF 45 per month. Major providers include Cablecom (☏ 0800-660 800, 🖳 www.cablecom.ch), Datazug (☏ 041-748 49 59, 🖳 www.datazug.ch) and Quickline (☏ 0800-841 020, 🖳 www.quickline.com). For a map showing providers by canton, visit 🖳 www.cablemodem.ch and click on 'Anbieter-/Provider-Liste' at the top of the page. Cable isn't available in rural areas.

It's also possible to access the internet via a mobile phone. Check with your mobile service provider for the latest information and rates.

---

### ☑ SURVIVAL TIP

Most Swiss websites have French, German and Italian versions (German is often the default) and many are also in English; look for the language option buttons, usually located at the top of the screen or shown by flag icons.

---

## TELEVISION & RADIO

Television (TV) and radio services in Switzerland are operated by the Swiss Broadcasting Corporation (*Schweizerische Radio und Fernsehgesellschaft/SRG, Société Suisse de Radiodiffusion et Télévision/SSR*), which is a private, non-profit company and a public service financed by advertising and licence fees.

## Television

The quality of Swiss TV leaves much to be desired, although it's no worse than the fare served up in most other European countries. The German-speaking Swiss reportedly watch less TV than almost anyone in Europe, and other Swiss also watch much less TV than the European average. The choice of Swiss TV stations has increased in the last few years with the introduction of a number of local cable TV companies. Cable TV is available throughout the country, and some 90 per cent of homes in Switzerland receive their TV programmes via a communal aerial or cable. Due to the wide availability of cable TV, satellite TV (see page 245) isn't common in Switzerland, although it's popular with expatriates. TV programmes are listed in daily and weekly newspapers and published in weekly TV magazines.

### Cable Television

Cable TV (*Gemeinschaftsantenne, antenne collective*) is available in most areas of Switzerland, but is restricted to towns and buildings wired for cable. Around 90 per cent or some 3mn Swiss households are connected to a communal antenna or a cable network (only Belgium and the Netherlands have more households with cable). The largest cable TV company is Cablecom (🖳 www.cablecom.ch), with over 1.5mn TV customers; it also provides broadband internet access and mobile and fixed network telephony.

Cable TV consists of cable relays of Swiss and foreign national TV stations, dedicated cable-only stations and satellite stations. The average Swiss household can receive around 40 TV channels, although some areas receive many more, e.g. 70 in Geneva. English-language cable TV stations are widely available and include CNN International, Eurosport, MTV Europe and NBC Superchannel. Digital TV is available in most areas through a cable provider and usually includes the British BBC1 and BBC2 channels.

Cable TV isn't available in remote areas of Switzerland and may not be available in older buildings and small towns and villages. If you want to receive English-language cable TV, check that it's available (and which stations) before signing a lease. When available, all you need to do to receive cable TV is to connect your TV aerial to a cable wall socket.

You can check whether cable TV is available via Swiss Cable (💻 www.swisscable.ch) by simply entering the address of an apartment that you're planning to buy or rent.

Cable TV usually costs between CHF 20 (analogue) and CHF 25 (digital) per month, depending on the channels provided, and is included in your apartment's monthly charges or billed annually. If you don't own a TV, you may be able to get the cable TV company to seal the aerial outlet and thus avoid paying the monthly rental charge. This is easy enough if you live in a house, but may be impossible if you live in an apartment, where cable TV costs are shared and included in your apartment's charges.

In addition to unscrambled cable TV channels, scrambled TV channels are available in many areas. Like some satellite TV stations (see below), you require a decoder to receive them (which can be installed by most TV shops) and must pay a monthly subscription.

### TV via Broadband

In common with many countries, Switzerland offers a digital TV service delivered via a broadband phone line or cable connection, including high definition TV (HDTV). You can receive digital TV from a number of providers including Cablecom (☎ 0800-668 866, 💻 www.cablecom.ch), Datazug (☎ 041-748 49 59, 💻 www.datazug.ch), Quickline (☎ 0800-841 020, 💻 www.quickline.com) and Swisscom (☎ 0800-800 800, 💻 www.swisscom.ch), all of whom also provide telephone and broadband internet services.

A typical digital TV service is provided by Swisscom (called Bluewin), featuring over 140 TV channels, 130 national and international radio stations, a wide variety of Internet radio stations and over 500 films on demand. Various subscriptions are available, the most expensive of which is Bluewin TV Plus, costing CHF 29 per month plus the installation fee.

### Satellite TV

There are a number of satellites positioned over Europe, carrying over hundreds of TV stations broadcasting in a variety of languages. Although very popular in the UK and Ireland, most of Switzerland has cable TV and therefore satellite TV is mainly of interest to expatriates, e.g. those who wish to receive Sky Television.

### Sky Television

In order to receive Sky television in Switzerland (or anywhere else) you need a Sky digital receiver (digibox) and a dish. There are two ways to obtain the equipment and the necessary Sky 'smart' card. You can subscribe in the UK or Ireland (personally, if you have an address there, or via a friend) and then take the Sky receiver and card to Switzerland. Alternatively, you can buy a digibox and obtain a Sky card from a number of companies (see below) in Switzerland, although strictly speaking it's illegal to access encrypted Sky programming there. However, it's possible to receive UK-based, free-to-air (FTA) programming on the same satellite that broadcasts Sky digital, without a Sky card.

You must subscribe to Sky to receive most English-language channels, other than the free-to-air UK channels (BBC1, BBC2, ITV1, CH4 and CH5), Sky News, CNN, Eurosport and a few other channels. If you subscribe to the basic Sky package, costing around GB£15 per month, you'll have access to around 100 channels. Various packages are available, costing up to GB£43.50 per month (more for HDTV), for which you'll have access to the Movie and Sports channels. For further information, see 💻 www.sky.com.

A bonus for Sky subscribers is the availability of radio stations, including all the UK national BBC stations (see **Radio** below).

### Location & Installation

To be able to receive programmes from any satellite, there must be no obstacles between the satellite and your dish, i.e. no large obstacles such as trees, buildings or mountains must obstruct the signal, so check before renting an apartment or buying a home. If it faces the right way, you can have a dish set into a concrete block and installed on a balcony. However, before buying or erecting a satellite dish – or even before buying or renting a home – check whether it's possible to install a dish and whether you require permission from your landlord or a permit from the local authorities.

Dishes (85-90cm is best for Switzerland) can usually be mounted in a variety of unobtrusive positions and can be painted or patterned to blend in with the background. New apartment blocks may be fitted with at least one communal satellite dish. If you need your own dish, it's best to have it installed by a professional. There are many companies in Switzerland; see 🖳 http://geneva. angloinfo.com for a list, or Google 'Sky TV in Switzerland'.

## Radio

The good news for radio fans is that radios have the same standards the world over, although bandwidths vary. FM (VHF) stereo stations flourish in Switzerland, and Medium Wave (MW or AM) and Long Wave (LW) bands are also used throughout Europe. A Short Wave (SW) radio is useful for receiving international stations such as the BBC World Service, Voice of America, Radio Canada and Radio Sweden. The BBC World Service and the Voice of America are also available via cable radio in many areas (see below). Portable digital radios (DAB) provide good reception, particularly on short wave, and expensive 'professional' receivers are capable of receiving stations from almost anywhere.

If you're interested in receiving radio and TV stations from further afield, you should obtain a copy of the *World Radio TV Handbook* (WRTH Publications, 🖳 www.wrth.com).

### Cable Radio

If your apartment is wired for cable TV (see above), it will also be wired for cable radio,

providing reception of around 30 stereo stations. Many cable networks provide the BBC World Service, BBC Foreign Language Service, Voice of America, Swiss Radio International (English service) and Sky Radio, in addition to a wide selection of FM stereo stations from Switzerland (national and local), Austria, France, Germany and Italy. All you need do is connect your radio or hi-fi tuner aerial to a special wall socket (cables are available from TV stores).

## Television & Radio Licences

A TV licence (*Fernsehempfangskonzession*, *concession de réception de télévisuelle*) costs CHF 24.40 per month or CHF 73.25 per quarter (CHF 293 per year) and a radio licence (*Radioempfangskonzession, concession de réception radio*) CHF 14.10 per month or CHF 42.25 per quarter (CHF 169 per year), both of which are required by all owners of TVs and radios (including car radios) in Switzerland. If you need both a TV and radio licence, the cost is CHF 38.50 per month or CHF 115.50 per quarter (CHF 462 per year). Both radio and TV licence registration can be done together by contacting Billag (☎ 0844-834 834, 🖳 www. billag.ch) and can be paid by direct debit.

The licence fee covers any number of TVs and radios owned or rented by you, irrespective of where they're located, e.g. holiday homes, motor vehicles or boats, but not TVs and radios in a workplace, which should be covered by your employer's licence. Registration must be made within 14 days of buying or importing a TV or radio, otherwise you'll be fined if you're caught without a licence when an inspector calls. However, if a TV is used only for DVD playback or as a computer monitor, no licence fee is payable – but it mustn't be capable of receiving TV broadcasts. If your have a computer with RealPlayer or Media Player installed, a cell phone which can receive radio, or a Walkman or any other radio-receiving device, then you must pay the fee!

# UTILITIES

Utilities include electricity, gas and water services (*Städtische Werke-Elektrizität, Gas und Wasser, centrale des services techniques: électricité, gaz, eau/services industriels*). This section also includes information about central heating, the cost of which may be included in your apartment's monthly charges (*Nebenkosten/NK, charges/frais immobiliers*).

## Registration & Billing

You don't always need to apply to your local electricity, gas and water companies to have your supply connected and/or transferred to your name. This may be done automatically by your landlord or community, although a deposit (e.g. CHF 250) is required in some areas.

You're billed quarterly and can pay your bills by direct debit from a bank account. You may receive a single bill for your electricity, gas, water and sewerage, or separate bills. Meters are usually read every six months, so that the first bill received in a six-month period (i.e. after three months) is an estimate, and the second bill contains an itemised list of your actual consumption and costs. If you think the estimate is wildly inaccurate, you can ask for an adjustment.

## Electricity

The electricity supply in Switzerland is 220 volts AC, 10 amps maximum, with a frequency of 50 hertz (Hz). This is suitable for all electrical equipment with a power consumption of up to 2,200 watts. For equipment with a higher power consumption (e.g. oven, washing machine, dishwasher, etc.), a single or three-phase 380 volts AC, 20-amp supply is necessary.

A low-cost electricity rate is in operation from around 8pm to 6 or 7am, Mondays to Fridays, Saturday afternoons and all day on Sundays, depending on the area and the time of the year, which are good times to run a washing machine, dryer or dishwasher.

## Converters & Transformers

Electrical equipment rated at 110 volts AC (for example from the US) without a voltage switch requires a transformer to convert it to 220 volts AC, which are available from electrical retailers in Switzerland. Some electrical appliances (e.g. electric razors and hair dryers) are fitted with a 110/220 volt switch. Check for the switch, which may be inside the casing, and make sure that it's switched to 220 volts before connecting it to the power supply.

## Fuses, Plugs & Bulbs

Most apartments and all houses have their own fuse boxes, which may be of two types. Older houses may have screw fuses with a coloured disk, which when it isn't displayed indicates that the fuse has blown. These fuses, which have different amp ratings, can be purchased in electrical stores and supermarkets. The other type of fuse, found in newer houses and apartments, consists of a simple switch, which when a circuit is overloaded, trips to the OFF position. After locating and remedying the cause, simply switch it back to the ON position.

Switzerland has three different plug configurations with two, three or five contact points (including the earth) and a 16-amp rating. Modern Swiss plugs are of the two- or three-pin or two-pin/earth socket type. Pins are round with a 4mm diameter, with live and neutral pins 2cm apart. Electric light bulbs are of the Edison screw type. Bayonet-fitting bulbs for British-type lamp fittings aren't available in Switzerland but can be purchased in France. As in EU countries, from 1st January 2010, only energy-efficient electric light bulbs will be sold in Switzerland.

---

 **Caution**

In most cantons, only a qualified electrician is allowed to install electrical wiring and fittings, particularly in connection with fuse boxes.

## Gas

Gas is piped from Germany, the Netherlands and France to the major Swiss cities, but isn't used in many homes, although its use is rising and it now accounts for around 15 per cent of total energy consumption (mainly industrial). If you want to cook by gas, you may be able to find a house or apartment that has it, or you can buy a combined electric/gas cooker, where the gas is provided by gas bottles.

## Water

Water is usually hard in Switzerland with a high calcium content, which means that you'll need a copious supply of decalcification liquid to keep your kettle, iron and other equipment and utensils clean. Stainless steel pots and pans stain quickly when used to boil water, and should be cleaned soon after use. Tap and shower filters must be decalcified regularly. You can have decalcification equipment installed in your water system, which is rarely fitted as standard equipment in apartments. There are various systems available, most of which are expensive and not all are very effective. Distilled water, or water melted from ice from your refrigerator or freezer, should be used in steam irons (mineral water is also okay).

Water rates are calculated by one of two methods. If your apartment has a water meter, you're billed for the amount of water you use. Otherwise, you pay a fixed rate according to the size of your house or apartment and possibly the number of taps. In Zurich, water costs around CHF 2.50 per cubic metre – there have been large increases in some areas in recent years.

---

☑ SURVIVAL TIP

In Switzerland, the left tap is always the hot water tap.

---

### Security Measures

Before moving into a new home you should check where the main stop-valve or stopcock is located, so that you can turn off the water in an emergency. If the water stops flowing for any reason, you should ensure that all the taps are turned off to prevent flooding when the supply starts again. In community properties, the tap to turn the water on or off may be located outside the building.

When leaving a property empty for an extended period, particularly during the winter when there's the possibility of freezing, you should turn off the main stopcock, switch off the system's controls and drain the pipes, toilets (you can leave salt in the toilet bowls to prevent freezing) and radiators. It's also recommended to have your cold water tank and the tank's ball valves checked periodically for corrosion, and to check the hosing on appliances such as washing machines and dishwashers. It can be very expensive to repair the damage if a pipe bursts, particularly if the leak goes undiscovered for a long time!

## Central Heating

Most apartments in Switzerland have central heating (*Zentralheizung*, *chauffage central*), the cost of which is included in your extra costs and can be expensive. Heating is usually switched on in the autumn and off in the spring by the caretaker or landlord, or it may be thermostatically controlled all year round (you can usually set the temperature in your own apartment and switch off individual radiators). In most apartment blocks, the cost of heating for the whole building is divided among tenants according to their apartment size, while in others radiators may be individually metered, so you pay only for the heating you use. All modern apartments have under-floor heating.

## WASTE DISPOSAL

Switzerland produces around 720kg of waste per head of population annually, around half of which is recycled. The country has one of the highest rates of waste recycling in the world, and most Swiss religiously sort their rubbish (where there's muck, there's money!), which in many cases is obligatory. Recycling is a way of life in Switzerland, where there's a successful national campaign to reduce household waste under the slogan 'reduce, reuse and recycle' (see **Recycling** below). Large apartment blocks may have different coloured bins for different types of waste.

For non-recyclable waste, most apartments have large rubbish disposal bins in which rubbish must be deposited in special plastic bags (*Kehrichtsäcke, sacs à ordures*). In most communities, you must use only 'official' (taxed) bags, usually coloured and printed with the community name, sold in local stores and supermarkets (only at the checkout to prevent theft!). Regular rubbish bags aren't official, and cannot be deposited in the rubbish disposal bins in most communities, unless they have a 'tax stamp' attached – in some areas, you must buy 'tax stamps' (sold at the town hall or other council offices), which are affixed to regular rubbish bags before disposal. Rubbish is usually collected weekly.

Rubbish bags come in various sizes (e.g. 17, 35, 60 and 110 litres), each with a different tax, e.g. CHF 2 (35-litre) to CHF 6.30 (110-litre) each, which varies according to the community. Waste deposited in these bags is usually restricted to materials that can be incinerated. If you use unofficial rubbish bags, they won't be collected and the local waste 'detective' may track you down and fine you, e.g. CHF 100 (you have been warned!).

The aim is to encourage recycling and avoid the unnecessary use of wrapping and packaging, which prompts most people to deposit unwanted packaging in supermarket bins specially provided for this purpose. It must be working, as since the tax was introduced, waste has been reduced by as much as 50 per cent in some areas. Some communities, however, charge residents an annual waste tax, e.g. CHF 30, irrespective of the amount of waste they generate.

In some communities you may need to buy a dustbin (garbage can), which is usually emptied once a week.

## Recycling

Many kinds of waste are recycled or reused in Switzerland, and all major towns and cities have recycling centres. Some cities organise a home pick-up of certain recyclable waste – you can obtain a schedule from your local council, which may also be published online. There's a charge for the collection of some waste.

The following waste is recycled in most communities:

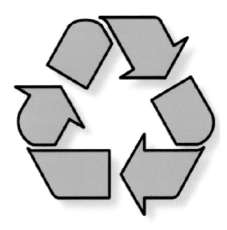

◆ Paper and cardboard should be tied in bundles with string and shouldn't include any plastic or metal, e.g. covers or bindings. Don't pack papers into paper or plastic bags for street pick-up as this isn't permitted. Collection is organised by the community each month (for paper and cardboard), although in some communities there are no collections and it must be deposited in a special container or storage area.

◆ Large objects, for example, old furniture, carpets, skis and appliances, are collected periodically (e.g. once a month) in some areas (or on request), usually just after the official house moving dates (dates are announced in local newspapers). Second-hand 'junk' and furniture stores, often operated in aid of charities such as the Red Cross or Salvation Army, may collect old furniture free of charge.

◆ Bottles and glass should be deposited in bottle banks provided in all towns and villages. Bottle banks are divided into sections for green, brown and white bottles. Their use may be restricted; for example, no deposits between 8pm and 7 or 8am and on Sundays and public holidays (or as listed). Some bottle banks are reserved for large bottles (0.5l or larger) of all colours, which are washed and reused. Switzerland is the world leader in glass recycling with an over 90 per cent recovery rate. However, there's a returnable deposit of CHF 0.30 to 0.50 on most one-litre glass bottles, so don't throw them away but return them to the store!

◆ Tin cans can be taken to collection areas or deposited in can-crunching machines.

They should be washed and squashed flat after the label, lid and base have been removed, and should be deposited only in the specified container.

♦ Household cooking oils shouldn't be flushed down sinks as they clog the pipes. Most communities have oil bins and designated dumps for motor oil.

♦ Hazardous and toxic waste, such as chemicals, paints, thinners and varnishes, can be returned to the point of sale or taken to a hazardous waste collection point.

♦ Batteries should be returned to retailers, who must provide containers; or taken to a designated dump (some are recycled). Car batteries should be returned to a garage.

♦ Aluminium (e.g. cans, tops and frozen food containers) may be taken to collection areas. A magnet is built into containers for aluminium waste: if it's magnetic, it isn't aluminium.

♦ Vegetable or organic waste, including garden rubbish, may be collected and used as compost (designated green bins may be provided next to your housing rubbish bins) – or you can make your own compost heap if you have a garden.

♦ Old clothes are collected by charitable organisations, usually once or twice a year. You usually receive special bags (e.g. Tex-Aid in Zurich) by mail. In some communities, women's groups organise a clothes exchange once or twice a year and collect and sell nearly-new clothing for a small commission. Old shoes are collected by local shoe stores in some towns and sent to third-world countries (opticians may also collect old prescription spectacles for the same purpose).

♦ Unused medicines and poisons should be returned for disposal to a chemist (pharmacy) or to the shop where they were purchased.

♦ Old electronics products, computers, household appliances and tyres can be returned to the vendor, who must take them back (but may charge for the service); although when buying new appliances, such as a refrigerator, the vendor may take your old one away free of charge.

♦ Plastic (PET) bottles must be flattened and deposited at the PET bottle drop at the store where you bought them.

In communities with a recycling centre, there are sometimes collection bins for other types of plastic, e.g. soft PVC, metal (other than that specified above), electrical apparatus, mineral items, books (which other people can take for free), and various other waste such as cork, broken flower pots, china, etc.

All communities publish instructions regarding what to do with different waste, and a list of waste collection times and depots. Many large stores, e.g. Coop, Manor and Migros, have collection bins for aluminium, batteries, tins and certain types of bottles.

---

▲ **Caution**

The indiscriminate dumping of rubbish is strictly forbidden in Switzerland.

---

Fête de l'Escalade. Geneva

# APPENDICES

## APPENDIX A: USEFUL ADDRESSES

### Swiss Embassies Abroad

The following list contains a selection of Swiss embassies abroad. For a complete list, see the Federal Department of Foreign Affairs website (🖥 www.eda.admin.ch/eda/en/home/reps.html).

**Albania:** Rruga e Elbasanit 81, Tirana (☎ +355-4-223 48 88, 🖥 www.eda.admin.ch/tirana).

**Andorra:** c/o Crowne Plaza Andorra, Carrer Prat de la Creu, 88, 500 Andorra la Vella (☎ +376-871 385).

**Argentina:** Avenida Santa Fe 846, 12° piso, 1059 Buenos Aires (☎ +54-11-4311 6491, 🖥 www.eda.admin.ch/buenosaires).

**Australia:** 7 Melbourne Avenue, Forrest, ACT 2603 (☎ +61-2-6162 8400, 🖥 www.eda.admin.ch/australia).

**Austria**: Prinz-Eugen-Strabe 7, 1030 Vienna (☎ +43-1-795050, 🖥 www.eda.admin.ch/wien).

**Belgium:** Rue de la Loi 26, bte 9, 1040 Brussels (☎ +32-2-285 4350, 🖥 www.eda.admin.ch/bruxelles).

**Bosnia and Herzegovina:** Josipa Stadlera 15, 71000 Sarajevo (☎ +387-33-275 850, 🖥 www.eda.admin.ch/sarajevo).

**Brazil:** SES, Avenida das Nações, Lote 41, 70448-900 Brasilia/DF (☎ +55-61-3443 5500, 🖥 www.eda.admin.ch/brasilia).

**Bulgaria:** ul. Chipka 33, 1504 Sofia (☎ +359-2-942 0100, 🖥 www.eda.admin.ch/sofia).

**Canada:** 5 Marlborough Avenue, Ottawa, Ontario K1N 8E6 (☎ +1-613-235 1837, 🖥 www.eda.admin.ch/ottawa).

**Chile:** Américo Vespucio Sur 100, piso 14, Santiago, Las Condes (☎ +56-2-928 0100, 🖥 www.eda.admin.ch/santiago).

**China:** Sanlitun Dongwujie 3, Beijing (☎ +86-10-8532 8888, 🖥 www.eda.admin.ch/beijing).

**Croatia:** Bogoviceva 3, 10000 Zagreb (☎ +385-1-487-8800, 🖥 www.eda.admin.ch/zagreb)

**Cyprus:** Medcon Tower, 6th floor, 46, Themistocles Dervis Street, 1066 Nicosia (☎ +357-22-466800, 🖥 www.eda.admin.ch/nicosia).

**Czech Republic:** Pevnostn 7, 16201 Prague 6 (☎ +420-220-400 611, 🖥 www.eda.admin.ch/prag).

**Denmark:** Amaliegade 14, Copenhagen (☎ +45-33-141796, 🖥 www.eda.admin.ch/copenhagen).

**Estonia:** Tuvi 12-28, 10119 Tallinn (☎ +372-6-313 041).

**Finland:** Uudenmaankatu 16A, 00120 Helsinki (☎ +358-9-622 9500, 🖥 www.eda.admin.ch/helsinki).

**France:** 142, Rue de Grenelle, 75007 Paris (☎ +33-1-49-556700, 🖥 www.eda.admin.ch/paris).

**Germany:** Otto-von-Bismarck-Allee 4A, 10557 Berlin (☎ +49-30-390 4000, 🖥 www.eda.admin.ch/berlin).

**Greece:** Rue Iassiou 2, 115 21 Athens (☎ +30-210-723 0364, 🖥 www.eda.admin.ch/athens).

**Hungary:** Stefánia ùt. 107, 1143 Budapest (☎ +36-1-460 7-40, 🖥 www.eda.admin.ch/budapest).

**Iceland:** Laugavegi 13, 101 Reykjavik (☎ +354-551 7172).

**India:** Nyaya Marg, Chanakyapuri, New Delhi 110 021 (☎ +91-11-2687 8372, 🖥 www.eda.admin.ch/newdelhi).

**Indonesia:** Jl. H.R. Rasuna Said, Blok X 3/2, Kuningan, Jakarta-Selatan 12950 (☎ +62-21-525 6061, 🖥 www.eda.admin.ch/jakarta).

**Iran:** 2 Yasaman Street, Sharifi Manesh Avenue, Elahieh, Tehran (☎ +98-21-2200 8333, 🖥 www.eda.admin.ch/tehran).

**Ireland:** 6, Ailesbury Road, Ballsbridge, Dublin 4 (☎ +353-1-218 6382, 🖥 www.eda.admin.ch/dublin).

**Israel:** 228 Hayarkon Street, 63405 Tel Aviv (☎ +972-3-546 4455, 🖥 www.eda.admin.ch/telaviv).

**Italy:** Via Barnaba Oriani 61, 00197 Roma (☎ +39-6-809571, 🖥 www.eda.admin.ch/roma).

**Japan:** 5-9-12 Minami-Azabu, Minato-ku, Tokyo 106-8589 (☎ +81-3-5449 8400, 🖥 www.eda.admin.ch/tokyo).

**Korea (Republic):** 32-10 Songwol-dong, Jongro-ku, Seoul 110-101 (☎ +82-2-739-9511, 🖥 www.eda.admin.ch/seoul).

**Latvia:** Elizabetes iela 2, 1340 Riga (☎ +371-6733 8351, 🖥 www.eda.admin.ch/riga).

**Lithuania:** Lvovo 25, 09320 Vilnius (☎ +370-5203 1360)

**Luxumbourg:** Forum Royal, 25A, Boulevard Royal, 2449 Luxembourg (☎ +352-227 474, 🖳 www.eda.admin.ch/luxumbourg).

**Malaysia:** 16, Pesiaran Madge, 55000 Kuala Lumpur (☎ +60-3-2148 0622, 🖳 www.eda.admin.ch/kualalumpur).

**Malta:** 6 Zachary-Street, Valletta (☎ +356-21-244 159).

**Mexico:** Torre Optima, piso 11, Paseo de las Palmas Nr. 405, Lomas de Chapultepec, 11000 Mexico DF (☎ +52-55-91 784 370, 🖳 www.eda.admin.ch/mexico).

**Monaco:** c/o UBS (Monaco) SA, 2 avenue de Grande Bretagne, 98007 Monaco Cedex (☎ +377-93-155 882).

**Netherlands:** Lange Voorhout 42, 2514 EE Den Haag (☎ +31-70 364 2831, 🖳 www.eda.admin.ch/denhaag).

**New Zealand:** Maritime Tower, 10 Customhouse Quay, Level 12, Wellington (☎ +64-4-472 1593, 🖳 www.eda.admin.ch/wellington).

**Norway:** Bygdoy Allé 78, 0244 Oslo (☎ +47-22-542 390, 🖳 www.eda.admin.ch/oslo).

**Philippines:** 24th Floor, Equitable Bank Tower, 8751, Paseo de Roxas, 1226 Makati City, Metro Manila (☎ +63-2-757 9000, 🖳 www.eda.admin.ch/manila).

**Poland:** Aleje Ujazdowskie 27, 00-540 Warsaw (☎ +48-22-628 0481, 🖳 www.eda.admin.ch/warsaw).

**Portugal:** Travessa do Jardim, no. 17, 1350-185 Lisboa (☎ +351-213-944 090, 🖳 www.eda.admin.ch/lisbon).

**Romania:** Str. Grigore Alexandrescu 16-20, 4th Floor, 010626 Bucharest (☎ +40-21-206 1600, 🖳 www.eda.admin.ch/bucarest).

**Russia:** Per. Ogorodnaya Sloboda 2/5, 101000 Moscow (☎ +7-495-258 3830, 🖳 www.eda.admin.ch/moscow).

**Saudi Arabia:** Diplomatic quarter, Riyadh 11693 (☎ +966-1-488 1291, 🖳 www.eda.admin.ch/riad).

**Serbia:** Bircaninova 27, 11001 Belgrade (☎ +381-11-3065 820, 🖳 www.eda.admin.ch/belgrade).

**Singapore:** 1, Swiss Club Link, Singapore 288162 (☎ +65-6468 5788, 🖳 www.eda.admin.ch/singapore).

**Slovakia:** Tolsteho ul.9, 81106 Bratislava 1 (☎ +421-2-59-301 111, 🖳 www.eda.admin.ch/bratislava).

**Slovenia:** Trg republike 3, 6th floor, 1000 Ljubljana (☎ +386-1-200 8640, 🖳 www.eda.admin.ch/ljubljana).

**South Africa:** 225 Veale Street, Parc Nouveau, New Muckleneuk 0181 (☎ +27-12-452 0660, 🖵 www.cda.admin.oh/protoria).

**Spain:** Calle de Núñez de Balboa 35 A, 7.°, Edificio Goya, 28001 Madrid (☎ +34-91-436 3960, 🖵 www.eda.admin.ch/madrid).

**Sri Lanka:** 63, Gregory's Road, Colombo 7 (☎ +94-11-269 5117, 🖵 www.eda.admin.ch/colombo).

**Sweden:** Valhallavägen 64, 100 41 Stockholm (☎ +46-8-676 7900, 🖵 www.eda.admin.ch/stockholm).

**Thailand:** 35 North Wireless Road, Bangkok 10330 (☎ +66-2-253 0156, 🖵 www.eda.admin.ch/bangkok).

**Turkey:** Atatürk Bulvari No:247, PK 25, Kavaklidere 06692, Ankara (☎ +90-312-457 3100, 🖵 www.eda.admin.ch/turkey).

**Ukraine:** vul. Kozyatynska 12, 01015 Kyiv (☎ +380-44-281 6128, 🖵 www.eda.admin.ch/kiev).

**United Kingdom:** 16-18 Montagu Place, London W1H 2BQ (☎ +44-20-7616 6000, 🖵 www.eda.admin.ch/london).

**United States of America:** 2900 Cathedral Ave. NW, Washington DC 20008 (☎ +1-202-745-7900, 🖵 www.eda.admin.ch/washington).

**Uruguay:** Casilla de Correo 12261, 11300 Montevideo-Pocitos (☎ +598-2-711 5545, 🖵 www.eda.admin.ch/montevideo).

## Swiss Government Departments & Organisations

**Federal Audit Office**, Monbijoustrasse 45, 3003 Berne (☎ 031-323 11 11, 🖵 www.efk.admin.ch).

**Federal Customs Administration,** Oberzolldirektion, Monbijoustr. 40, CH-3003 Berne (☎ 031-322 65 11, 🖵 www.ezv.admin.ch).

**Federal Department of Defence, Civil Protection and Sport**, Bundeshaus Ost, CH-3003 Berne (☎ 031-322 21 11, 🖵 www.vbs.admin.ch).

**Federal Department of Economic Affairs**, Federal Palace East Wing, CH-3003 Berne (☎ 031-322 20 07, 🖵 www.evd.admin.ch).

**Federal Department of the Environment, Transport, Energy and Communications** (☎ 031-322 55 11, 🖵 www.uvek.admin.ch).

**Federal Department of Finance**, Bundesgasse 3, CH-3003 Berne (☎ 031-322 21 11, 🖵 www.efd.admin.ch).

**Federal Department of Foreign Affairs**, Bundeshaus West, CH-3003 Berne (☎ 031-322 21 11, 🖵 www.ede.admin.ch).

**Federal Department of Home Affairs,** General Secretariat GS-FDHA, Schwanengasse 2, CH-3003 Berne (☎ 031-322 80 41, 🖥 www.edi.admin.ch).

**Federal Department of Justice and Police**, Information services, Federal Palace, West Wing, CH-3003 Berne (☎ 031-322 21 11, 🖥 www.ejpd.admin.ch).

**Federal Office of Housing**, Storchengasse 6, 2540 Granges (☎ 032-654 91 11, 🖥 www.bwo.admin.ch).

**Federal Office for Migration.** Quellenweg 6, CH-3003 Berne-Wabern (☎ 031-325 11 11, 🖥 www.bfm.admin.ch).

**Federal Office for Social Insurance,** Effingerstr. 20, CH-3003 Berne (☎ 031-322 90 11, 🖥 www.bsv.admin.ch).

**Federal Statistical Office**, Library, Espace de l'Europe 10, CH-2010 Neuchâtel (☎ 032-713 60 54, 🖥 www.bfs.admin.ch).

**Federal Tax Administration**, Eigerstr. 65, CH-3003 Berne (☎ 031-322 71 41, 🖥 www.estv.admin.ch).

**Federal Veterinarians Office,** Schwarzenburgstr. 155, CH-3003 Berne (☎ 031-323 30 33, 🖥 www.bvet.admin.ch).

**Osec, Business Network Switzerland,** Stampfenbachstrasse 85, CH-8021 Zurich (☎ 044-365 51 51, 🖥 www.osec.ch). The umbrella organisation for the promotion of exports, imports and investments, as well as the promotion of Switzerland as a business location.

**Swiss Broadcasting Corporation (SRG),** Belpstrasse 48, CH-3000 Berne 14 (☎ 031-350 91 11, 🖥 www.srg.ch).

**Swiss Portal**, Federal Chancellery, e-Government Section, Gurtengasse 5, CH-3003 Berne (☎ 031-324 30 00, 🖥 www.ch.ch).

**Switzerland Tourism (ST),** PO Box 695, CH-8027 Zurich (☎ 0800-100 200 30/044-288 11 11, 🖥 www.myswitzerland.com).

**Swiss Radio International,** Giacomettistr. 1, CH-3000 Berne 15 (☎ 031-350 92 22, 🖥 www.swissinfo.org).

## Cantonal Real Estate Purchase Authorisation Bodies

**Aargau:** Departement Volkswirtschaft und Inneres des Kantons Aargau, Justizabteilung, Sektion Grundbuch & Notariat, Bleichemattstrasse 1, CH-5001 Aarau (☎ 062-835 14 64, ✉ matthias.vonarx@ag.ch).

**Appenzell Innerrhoden:** Departement Volks- und Landwirtschaft des Kantons Appenzell Ausserrhoden, Regierungsgebäude, CH-9102 Herisau (☎ 071-353 64 50, ✉ daniel.kobler@ar.ch).

**Appenzell Outerrhoden:** Volkswirtschaftsdepartement des Kantons Appenzell Innerrhoden, Marktgasse 2, CH-9050 Appenzell (☎ 071-788 96 60, ✉ wirtschaft@ai.ch).

**Basle-City:** Präsidialdepartement des Kantons Basel-Stadt, Schlichtungsstelle für Mietstreitigkeiten, Utengasse 36, Postfach, CH-4005 Basle (☎ 061-267 85 36, ✉ ernst.jost@bs.ch).

**Basle-Country:** Bau- und Umweltschutzdirektion des Kantons Basle-Landschaft, Rheinstrasse 29, 4410 CH-Liestal (☎ 061-552 53 53, ✉ christine.bobst@bl.ch).

**Berne:** Government Representatives (26 districts) Supervisory uthority: beco – Berner Wirtschaft Marktaufsicht, Laupenstrasse 22, CH-3011 Berne (☎ 031-633 50 93, ✉ christoph.gugger@vol.be.ch).

**Fribourg:** Kommission für den Erwerb von Grundstücken durch Personen im Ausland des Kantons Freiburg, p.a. Volkswirtschafts-, Verkehrs- und Energiedirektion des Kantons Freiburg, Joseph-Piller-Strasse 13, CH-1701 Freiburg (☎ 026-322 03 23, ✉ hauser@avopartner.ch).

**Geneva:** Département de l'économie et de la santé du Canton de Genève, Case postale 3984, CH-1211 Geneva 3 (☎ 022-327 29 39, ✉ francois.panosetti@etat.ge.ch).

**Glarus:** Departement für Volkswirtschaft und Inneres des Kantons Glarus, Zwinglistrasse 6, CH-8750 Glarus (☎ 055-646 66 00, ✉ volkswirtschaftinneres@gl.ch).

**Graubunden:** Grundbuchinspektorat und Handelsregister des Kantons Graubünden, Rohanstrasse 5, CH-7001 Chur (☎ 081-257 24 85, ✉ sekretariat @giha.gr.ch).

**Jura:** Département des finances, de la justice et de la police du Canton du Jura, Service juridique, Rue du 24-Septembre 2, CH-2800 Delémont (☎ 032-420 56 35, ✉ denis.allimann@jura.ch).

**Lucerne:** Government representatives (5 districts) Supervisory authority: Justiz- und Sicherheitsdepartement des Kantons Luzern, Rechtsdienst, Bahnhofstrasse 15, CH-6002 Lucerne (☎ 041-228 57 93, ✉ peter.wipraechtiger@lu.ch).

**Neuchâtel:** Commission pour la sanction d'acquisitions immobilières par des personnes à l'étranger du Canton de Neuchâtel, p.a. Inspectorat du registre foncier du Canton de Neuchâtel, Rue du Tivoli 22, Case postale 39, CH-2003 Neuchâtel (☎ 032-889 61 40, ✉ jean-marc.gicot@ne.ch).

**Nidwalden:** Justiz- und Sicherheitsdirektion des Kantons Nidwalden, c/o Rechtsdienst, Dorfplatz 2, CH-6370 Stans (☎ 041-618 79 14, ✉ armin.eberli@nw.ch).

**Obwalden:** Volkswirtschaftsdepartement des Kantons Obwalden, Volkswirtschaftsamt, St. Antoniusstrasse 4, Postfach 1264, CH-6061 Sarnen (☎ 041-666 62 20, ✉ volkswirtschaftsamt@ow.ch).

**St. Gallen:** Grundbuchinspektorat des Kantons St. Gallen, Oberer Graben 32, CH-9001 St. Gallen (☎ 071-229 37 35, ✉ ernst.kurer@sg.ch).

**Schaffhausen:** Volkswirtschaftsdepartement des Kantons Schaffhausen, Mühlentalstrasse 105, CH-8200 Schaffhausen (☎ 052-632 74 01, ✉ gbamt@ktsh.ch).

**Schwyz:** Volkswirtschaftsdepartement des Kantons Schwyz, Bahnhofstrasse 15, Postfach 1180, CH-6431 Schwyz (☎ 041-819 18 18, ✉ vd@sz.ch).

**Solothurn:** Amtschreiberei-Inspektorat des Kantons Solothurn, Bielstrasse 9, Postfach 364, CH-4502 Solothurn (☎ 032-627 75 80, ✉ philipp.adam@fd.so.ch).

**Thurgau:** Departement für Inneres und Volkswirtschaft des Kantons Thurgau, Rechtsdienst, CH-8510 Frauenfeld (☎ 052-724 23 79, ✉ beat.andrist@tg.ch).

**Ticino:** Autorità di prima istanza LAFE, c/o Ufficio dei Registri (8 districts), Supervisory authority, Commissione di sorveglianza del Cantone Ticino per l'applicazione della LAFE, c/o Ufficio dei Registri di Lugano, Via Bossi 2A, CH-6901 Lugano (☎ 091-815 54 10, ✉ arnaldo.caccia@ti.ch).

**Uri:** Volkswirtschaftsdirektion des Kantons Uri, Klausenstrasse 4, CH-6460 Altdorf (☎ 041-875 24 01, ✉ christoph.mueller@ur.ch).

**Valais:** Dienststelle für Grundbuchämter und Geomatik des Kantons Wallis, Rechts- und Verwaltungsamt, Avenue Ritz 24, CH-1951 Sion (☎ 027-606 28 50, ✉ melanie.morand@admin.vs.ch).

**Vaud:** Commission foncière du Canton de Vaud, Section II, Rue de la Paix 6, CH-1014 Lausanne (☎ 021-316 24 83, ✉ olivier.dind@.vd.ch).

**Zug:** Volkswirtschaftsdirektion des Kantons Zug, Verwaltungsgebäude 1, Aabachstrasse 5, Postfach 857, CH-6301 Zug (☎ 041-728 55 06, ✉ peter.muellhaupt@vd.zg.ch).

**Zurich:** District council (12 districts) Supervisory authority: Volkswirtschaftsdirektion des Kantons Zürich, Amt für Wirtschaft und Arbeit Erwerb von Grundstücken durch Personen im Ausland, Walchestrasse 19, CH-8090 Zurich (☎ 043-259 26 26, ✉ awa@vd.zh.ch).

## Cantonal Tax Offices

### Federal Tax Office

For general information about taxation in Switzerland, contact the Swiss Federal Tax Administration (*Eidgenössische Steuerverwaltung, Administration fédérale des contributions*), Eigerstr. 65, CH-3003 Berne (☎ 031-322 7106, 🖥 www.estv.admin.ch).

**Aargau:** Kantonales Steueramt, Telli-Hochhaus, CH-5004 Aarau (☎ 062-835 2530, 🖥 www.steuern.ag.ch).

**Appenzell-Ausserrhoden:** Herisau (AR) Address: Kantonale Steuerverwaltung, Gutenberg-Zentrum, CH-9102 Herisau (☎ 071-353 62 90, 🖥 www.appenzellerland. ch/verwaltung).

**Appenzell-Innerrhoden:** Kantonale Steuerverwaltung, Marktgasse 2, CH-9050 Appenzell (☎ 71-788 9401, 🖳 www.ai.ch/_d/verwaltung/finanzen.shtml).

**Basle-Land:** Kantonale Steuerverwaltung, Rheinstr. 33, CH-4410 Liestal (☎ 061-925 51 11, 🖳 www.baselland.ch/index.htm).

**Basel-Stadt:** Kantonale Steuerverwaltung, Fischmarkt 10, CH-4001 Basle (☎ 061-267 81 81, 🖳 www.steuer.bs.ch).

**Berne:** Kantonale Steuerverwaltung, Münstergasse 3, CH-3011 Berne (☎ 0848-844 411, 🖳 www.sv.fin.be.ch).

**Fribourg:** Kantonale Steuerverwaltung, Rue Joseph Piller 13, CH-1701 Fribourg (☎ 026-305 11 11, 🖳 www.fr.ch/scc).

**Geneva:** Administration fiscale cantonale, Rue du Stand 26, CH-1211 Geneva 3 (☎ 022-327 70 00, 🖳 www.geneve.ch/df/html/vos_impots.html).

**Glarus:** Kantonale Steuerverwaltung, Hauptstrasse 11/17, CH-8750 Glarus (☎ 055-646 61 50, 🖳 www.gl.ch/finanzdirektion/index.htm).

**Graubunden:** Kantonale Steuerverwaltung, Steinbruchstrasse 18/20, CH-7000 Chur (☎ 081-257 33 32, 🖳 www.stv.gr.ch).

**Jura:** Service cantonal des contributions, Rue de la Justice 2, CH-2800 Delémont (☎ 32-420 5530, 🖳 www.ju.ch/index_etat.html).

**Lucerne:** Kantonale Steuerverwaltung, Buobenmatt 1, CH-6002 Lucerne (☎ 41-228 56 43, 🖳 www.steuernluzern.ch).

**Neuchâtel:** Administration cantonale des contributions, Rue du Docteur-Coullery 5, CH-2300 La Chaux-de-Fonds (☎ 032-889 64 20, 🖳 www.ne.ch/neat/site/jsp/rubrique/rubrique.jsp?StyleType=marron&CatId=67).

**Nidwalden:** Kantonales Steueramt, Bahnhofplatz 3, CH-6371 Stans (☎ 041-618 71 27, 🖳 www.nw.ch/index_regierung_d.html).

**Obwalden:** Kantonale Steuerverwaltung, St. Antonistrasse 4, CH-6061 Sarnen (☎ 041-666 62 94, 🖳 www.ow.ch/index_regierung_d.html).

**St-Gallen:** Kantonale Steuerverwaltung, Davidstr. 41, CH-9002 St. Gallen (☎ 071-229 41 21, 🖳 www.steuern.sg.ch).

**Schaffhausen:** Kantonale Steuerverwaltung, VGM Mühlentalstr. 105, CH-8201 Schaffhausen (☎ 52-632 71 11, 🖳 www.sh.ch/kanton).

**Schwyz:** Kantonale Steuerverwaltung, Bahnhofstrasse 15, CH-6431 Schwyz (☎ 041-819 11 24, 🖳 www.sz.ch/rv/index.html).

**Solothurn:** Kantonale Steuerverwaltung, Werkhofstrasse 29c, CH-4509 Solothurn (☎ 032-627 87 87, 🖳 www.so.ch/fd/stv).

**Thurgau:** Kantonale Steuerverwaltung, Schlossmühlestr. 15, CH-8501 Frauenfeld (☎ 052-724 11 11, 🖳 www.tg.ch/steuern).

**Ticino:** Amministrazione cantonale delle contribuzioni, Viale S.Franscini 6, CH-6500 Bellinzona (☎ 091-814 39 58, 🖳 www.ti.ch/dfe/dc).

**Uri:** Kantonale Steuerverwaltung, Haus Winterberg, CH-6460 Altdorf (☎ 041-875 2244, 🖳 www.ur.ch/start.asp?level=10).

**Valais:** Administration cantonale des contributions, Avenue de la Gare 35, CH-1951 Sion (☎ 027-606 24 51, 🖳 www.vs.ch/navig2/FinanceEconomie/de/Frame129.htm).

**Vaud:** Administration cantonale des impôts, Route de Chavannes 37, CH-1014 Lausanne (☎ 021-316 21 21, 🖳 www.aci.vd.ch).

**Zug:** Kantonale Steuerverwaltung, Bahnhofstrasse 26, CH-6301 Zug (☎ 041-728 33 11, 🖳 www.zug.ch/tax).

**Zurich:** Kantonales Steueramt, Bändliweg 21, Postfach, CH-8090 Zurich (☎ 043-259 4050, 🖳 www.steueramt.zh.ch).


## Real Estate Organisation

**Federation of French-Speaking Real Estate Agents** (Fédération Romande Immobilière/FRI), rue du Midi 15, CP 5607, CH-1002 Lausanne (☎ 021-341 41 42, 🖳 www.fri.ch).

**Geneva Real Estate Agents** (Genève Immobilière), Plurality Presse SA, 8 rue Jacques-Grosselin, CH-1227 Carouge, Geneva (☎ 022-307 02 20, 🖳 www.geneveimmobilier.ch/gi).

**House Forum** (Haus-Forum), Swissforums AG, Eisenbahnstrasse 11, CH-4901 Langenthal (☎ 062-916 40 00, 🖳 www.haus-forum.ch). The largest house-building database in Switzerland.

**Rent Law**, Mietrechtspraxis, Verlag und Seminare, Postfach, CH-8026 Zurich (☎ 043-243 40 50, 🖳 www.mietrecht.ch). Everything you need to know about tenancy law (in German).

**Schweizerischen Verband für Wohnbau-und Eigentumsförderung** (SWE, Guggistrasse 7, CH-6002 Lucerne, ☎ 041-317 05 60, 🖳 www.swe-wohnen.ch).

**Swiss Home Owners Association** (Hauseigentümerverband Schweiz/HEV), Seefeldstrasse 60, Postfach, CH-8032 Zurich (☎ 44-254 90 20, 🖳 www.hev-schweiz.ch).

**Swiss Housing Association** (Schweizerischen Verbandes für Wohnungswesen/SVW), Bucheggstrasse 109, Postfach, CH-8042 Zurich (☎ 044-362 42 40, 🖳 www.svw.ch).

**Swiss Housing Organisation** (Hausverein Schweiz), HabitatDurable, Zentralsekretariat, Bollwerk 35, Postfach 6515, CH-3001 Berne (☎ 031-311 50 55, 🖳 www.hausverein.ch).

**Swiss Real Estate Association** (Schweizerischer Verband der Immobilienwirtschaft/SVIT, Association suisse de l'économie immobilière), Puls 5, Giessereistr. 18, CH-8005 Zurich (☏ 044-434 78 82, 🖥 www.svit.ch).

**Swiss Union of Real Estate Professionals** (French-speaking cantons), Union suisse des professionnels de l'immobilier/USPI, Case Postale 1215, CH-1001 Lausanne (☏ 021-796 33 00, 🖥 www.uspi.ch).

**Tenants Associations**: German-speaking cantons, Mieterverband (☏ 0900-900 800, 🖥 www.mieterverband.ch); French–speaking cantons, ASLOCA (🖥 www.asloca.ch); Italian-speaking Ticino, ASI (☏ 091-967 51 44, 🖥 www.asi-infoalloggio.ch).

## Miscellaneous

**The Automobile Club of Switzerland (ACS):** Wasserwerkgasse 39, CH-3000 Berne 13 (☏ 031-328 31 11, 🖥 www.acs.ch).

**Basle-EuroAirport** (☏ 061-325 31 11, 🖥 www.euroairport.com).

**British Swiss Chamber of Commerce:** Bellerivestr. 209, CH-8008 Zurich (☏ 044 422 31 31, 🖥 www.bscc.ch).

**Geneva Airport** (☏ 022-717 71 11, 🖥 www.gva.ch/en).

**Health.ch AG**, Dorfstr. 24, 8700 Küsnacht (☏ 043-541 15 21, 🖥 www.doctor.ch). Internet site containing lists of doctors, dentists, pharmacies and clinics throughout Switzerland.

**Mobility Carsharing Schweiz:** Gütschstrasse 2, PO Box, CH-6000 Lucerne 7 (☏ 0848-824 812, 🖥 www.mobility.ch).

**REGA (air rescue service):** Administration und Secretariat, Rega Center, PO Box 1414, CH-8058 Zurich Airport (☏ 044-654 37 37, 1414 in an emergency or +41-333 333 333 if your mobile phone doesn't have a SIM card from a Swiss network provider, 🖥 www.rega.ch).

**STA Travel:** Ankerstr. 112, CH-8026 Zurich (☏ 058-450 40 50, 🖥 www.statravel.ch).

**Swiss Accidents and Insurance (SUVA):** Fluhmattstr. 1, CH-6002 Lucerne (☏ 0848-830 830, 🖥 www.suva.ch).

**Swiss-American Chamber of Commerce:** Talacker 41, CH-8001 Zurich (☏ 043-443 72 00, 🖥 www.amcham.ch).

**Swiss Hotel Association (SHV):** Monbijoustr. 130, PO Box, CH-3007 Berne (☏ 031-370 41 11, 🖥 www.swisshotels.ch).

**Swiss International Air Lines** (☏ 041-848 700 700, 🖥 www.swiss.com).

**Swiss Railways** (☏ 0900-300 300, 🖥 www.sbb.ch.en).

**Swiss Red Cross:** Rainmattstr. 10, CH-3001 Berne (☏ 031-387 71 11, 🖥 www.redcross.ch).

**Swiss Television** (Schweizer Fernsehen), Kundendienst, Postfach, CH-8052 Zurich (☎ 044-305 66 11, ⌨ www.sf.tv).

**Touring Club of Switzerland (TCS):** Ch. de Blandonnet 4, PO Box 820, CH-1214 Vernier (☎ 0800-801 000, ⌨ www.tcs.ch).

**Transport Club of Switzerland (VCS):** Lagerstr. 18, PO Box, CH-3360 Herzogenbuchsee (☎ 0848-611 611, ⌨ www.verkehrsclub.ch).

**Zurich Airport** (☎ 0900-300 313, ⌨ www.zurich-airport.com).

## Swiss Magazines in English

**Inside Switzerland magazine,** Schweizer + Davies Media GmbH, Technoparkstrasse 1, CH-8005 Zurich (☎ 044-445 35 35, ⌨ www.insidemagazine. ch). Quarterly magazine targeted at Switzerland's 'style-conscious international people'.

**Swiss magazine**, Ambient Media, Airpage AG, Aathalstrasse 34, CH-8610 Uster-Zurich (☎ 043-311 3000, ⌨ www.swiss.com/web/en/services/on_board/Pages/swiss_magazine.aspx). Magazine of Swiss International Air Line, published ten times a year.

**Swiss News magazine,** Swiss Businesspress SA, Köschenrütistrasse 109, CH-8052 Zurich (☎ 044-306 4700, ⌨ www.swissnews.ch). Swiss monthly news and events magazine.

**Swiss Political Science Review**, PO Box 1470, CH-8040 Zurich (☎ 044-491 21 30, ⌨ http://new.spsr.ch).

**Swiss Review**, Alpenstrasse 26, CH-3006 Berne (☎ 031-356 61 10, ⌨ www.revue. ch). Magazine for the Swiss abroad.

**Swiss Style magazine,** CP 2024, 1227 Carouge (☎ 0900-576 444, ⌨ www. swissstyle.com). Swiss lifestyle magazine published by Anglophone Telephone Information Services.

# APPENDIX B: USEFUL WEBSITES

See also the websites listed for individual cantons in **Chapter 2**.

## Government

**Directory of Administrative Authorities** (🖥 www.ch.ch/verzeichnis/index. html?lang=en#). Federal, cantonal and communal authorities.

**Federal Government** (🖥 www.admin.ch). The website of the Swiss government with links to all state departments.

**Federal Office of Housing** (🖥 www.bwo.admin.ch).

**Federal Office for Migration** (🖥 www.bfm.admin.ch). Provides information on work and residence permits.

**Swiss Embassies** (🖥 www.eda.admin.ch/eda/en/home/reps.html). Contact details and links to Swiss embassy websites.

**Swiss Emigration** (🖥 www.swissemigration.ch). Information about living and working in Switzerland.

**The Swiss Portal** (🖥 www.ch.ch). A wealth of practical information provided by the Swiss government.

**SwissInfoDesk** (🖥 www.nb.admin.ch). Information about Switzerland from the Swiss National Library (NL).

**Swiss Parliament: Federal Assembly** (🖥 www.parlament.ch/e/pages/default. aspx).

**Swiss Parliament: Federal Council** (🖥 www.admin.ch/br/index.html?lang=en).

**Swiss Statistics** (🖥 www.bfs.admin.ch/bfs/portal/en/index.html).

## Business

**British Swiss Chamber of Commerce** (🖥 www.bscc.ch).

**Chambers of Commerce & Industry** (🖥 www.cci.ch/en/map.htm).

**Doing Business** (🖥 www.doingbusiness.org/ExploreEconomies/?economyid=182). Provides objective measures of business regulations and their enforcement.

**Infonautics Business Directory** (🖥 www.swissdir.ch). Index of Swiss Business, Companies, Hotels and Tourism.

**Osec, Business Network Switzerland** (💻 www.osec.ch). The umbrella organisation for the promotion of exports, imports and investments, as well as the promotion of Switzerland as a business location.

**Swiss-American Chamber of Commerce** (💻 www.amcham.ch).

**Swiss Business Hub USA** (💻 www.swissbusinesshub.org). Trade Commissions of Switzerland to the US.

**Swiss Business School** (💻 www.sbs.edu). One of the world's leading business schools (situated in Zurich).

**Swiss Firms** (💻 www.swissfirms.ch/en). Promotes member companies of the Swiss Chambers of Commerce and supports them in their daily business activities.

**Swiss Network** (💻 www.swissnetwork.com). Portal for business and investments in Switzerland.

## Education & Families

**All for Kids** (💻 www.allforkids.ch). Fun learning and creative products in English for families in Switzerland.

**Bilingual Middle School** (💻 www.bilingual-middleschool.ch). German-English primary school in Zurich.

**CRUS** (💻 www.crus.ch/information-programme/study-in-switzerland.html?L=2). Information about study in Switzerland from the Rectors' Conference of Swiss Universities.

**Educa** (💻 www.educa.ch). Covers all levels of the Swiss education system.

**Education in Switzerland** (💻 www.about.ch/education/index.html). Information about the Swiss school system.

**English Teachers Association Switzerland** *(*💻 www.e-tas.ch).

**Geneva Association of Private Schools** (💻 www.agep.ch/eng).

**Gymboree** (💻 www.gymboree.ch). Play, music & arts' classes for infants to five years with classes in Basle, Geneva and Zurich.

**International School of Central Switzerland** (💻 www.isocs.ch). New international school located in Cham, Zug.

**International Schools in Switzerland** (💻 http://switzerland.english-schools.org).

**ISW International School Winterthur** (💻 www.iswinterthur.ch). International school offering the International Baccalaureate (IB) examination.

**Lake Geneva Swiss Private Schools** (💻 www.avdep.ch/default.cfm?lng=2).

**The Learning Place** (💻 www.thelearningplace.ch). Language school in Zug.

**Mothering Matters** (⌨ www.mmjournal.com). Devoted to parenting in Switzerland.

**Swiss Education Group** (⌨ www.swisseducation.com). The leading Swiss provider of hotel management schools.

**Swiss Federation of Private Schools** (⌨ www.swiss-schools.ch).

**Swiss International School** (⌨ www.iszn.ch/en/index.php). Zurich North international school is an IB World School that offers students an international education in the English language.

## Finance & Mortgages

**Comparis** (⌨ www.comparis.ch/hypotheken). Insurance and mortgage comparisons online.

**Credit Suisse** (⌨ www.credit-suisse.com/ch/en). Credit Suisse in English.

**Homegate** (⌨ www.homegate.ch). Mortgage rate comparison (French/German only).

**Swiss Banking** (⌨ www.swissbanking.ch). Swiss Bankers' Association website where the Swiss banking system is explained.

**Swiss Cantonal Banks** (⌨ www.kantonalbank.ch/e/index.php). An association of 24 Swiss cantonal banks offering a wide range of banking services and mortgages.

**Swiss Federal Banking Commission** (⌨ www.finma.ch/archiv/ebk/e/index.html).

**Union Bank of Switzerland** (⌨ www.ubs.com). UBS in English.

**Zurich Insurance** (⌨ www.zurich.ch/site/en.html). Zurich insurance and mortgages.

## Living & Working

**Anglo Info** (⌨ http://geneva.angloinfo.com). The website of Anglophone (☎ 0900-576 444), the Swiss information service for expatriates.

**Anglo Swiss Clubs** (⌨ www.angloswissclubs).

**Auris Relocation** (⌨ www.aurisrelocation.com). Swiss specialist relocation company.

**Basel Expats** (⌨ http://baselexpats.com). Local and general info for expats.

**Crown Relocation** (⌨ www.crownrelo.com). A division of the Crown Worldwide Group established in 1965.

**English Forum** (⌨ www.englishforum.ch). English-language community forum.

**Expats in Switzerland** (⌨ www.expatinch.com). Wide range of useful information.

**Geneva Info** (⌨ www.geinfo.ch). Geneva information for expats.

**Geneva Lunch** (⌨ http://genevalunch.com). Community 'newspaper' for the Lake Geneva region.

**Geneva Welcome Centre** (💻 www.cagi.ch). Website of CAGI, which helps find accommodation for international civil servants, members of permanent missions, consulates, NGOs and their families.

**Glocals** (💻 www.glocals.com). Social networking website. Began life as 'genevalocals', but now covers the whole of Switzerland.

**Keller Relocation** (💻 www.keller-swiss-group.com). Removals and relocation for the whole of Switzerland and worldwide.

**Know it All** (💻 www.knowitall.ch). The ultimate guide to daily life for English-speakers in the Geneva, Vaud and neighbouring French areas.

**Local** (💻 www.local.ch). Find regional information at a glance, e.g. phone numbers, events and classifieds, anywhere in Switzerland.

**Migros Online** (💻 www.leshop.ch). Shop at Migros from the comfort of your home (in English).

**Survival Books** (💻 www.survivalbooks.net). Publisher of *Living and Working in Switzerland* and *Buying or Renting a Home in Switzerland*.

**Swiss Association of Relocation Agents** (💻 www.sara-relocation.com).

**SwissConnex** (💻 www.swissconnex.ch). A portal that links to many sites covering health, tourism, sports and business.

**Switzerland is Yours** (💻 www.switzerland.isyours.com). Micheloud & Cie's website offering financial and immigration services for newcomers.

**Taxation** (💻 www.taxation.ch). Swiss taxation website.

**XpatXchange** (💻 www.xpatxchange.ch). Excellent one-stop site for English-speaking expats in Switzerland.

**Zurich Expats** (💻 http://zurichexpats.com). Info for expats living and working in Zurich.

## Media

**24 Heures** (💻 www.24heures.ch). Leading French-language magazine.

**Annonce 24 Heures** (💻 http://annonces.24heures.ch). Small ads website.

**Basler Zeitung** (💻 www.baz.ch). The online version of *Basler Zeitung*, covering mainly the northwest of Switzerland. In German, but with many articles are translated into English.

**Berner Zeitung** (💻 www.bernerzeitung.ch). Berne's leading newspaper (German).

**Bergli Books** (💻 www.bergli.ch). Specialist Swiss publisher of books about Switzerland and the Swiss for expatriates.

**Blick** (⌨ www.blick.ch). Switzerland's leading tabloid newspaper (in German).

**Cosmopolis** (⌨ www.cosmopolis.ch/english/archives.htm). Current affairs and culture magazine.

**The Economist** (⌨ www.economist.com/countries/switzerland). English business magazine Contains interesting in-depth articles about Switzerland.

**Gourmet World** (⌨ www.gourmet-verlag.ch). German-language food magazine.

**Hello Switzerland** (⌨ www.helloswitzerland.ch). Swiss culture, politics, tourism and events – free quarterly magazine published by Network Relocation.

**Inside Switzerland magazine** (⌨ www.insidemagazine.ch). Quarterly magazine targeted at Switzerland's 'style-conscious international people'.

**Le Temps** (⌨ www.letemps.ch). Leading French-language newspaper.

**Marmite** (⌨ http://marmite.ch). Food and drink magazine in German.

**Le Matin** (⌨ www.lematin.ch). Popular French-language newspaper.

**News** (⌨ www.news.ch). Excellent news website (German only).

**Neue Zürcher Zeitung** (⌨ www.nzz.ch). The leading national newspaper in Switzerland, mainly Zurich focused (German).

**Swissinfo** (⌨ www.swissinfo.org). National and international news provided by Swiss Radio International.

**Swiss News magazine** (⌨ www.swissnews.ch). Swiss monthly news and events magazine for expats.

**Swiss Newspapers Online** (⌨ www.onlinenewspapers.com/switzerl.htm). The most comprehensive list of Swiss national and regional newspapers in A-Z order.

**Swiss Television** (⌨ www.srgssrideesuisse.ch/en). Switzerland's national radio and television company.

**Swisster** (⌨ www.swisster.ch). News website dedicated to the English-speaking expatriate community in Switzerland.

**Tribune de Genève** (⌨ www.tdg.ch). Geneva's leading newspaper.

**Zeitung** (⌨ www.zeitung.ch). Index of Swiss newspapers published in German.

## Miscellaneous

**About Switzerland** (⌨ www.about.ch). General information about Switzerland.

**Comparis** (⌨ www.comparis.ch). Provides interactive comparisons of insurance premiums, telephone and bank charges (etc.).

**Dignitas** (⌨ www.dignitas.ch). The Swiss organisation that assists those with terminal or incurable illnesses to end their lives with dignity.

**Directories** (⌨ www.directories.ch). Swiss online telephone book.

**Eat Smoke Free** (⌨ www.eatsmokefree.ch). A directory of Swiss restaurants that are non-smoking or that have separate dining rooms for non-smokers.

**English Forum** (⌨ www.englishforum.ch). A forum for English speakers throughout Switzerland.

**Feiertagskalender** (⌨ www.feiertagskalender.ch). Lists public holidays for each canton.

**Health.ch AG** (⌨ www.doctor.ch). Lists of doctors, dentists, pharmacies and clinics throughout Switzerland.

**Meteo Schweiz** (⌨ www.meteoswiss.admin.ch). Swiss weather from the Federal Office of Meteorology and Climatology

**My Swiss Alps** (⌨ www.myswissalps.com). Everything you ever wanted to know about the Swiss Alps.

**REGA** (⌨ www.rega.ch). Swiss air rescue service.

**Ricardo** (⌨ www.ricardo.ch). Switzerland's most popular auction site.

**Search** (⌨ www.search.ch). Search engine for Swiss websites.

**Swiss Ski** (⌨ www.swiss-ski.ch). Website of the Swiss Ski Federation.

**Swiss Red Cross** (⌨ www.redcross.ch).

**Swissworld** (⌨ www.swissworld.org). Provides information on Switzerland's history, the political system, culture and society – and on the history of chocolate production in Switzerland.

**Swiss Airports** (⌨ www.airport.ch). Swiss airports portal.

**Traveling** (⌨ www.traveling.ch/index2.php?title=city). A useful index of Swiss towns/cities with links to their websites.

**Wikipedia** (⌨ http://en.wikipedia.org/wiki/Switzerland). Wikipedia pages for Switzerland.

**Yoodle** (⌨ www.yoodle.ch). Swiss search engine.

## Property Rental & Purchase

**Alle Immobilien** (⌨ www.alle-immobilien.ch). Buy or rent property (English version).

**Anibis** (⌨ www.anibis.ch/c/15). Classified property ads in French (Suisse romande).

**Anzeiger** (⌨ www.anzeiger.ch). Buy or rent property – browse by canton. German only.

**Comparis** (⌨ www.comparis.ch/immobilien/intro.aspx). One of Switzerland's leading websites for buying and renting property. English version.

**Dream Chalet** (⌨ www.dreamchalet.nl). Dutch website for Swiss property investors.

**Geneva Immobilier** (⌨ www.geneveimmobilier.ch). Geneva association of around 30 real estate agents.

**Global Property Guide** (⌨ www.globalpropertyguide.com/Europe/Switzerland). Useful information about Swiss real estate for investors.

**Haus Forum** (⌨ www.haus-forum.ch). The largest house-building database in Switzerland.

**HEV Immo** (⌨ www.hev-immo.ch/hev/home/estate/index.htm). Property sales by the Hauseigentümerverband Schweiz.

**Homegate** (⌨ www.homegate.ch). Comprehensive database of apartments and houses for rent or sale. English version.

**Home Styling by Ursula** (www.homestyling-by-ursula.ch).

**Immobilienmakler** (⌨ www.die-immobilienmakler.ch). Find a real estate agent anywhere in Switzerland.

**Immo Click** (⌨ www.immoclick.ch). Buy or rent property (French/German only).

**Immo Galaxy** (⌨ www.immogalaxy.ch/e). Largest real estate agent in Ticino.

**ImmoMarkt Schweiz** (⌨ www.immomarktschweiz.ch). Property sales by 15 cantonal banks.

**Immo-Net** (⌨ www.immo-net.ch). Buy or rent property (French/German only).

**Immo Scout** (⌨ www.immoscout24.ch). Buy or rent a home (English version).

**Immo Search** (⌨ http://immo.search.ch). Buy or rent property (French/German only).

**In-lease** (⌨ www.in-lease.com). Furniture rental services.

**Rent Law** (⌨ www.mietrecht.ch). Everything you need to know about tenancy law (in German).

**Swiss Architects** (⌨ www.swiss-architects.com). Find a local architect.

**Swiss Property** (⌨ www.swissproperty.co.uk). Swiss property sales for investors.

**Swiss Getaway** (⌨ www.swissgetaway.com). Swiss property specialist for foreign investors.

**Swiss Real Estate Association** (⌨ www.svit.ch). The professional body for Swiss real estate agents.

**Tenants' Associations** (German-speaking cantons, ⌨ www.mieterverband.ch, French–speaking cantons, ⌨ www.asloca.ch, Italian-speaking Ticino, ⌨ www.asi-infoalloggio.ch).

**USPI** Geneva (⌨ www.uspi-ge.ch). Union of real estate agents in Geneva.

**WG Zimmer** (🖥 www.wgzimmer.ch/home.cfm?land=CH&lang=D). Switzerland's largest flatshare website.

## Travel & Tourism

**The Automobile Club of Switzerland** (🖥 www.acs.ch). Motoring organisation.

**Inforoute** (🖥 www.inforoute.ch). Up-to-date traffic information on Swiss motorways, alpine passes and tunnels.

**Mobility Carsharing Schweiz** (🖥 www.mobility.ch). Enjoy the benefits of car use without the costs and hassles of ownership.

**My Switzerland** (🖥 www.myswitzerland.com/en). Swiss national tourist office website with comprehensive information and links to accommodation, transport, sports facilities, events etc.

**Out and About** (🖥 www.outandabout.ch). Leisure guide for the greater Zurich area.

**STA Travel** (🖥 www.statravel.ch). Student travel agent with travel shops throughout Switzerland.

**Swiss Hotel Association** (🖥 www.swisshotels.ch).

**Swiss International Air Lines** (🖥 www.swiss.com).

**Swiss Railways** (🖥 www.sbb.ch). Train schedules and personalized timetables.

**Swiss Travel System** (🖥 www.swisstravelsystem.com). Travel passes for visitors.

**Switzerland.com** (🖥 www.switzerland.com). Wealth of general information about Switzerland from Switzerland Tourism.

**Touring Club of Switzerland** (🖥 www.tcs.ch). Motoring organisation.

Skiing is fun!

# APPENDIX C: WEIGHTS & MEASURES

Switzerland uses the metric system of measurement. Those who are more familiar with the imperial system will find the tables on the following pages useful. Some comparisons shown are only approximate, but are close enough for most everyday uses.

In addition to the variety of measurement systems used, clothes sizes often vary considerably with the manufacturer – as we all know only too well! Try all clothes on before buying and don't be afraid to return something if, when you try it on at home, you decide it doesn't fit (most shops will exchange goods or give a refund).

| Women's Clothes | | | | | | | | | |
|---|---|---|---|---|---|---|---|---|---|
| Continental | 34 | 36 | 38 | 40 | 42 | 44 | 46 | 48 | 50 | 52 |
| UK | | 8 | 10 | 12 | 14 | 16 | 18 | 20 | 22 | 24 | 26 |
| US | | 6 | 8 | 10 | 12 | 14 | 16 | 18 | 20 | 22 | 24 |

| Pullover's | | | | | | | | | | | | |
|---|---|---|---|---|---|---|---|---|---|---|---|---|
| | Women's | | | | | | Men's | | | | | |
| Continental | 40 | 42 | 44 | 46 | 48 | 50 | 44 | 46 | 48 | 50 | 52 | 54 |
| UK | 34 | 36 | 38 | 40 | 42 | 44 | 34 | 36 | 38 | 40 | 42 | 44 |
| US | 34 | 36 | 38 | 40 | 42 | 44 | sm | med | | lar | xl | |

| Men's Shirts | | | | | | | | | |
|---|---|---|---|---|---|---|---|---|---|
| Continental | 36 | 37 | 38 | 39 | 40 | 41 | 42 | 43 | 44 | 46 |
| UK/US | 14 | 14 | 15 | 15 | 16 | 16 | 17 | 17 | 18 | - |

| Men's Underwear | | | | | | |
|---|---|---|---|---|---|---|
| Continental | 5 | 6 | 7 | 8 | 9 | 10 |
| UK | | 34 | 36 | 38 | 40 | 42 | 44 |
| US | | sm | med | | lar | xl | |

**NB:** sm = small, med = medium, lar = large, xl = extra large

| Children's Clothes | | | | | | |
|---|---|---|---|---|---|---|
| Continental | 92 | 104 | 116 | 128 | 140 | 152 |
| UK | 16/18 | 20/22 | 24/26 | 28/30 | 32/34 | 36/38 |
| US | 2 | 4 | 6 | 8 | 10 | 12 |

| Children's Shoes | |
|---|---|
| Continental | 18 19 20 21 22 23 24 25 26 27 28 29 30 31 32 |
| UK/US | 2  3 4  4 5  6  7 7 8  9  10 11  11 12 13 |
| Continental | 33 34 35 36 37 38 |
| UK/US | 1  2  2  3  4  5 |

| Shoes (Women's & Men's) | |
|---|---|
| Continental | 35  36  37 37 38  39  40  41 42  42 43  44 |
| UK | 2  3  3  4  4  5  6  7  7  8 9  9 |
| US | 4  5  5  6  6  7  8  9  9  10 10  11 |

| Weight | | | |
|---|---|---|---|
| **Imperial** | **Metric** | **Metric** | **Imperial** |
| 1oz | 28.35g | 1g | 0.035oz |
| 1lb* | 454g | 100g | 3.5oz |
| 1cwt | 50.8kg | 250g | 9oz |
| 1 ton | 1,016kg | 500g | 18oz |
| 2,205lb | 1 tonne | 1kg | 2.2lb |

| Area | | | |
|---|---|---|---|
| **British/US** | **Metric** | **Metric** | **British/US** |
| 1 sq. in | 0.45 sq. cm | 1 sq. cm | 0.15 sq. in |
| 1 sq. ft | 0.09 sq. m | 1 sq. m | 10.76 sq. ft |
| 1 sq. yd | 0.84 sq. m | 1 sq. m | 1.2 sq. yds |
| 1 acre | 0.4 hectares | 1 hectare | 2.47 acres |
| 1 sq. mile | 2.56 sq. km | 1 sq. km | 0.39 sq. mile |

| Capacity | | | |
|---|---|---|---|
| **Imperial** | **Metric** | **Metric** | **Imperial** |
| 1 UK pint | 0.57 litre | 1 litre | 1.75 UK pints |
| 1 US pint | 0.47 litre | 1 litre | 2.13 US pints |
| 1 UK gallon | 4.54 litres | 1 litre | 0.22 UK gallon |
| 1 US gallon | 3.78 litres | 1 litre | 0.26 US gallon |

**NB:** An American 'cup' = around 250ml or 0.25 litre.

| Length | | | |
|---|---|---|---|
| **British/US** | **Metric** | **Metric** | **British/US** |
| 1in | 2.54cm | 1cm | 0.39in |
| 1ft | 30.48cm | 1m | 3ft 3.25in |
| 1yd | 91.44cm | 1km | 0.62mi |
| 1mi | 1.6km | 8km | 5mi |

| Temperature | |
|---|---|
| **°Celsius** | **°Fahrenheit** |
| 0 | 32  (freezing point of water) |
| 5 | 41 |
| 10 | 50 |
| 15 | 59 |
| 20 | 68 |
| 25 | 77 |
| 30 | 86 |
| 35 | 95 |
| 40 | 104 |
| 50 | 122 |

### Temperature Conversion

**Celsius to Fahrenheit:** multiply by 9, divide by 5 and add 32. (For a quick and approximate conversion, double the Celsius temperature and add 30.)

**Fahrenheit to Celsius:** subtract 32, multiply by 5 and divide by 9. (For a quick and approximate conversion, subtract 30 from the Fahrenheit temperature and divide by 2.)

**NB:** The boiling point of water is 100°C / 212°F. Normal body temperature (if you're alive and well) is 37°C / 98.6°F.

| Power | | | |
|---|---|---|---|
| **Kilowatts** | **Horsepower** | **Horsepower** | **Kilowatts** |
| 1 | 1.34 | 1 | 0.75 |

| Oven Temperature | | |
|---|---|---|
| **Gas** | **Electric** | |
| | **°F** | **°C** |
| - | 225–250 | 110–120 |
| 1 | 275 | 140 |
| 2 | 300 | 150 |
| 3 | 325 | 160 |
| 4 | 350 | 180 |
| 5 | 375 | 190 |
| 6 | 400 | 200 |
| 7 | 425 | 220 |
| 8 | 450 | 230 |
| 9 | 475 | 240 |

| Air Pressure | |
|---|---|
| **PSI** | **Bar** |
| 10 | 0.5 |
| 20 | 1.4 |
| 30 | 2 |
| 40 | 2.8 |

# APPENDIX D: AIRLINE TABLES

The flights listed below are mostly direct (no stops) scheduled flights that operate all year round.

## Direct Scheduled Flights from the UK & Ireland to Switzerland

### Basle-Mulhouse-Freiburg

| Fly From | Airline(s) |
| --- | --- |
| London City | Swiss, British Airways |
| London Gatwick | Easyjet |
| London Heathrow | BA |

### Berne

| Fly from | Airline(s) |
| --- | --- |
| Southampton | Flybe |

### Geneva

| Fly From | Airline(s) |
| --- | --- |
| Belfast | Easyjet |
| Birmingham | Bmibaby, Easyjet |
| Blackpool | Jet2 |
| Bournemouth | Easyjet |
| Bristol | Easyjet |
| Cardiff | Bmibaby |
| Cork | Aer Lingus |
| Doncaster/Sheffield | Thompson Airways |
| Dublin | Aer Lingus, Primera Air |
| East Midlands | Bmibaby, Easyjet |
| Edinburgh | Easyjet, Flyglobespan |
| Exeter | Flybe |
| Glasgow | Easyjet |
| Guernsey | Blue Islands |
| Isle of Man | Flybe |
| Jersey | Blue Islands, Flybe |
| Leeds/Bradford | Jet2 |

| Liverpool | Easyjet |
| London City | BA, Swiss |
| London Gatwick | BA, Easyjet, Flythomascook, Viking |
| London Heathrow | BA, Qantas, Swiss |
| London Luton | Easyjet |
| London Stansted | Easyjet |
| Manchester | Bmibaby, Easyjet, Flythomascook, Jet2, Saudi Arabian Airlines, Viking |
| Newcastle | Easyjet |
| Newquay | Flybe |
| Norwich | Flybe |
| Southampton | Flybe |

## Sion

| **Fly From** | **Airline(s)** |
| London-Stansted | Snowjet |

## St Gallen-Altenrhein

| **Fly From** | **Airline(s)** |
| London Heathrow | Austrian Airlines |

## Zurich

| **Fly From** | **Airline(s)** |
| Birmingham | Swiss |
| Dublin | Aer Lingus, |
| Edinburgh | Bmibaby |
| Guernsey | Blue Islands |
| Jersey | Blue Islands |
| London City | Austrian Airlines, BA, Swiss |
| London Gatwick | Aer Lingus, Easyjet |
| London Heathrow | Air Seychelles, BA, Japan Airlines, Qantas, Swiss |
| London Luton | Easyjet |
| Manchester | Swiss |

## Airline Contacts

| Airline | Contact Tel. Number(s) & Website |
|---------|----------------------------------|
| Aer Lingus | ☎ (Ireland) 0818-365 000<br>☎ (Switzerland) +41-442-86 99 33<br>💻 www.aerlingus.com |
| Air Seychelles | ☎ (UK) 01293-596 655<br>☎ (Switzerland) +41-43-816 68 34<br>💻 www.airseychelles.co.uk |
| Austrian Airlines | ☎ (UK) 020-7766 0300<br>☎ (Switzerland) +41-44-286 80 88<br>💻 www.aua.com |
| BA | ☎ (UK) 0844-493 0787<br>☎ (Switzerland) +41-848-845 845<br>💻 www.britishairways.com |
| Blue Islands | ☎ (UK/CI) 08456-202 122<br>☎ (Non UK/CI) +44-1481-727567<br>💻 www.blueislands.com |
| Bmibaby | ☎ (UK) 0905-828 2828<br>☎ (Non UK) + 44 845 810 11 00<br>💻 www.bmibaby.com |
| Easyjet | ☎ (UK) 08712-882 236<br>☎ (Switzerland) +41-900-000 195<br>💻 www.easyjet.com |
| Flybe | ☎ (UK) 0871-700 2000<br>☎ (Non UK) +44-1392-268 513<br>💻 www.flybe.com |
| Flyglobespan | ☎ (UK) 0871-271 9000<br>☎ (Non UK) +44-141-332 3233<br>💻 www.flyglobespan.co.uk |
| Flythomascook | ☎ (UK) 0871-230 2406<br>☎ (Switzerland) +41-43-816 2211<br>💻 www.book.flythomascook.com |
| Japan Airlines | ☎ (UK) 0845-7-747 700<br>☎ (Non UK) +44-20-7660 0348<br>💻 www.uk.jal.com |

Jet2                                ☎ (UK) 0906-302 0660
                                    ☎ (Non UK) +44-203-031 8103
                                    ⌨ www.jet2.com

Qantas                              ☎ (UK) 0845-774 7767
                                    ☎ (Switzerland) +41-22-567 51 61
                                    ⌨ www.qantas.com.au

Snowjet                             ☎ (UK) 020-8652 1222
                                    ☎ (Switzerland) +41-27-329 0600
                                    ⌨ www.snowjet.co.uk

Swiss                               ☎ (UK) 0845-601 0956
                                    ☎ (Switzerland) +41-848-700 700
                                    ⌨ www.swiss.com

Titan Airways (Snowjet)             ☎ (London) 020-7928 3131
                                    ☎ (Stansted) 01279-680 616
                                    ⌨ www.titan-airways.com

United Airlines                     ☎ (UK) 0845-844 4777
                                    ☎ (Zurich) +41-43-816 22 11
                                    ⌨ www.united.com

## Airport Contacts

| Airport | Contact Tel. Number(s) & Website |
| --- | --- |
| Belfast City | ☎ 028-9448 4848<br>⌨ www.bial.co.uk |
| Birmingham | ☎ 0121 767 5511<br>⌨ www.bhx.co.uk |
| Blackpool | ☎ 0844-482 7171<br>⌨ www.blackpoolinternational.com |
| Bournemouth | ☎ 01202-364 000<br>⌨ www.bournemouthairport.com |
| Bristol | ☎ 0871-334 4344<br>⌨ www.bristolairport.co.uk |
| Cardiff | ☎ 01446-711111<br>⌨ www.tbicardiffairport.com |

| Cork | ☎ 021-431 3131 |
| | 🖥 www.corkairport.ie |
| Dublin | ☎ 01-814 1111 |
| | 🖥 www.dublinairport.com |
| East Midlands | ☎ 0871-919 9000 |
| | 🖥 www.eastmidlandsairport.co.uk |
| Edinburgh | ☎ 0870-040 0007 |
| | 🖥 www.edinburghairport.com |
| Exeter | ☎ 0871-282 0990 |
| | 🖥 www.exeter-airport.co.uk |
| Glasgow | ☎ 0870-040 0008 |
| | 🖥 www.glasgowairport.com |
| Guernsey | ☎ 01481-237766 |
| | 🖥 www.guernsey-airport.gov.gg |
| Isle of Man | ☎ 01624-821600 |
| | 🖥 www.iom-airport.com |
| Jersey | ☎ 01534-446000 |
| | 🖥 www.jerseyairport.com |
| Leeds/Bradford | ☎ 0871-288 2288 |
| | 🖥 www.leedsbradfordairport.co.uk |
| Liverpool | ☎ 0871-521 8484 |
| | 🖥 www.liverpoolairport.com |
| London City | ☎ 020-7646 0088 |
| | 🖥 www.londoncityairport.com |
| London Gatwick | ☎ 0844-335 1802 |
| | 🖥 www.gatwickairport.com |
| London Heathrow | ☎ 0870-000 0123 |
| | 🖥 www.heathrowairport.com |
| London Luton | ☎ 01582-405100 |
| | 🖥 www.london-luton.co.uk |

London Stansted    ☎ 0870-000 0303
                   🖥 www.stanstedairport.com

Manchester         ☎ 08712-710 711
                   🖥 www.manchesterairport.co.uk

Newcastle          ☎ 0871-882 1121
                   🖥 www.newcastleairport.com

Norwich            ☎ 01603-428700
                   🖥 www.norwichairport.co.uk

Southampton        ☎ 0870-040 0009
                   🖥 www.southamptonairport.com

## Scheduled Flights From North America

### Basle-Mulhouse-Freiburg

| From | Airline(s) |
| --- | --- |
| Montreal | Air Transat |
| Seattle | Condor |

### Geneva

| From | Airline(s) |
| --- | --- |
| Newark | Continental |
| New York JFK | Swiss, United Airlines |
| Seattle | Condor |
| Toronto | Air Canada |
| Washington-Dulles | United |

### Zurich

| From | Airline(s) |
| --- | --- |
| Atlanta | Delta, KLM, NWA |
| Los Angeles | Lufthansa, Swiss, United Airlines |
| Newark | Continental, Swiss |
| New York JFK | Delta, NWA, Swiss, United Airlines |
| Seattle | Condor |
| Toronto | Air Canada, Swiss |

## Airline Contacts

| Airline | Contact Tel. Number(s) & Website |
|---|---|
| Air Canada | ☎ (Canada & USA) 1-888-247 2262<br>☎ (UK) 0871-220 1111<br>🖥 www.aircanada.com |
| Air Transat | ☎ (General) 1-877-872 6728<br>☎ (Local to Montreal) 514-636 3630<br>🖥 www.airtransat.ca |
| Condor | ☎ (Canada & USA) 1-800-364-1667<br>☎ (Germany) +49-180-5707 202<br>🖥 www.11.condor.com |
| Continental | ☎ (USA) 1-800-231.0856<br>☎ (UK) 0845-607 6760<br>🖥 www.continental.com |
| Delta | ☎ (USA) 1-800-323 2323<br>☎ (UK) 0800-414 767<br>🖥 www.delta.com |
| KLM | ☎ (Atlanta) 1-866-434 0320<br>☎ (UK) 08705-074 074<br>🖥 www.klm.com |
| Lufthansa | ☎ (Los Angeles) 1-800-399-5838<br>☎ (UK) 01871-945 9747<br>🖥 www.airport-la.com |
| NWA | ☎ (USA) 1-800-225 2525<br>☎ (UK) 08705-074074<br>🖥 www.nwa.com |
| Swiss | ☎ (USA) 1-877-359 7947<br>☎ (UK) 0845-601 0956<br>🖥 www.swiss.com |
| United Airlines | ☎ (USA) 1-718-244 2800<br>☎ (UK) 0845-8444 777<br>🖥 www.united.com |

## Airport Contacts

| Airport | Contact Tel. Number(s) & Website |
|---------|-----------------------------------|
| Atlanta | ☎ 1-800-897 1910<br>💻 www.atlanta-airport.com |
| Los Angeles | ☎ 1-310-646 5252<br>💻 www.lawa.org/lax |
| Montreal | ☎ 1- 800-465 1213<br>💻 www.admtl.com |
| Newark | ☎ 1- 973-961 6000<br>💻 www.panynj.gov/airports/newark-liberty |
| New York JFK | ☎ 1-718-244 4444<br>💻 www.jfk-airport.net |
| Seattle | ☎ 1-800 787 1965<br>💻 www.portseattle.org |
| Toronto | ☎ 1-866-207 1690<br>💻 www.gtaa.com |

## Direct Flights to Switzerland

### From North America:

| From | Basle | Geneva | Zurich |
|------|-------|--------|--------|
| Atlanta | | | ● |
| Los Angeles | | | ● |
| Montreal | ● | | |
| Newark | | ● | ● |
| New York JFK | | ● | ● |
| Seattle | ● | ● | ● |
| Toronto | | | ● |

## From UK/Ireland:

| From | Basle | Berne | Geneva | St Gallen-Alt | Zurich |
|---|---|---|---|---|---|
| Belfast City | | | ● | | |
| Birmingham | | | ● | | |
| Blackpool | | | ● | | |
| Bournemouth | | | | ● | |
| Bristol | | | ● | | |
| Cardiff | | | ● | | |
| Cork | | | ● | | |
| Dublin | | | ● | | ● |
| East Midlands | | | | ● | |
| Edinburgh | | | ● | | ● |
| Exeter | | | ● | | |
| Glasgow | | | ● | | |
| Guernsey | | | | | ● |
| Isle of Man | | | ● | | |
| Jersey | | | ● | | ● |
| Leeds/Bradford | | | ● | | |
| Liverpool | | | ● | | |
| London LCY | ● | | ● | | ● |
| London LGW | ● | | ● | | ● |
| London LHR | ● | | ● | ● | ● |
| London LTN | | | ● | | ● |
| London STN | ● | | ● | | |
| Manchester | ● | | ● | | ● |
| Newcastle | | | ● | | |
| Norwich | | | ● | | |
| Southampton | | ● | ● | | |

# APPENDIX E: MAPS

**Physical:**

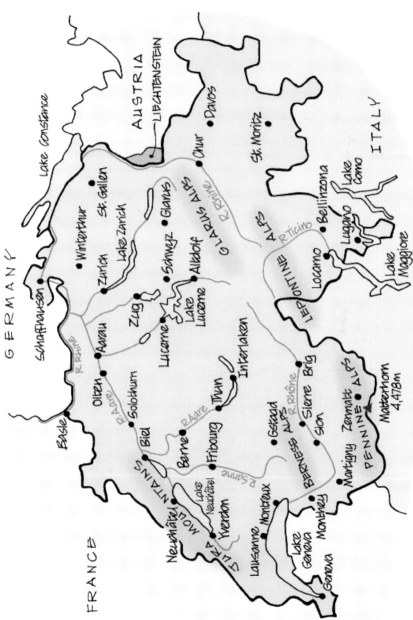

**Major Roads:**

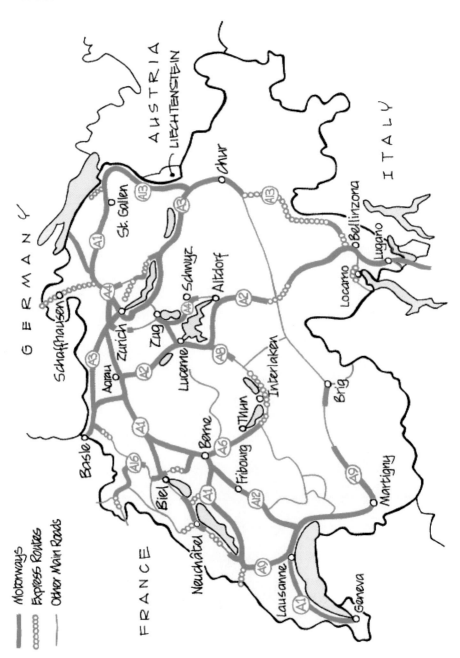

## Railways & Airports:

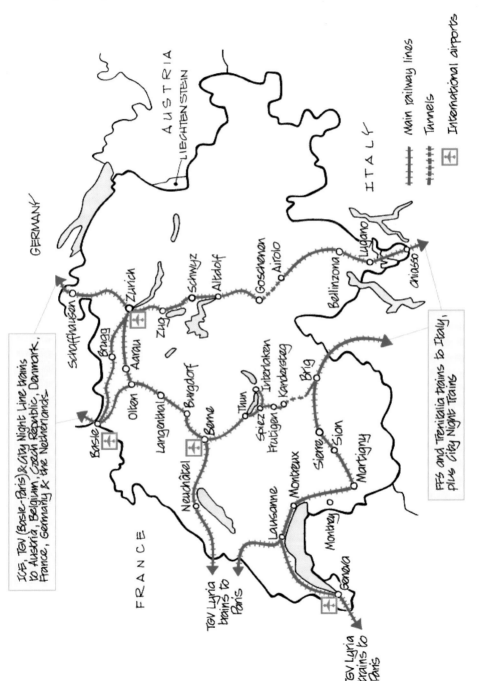

Mt Pilatus, Lucerne

# APPENDIX F: GLOSSARIES

## FRENCH-ENGLISH

### A

**A débattre:** negotiable.

**A rénover:** for renovation (possibly a euphemism for 'a ruin').

**Abonnement:** standing charge, e.g. for electricity, gas, telephone or water services.

**Acheter:** buy.

**Acompte:** deposit (non-refundable). If a deposit is described as *acompte* neither party can withdraw and the sale can be legally enforced.

**Acte de vente:** deed of sale or conveyance document.

**Administration fiscale:** tax authorities.

**Agence immobilière:** real estate agency.

**Agent immobilier:** real estate agent.

**Agglomération:** refers to cities and their suburbs.

**Amortissement:** amortisation.

**ancien:** old building.

**année de la construction:** year of construction.

**Appartement:** apartment or flat.

**Appartement bourgeois:** spacious (usually 19th century) apartment with separate servant's quarters (*chambre de bonne*).

**Appartement de standing:** a luxury (usually modern) apartment. Also called a *grand standing*.

**armoires murales:** wall cupboards.

**Ascenseur:** lift or elevator.

**Assurance ménage et responsabilité civile:** fully comprehensive (all-risk) household insurance .

**Atelier:** workshop.

**Attique:** apartment under the roof, also referred to as a 'penthouse'. A attic itself isn't called an *attique* but a *grenier* or *combles*.

**Authentique:** authentic, i.e. a document signed in the presence of a notary and authenticated by him.

**Avec tout confort:** with all mod. cons.

**Avocat:** lawyer or solicitor.

### B

**Bail:** contract, lease (variations include *bail à loyer*, *bail d'habitation* and *contrat de bail*).

**Bail commercial:** leaseback agreement.

**Bailleur:** lessor, e.g. owner, landlord or an agent (who signs the *bail* or contract on the owner's behalf).

**Balcon:** balcony.

**Ballon (à eau chaude)**: hot water tank (also referred to as a 'boiler' in French).

**Banlieue:** suburb.

**Bâtiment:** building.

**Bilan (de santé immobilier)**: (house) survey.

**Bi-propriété:** shared ownership.

**Bois/Boiserie:** wood/woodwork.

**Bon état:** good condition.

**Bourg:** small town or large village.

**Box:** lock-up garage in an underground car park (*parking souterrain*).

**Bricolage:** building, repairs and do-it-yourself (DIY) supplies.

**Brique:** brick.

**Buanderie:** wash house, laundry or utility room.

**Bungalow/de plain pied:** single storey, bungalow.

**Bureau:** study.

**Bureau de vente:** sales office.

# C

**Cabinet:** small room.

**Cabinet WC:** toilet.

**Cachet:** home with character or special appeal, such as *parquet* floors, *moulures* (cornices) or a *cheminée* (fireplace, possibly marble).

**Cadastre:** land registry/land registration.

**(à la) Campagne:** in the country.

**Canton:** county or state. Switzerland is comprised of 26 cantons.

**(de) Caractère:** characterful – may be a euphemism for odd or dilapidated, but can mean a home with *cachet*.

**Carrelé:** tiled.

**Carrelage:** tiling (usually floor).

**Caution:** guarantee or security deposit.

**Cave en sous-sol:** cellar.

**Cédule hypothécaire:** mortgage note.

**Centre foncier:** land office.

**Centre des impôts:** tax office. Also called a *bureau des impôts* or *hôtel des impôts*.

**Cession:** transfer of ownership or rights, including property.

**Chambre (ch):** bedroom.

**Chambre à coucher:** bedroom.

**Chambre d'ami:** guest room.

**Chambres d'hôtes:** bed and breakfast establishment.

**Charges:** extra costs for utilities such as electricity, gas, (hot) water, satellite TV, insurance, maintenance and other services.

**Charges comprises (cc):** extra costs including building charges.

**Charges locatives:** monthly fees for collective amenities.

**Chaudière:** boiler (water heater).

**Chauffage (central):** heating (central).

**Chauffage collectif:** communal or shared heating, e.g. in an apartment block.

**Chauffe-eau:** gas water heater or hot water tank.

**Cheminée:** fireplace or chimney, usually in working order.

**Citerne à eau:** water tank.

**Citerne à gaz:** gas tank, e.g. for central heating.

**Climatisation:** air-conditioning.

**Clôture:** fence.

**Combles:** loft; roof space.

**Commission comprise (C/C):** commission included, e.g. the sale price of a property including the agent's commission.

**Commission foncière:** local administrative body which decides whether a non-European Swiss resident can buy a house with more than 3,000m² of land.

**Commission non comprise:** commission not included.

**Commune:** town, village, district or parish. Also similar to a neighbourhood.

**Compromis de vente:** preliminary sales' contract for a property.

**Comptable:** accountant.

**Comptant:** payable in cash without a loan.

**Compte séquestre:** deposit held in a special escrow account pending fulfillment of certain conditions.

**Compteur:** meter (electricity/gas/water).

**Concierge:** caretaker/porter of an apartment block. He's usually a repair man rather than someone who runs errands or sources goods and services for tenants/owners.

**Conservateur des hypothèques:** district land register.

**Constructible:** land available for building purposes.

**Contrat:** contract.

**Contrat préliminaire:** preliminary contract. Same as a *contrat de réservation*.

**Contrat de réservation:** promissory contract to buy a property off-plan before it's built.

**Convention:** agreement.

**Copropriété:** co-ownership of communal property, equivalent to a US condominium.

**Corps de bâtiments:** group of buildings.

**Cour (intérieure):** yard or courtyard (interior).

**Cuisine:** kitchen.

**Cuisine aménagée/équipée:** built-in or fitted kitchen with cupboards and appliances.

**Cuisine américaine/cuisine ouverte:** American-style (open-plan) kitchen.

**Cuisinière:** cooker/stove.

**Cuve:** tank, e.g. for water, gas or oil.

# D

**Déménagement:** moving house.

**Demeure:** any dwelling, but it normally refers to a grand country house with extensive grounds.

**Dépendance:** outbuilding, including separate servants' quarters, barns, boathouse, sheds, kennels, etc.

**Dépôt de garantie:** the deposit paid when buying or renting a property.

**Digicode:** security door with a digital entry keypad.

**Disponibilité:** availability. The best is *tout de suite* or *selon accord*, meaning immediately or as agreed.

**Domicile fiscal:** main residence for tax purposes.

**Douche:** shower.

**Droit de passage:** right of way.

**Droits d'enregistrement:** stamp duty on a property purchase which is usually paid by the buyer.

**Droits de mutation:** transfer tax.

**Droits de succession:** inheritance tax.

**Duplex:** apartment or maisonette on two floors.

# E

**Eau:** water.

**Eau chaude collective:** shared hot water supply, e.g. in an apartment block.

**Eaux usées:** drain or waste water.

**Enregistrement:** stamp duty.

**Entrée:** entry, hallway.

**Entrepreneur de construction:** building consortium or contractor.

**Entretien:** maintenance.

**Escalier:** stairway.

**Étage/niveau:** floor or storey.

**État:** condition. *Bon état* (good), *état neuf* (like new), *excellent état* (excellent) or *mauvais état* (poor or terrible).

**États des lieux:** inventory. *Etat des lieux d'entrée* is the inventory at the start of a lease and *Etat des lieux de sortie* is the inventory when you leave.

**Expert de bâtiment:** surveyor.

**Expert foncier:** valuer.

**Expert géomètre:** land surveyor.

**Expertise:** survey or valuation.

**Exposé sud:** south facing.

# F

**Facture:** bill.

**Fenêtre:** window.

**Fenêtre en baie:** bay window.

**Ferme:** farm.

**Forfait:** fixed price or contract with an all-in price.

**Forfait fiscal:** lump sum income tax.

**Fosse septique/traditionnelle:** septic tank.

**Fosse à toutes eaux:** septic tank which filters all household waste water and discharges it underground.

**Frais:** fees.

**Frais compris:** fees included.

**Frais de dossier:** the arrangement fee charged by a bank for establishing a mortgage.

**Frais de mutation:** change of hands fee.

**Frais de notaire:** same as *frais d'acte*.

# G

**Garage:** private lock-up garage, which may be attached to a house or townhouse. A *box* is a *garage* in a *parking souterrain* (underground garage).

**Garantie:** deposit. Usually three months' rent, but sometimes less.

**Gardien/gardienne:** guardian (male/female), caretaker or superintendent.

**Gaz de ville:** mains gas.

**Gentilhommière:** small manor house, originally a gentleman's country seat.

# H

**Habitation:** dwelling.

**Halle d'entrée:** hallway, entrance.

**Honoraires:** fees.

**Hors frais/taxes:** fees (*frais*) or taxes not included.

**Hôtel de ville:** town hall in cities and large towns. See also *Mairie*.

**Hôtel particulier:** elegant townhouse or mansion, sometimes better described as a palace.

**Hypothèque:** mortgage or loan on a property.

# I

**Immeuble:** building or residence (immovable property).

**Immobilier:** real estate; property.

**Impôt:** tax.

**Indemnité de l'immobilisation:** down payment on a preliminary contract of sale, usually 10 per cent of the price.

**Installation:** fixture or fitting.

**Installation électrique:** wiring.

**Inventaire détaillé/état des lieux:** an inventory of the contents and condition of a rented property.

# J

**Jardin/Jardinier:** garden/gardener.

**Jardin d'hiver:** winter garden or conservatory.

**Jouissance:** possession (or taking possession) or tenure.

**Jumelle:** semi-detached house (UK), duplex (US).

# L

**Lavabo:** sink.

**Lave/sèche linge:** washer/dryer.

**Lex Friedrich:** federal law that restricts the sale of real estate to foreigners.

**Living:** living room.

**Localité:** area, location.

**Location:** tenancy.

**Location vente:** renting a property while buying some of the equity.

**Locataire:** tenant (can be an individual or several people).

**Logement:** lodging, accommodation.

**Logement meublé:** furnished rental.

**Loggia:** covered terrace.

**Lotissement:** housing estate.

**(à) Louer:** to rent, hire or let.

**Loyer:** rent/rental.

**Lucarne:** dormer window or skylight.

**Lumineuse:** light (airy).

# M

**Maçon:** builder such as a bricklayer or stone mason.

**Maçonnerie:** brick or stonework.

**Mairie:** town hall (or equivalent in village).

**Maison:** house.

**Maison à étage:** two-storey house.

**Maison d'amis:** second or holiday home.

**Maison bourgeoise:** large period house designed for the professional classes during the 19th century.

**Maison de campagne:** house in the country.

**Maison de caractère:** house of character, often with a dovecote or pigeon tower.

**Maison en carré:** house built around a courtyard.

**Maison de chasse:** hunting lodge, usually located on the edge of a forest.

**Maison individuelle:** detached house.

**Maison jumelle:** semidetached or duplex house that shares a wall with its neighbour.

**Maison de maître:** gentleman's mansion or imposing house, usually a few centuries old.

**Maison mitoyenne:** semi-detached house.

**Maison neuve:** new house.

**Maison villageoise:** townhouse or terraced house in a village, usually 150 years old or older.

**Maisonette:** cottage.

**Maître:** title used when addressing a *notaire*.

**Maître d'oeuvres:** master builder, clerk of works or project manager.

**Manoir:** manor house.

**Menuisier:** carpenter or joiner.

**Meublé/équipé:** furnished. Unfurnished is *non-meublé*.

**Meubles:** furniture.

**Mode de paiement:** method of payment.

**(à la) Montagne:** in the mountains.

**Monument historique:** listed building.

**Moquette:** fitted or wall-to-wall carpet.

**Moulin:** mill/watermill.

**Mur:** Wall.

**Mur mitoyen:** wall shared with another property.

# N

**Nantissement:** collateral or security for a loan.

**Net vendeur:** the amount the vendor receives, excluding any agent's fees.

**Nettoyage pour remise d'appartement:** removal (moving house) cleaning.

**Nombre de pieces:** total number of rooms including reception and bedrooms.

**Non-meublé:** unfurnished.

**Notaire:** notary public. The legal professional who handles the conveyance for all property sales in Switzerland (similar to a British solicitor or an American property lawyer).

**Nouvelle propriété:** property under five years old..

# O

**Offre d'achat:** offer to buy.

**Offre de vente:** offer of sale.

# P

**P:** abbreviation for *pièces* used by estate agents and in property advertisements, followed by a figure indicating the number of main rooms, i.e. excluding kitchen, bathrooms, toilets, etc.

**Parcelle:** plot (of land).

**Parking (à proximité):** parking usually indicates a private car park, while *parking à proximité* refers to street parking in the neighbourhood.

**Parking souterrain:** parking space in an underground garage. A *box* is a private *garage* in a *parking souterrain*.

**Pavillon:** small detached or semidetached house, usually located on the outskirts of a town or village.

**Pays:** country or the countryside.

**Pelouse:** lawn.

**Penderie:** wardrobe or hanging space.

**Permis de construire:** building permit.

**Pièce:** room.

**Pièces en enfilade:** this means that to access a room you must go through another, as opposed to separate access from a corridor.

**Pièces de réception:** the rooms used to entertain.

**Pièce principale:** main room.

**Pierre (du pays):** stone (local).

**Pierre de taille (pdt):** stone building.

**Pignon:** gable.

**Piscine:** swimming pool (a *piscine couverte* is an indoor pool).

**Place de parc:** parking space (open air).

**Plafond:** ceiling.

**Plain-pied:** single storey building, bungalow.

**Plan d'amortissement:** schedule for paying off a mortgage.

**Plan cadastral:** cadastral plan showing the dimensions of a property's land area.

**Plan de financement:** plan or schedule of purchase payments, e.g. in stages when buying a new property.

**Plancher:** wooden floor.

**Pleine propriété:** freehold.

**Port/Plage privé:** private port (for boats) or beach, e.g. on a lake.

**Porte:** door.

**Portes-fenêtres:** French windows.

**Potager:** kitchen garden.

**Poubelle(s):** dustbin or garbage can.

**Poutre:** beam (wooden); *poutres apparentes* are exposed beams.

**Prêt:** loan.

**Prêt immobilier:** mortgage.

**Prix:** price.

**Prix déclaré:** the price of a property declared to the authorities.

**Prix fermé:** fixed price (non-negotiable).

**Prix de vente:** selling (or asking) price.

**Procuration:** power of attorney. Also known as a *mandat* or *pouvoir*.

**Projet d'acte:** draft conveyance deed.

**Promoteur:** property developer.

**Propriétaire:** landlord or owner (refers to anyone who owns a house that he lives in).

**Propriété:** property, usually large with extensive grounds, but not as grand as a *domaine*.

**Propriété à restaurer:** property for restoration.

**Propriété en ruines:** property in ruins.

**Propriétés baties:** developed or built property.

**Propriété par étage:** condo, condominium, freehold apartment.

**Publicité foncière:** obligatory registration of a property at the land registry.

**Puisard:** cesspool or sump.

**Puissance:** electricity power rating (in kilowatts).

# Q

**Quartier:** district, neighbourhood.

**Quincaillerie:** hardware store or ironmonger's.

**Quittance:** receipt.

# R

**à Raffraîchir:** to 'refresh' or renovate. May mean a house is in need of a lot of work and is in poor condition.

**Ramoneur:** chimney sweep.

**Rangement:** storage area, built-in cupboards.

**Récent:** built in the last decade.

**Réduit:** box room.

**Refait à neuf:** rebuilt.

**Réfection:** reconstruction.

**Réfrigérateur:** refrigerator (often shortened to *frigo*).

**Régie:** building management company which represents the landlord (owner).

**Registre foncier/Cadastre:** the official Swiss land registry where a record is kept of who owns land and buildings.

**Règlement de copropriété:** the document containing the rules and regulations of a *copropriété* building.

**Remis:** storeroom.

**Remise des clefs:** handing over keys to a new owner.

**Rénovation:** renovation. Usually means that a house is in poor condition and requires a lot of work,

**Réservation:** deposit (in a *contrat de réservation*).

**Réservoir:** water tank.

**Résidence:** building.

**Résidence principale:** main or principal home.

**Résidence secondaire:** second or holiday home.

**Résiliation:** cancellation (of'contract). A *résiliation anticipée* is when you want to leave before the end of your lease.

**Responsabilité civile propriétaire:** third party liability of homeowners for which insurance is mandatory.

**Révision de loyer:** a revision or review of the rent payable on a property.

**Renouvellement:** the renewal of a rental contract (lease).

**Rez-de-chaussée:** ground floor; if there are split levels, the lower ground floor is the *rez inférieur* and the upper ground floor the *rez supérieur*.

**Ruine:** ruin or run-down property. A property in need of restoration, renovation and modernisation is referred to as a *propriété en ruines* or a *propriété à restaurer*.

**Rustico:** basic stone (usually slate) mountainside shack, e.g. in Ticino, used as a holiday home.

# S

**Sacs à ordures:** rubbish/garbage bag.

**Salle:** room, usually very large (*grande pièce*).

**Salle de bain (baignoire):** bathroom.

**Salle de douche/d'eau:** shower room.

**Salle à manger:** dining room.

**Salle de séjour:** living room.

**Salon:** sitting room, lounge or drawing room.

**Sanitaire:** bathroom or plumbing.

**Sanitation:** sanitation or main drainage.

**Sans vis-à-vis:** not overlooked.

**Séjour:** living/sitting room.

**Séjour cathédrale:** living room with no room above.

**Séjour principal:** main or principal residence.

**Servitudes:** building regulations, rights of way or easements.

**Situation:** location or neighbourhood. *Situation calme* or *situation tranquille* (no noise), *situation centrale* (central location) or *à deux pas de ...* (a stone's throw from ....), *situation dominante* (commanding the whole neighbourhood, usually from high ground) and *situation protégée* (sheltered or protected).

**Sol:** ground.

**Source:** spring (a *sourcier* is a water diviner).

**Sous-sol:** basement often used as a garage or cellar.

**Sous terrain:** below ground level.

**Studio:** one-room apartment or bed-sitter.

**Surface habitable/surface de plancher:** habitable area excluding terraces, balconies, cellars, store rooms, etc. (A much better guide to the size of an apartment than the number of rooms.)

**Superficie du terrain:** surface of land.

**Surface utile:** habitable area including terraces, balconies, etc.

**Syndicat (des copropriétaires):** the committee appointed to manage a community development (*copropriété*).

**Système de chauffage:** heating system.

# T

**Tapis:** rug or carpet. A fitted (wall-to-wall) carpet is a *moquette*.

**Taux (d'imposition communal):** city tax rate or local income tax. Similar to property tax or rates levied in other countries.

**Témoin:** show apartment or house (*appartement/maison témoin*).

**Terrain:** grounds or land.

**Terrain à bâtir:** building site for sale.

**Terrasse:** terrace, paved area or large balcony.

**Titre de propriété:** title deed.

**Toilettes:** toilet or lavatory (public).

**Toit/Toiture:** roof/roofing.

**Toit en terrasse:** flat roof.

**Tout confort:** well equipped.

**Tout à l'égout:** mains drainage system.

**Toutes taxes:** including taxes.

**Triplex:** maisonette on three floors.

# U

**Urbanisme:** town planning.

**Usufruct/Usufruit:** legal term for a life interest in a property.

# V

**Valuer:** value.

**Valeur cadastrale:** assessment of a property's value for land tax purposes.

**Valeur fiscale:** the value determined by the city council for the purpose of levying property taxes. It's invariably much lower than the actual market value.

**Valeur de rendement:** the value used to calculate the rentable value of a property.

**Valeur locative:** fictitious rental amount for property owners (for taxes).

**Valeur vénale:** market value.

**Vendeur:** vendor/seller.

**Vendre, à vendre, vente:** to sell, for sale, a sale.

**Vente en état futur d'achèvement:** sale of a property off plan (on plan) before it is built.

**Vente à réméré:** sale which is subject to a right of repurchase.

**Vente sous conditions suspensives:** sale subject to special conditions, e.g. the sale of an existing property.

**Viabilisé:** (plot) having mains water and electricity connections.

**Vente à tenure:** sale of usufruct.

**Véranda:** conservatory, sun-room or extension.

**Verger:** orchard.

**Vieille maison:** old house.

**Villa:** detached house (usually modern) with a garden.

**Ville:** town.

**Volet (roulant):** shutter (roller).

**Volume:** the volume of a building can be the *volume bâti* (overall volume of the building), or the *volume habitable/ volume utilisable* (the usable volume taking into accounts walls, etc.). When *volume SIA* (*Société Suisse des Ingénieurs et des Architectes*) is stated it means the official SIA method of computing the volume of buildings has been used.

**Vue imprenable:** unobstructed view. *You* may also come across *vue sur les Alpes* (mountain view), *vue sur le lac* (lake view), *vue sur la rade* (road view), or the most prized of all, *vue panoramique* (panoramic view).

# W

**WC séparées:** separate toilet.

# GERMAN-ENGLISH

## A

**ab sofort:** available immediately.

**Abstellplatz:** outside (uncovered) parking space.

**Abstellraum:** storage room.

**Altbau/AB:** older building (*Neubau/NB* = new).

**Altersresidenz:** senior citizens home.

**Angebot:** offer.

**Angebaut/einzeitig angebaut:** refers to a row house, duplex, etc., where one side of the house is built on to another house, semi-detached (UK).

**Ankauf:** buy, purchase.

**Ankleidezimmer:** dressing room or walk-in closet.

**Anzahlung:** down payment, deposit.

**Amortisieren:** amortisation. The gradual process of systematically reducing debt in equal payments (as in a mortgage) comprising both principal and interest, until the debt is paid in full.

**Apartment/Appartement (App.):** studio apartment/flat, bedsit.

**Architekt:** architect.

**Are:** 100 square metres.

**Atelier:** studio (apartment).

**Attikawohnung:** attic or top floor apartment.

**Aufzug:** elevator or lift.

**Aussicht:** view (*herrliche Aussicht* = great view, *schöne Aussicht* = beautiful view – they don't usually mention the car lot or city dump!).

**Ausstattung:** equipment, furnishings.

## B

**Backofen:** oven (literally 'baking oven').

**Bad:** bath (refers to both the bathroom and the bathtub).

**Badewanne:** bath tub.

**Badezimmer:** bathroom.

**Balkon:** balcony (*gedeckte Balkon* = covered balcony).

**Bankgarantie:** bank guarantee.

**Bankspesen:** bank fees/charges.

**Bastelraum:** play or work room in the cellar, sometimes with running water, but usually without windows – also referred to as a *Hobbyraum* (hobby room).

**Bauernhof:** farm.

**Bauernhaus:** farmhouse (*Bauernhausteil* = part of a farmhouse when the farmhouse is a two-family house).

**Bauabnahme:** acceptance of construction work, completion.

**Baubewilligung:** building permit.

**Baujahr (Bj.):** year of construction.

**Bauland:** building land.

**Bauplan:** building plan.

**Besucherparkplatz:** visitor parking.

**Betriebskosten:** running or operating costs.

**Beurkundung:** (*Notarbeurkundung*) notarisation.

**bevorzugte Lage:** preferred area.

**bezugsfertig:** ready for occupancy, vacant possession.

**Boden:** ground, terrain.

**Bungalow:** single-storey house.

## C

**charaktervoll:** characterful – may be a euphemism for odd or dilapidated, but may mean a home with special appeal.

**(mit) Charm:** with charm or character.

**Cheminée:** chimney, open fireplace (*Warmluft-Cheminée* = a fireplace with a ventilator).

# D

**Dach:** roof.

**Dachgeschoss:** attic, loft.

**Dachwohnung:** attic apartment, penthouse.

**Dachmaisonettewohnung:** duplex attic apartment.

**Dauerauftrag:** (bank) standing order.

**(Zimmer) Decke:** ceiling.

**unter Denkmalschutz:** protected (listed) building or monument.

**Doppelfenster:** double glazing (triple glazing = *Dreifachverglasung*).

**Doppelgarage:** two-car garage.

**Doppelwaschbecken:** double sinks (in the bathroom).

**Dreifachverglasung:** triple glazing.

**Dusche:** shower.

# E

**Eigenbedarf:** personal use.

**Eigenheim:** private residence/home; freehold house.

**Eigenmietwert:** fictitious rental amount (for taxes).

**Eigentümer:** owner, property owner.

**Eigentumsübertragung:** deed transfer.

**Eigentumsurkunde:** title deed.

**Eigentumswohnung:** condo, condominium, freehold apartment.

**einbau-:** built-in (prefix); *Einbauküche* = built-in kitchen, *Einbauschränke* = built-in cabinets.

**Einfamilienhaus (EFH):** single-family house.

**Eingang:** entrance, entry (*eigener Eingang* = separate entrance, *privater Eingang* = private entrance; also entrée).

**Einkommenssteuer:** income tax.

**Einliegerwohnung:** self-contained apartment/flat inside or attached to a house, e.g. a granny flat or guest apartment.

**Einrichtungen:** facilities, e.g. bathroom.

**Einstellplatz:** car parking space (*überdachter Einstellplatz* = covered space or car port).

**Einzimmerwohnung:** one-room apartment.

**Einzugstermin:** moving in date.

**Elektriker:** electrician.

**Erdgeschoss (EG):** ground floor.

**Erneuerungsfond:** renovation or sink fund for a community property, e.g. a block of flats.

**Erstbezug:** first occupancy (new property or after major renovations).

**Esszimmer:** dining room.

**Etage:** floor (story); *in der vierten Etage* = on the 4th floor.

**Etagenwohnung (ETW):** apartment/suite occupying an entire floor.

# F

**Fenster:** window.

**Fensterläden:** shutters

**Ferienhaus:** vacation home, holiday flat (also *Ferienwohnung*).

**Festpreis:** fixed/firm price, non-negotiable.

**Finanzierung:** financing.

**Fläche:** area (size).

**frei:** available, vacant (*frei ab...* = available as of..., *frei ab sofort* = available immediately).

**freistehend (freist.):** free-standing, non-attached.

**Fussboden:** floor, flooring (*Parkettfußboden* = wood floors, parquet).

**Fussbodenbelag:** flooring, floor covering.

# G

**Galerie:** a roofed arcade or gallery with open sides.

**Garage:** garage (*Doppelgarage* = two-car garage).

**Garagenplatz:** parking space in a covered/secure garage.

**Garantie:** guarantee or warranty, e.g. on a new house.

**Garten:** garden, yard.

**Gartenanteil:** small garden, yard.

**Gartenbenutzung:** use of garden.

**Gartenmitbenutzung:** shared garden.

**Gartensitzplatz:** patio or terrace.

**Gärtner:** gardener.

**Gäste-WC:** guest toilet, restroom.

**Gebäude:** large building.

**Gebiet:** region, district.

**Gebühren:** fees.

**gehoben(e):** above average.

**Gemeinde:** community, municipality.

**Gemütlich:** cosy.

**gepflegt:** well cared for, in good shape.

**geräumig:** spacious.

**Geschirrspülmaschine:** dishwasher.

**Geschoss:** storey, floor.

**Gewerbeobjekt:** commercial property.

**Glaskeramikherd:** ceramic glass hob/stove top.

**Granitabdeckung:** granite counter-tops (kitchen).

**Grundbuch:** land/real estate register.

**Grundgebühr:** standing charge, e.g. for electricity, gas, telephone or water services.

**Grundriss:** floor plan.

**Grundstück:** land, plot.

**Grundstückgewinnsteuer:** capital gains tax on real estate.

**Grösse:** size, area (indicated in square metres, i.e. m² or qm).

# H

**Handänderungssteuer:** transfer tax.

**Handlungsvollmacht:** proxy/power of attorney.

**Handwerker:** handyman, skilled worker, craftsman.

**Hauptwohnsitz:** principal residence or main domicile.

**Haus (Häuser):** house (houses). *Das Haus* can also mean a building.

**Hausordnung:** house rules/regulations, e.g. in an apartment block.

**Haustiere:** pets (*keine Haustiere* = no pets, *Haustiere erlaubt* = pet friendly).

**Hauswart:** caretaker/janitor, apartment manager (Am.).

**Heimatschutz:** national heritage protection.

**Heizkosten:** heating costs.

**Heizung:** heating.

> **Elektroheizung:** electric heating.
>
> **Fussbodenheizung:** under-floor heating.
>
> **Gasheizung:** gas heating.
>
> **Ölheizung:** oil heating.
>
> **Zentralheizung:** central heating.

**Herd:** oven, cooker (*Elektroherd* = electric cooker, *Gasherd* = gas cooker).

**Hobbyraum:** hobby room (usually a room in the cellar).

**Hof:** courtyard.

**Holz:** wood.

**Holzbalken:** wooden beams.

**Holzboden:** wooden floor.

**Holzofen:** wood-burning stove.

**Hypothek:** mortgage.

**Hypothekenbrief:** mortgage deed (also *Schuldbrief*).

**Hypothekarzins:** mortgage interest.

# I

**Immobilie:** property, house, piece of real estate.

**Immobilien:** real estate.

**Immobilienbüro (geschäft):** real estate office (agency).

**Immobilienmakler:** real estate broker, realtor, also *Immobilientreuhänder*.

**Immobilienmarkt:** real estate market.

**Innenausstattung/Innenausbau:** interior decoration.

**isoliert:** insulated.

**IP-Bau-Grobdiagnose:** computer program used to determine or appraise the value of (older) buildings.

**inklusive(inkl.):** included, including.

**Isolierung:** insulation.

**Isolierverglasung:** insulated glass (windows).

# J

**jährlich:** annually, yearly.

# K

**Kabelanschluss:** cable TV (hook-up).

**Kacheloffen:** tiled stove,

**Kamin:** fireplace, hearth.

**Kanton:** county or state. Switzerland is comprised of 26 *Kantons*.

**Kantonssteuer:** canton tax.

**Kapitalertragssteuer:** capital gains tax.

**Kataster:** land register/registry.

**Käufer:** buyer.

**Kaufpreis (KP):** selling price, purchase price.

**Kaufvertrag:** sales contract.

**Kaution:** deposit (*Mietzinskaution* = rent desposit).

**Kehricht:** garbage.

**Kehrichtgebüh**r: garbage collection fees.

**Kehrichtsack:** rubbish/garbage bag.

**Keller:** basement, cellar.

**Kellerraum:** basement room (also doubles as a nuclear shelter).

**Kinderzimmer:** child's bedroom.

**kinderfreundlich, familenfreundlich:** children welcome, kids OK.

**(Kinder)spielplatz:** children's playground.

**Kirchensteuer:** church tax.

**Kleiderschrank (-schränke):** wardrobe(s), clothes closet.

**klein:** small.

**Kleinanzeige:** classified ad.

**Klimaanlage:** air-conditioning.

**Kochnische:** kitchenette.

**Komfort (mod. Komf.):** modern conveniences.

**Konto:** (bank) account.

**Kostenanschlag:** estimate (of costs).

**Küche:** kitchen.

**Kühlschrank:** refrigerator.

**kündigen/beenden (einen Vertrag):** to give notice/terminate (a contract).

# L

**Lage:** location (*ruhige Lage* = quiet location, *zentrale Lage* = central location).

**Laminat:** laminate flooring.

**Landhaus:** country house.

**ländlich:** rural.

**Lärm:** noise.

**Landwirtschaft/Landwirtschaftszone:** agriculture/zoned for agriculture.

**Lex Friedrich:** federal law that restricts the sale of Swiss real estate to foreigners.

**Liegenschaft:** property, real estate property.

**Liegenschaftsteuer:** building tax.

**Luftschutzkeller:** bomb shelter.

**Luxus/luxuriös (lux):** luxurious, luxury.

# M

**Makler:** broker, realtor.

**Maisonette:** maisonette apartment, small duplex apartment.

**Mängelliste:** list of faults found during an inventory (also *Hauszustand*).

**Mansarde:** mansard, attic apartment, garret.

**Mauer:** wall (exterior).

**Maurer:** bricklayer.

**Mehrfamilienhaus (MFH):** multi-family dwelling, apartment house.

**Mehrwertsteuer (MWSt):** value added tax.

**Miele-Geräte:** appliances made by Miele (the manufacturer – other high-end appliances may also be mentioned in ads.).

**Miete/Mietpreis, Mietzins:** rent.

**mieten:** to rent.

**Mieter:** tenant.

**Mietgarantie:** proof of ability to pay rent.

**Mietwohnung:** rented apartment or house.

**Mietzinskaution:** deposit (also *Mietzindepot*).

**Minergie:** quality label for low-energy consumption (building).

**Mittagsruhe:** period of quiet (after lunch).

**Möbel:** furniture.

**möbliert:** furnished (*voll möbl.* = fully furnished).

**möbliertes Zimmer:** furnished room.

**möbilierte Wohnung:** furnished apartment.

**monatlich:** monthly.

**Monatsmiete:** monthly rent, month's rent (*2 MM Kaution* = deposit of two months' rent).

**Mülltonne:** garbage or trash can.

**Musterhaus:** model or show home.

# N

**Nachbar:** neighbour.

**Nachmieter:** someone who takes over the lease.

**nach Süden:** south-facing.

**Naherholungsgebiet:** local recreation area, nature.

**Naturschutzgebiet:** conservation area (rural).

**Natursteinboden:** natural stone floors.

**Nebenkosten (NK):** extra costs, utility costs (not included in rent).

**netto:** net, after expenses and/or tax (*brutto* = gross, before expenses).

**Neubau/NB:** new house, new building (*Altbau/AB* = old).

**neuwertig:** like new.

**Nichtraucher (NR):** non-smoker.

**Notar:** notary; the legal professional who handles the conveyance for all property sales in Switzerland (similar to a British solicitor or an American property lawyer).

**Notfall:** emergency.

**Nutzfläche:** usable floor space.

# O

**Obergeschoss (OG):** upper floor (**4OG** = fourth upper floor).

**offener Kamin:** open fireplace.

**Offerte:** offer.

**Ort:** city, town.

**Ortsteil:** suburb, part of town.

# P

**Parkett/Parkettfussboden:** wooden parquet flooring.

**Parkplatz:** parking area, parking space.

**Pauschalbesteuerung:** estimated lump-sum income tax.

**Plattenboden/Plättliboden:** tiled floors.

**Postleitzahl (plz):** postcode, zip code.

**Preis:** price.

**Provision:** commission (fee).

**provisionsfrei:** no commission.

**Putzfrau:** cleaning lady.

# Q

**Quadratmeter(m2):** square meter (qm, m²). The area of a property is usually

shown in ads. in square metres, i.e. 100qm = approx. 1,000ft².

**Quellensteuer:** tax at source (direct income tax).

**Quittung:** receipt (also *Beleg*).

# R

**Rasen:** lawn.

**Raumhöhe:** ceiling height.

**Rechnung:** bill, check, invoice.

**Rechtsanwalt:** lawyer/solicitor.

**Reduit:** storage room, pantry.

**Reihenhaus:** townhouse, terraced or row house (*Reihenendhaus/REH* = end terrace house, *Reihenmittelhaus/RMH* = middle terrace house).

**Rollstuhlgängig:** wheelchair accessible.

**Renovierung:** renovation.

**renovierungsbedürftig:** needs renovation.

**Reservationsvereinbarung/ Reservationsvertrag:** pre-sale contract.

# S

**saniert, renoviert:** renovated, remodelled.

**Sanierung:** renovation, remodelling.

**S-Bahn (S):** commuter rail, metro.

**Schätzung:** estimate.
**Schlafzimmer:** bedroom.

**Schloss:** castle, palace.

**Schnäppchenpreis:** a steal, bargain.

**Schlüssel:** key.

**Schlüsselfertig:** ready to move in.

**Schuldbrief:** mortgage deed.

**Schwimmbad:** swimming pool.

**selbstständig:** independent, stand-alone.

**separat:** separate, separately.

**Sicherheit:** security (also for a loan).

**Sicherheitsschalter:** electricity overload trip switch or circuit breaker.

**Solaranlage:** solar heating system (for hot water).

**Spesen:** fees.

**Staatssteuer/Kantonssteuer:** cantonal income tax.

**Stadt:** city, town.

**Stadtplanung:** town planning.

**städtisch:** urban.

**der Stadtteil:** part, section of city.

**Steinboden:** stone floors.

**Stempelgebühr:** stamp duty.

**Steuer:** tax.

**Steuerabzug:** tax deduction.

**Steueramt:** local tax office.

**Steuerberater:** tax accountant.

**Steuerfuss:** tax rate/index.

**steuergünstig:** attractive tax-wise, low taxes.

**Steuerrechnung:** tax bill.

**Stock:** floor, storey.

**Stockwerkeigentum:** freehold apartment, literally 'floor owner' – refers to an apartment in a multi-family apartment building.

**Storen:** built-in shutters.

**Strand:** beach, e.g. on a lake.

**Strasse (Str):** street.

**Strom:** electricity.

**Studiowohnung:** studio apartment.

# T

**Teppich:** carpet.

**Teppichboden:** carpeted floor, wall-to-wall carpeting.

**Terrasse:** terrace, patio.

**Tiefgarage/Tiefgaragenplatz:** underground parking, lower-level garage space.

**Tierhaltung:** pets OK.

**Toilette:** toilet, WC (also *Klosett*).

**Tragbarkeitsberechnung:** feasibility, qualifying for a mortgage.

**Traumhaus/Traumwohnung:** dream home.

**Treppe/Treppenhaus:** stairs, staircase.

**Tür:** door.

# U

**Ueberbauung:** housing development.

**übertragbar:** transferable, e.g. a lease or mortgage.

**umgebaut:** converted (*ausgebaut* = loft).

**Umbau:** reconstruction, renovation or remodel.

**umbauen:** remodel.

**Umgebung:** area, neighbourhood, surroundings.

**unmöbiliert:** unfurnished.

**Umschwung:** surroundings.

**Umzug:** moving house.

**Umzugsreinigung:** removal (moving house) cleaning.

**Unverbaubarer Aussicht:** no buildings will obstruct views – ever.

**Untergeschoss (UG):** basement, lower level.

**Unterhaltskosten:** upkeep expenses, running costs.

**Untermiete:** sublease.

# V

**V-Zug-Geräte:** appliances made by V-Zug, for example V-Zug Backofen (oven).

**Veranda:** conservatory, sun-room or extension.

**nach Vereinbarung (nV):** as agreed.

**Verfügbar ab** = available from (date).

**Verhandlungbasis (VB):** negotiable price or best offer.

**Verkaufspreis:** asking or selling price.

**(zu) verkaufen:** for sale.

**Verkäufer:** seller, vendor.

**verkäuflich/veräusserlich:** negotiable (not negotiable = *nicht verkäuflich/ veräusserlich*).

**(zu) vermieten:** for rent.

**Vermieter:** landlord.

**Vermögenssteuer:** wealth tax.

**Verrechnungssteuer:** withholding tax (from investment income).

**Versicherung:** insurance; *Bauherrenhaftpflicht* = builders' liability insurance, *Bauwesenversicherung* = construction insurance, *Bauzeitversicherung* = construction time insurance, *Gebäudeversicherung* = building insurance, *Gebäudehaftpflichtversicherung* = building liability insurance, *Hausratversicherung* = household insurance, *Privathaftpflichtversicherung* = private liability insurance.

**verstärkte Tür:** armoured door.

**Vertrag:** contract, agreement (*Mietvertrag* = rental contract or lease agreement).

**Vorbau/Vordach:** porch.

**vorhanden:** available, provided.

# W

**Wand:** wall (interior).

**Waschküche:** utility or laundry room.

**Waschmaschine:** washing machine.

**Wasser:** water.

**Wasserenthärtungsanlage:** water decalcifcation unit.

**Wassergebühren:** water fees.

**Wasserverbrauch:** (amount) of water used.

**WC:** toilet (water closet).

**Weitsicht:** view (in the distance).

**Werkstatt:** workshop.

**Wintergarten:** winter garden (US sunroom).

**Wohnfläche:** living area, usable space.

**Wohngemeinschaft (WG):** flat share, shared flat.

**Wohnort:** place of residence.

**Wohnsitz:** domicile.

**Wohnung (Whg):** apartment, flat, dwelling.

**Wohnung zu vermieten:** apartment or house to rent.

**Wohnungssuche:** house hunting.

**Wohnzimmer:** living room, lounge.

# Z

**Zähler (Strom/Gas/Wasser):** meter (electricity/gas/water).

**Zahlungsauftrag:** (bank) payment order.

**Zentralheizung:** central heating.

**Zimmer (Zi):** room.

**Zimmer mit (eigenem) Bad:** room with bath (en suite).

**Zinsen:** interest (percentage).

**Zustand:** condition (*guter Zustand* = good condition, *schlechter Zustand* = poor condition).

**Zweifamilienhaus (ZFH):** duplex, two-family house.

**Zweitliegenschaft:** second home.

Notre-dame Cathedral, Lausanne

# INDEX

Survival Books was established in 1987 and by the mid-'90s was the leading publisher of books for people planning to live, work, buy property or retire abroad.

From the outset, our philosophy has been to provide the most comprehensive and up-to-date information available. Our titles routinely contain up to twice as much information as other books and are updated frequently. All our books contain colour photographs and some are printed in two colours or full colour throughout. They also contain original cartoons, illustrations and maps.

Survival Books are written by people with first-hand experience of the countries and the people they describe, and therefore provide invaluable insights that cannot be obtained from official publications or websites, and information that is more reliable and objective than that provided by the majority of unofficial sites.

Survival Books are designed to be easy – and interesting – to read. They contain a comprehensive list of contents and index and extensive appendices, including useful addresses, further reading, useful websites and glossaries to help you obtain additional information as well as metric conversion tables and other useful reference material.

Our primary goal is to provide you with the essential information necessary for a trouble-free life or property purchase and to save you time, trouble and money.

We believe our books are the best – they are certainly the best-selling. But don't take our word for it – read what reviewers and readers have said about Survival Books at the front of this book.

**Order your copies today by phone, fax, post or email from:**
**Survival Books, PO Box 3780, Yeovil, BA21 5WX, United Kingdom.**
**Tel: +44 (0)1935-700060, email: sales@survivalbooks.net,**
**Website: www.survivalbooks.net**

# Buying a Home Series

B uying a home abroad is not only a major financial transaction but also a potentially life-changing experience; it's therefore essential to get it right. Our Buying a Home guides are required reading for anyone planning to purchase property abroad and are packed with vital information to guide you through the property jungle and help you avoid disasters that can turn a dream home into a nightmare.

The purpose of our Buying a Home guides is to enable you to choose the most favourable location and the most appropriate property for your requirements, and to reduce your risk of making an expensive mistake by making informed decisions and calculated judgements rather than uneducated and hopeful guesses. Most importantly, they will help you save money and will repay your investment many times over.

Buying a Home guides are the most comprehensive and up-to-date source of information available about buying property abroad – whether you're seeking a detached house or an apartment, a holiday or a permanent home (or an investment property), these books will prove invaluable.

**For a full list of our current titles, visit our website at www.survivalbooks.net**

# Living and Working Series

Our Living and Working guides are essential reading for anyone planning to spend a period abroad – whether it's an extended holiday or permanent migration – and are packed with priceless information designed to help you avoid costly mistakes and save both time and money.

Living and Working guides are the most comprehensive and up-to-date source of practical information available about everyday life abroad. They aren't, however, simply a catalogue of dry facts and figures, but are written in a highly readable style – entertaining, practical and occasionally humorous.

Our aim is to provide you with the comprehensive practical information necessary for a trouble-free life. You may have visited a country as a tourist, but living and working there is a different matter altogether; adjusting to a new environment and culture and making a home in any foreign country can be a traumatic and stressful experience. You need to adapt to new customs and traditions, discover the local way of doing things (such as finding a home, paying bills and obtaining insurance) and learn all over again how to overcome the everyday obstacles of life.

All these subjects and many, many more are covered in depth in our Living and Working guides – don't leave home without them.

*The Expats' Best Friend!*

# Culture Wise Series

Our **Culture Wise** series of guides is essential reading for anyone who wants to understand how a country really 'works'. Whether you're planning to stay for a few days or a lifetime, these guides will help you quickly find your feet and settle into your new surroundings.
**Culture Wise** guides:

- Reduce the anxiety factor in adapting to a foreign culture
- Explain how to behave in everyday situations in order to avoid cultural and social gaffes
- Help you get along with your neighbours
- Make friends and establish lasting business relationships
- Enhance your understanding of a country and its people.

People often underestimate the extent of cultural isolation they can face abroad, particularly in a country with a different language. At first glance, many countries seem an 'easy' option, often with millions of visitors from all corners of the globe and well-established expatriate communities. But, sooner or later, newcomers find that most countries are indeed 'foreign' and many come unstuck as a result. **Culture Wise** guides will enable you to quickly adapt to the local way of life and feel at home, and – just as importantly – avoid the worst effects of culture shock.

*Culture Wise – The Wise Way to Travel*

**The essential guides to Culture, Customs & Business Etiquette**

# Other Survival Books

**The Best Places to Buy a Home in France/Spain:** Unique guides to where to buy property in Spain and France, containing detailed regional profiles and market reports.

**Buying, Selling and Letting Property:** The best source of information about buying, selling and letting property in the UK.

**Earning Money From Your French Home:** Income from property in France, including short- and long-term letting.

**Investing in Property Abroad:** Everything you need to know and more about buying property abroad for investment and pleasure.

**Life in the UK - Test & Study Guide:** essential reading for anyone planning to take the 'Life in the UK' test in order to become a permanent resident (settled) in the UK.

**Making a Living:** Comprehensive guides to self-employment and starting a business in France and Spain.

**Renovating & Maintaining Your French Home:** The ultimate guide to renovating and maintaining your dream home in France.

**Retiring in France/Spain:** Everything a prospective retiree needs to know about the two most popular international retirement destinations.

**Running Gîtes and B&Bs in France:** An essential book for anyone planning to invest in a gîte or bed & breakfast business.

**Rural Living in France:** An invaluable book for anyone seeking the 'good life', containing a wealth of practical information about all aspects of French country life.

**Shooting Caterpillars in Spain:** The hilarious and compelling story of two innocents abroad in the depths of Andalusia in the late '80s.

**For a full list of our current titles, visit our website at www.survivalbooks.net**

# PHOTO

# CREDITS

## www.shutterstock.com

Pages 123 © Leigh, 131 © Zsolt Nyulaszi, 132 © billblakey, 140 © STILLFX, 145 © Aleksey Fursov, 153 © Tomasz Trojanowski, 154 © kristian sekulic, 159 © Wojciech Burda, 168 © Tipylashin Anatoly, 171 © Cyril Hou, 182 © Mashe, 188 © Stankevich, 190 © Stuart Miles, 193 © Scott Maxwell/LuMaArt, 205 © Thomas M Perkins, 212 © Thomas M Perkins, 215 © Jiri Vaclavek, 227 © Bryce Newell, 230 © Perov Stanislav, 242 © Andrey Armyagov, 245 © White Smoke, 246 © amfoto, 318 © Pichugin Dmitry, 319 © Zaporozhchenko Yury.

## Peter Farmer

© Pages 89, 99, 100, 114, 134, 149, 150, 197, 210, 228, 237, 238, 241.

## Wikipedia

© Pages 19, 38, 30, 44, 50, 84, 87, 90, 93.

# Buying a Home
# Series